Benefit-Cost Analysis

Benefit-Cost Analysis

Analysis

A Political Economy Approach

A. Allan Schmid
MICHIGAN STATE UNIVERSITY

Westview Press
BOULDER, SAN FRANCISCO, & LONDON

Copyright © 1989 by Westview Press, Inc.

Published in 1989 in the United States of America by Westview Press, Inc., 5500 Central Avenue, Boulder, Colorado 80301, and in the United Kingdom by Westview Press, Inc., 13 Brunswick Centre, London WC1N 1AF, England

Library of Congress Cataloging-in-Publication Data
Schmid, A. Allan.
  Benefit-cost analysis.
  Bibliography: p.
  Includes index.
  1. Economic development projects--Cost effectiveness.
2. Economic development projects--Evaluation. I. Title.
HD47.4.S36 1989   338.9'0068'1   88-5782
ISBN 0-8133-0732-5

Printed and bound in the United States of America

The paper used in this publication meets the requirements of the American National Standard for Permanence of Paper for Printed Library Materials Z39.48-1984.

10   9   8   7   6   5   4   3   2   1

To my family and loves:
Florence, Kay, Elizabeth, Kevin, Emily, Jordan, Charles, Cindy,
Lindsay, Thomas, Susan, John, Diane, James, Patrick, Daniel,
those in our memories, and those yet to be born

Contents

List of Tables and Figures   xi
Foreword, *Warren J. Samuels*   xiii
Acknowledgments   xix

1   Introduction   **1**

    1.1.   Demand for Systematic Analysis:
        Implication for Second Best, 4
    1.2.   Steps in Analysis, 4
    1.3.   Skills of the Applied Economist, 6

2   Public Investment: Rationales and Objectives   **9**

    2.1.   High Exclusion Cost Goods, 12
    2.2.   Joint-Impact Goods, 12
    2.3.   Consumer Surplus, 13
    2.4.   Information and Uncertainty, 14
    2.5.   Externalities, 15
    2.6.   Market Imperfections, 16
    2.7.   Income Redistribution, 16
    2.8.   Inefficient Markets and Inefficient Government, 17
    2.9.   Levels of Analysis and System Extent, 18

3   Program Information Structure   **21**

    3.1.   Micro and Macro Perspectives, 21
    3.2.   Consequences of Input versus Impact
        Budget Formats, 22
    3.3.   Formulation of Output and Impact Categories
        for Projects, Programs, and Budgets, 25
    3.4.   Risk-Benefit Analysis, 39
    3.5.   Formulation of Units and Scales, 42
    3.6.   Formulation of Cost Categories, 43

4   Estimating Project Effects   **47**

4.1.   Threats to Internal Validity, 47
4.2.   Quasiexperimental Designs, 48
4.3.   Threats to External Validity, 54
4.4.   Choice and Weight of the Evidence, 55

5   Valuation of Direct Effects   **59**

5.1.   Market Analogy (Substitute Products) Method, 60
5.2.   Intermediate Good Method, 62
5.3.   Cost Saving Method, 66
5.4.   Access Cost-Quantity Demanded Method, 73
5.5.   Rent and Hedonic Price Methods, 79
5.6.   Alternate Cost Method, 84
5.7.   Bidding Games and Surveys, 86
5.8.   Systematic Choice among Multiple Outputs of Public
        Projects without Prices, 95
5.9.   Conclusion, 101

6   Opportunity Cost Adjustments   **105**

6.1.   Introduction, 105
6.2.   Taxation and Tariffs, 106
6.3.   Monopoly, Subsidy, and Economies of Scale, 109
6.4.   Foreign Exchange, 111
6.5.   Labor and Capital Goods, 115
6.6.   Conclusion, 134

7   Valuation of Nonmarginal Projects   **137**

7.1.   Conceptualizing a Welfare Measure of Change
        in Price, 139
7.2.   Policy Problems, 144
7.3.   Resource Savings and Asset Mobility, 146
7.4.   Project Firm as Intramarginal Firm, 150
7.5.   Regulatory Applications, 152
7.6.   What Governments Do, 152
7.7.   Conclusion, 153

8   Distribution Effects   **157**

8.1.   Introduction: Alternative Means for Distribution, 157
8.2.   Pricing of Marketed Output, 158
8.3.   Cost Sharing, 161

8.4.   Allocation of Joint Cost, 162
8.5.   Pecuniary Interdependencies (Externalities), 167
8.6.   Technological Interdependencies, 168
8.7.   Cash versus In-Kind Transfers, 169
8.8.   Distributive Weights, 170
8.9.   Grants Account Display, 172
8.10. What Governments Do, 179
8.11. Conclusion, 188

9   Valuation over Time and Selection Criteria   **191**

9.1.   Introduction to Time Preference, 191
9.2.   Time Preference Determinants, 195
9.3.   Investment Criteria, 198
9.4.   Choice of Discount Rate, 210
9.5.   What Governments Do, 220
9.6.   Second-Best Segmented Budgets, 221
9.7.   Summary and Conclusion, 223

10   Uncertainty   **235**

10.1. Introduction, 235
10.2. Mathematical Expectation, 235
10.3. Risk Trade-Offs Revealed, 246
10.4. Decision Rules without Mathematical
       Probabilities, 250
10.5. The Unknowable, 253
10.6. Matching Risk Decision Rules to People's
       Judgments, 253
10.7. What Governments Do, 256
10.8. Institutions and Incentives, 262
10.9. Project Implementation and Management:
       The Case for Flexibility, 263
10.10. The Need for Political Choice, 264

11   The Political Economy of Budgeting   **267**

11.1   Appropriations Decision Structure and
       Performance, 267
11.2. Bargaining, Decision Levels, and Program
       Budgeting, 272
11.3. Rewards for Display of Alternatives, 277
11.4. Program Budgeting and Value Judgments, 278
11.5. Conclusion, 282

12   Conclusion: Systematic Analysis in Perspective   285

12.1. The Role of Analysis, 285
12.2. Program Information Structure, 288
12.3. Estimating Project Effects, 290
12.4. Pricing Benefits and Costs, 290
12.5. Adjusting Opportunity Cost, 293
12.6. Nonmarginal Projects, 295
12.7. Distributional Comparisons, 296
12.8. Valuation over Time, 296
12.9. Uncertainty, 297
12.10. Public Choice Affects Relational Values, 298
12.11. Role of Property Rights in Exchange and Grants:
       Externalities, 299
12.12. Systems Analysis and Public Choice, 301
12.13. Conclusion, 304

References and Bibliography   307
Author Index   337
Subject Index   345

Tables and Figures

Tables

3.1	Example of an input budget for schools	23
3.2	Example of a program budget	39
5.1	National park visits	75
5.2	Cost saving versus alternate cost methods	86
5.3	Method A using physical output units	97
5.4	Method B using index of relative outputs	97
6.1	Adjustment of market prices with taxes, tariffs, and foreign exchange controls	108
6.2	Gross flows table	125
8.1	Allocation of costs by separable costs-remaining benefits method	164
8.2	Hypothetical display of grants budget performance for a target group	174
9.1	Alternative projects cash flow	192
9.2	Schedule of investment returns at different interest rates and investment criteria	201
9.3	Incorporating reinvestment to a terminal value	204
10.1	Present value of net income with alternative futures	236
10.2	Comparison of expected value and utility	240
10.3	Occupational risk payoff matrix	247
10.4	Net income payoff matrix	250
10.5	Minimum payoff	251
10.6	Regret matrix and maximum regret	251
10.7	Payoff matrix for pesticide regulations	261

Figures

3.1 Cost-dose associated with regulatory alternatives
and trade-off function 41
3.2 Cost-dose associated with regulatory alternatives and dose
reduction demand curve 41

5.1 Derivation of time-cost trade-off rate arising from
selection between two modes 70
5.2 Demand curve derived from cost-behavior data 76

6.1 Types of indirect benefits illustrated with navigation project 122

7.1a Relationship of ordinary, compensated, and all-or-nothing
demand curves 138
7.1b Measures of price change effects 138
7.2 Impact of a project reducing costs of all firms equally 147
7.3 Impact of a project whose costs are lower than previous
marginal firms 149
7.4 Impact of a project reducing costs of all firms differentially 152

9.1 Consumption in two periods with two choices 193
9.2 Relation of present and future value to the rate of discount 194

10.1 Utility functions 238
10.2 Gambler's indifference maps 242

Foreword

Economists have long been known for their disciplinary epigram that there is no such thing as a free lunch. Economists tend to be, in the words of Lord Balfour, chilling skeptics. This is because they understand that everything has its opportunity cost, the forgone opportunities sacrificed in making a particular choice or undertaking any particular line of action. Another way of making the point is to say that the meaning of anything derives from an understanding of both its strengths and limitations.[1]

Benefit-cost analysis, or BCA, has both strengths and limitations (the latter correlative to the former), and both derive from the fundamental design or nature of the tool itself. Looked at a bit differently, BCA shares the characteristics of most economic analyses, which are of the nature of models. A model is a set of variables and a set of relationships, the combination of which is used to address a problem or set of problems. Not all possible variables are included in any one model, and not all possible relationships are hypothesized in any one model. Thus, there can be many models, with varying sets of variables and varying sets of relationships adduced to exist among the variables, and also quite different models that address quite different problems. Furthermore, because they include neither all variables nor all possible relationships between the variables actually included, models do not presume to replicate or substitute for the real world in all its variegated and kaleidoscopic complexity. One important consequence is that estimation or prediction within the context of a model is different from estimation or prediction in the real world.

$P = MV/T$, the equation frequently used to state the quantity theory of money, is a model. It attempts to explain the price level, P, in terms of the three other aggregative variables M, V, and T (somehow specifically defined) in certain ways. There are other models capable of addressing the determination of the price level and also several ways of utilizing (making further assumptions about) M, V, and T. Moreover, the model itself cannot determine what will happen to the price level in the future in the real world, and even with additional data and/or assumptions the predictive capacity of the model is problematic and controversial. It will not escape the reader that whatever one thinks about the nature of economic reality (whatever that phrase may connote), there is inescapable subjectivity present in determining (1) that the problem on which to focus is the price level; (2) that this, rather than some other model, is the one worth using; (3) what the further, amplificatory assumptions should be; and so on. The use, then, of the quantity theory of money is laden with all sorts of implicit qualifications; that is to say, it has a distinctive set of strengths and limitations. So it is with benefit-cost analysis.

Alas, because economists are human beings and share the capacity for myopia with their fellow human beings, including the presumption of the validity of those techniques that constitute the tools of the discipline, there are both sophisticated and naive understandings and usages of techniques such as benefit-cost analysis. Even when used correctly and with a sense of its limitations, the technical analytic meaning and policy significance of BCA derive from both its strengths and limitations. When used in an improper, naive, or question-begging way, the situation is serious to the point of grievous numerology. It is the genius of this book to seriously indicate how to avoid such naivete and misuse.

The attractiveness and wide use of benefit-cost analysis derive from several sources. First, economists (1) typically very much want to have something significant to say about policy and (2) are expected by noneconomists to have something important to say about policy. Second, inasmuch as economics deals with prices, costs, benefits, and the details of complex decision making under the rubric of constrained maximization, it is to be expected that the status of the discipline, in the minds of both economists and noneconomists, would depend on the abilities of its practitioners to apply those concepts to real world problems. Third, BCA appears particularly coherent and persuasive because of the concatenation of two circumstances: the predominance of utilitarian modes of thought and of pecuniary, calculatory ways of life--so much so that the two tend to merge in our understanding. Fourth, it must be acknowledged that BCA is a technique that readily accommodates those analysts and policy makers who want to wrap the policy implications of their subjective policy preferences in the cloth of seemingly objective technique, so that (to change the metaphor) policy masquerades as science for purposes of legitimation and political mobilization or consensus formation. Those who want to control policy seek, in part, to control the definition of reality, and BCA has been an object of capture and use so as to define reality in some preferred way rather than another. So, far from being wholly and solely an objective tool, BCA has been part of the processes of argument and social control, not transcendental to either.

What distinguishes Allan Schmid's book is his effort to present BCA as a tool of analysis and not as a neutral black box substitute for policy making. He demonstrates that BCA is more complex and at all stages more laden with fundamental assumptions than is sometimes seriously presented in the textbooks or, more widely, realized or acknowledged by its practitioners. In one sense, it is true that BCA is a neutral tool. Like a computer, one gets out of it what one puts into it; like a hammer, what it does and accomplishes depends on its use. But this means that in another sense, if one understands the tool as also comprising its users' subjective uses of it, it is not neutral; it is an extension, and instrument, of the user. In other words, the meaning of BCA depends on the sum of its strengths and its limitations. This point has never been briefly stated so well as by John Maynard Keynes in his introduction to the volumes in the Cambridge Economic Handbook series in the period between the two world wars: "The Theory of Economics does not furnish a body of settled conclusions immediately applicable to policy. It is a method rather than a doctrine, an apparatus of the mind, a technique of thinking, which helps its possessor to draw correct conclusions." One has only to add that the "correctness" of the conclusions derives not solely from the technique of analysis per se but also, and arguably much more so, from the data that one uses in conjunction with the technique.

Schmid demonstrates the subjectivism--the choices--that *inexorably* characterize the use of BCA. He does this by a holistic attention to the details of use that must also be seen as constituting the technique. BCA is a tool that enables its user to make choices; these choices are not made on the basis of the technique alone but on the basis of the subjective inputs that are conjoined with the technique. Schmid's frank and nonapologetic, indeed rather robust, holism enables the reader and the user of BCA to recognize what it is that he or she is doing when using BCA.

It may well be felt that the foregoing emphasis on subjectivism is ironic considering the belief that BCA is an objective technique for policy making, one that is independent of ideology, values, and personal fancy. Well, it is the forte of Schmid's presentation to void that feeling and to dispel any such pretense. BCA is a useful framework for organizing information-- information that is largely subjective--but it is not the Holy Grail. Another way of making the point is to note the Humean proposition that one cannot derive an "ought" from an "is" alone; one needs additional normative premises. The points here are that BCA structures data and relationships in certain ways, that BCA uses highly subjective data to begin with, and that BCA does what its users have it do and show what they have it show-- whether they are aware of it or not.

This will not surprise the policy analyst who is sensitive to the fact that policy-making practice tends to shift between (1) the ideological practitioner who uses techniques selectively to ground certain desired policy results, that is, as a means to support their ideological fortress and advancement of their normative program, and (2) the technician who abjures consideration of normative premises (in which the ideologist revels) in favor of techniques of analysis that appear, or may be made to appear, value free. The human mind frequently desires the anxiety-avoiding comfort of ready-made solutions to problems that are thereby no longer problems; the ideologists find these solutions in their ideologies and the technicians in their techniques. Thus is decision making, which is going on willy-nilly, shortcircuited, or obfuscated. Subjective, normative premises are inexorable. The ideologist applies those premises with which his or her fanaticism leads him or her to identify; the technician may well be unaware of the presence of such premises. The conclusions of BCA are tautological with and give effect to the subjective, normative inputs (premises) made a part of it.

BCA in public affairs is in some respects similar to ordinary individual decision making and in some respects not. Individuals determine, on the basis of their own view of the world and subjective preferences, the costs and benefits to them of alternative choices or lines of action. Presumably in some sense they practice constrained decision making. When it comes to public sector decision making, the logic of the foregoing still applies, but the circumstance is significantly altered. Instead of one given decision maker who has to calculate and compare his or her benefits and costs, we now have the problem of determining, or finding proxies for, the world views and subjective social preferences of a variety of individuals and subgroups. To assume a consensus is to beg the question at issue.

More is involved than that. In the case of the individual, he or she operates within a given environment and a given budget constraint, that is, within a given set of entitlements. The substance and/or sum of these entitlements in the future may change, depending upon decisions and choices made in the present (as well as the choices and actions of others, individually and aggregatively). In the case of collective decision making, it is fundamentally important to recognize that the exercise of BCA and other techniques of public investment decision making constitutes modes of (1) giving effect to existing rights, either otherwise given or selectively identified, and (2) determining and redetermining these rights. Let us consider the latter first. The subjective assumptions governing which--really whose--costs and benefits to include in BCA and in what magnitude are functional as assumptions as to whose interests count and how much. To say that someone's injuries are less than someone else's benefits and that therefore policy should be this or that is in fact to determine or redetermine rights--and therefore to determine and redetermine the distributions of income and wealth. Rights *do* need to be determined and redetermined. But what drives BCA is not the objective facts of the matter but the subjective identifications and quantifications that are the inputs of BCA. BCA is therefore a mode of creating and negating entitlements. Schmid's book makes this abundantly clear.

BCA is not only a mode for the creation and destruction of rights. It can also be a means of giving effect to and indeed reenforcing the existing structure or hierarchy of power. By using market prices and/or estimations of willingness to pay, which are directly or indirectly dependent on the existing distributions of income and wealth, BCA, or any other technique, can be used to generate one system of government policy and one system of justice for the rich and another system for the poor. This, too, is made clear in Schmid's book.

All this is to say that there is no way in which policy concerning rights-- whose interests will be given effect and made a cost to someone else, following the principle that there can be no free lunch--can be avoided. The policy determination--to give effect, perhaps selectively, to existing rights or claims of rights, or to redetermine rights--can be either buried or made clear, and that in part depends on how BCA is employed or required to be employed.

BCA can be used by all parties to any dispute. BCA will help form the structure of discourse but the conclusions will vary because the several parties will inject into BCA the different sentiments and social preferences that they had prior to and independent of BCA.

Schmid's book also makes clear that whatever one's ideological preferences or preconceptions, collective action is necessary; there always will be public policy, willy-nilly. The book also makes clear that the desire for rational deliberative decision making is sensible. The attractiveness of BCA is largely the result of the belief that it will properly satisfy that desire. But the book also makes clear that public policy, insofar as BCA is used in its formulation, is driven not so much by BCA as a technique itself but by the policy premises that are read into, or added to, BCA by the political analyst, even when the analyst would like to believe or to pretend that he or she is not doing so, because of either personal distaste for "politics" and/or "ideology" or efforts at political mobilization.

BCA, in short, is no substitute for politics understood as self-government and as a mode of working out collective decisions. Indeed, the great genius of BCA is not to determine compulsive, unique optimal solutions to problems but to facilitate the coherent identification and juxtaposition of competing subjectivities and their respective implications. That is why multiple benefit-cost analyses should be undertaken. BCA is a tool to aid in making comparisons between policies and in estimating the results of various policies, not to determine policy through an ostensible black box. In the context of BCA, benefits and costs do not exist independent of the subjective premises to which they give effect. Alternative subjective premises and their respective implications ought to be identified and laid bare through the adoption of alternative benefit-cost studies. Schmid fully understands this, and to this end suggests and warrants the use of distributive impact statements as a mode of accomplishing the same purpose. Nowhere is this more evident than in his treatment of the various types of externalities. Externalities are ubiquitous and reciprocal. The very identification of an externality gives effect to a presumption that one party to a reciprocal externality has an entitlement rather than the other party. At bottom there is an existential necessity of choice--choice that determines or redetermines whose interest will count, who will have what effective rights, which externality (of a reciprocal pair) will be realized, and thereby the distributions of income and wealth.

Should it be expected that every reader of this book and every user of BCA will always keep in mind all the complexities and all the associated assumptions that are involved in practicing BCA? Perhaps that is too much to expect of normal human beings; modesty tends to trade at a discount with hubris, even, perhaps especially, among professional experts. But it is not too much to demand of the policy process. Otherwise, that process is a game of pretense, a sham. The only way for such candor to be realized and maintained is for individual practitioners to be candid. And the matter most suitable for candor is the exercise of subjective choice in the use of BCA-- which even the use of BCA in making comparisons cannot avoid. To some uncertain extent, past use of BCA in government has been the result of parties successful in using it to establish the putative high ground in debate, as legislators and others have been swayed by the seeming objectivity residing in numbers calculated to several decimal points. But no party should have a monopoly on this technique. Allan Schmid's book is a splendid exposition of technical expertise and the candor with which that expertise should be utilized. It is not denigration of a technique to stress the limitations that help define its meaningfulness. It is, rather, the tribute that expertise pays to intellectual honesty.

Warren J. Samuels

Notes

1.   Ironically, this includes techniques for coping with both opportunity cost itself and the ubiquitous ignorance and uncertainty that decision making involves. But, alas, economists tend not to be skeptical enough of their own established techniques.

Acknowledgments

A work of scholarship is the result of interaction with many other scholars over a long period of time. I would like to acknowledge the intellectual stimulation of the members of the Spartan Group: Warren Samuels, James Shaffer, Robert A. Solo, Stephen Woodbury, and the late Dan Saks. Many thanks are also due to Alfred Birch, Roy Black, Josef Broder, Dan Bromley, Mark Cochrane, David Collard, Frank Convery, Steve Cooke, Ron Cotterill, Eric Crawford, Steve Dola, Ron Faas, Phil Favero, Gianluigi Galeotti, Glenn Johnson, George Johnston, Werner Kiene, George McDowell, Denton Morrison, Michael O'Higgins, Robert Proctor, Lindon Robison, C. T. Sandford, Judy Stallmann, Jim Tozzi, Gail Updegraff, Eileen van Ravenswaay, Phil Wandschneider, and William Ward. I appreciate the work of my secretaries, Nicole Alderman, Jeanette Barbour, Pat Neumann, and especially Cindy Robinson, who carefully prepared the camera-ready copy with advice from Chris Wolf. Thanks also go to the fine editorial team of Spencer Carr, Martha Leggett, Arline Keithe, and Alice Levine at Westview Press.

A. Allan Schmid

Benefit-Cost
Analysis

1

Introduction

Choice is the name of the game. Government sets the size of the public budget and decides which public projects it will invest in and which transfers and regulations it will implement. To do this systematically the government must have a procedure that displays the consequences of the alternatives. This book is an exposition of benefit-cost analysis (BCA), an analytic framework for organizing thoughts, listing the pros and cons of alternatives, and determining values for all relevant factors so that the alternatives can be ranked. A major question illuminated by this text is whether the results of such an analysis can instruct government--in the sense of telling it what it must do to avoid being labeled stupid, corrupt, irrational, and/or inefficient. How and when, we will ask, can the benefit-cost analyst label a particular governmental investment, policy, or regulation as *political* (in the pejorative sense) as opposed to *economic* (in the laudatory sense of being economically justified)?

This book will argue that BCA is much like a consumer information system. Consumer information neither tells consumers what to do nor tells them what they should want. However, it does tell them which products will perform in selected ways and at what costs. And this information, together with the independently arrived at wants, helps the consumer make intelligent choices.

Similarly, informed benefit-cost analysts cannot tell government what public projects to fund. They can provide an information system that illuminates and informs the decision-making process and that implements politically chosen objectives and facilitates public monitoring for consistency with objectives, even occasionally encouraging these objectives to be rethought. The adoption of this stance involves a clear understanding of the division of labor between analyst and politician. In this book, we differentiate, in particular, between questions involving political matters, for which the analyst must obtain answers from the political system, and questions that involve technical matters to be solved within the discipline of economics.

The distinction between efficiency and distribution (sometimes referred to as the allocation and distribution branches of economics) is central to most treatises on public investment analysis.[1] The government can implement the demands of sovereign consumers given the distribution of income and other property rights, or it can redistribute that income via projects which constitute transfers of goods in kind (or in cash grants). Much of the literature of public investment analysis is devoted to separating these effects, but this text will develop a different point of view. Instead of taking income and rights as independently given and to be implemented by BCA in a Pareto-better fashion, we will see income, rights, and the analytic rules of BCA emerge as interacting parts of the same structure. In practical terms, after all, a person's wealth is made up not only of titles to land and stock (factor ownership) but also of rules governing tax incidence and government spending (rules for project evaluation).

According to the potential Pareto-better criterion, a project should be implemented if the gainers can compensate the losers, or, put in terms of property rights, if the buyers of the goods can compensate the owners of the opportunities (inputs) used to produce the goods. One of the ingredients in the buyers' willingness to pay is their ownership of wealth. Essential to the equation is the legitimacy of ownership (rights) that produces the income behind the willingness to pay and the legitimacy of ownership (rights) of the inputs necessary to produce the good in question (Kennedy 1981).

If the present distribution of wealth is accepted, then taxes and public spending only serve to implement the allocative preferences of those with income. But if it is rejected (or continually being renegotiated), the spending of tax receipts is more like a stock dividend by which some of the owners get their share of the nation's net income. In this setting, a tax implements a social dividend to a stockholder to be named later (when the money is spent by the government, which acts as both rights giver and agent for the owner). And to push this account a step further, the appropriation process is a resolution of the conflict over who the stockholders are; that is, who owns the Treasury?

The process becomes hard to follow when the way in which the money is to be spent is part of the political agreement to implement a given group's ownership. Analysis would be simpler if basic ownership never changed or, if changed, was always done prior to analysis by changes in private property or lump-sum tax and direct income transfers (Musgrave 1969). But this is in fact not done, and any counsel to do so would be part of a power play to protect the *status quo*.

Welfare economics is concerned with evaluating whether any proposed change in government spending or regulation will improve total welfare. But as Hutchison (1964, 165) points out, "excessive claims for welfare economics have fostered the illusion of policies without politics, or that significant policy recommendations can be made without controversial value judgements." Welfare economics can produce policy conclusions only under the following conditions: Citizens must agree on the initial rights of the players. Second, government must be able to achieve any distribution of income and welfare it desires by using costless lump-sum taxation (Tresch 1981, Ch.4). Third, people must have identical preferences and income elasticities that equal unity (i.e., the elasticities are homothetic). These conditions are known as the first-best assumptions.

However, propositions and decision rules appropriate for a first-best world are often incorrect for the real world. This book works out the practical implications of second-best theory, which accepts the fact that government cannot achieve desired distribution with lump-sum taxes and, indeed, that public spending is one instrument used to achieve a desired distribution. A second-best analysis accounts for the following facts: taxes alter resource allocation and consumption; government uses budget constraints; government commandeers production inputs and distributes output free of charge or at prices below opportunity cost; monopoly power exists in the private sector, so some prices do not equal marginal opportunity cost. If the difference between first-best assumptions and second-best reality is not recognized, analysts will inevitably substitute their own implicit distributional judgments for those of elected participants in the political process.

Analysis is seen here as a means for systematically implementing politically chosen objectives on the size and content of production and its distribution. Analysis should show decision makers the specific choices that follow from more generally stated preferences chosen from outside the analytic system. The generality of preferences is, of course, a matter for political choice. The objectives can be stated so precisely that they imply specific projects and leave no role for further analysis. But complete systems analysis is utopian. Systematic analysis allows observers to determine the objectives being pursued and whether these objectives are pursued consistently or piecemeal over some chosen scope of application. The analysis should allow different groups with different interests to see how the government's proposed budget choices will affect them. The material to follow is, then, built on the premise that good analysis will facilitate widespread, informed public participation in decision making.

Government directs the allocation of resources not only via public spending projects but also by regulation. For example, a redirection of resources is accomplished by a rule requiring industry to install pollution control equipment, or by government paying for the equipment, or by a hospital treating those affected by the pollution. Systems analysis broadens the consideration of alternatives, although there are practical limits to placing all of policy analysis into the BCA framework. For example, a public firm might be created to compete with a private monopoly, and in that sense public projects would be a substitute for antitrust regulation. But it may not be useful to force all of antitrust analysis into the BCA format. So, even though most of the references in this book are to public spending projects, we show that the same principles apply to public regulations and tax spending (e.g., when reduced taxes are used to affect resource use and distribution).

1.1.   Demand for Systematic Analysis: Implication for Second Best

In the United States, government BCA reports are common in the areas of water and forest resources, regulatory action (especially relating to health and safety), and some human services. But the demand for systematic analysis should not be overestimated. Although many projects are studied, few are actually chosen according to how they fare under BCA. For example, water resource projects in the United States have been required to undergo a BCA since 1936, but Congress does not necessarily fund those with the highest returns. The analysis is used more to qualify a set of eligible projects rather than to establish the priority of members of the set. Similarly, the World Bank requires a BCA before it will make a loan, but its allocation of funds among countries has no systematic relation to relative rates of return.

There are several possible rationales for this behavior. The least charitable is that politicians do not wish to make the reasons for their choices explicit and subject to examination and public debate. The public itself may opt for self-delusion when faced with tough choices, such as health or safety for one group versus another. Another explanation is that there are many objectives that are not quantifiable and must be more flexibly and qualitatively assessed. Related to this are the information requirements of any analysis. The results of BCA must meet the test of practicality; that is, analysis and information must themselves be subject to BCA. Systems analysis makes political decisions more open and explicit, but some second-best compromises are necessary to deal realistically with information and management costs as well as political pressures.

1.2.   Steps in Analysis

The preparation of a report of the costs and benefits of public investments or regulations follows a series of logical steps, and this logic is reflected in the chapter titles of this book.

Theories of Public Investment: The first question is why a proposed investment should be made in the public rather than the private sector. The analyst working for a particular agency with an assigned task may not have to ask this question. Nevertheless, the rationale for public investment supplies the background for any subsequent analysis of particular projects. In Chapter 2 we analyze some of the more commonly expressed justifications for public investment and/or regulation, which frequently are based on particular characteristics of the project or service in question.

Program Information Structure: What does the project produce, and what are the physical units for measurement of its quantity? This question is often difficult to answer and is related to the goals and objectives of the public program. Its answer will facilitate or hinder comparison with other projects and regulatory programs across agencies. These issues, explored in Chapter 3, also provide a convenient context for a discussion of the contemporary practice of program budgeting.

Estimating Project Effects: The next step is to determine if the project's inputs caused a change in the outputs identified above in the program structure. The question is, did the project make the difference? Economists call this step estimating the physical production function, or more commonly known as program evaluation, which is a bit of a misnomer because it has little to do with values or prices. This is a specialized topic, and Chapter 4 will merely indicate the major threats to causal validity and familiarize the reader with alternative quasiexperimental designs.

Valuation of Direct Effects: After we know the product to be produced and the role of the project in its production, we must consider the valuation of any other products produced by the project and any inputs required. Chapters 5, 6, and 7 discuss side effects--what economists usually call "externalities." We argue that there is much confusion in the literature on this concept and that clarity can be obtained by careful attention to distributive and property rights issues. The resolution of these issues requires an explicit political choice among conflicting values of different individuals. An especially important problem, that of assigning values to effects when there is no market available to set them, is addressed in Chapter 5.

Opportunity Cost Adjustments: Even when prices exist, they might not reflect opportunity costs. Adjustments are often necessary because of taxation, monopoly, subsidies, foreign exchange, and labor policies. Projects not only produce goods and services directly used by consumers but they also indirectly affect employment and income of input suppliers and the subsequent processors of the direct output. These are often referred to as multiplier effects. Chapter 6 distinguishes regional gains from gains to the total economy. The use of unemployed resources is given special treatment.

Nonmarginal Projects: Particular attention will be given in Chapter 7 to the effect of project size on product prices. The discussion will be sensitive to how value (political) judgments enter into calculations of what is often asserted to be "net social gain."

Distribution Effects: The point has been made that the analysis and design of projects affect income distribution in many ways, some of which are often masked as net social gains. In Chapter 8, different ways of incorporating an explicit redistribution objective into project selection will be discussed. Systematic treatment of redistribution objectives has not previously been accomplished in the literature or practice. Topics discussed in this connection include tax incidence, pricing, and allocation of overhead costs in multiple-product projects.

Valuation over Time: Projects differ in the pattern and length of flow of benefits and costs. Alternative investment criteria and the role of the discount rate are explored in Chapter 9. Particular attention is given to the problems raised by capital rationing, and which interest groups' opportunity costs and reinvestment possibilities are given preference under real-world situations of disequilibrium.

Uncertainty: Projects also differ with respect to the predictability of outcomes. People do not always agree on the trade-off between different-sized benefits and their variance. One approach to irreducible uncertainty (discussed in Chapter 10) is to design, implement, and manage projects so that adjustments can be made as more information becomes available.

Political Economy of Budgeting: In the final two chapters, we return to the question of the demand for systematic analysis. Information is a resource to political bargainers, and no good study is neutral in its effect on conflict resolution. Resources for analysis have been growing, but use of the results in actual budget formulation is still limited. Reasons for this limitation and implications for the role of the analyst vis-a-vis the politician are explored. A final topic is the relationship of project analysis to budget formulation and national planning.

1.3. Skills of the Applied Economist

Public investment analysis places heavy demands on the skills of the applied economist. No subfield of economics is irrelevent. It is necessary to draw on production economics and theory of the firm to estimate benefits and size effects, industrial organization to adjust for effects of monopoly on prices, location and regional economics to estimate indirect effects on employment, macroeconomics and monetary policy to deal with discount rates, on international trade to take account of tariffs and foreign exchange policies, and so forth. Nor should we ignore the techniques of measurement from statistics for experimental design and contributions from other disciplines to facilitate implementation and management. No single book can address the necessary skills in detail. But it is possible to indicate which concepts and experience from these fields are particularly relevant for public investment analysis and to provide a framework for interpretation of information produced by other specialists when it is useful to apply such information to the choice of public investments.

This book discusses what BCA is and what it can do, provides guidelines for its proper use and interpretation. Some will see it as a critique of BCA, but that is a misunderstanding of our purposes. The book critiques not BCA itself, but only its presentations and practices that fail to be systematic, that do not recognize the costs of analysis, that ignore second-best reality, that misconceive or misapply important concepts, or that allow the analyst to usurp the job of politicians. It is a call to do BCA better than we have been doing it.

Notes

1. Treatises on BCA that provide background for this book but are not elsewhere cited are Aboucher (1985), Austin (1981), Cohn (1972), DeGarmo (1967), Dorfman (1965), Gittinger (1982), Howe (1971), Hufschmidt et al. (1983), Kendall (1971), Lal (1974), Mathur (1985), McKenzie (1983), Pearce (1984), Prest and Turvey (1965), Roemer and Stern (1975), Sinden and Worrell (1979), Smith (1986), Smith and Desvousges (1986), Squire and van der Tak (1975), Thompson (1980), Walsh (1985), and Wolfe (1973).

2

Public Investment: Rationales and Objectives

Decision makers may choose project options according to objectives. It is easy to say that we want to maximize utility or total welfare, but the task is far from straightforward. In a financial analysis, private managers may seek to maximize the flow of income over time. This flow is measured by financial accounts, and the individual does not ask what produced the prices for inputs and outputs that underlie the net income. But these prices are what they are partly because of property rights. Behind a consumer's willingness to buy (pay) is ownership of resources that produce income. And behind an input supplier's willingness to sell is the right to control that resource's use.

Because citizens care about the welfare of groups, government has the responsibility to create the rights that support willingness to buy and sell. It is also responsibe for creating the institutions that communicate and aggregate bids and offers. If some of these bids cannot be communicated in markets, and if costless lump-sum transfers are unavailable to implement distributive objectives, government may have to tax and spend to make its welfare objectives effective. Citizens do not really know what they are sovereign over until they know their private property rights (including those made effective by government regulation) as well as their rights in government appraisal of public projects, actual public taxes levied, and government spending programs.

Price is partly a function of rights. For example, the price of labor is influenced by unions and the right to bargain collectively. Workmen's compensation and occupational safety regulations also affect the cost of labor. These rights represent some compromise of conflicting interests. Suppose the objective of the ruling coalition is to increase the welfare of laborers whose union was not effective. One policy option would be to give unions the right to bargain for union shops in all states. Another would be a lump-sum income transfer. Both options may be unacceptable to the majority. Therefore the compromise is that all government building contracts must at least pay union wages, even if some would work for less as a result of individual bargaining. This is in fact the rights compromise prevailing in the United States. The price of labor can't be used when totaling the benefits and costs of governmental action unless the distribution of rights that produce the price is acceptable.

In principle, the government could alter the welfare of any group by direct tax transfers, by changing the group's bargaining rights in general, or by just changing wages in the public sector. Even if tax transfers had no transaction costs, we cannot assume that direct transfers are preferable without asking preferable for whom? Rights are whatever can be agreed to. These rights are not static; they change marginally and partially in the process of political compromise. Any theory that rules out certain kinds of rights is only a veiled presumption of the interests of the groups served by that theory.

To judge whether proposed public spending or regulation improves aggregate welfare we need a way to add up the costs and benefits to all individuals. An individual can make decisions by equating his or her marginal rate of substitution with price ratios. But the public can make decisions by summing changes in the quantities of goods multiplied by their prices only if distribution can be separated from resource allocation and if markets are perfect. Since income distribution affects relative prices, a sum of price times quantity is not relevant if that distribution is not acceptable. It is tempting to suggest that the key objective of public decision making is to make individual preferences count. But what do individuals have to count with? If analysts are to weight preferences by income, then each person's income must be legitimate. Some judgment about income distribution is implicit in any kind of BCA (Pearce and Nash 1981, 11).

If benefits and costs are accruing to different people with different incomes and preferences, a proposed project makes an improvement only if the gainers compensate the losers. This condition is called the *Pareto-better compensation test* and it ensures that if the original income distribution was acceptable, then subsequent action will not make things worse for anyone. However, this test requires ratification of some income distribution. The ability to compensate depends on prices that are influenced by income distribution.

In practice, it is impossible for government to administer the appropriate compensations without cost. So some economists have suggested that changes be regarded as improving welfare if gainers have the capacity to compensate the losers, even if this is not actually done. This test is referred to as the *potential Pareto-better compensation test* or the *Kaldor-Hicks test* after its best known proponents. It incorporates the value judgment that the resulting income distribution is acceptable. It is difficult to imagine citizens adopting this rule when they do not know who the parties are, and the test is often ambiguous when neither party can afford to buy the rights (opportunity) owned by the other party (see Section 5.7.4).

If government wishes to change the distribution of income, it could change rights universally via court rulings in negligence and liability, for example, or via regulation, or it may change the rights only in its own transactions. This last change is implemented through the rules for project analysis.

Many changes in the private market economy are not Pareto-better: People become unemployed and suffer losses to immobile assets; inflation reduces some people's real income; and the process of development, in general, creates losses for some. The policy issue is then, which losses are damages to rightful property? If you have a right, you are free of losses caused by the transactions of others. Implementation of a Pareto-better decision criteria requires ratification of the starting point for those rights. And this starting point is the domain of government in its rule making and spending decisions.

The Paretian approach to BCA assumes that some objectives command universal support and that the specific rules of BCA can be unambiguously deduced from these universals without further instructions from politicians. Whittington and MacRae, (1986, 677) note that the Paretian approach assumes "that the membership of a society or nation can be delimited without troublesome ambiguities and that membership is so much a matter of consensus that it need not be examined." This book makes no such presumption. We adopt an interactive political economy approach that accepts--indeed asks for--specific objectives reflecting the welfare desired for various groups. Ultimately, the objective of politicians is to reach a compromise among the conflicting welfare demands of groups such that the politicians may survive, and perhaps pursue other personal objectives.

This point of view is controversial but consistent with modern theoretical welfare economics literature.[1] After exploring the implications of second-best conditions, Boadway and Bruce (1984, 272) conclude that "to obtain a measure of welfare change in many-consumer economies which serves to rank all alternatives, there appears to be no alternative but to employ a social welfare function." This statement suggests that many questions must be asked of politicians before BCA system rules can be formulated. We call this practice the *necessity for public choice*.

An economic analysis to determine public choice would not be identical to a financial analysis even if there were perfect competition, because perfect competition does not settle all conflicts among people, and it is the role of government to affirm or alter all of the rights that influence willingness to buy and sell.[2] The purpose of BCA is not to replace the individual's decisions but to help government decide which individuals to count when the interests of those individuals conflict. Neither does BCA supplement efficiency objectives with distributive objectives, but it defines the rights that in turn define efficiency.

The specific techniques of BCA are used in various rationales for public investment. We briefly outline these reasons here. Later, when the specific techniques are discussed, we supply more detail. Some of these reasons for public sector investment include characteristics of products that may make them perform differently under private provision; high exclusion cost, joint-impact goods where marginal cost to another user is zero, transaction costs, and various other reasons, lumped together in the literature as externalities and market imperfections.[3]

2.1.   High Exclusion Cost Goods

People with income may not be able to get their preferences met with market trade when the desired product is a high exclusion cost good. Such goods, if they exist, are available to every person, whether or not he or she has helped pay for their production. Therefore, even people who think the product is worth its cost of production may not volunteer a bid. Instead they are tempted to be free riders and to hope that someone else will pay enough to get the good produced. For example, if a flood control dam is built, it will protect all downstream land in the flood plain. It is not possible to exclude a landowner from the benefit just because the owner claims it is not worth the cost. Because some demand may not be revealed by market bids, it is argued that government must build the project and finance it with taxes. This policy avoids the free rider but may well create the unwilling rider, who is not trying to hide preferences and truly does not want the product at its cost.

The task for analysis developed in Chapter 5, then, is to estimate what people would pay for these products if they were not trying to be free riders, which answers the question of whether total benefits exceed costs. (Depending on the incidence of taxes, however, it will not answer the question of whether each individual's benefit exceeds costs.) Recall that according to a "potential Pareto improvement" the relevant test for inclusion of a project in the public budget is whether total benefits exceed costs. When this Pareto improvement occurs, there is a capacity for the winners to compensate the losers, but whether this compensation is carried out is a matter of income distribution. This position urges government to increase total production regardless of whether distribution is altered. The decision to build a project must involve both the estimate of net benefit and the incidence of benefits and costs. Any decision to build a project providing high exclusion cost goods involves a political value judgment of the trade-off between the interests of the consumers, whose preferences are frustrated by their own and others' attempts to be free riders, and the interests of unwilling riders (taxpayers). Thus, the existence of high exclusion cost goods may be a rationale for public investment, but it is not sufficient without further conflict-resolving value judgments.

2.2.   Joint-Impact Goods

The cost function of some goods enables another consumer to be served with no additional cost. These goods are called *joint-impact* goods. They are also called *public* goods, but the term begs the question of whether such goods should be provided in the public sector. There is no problem here in getting a demand curve; rather, the problem lies in producer response under market institutions. The private producer attempts to maximize profits by selecting that quantity of output at which marginal cost equals marginal revenue. At this point the price given by the average revenue curve exceeds the marginal revenue. Propositions from welfare economics label this situation *Pareto-inferior*. Someone can be made better off and no one will be made worse off by expanding output to the point at which price equals marginal cost. Apparently, even though people could be excluded from use of the output, this exclusion would be a mistake as long as there is someone who places any value on the product, since it costs nothing to allow another user. The problem is that if the product is priced at zero, there is no way for a producer to obtain market reimbursement for the total costs paid.

Thus, it is argued that joint-impact goods should be provided by government with no charge at the point of use. Then, taxes must be used to finance the goods. When first-best costless lump-sum transfers are unavailable, it is not clear that price equal to marginal cost is Pareto-better. Again, depending on tax incidence, there may be unwilling participants-- people who must pay the tax but do not think the product is worth it. A public investment decision then requires a political resolution of this conflict. The problem raised by joint-impact goods is discussed in Chapter 8 on the distributive effects of product pricing and tax incidence. Similar problems occur with products that might not have zero marginal costs but that do have substantial economies of scale.

2.3. Consumer Surplus

If governments were to price joint-impact goods at zero, the estimate of total market receipts could not cover costs. Such projects will not look good compared with alternative investments. After all, it is not realistic to say that all joint-impact goods projects are undesirable. First-best theory suggests that the appropriate measure is not to estimate total value derived from a single price times quantity, but to estimate the maximum amount that might be extracted from consumers if each consumer were faced with a different take it or leave it price. This is considered to be the total area under the demand curve (rather than the area under a single price). This asserted utility in excess of what would have to be paid at a single price for all consumers is termed the *consumer surplus*.

Private producers of any good would be pleased to try to capture this surplus if they were allowed to use differential pricing. As a practical matter, the private producer could not invest and count on capturing all of the surplus because of problems with keeping different classes of consumers apart. So, even if private firms were permitted to use differential pricing, they could approach, but not make, the same investment returns and thus have the same project priorities as the public sector. Government can use a measure of consumer surplus to guide investment decisions and thus not worry about how the costs are actually going to be collected. Again, we see a rationale for public investment, but it requires a choice between conflicting groups in which costs and benefits are not matched for each person. The distinction between differential pricing and discriminatory pricing requires a value judgment.

Some theorists have suggested use of the consumer surplus concept when project output is so large that it affects prices. The project affects the rod by which the project is itself measured. In this situation the private investor considering the actual price that can be collected in the market may find other investments more attractive. It is possible that the total value of all output is actually less with the project than without it. It can be argued that government should make these investments anyway because consumers benefit by the lowered price. Chapter 7 examines the empirical and policy problems raised by consumer surplus.

2.4.   Information and Uncertainty

Capital markets are marked by capital rationing; labor markets are marked by unemployment. These otherwise competitive markets may not clear in the usual sense. In part, this is the result of costs of information and uncertainty as to future events and determination of quality (Stiglitz 1987a). Employers do not offer a wage appropriate for using the available productivity of all labor. Employers leave people unemployed because they cannot distinguish differences in individual labor quality. If they lowered wages to fit the productivity of the unemployed, their effective labor cost per unit of output may rise as average labor quality falls (adverse selection).

Lenders of money also may prefer to ration credit (leave some loan demand unmet) rather than raise interest rates. In the face of uncertainty about borrowers' success, raising rates may lower the lender's profits if the average quality of borrowers drops. In both the labor and capital markets, quality may depend on price in the face of uncertainty. Decentralized markets may fail to make economic use of some resources and opportunities.

Adjustment in nominal prices to reflect opportunity costs in labor markets is discussed in Chapter 6. The fact that government, like private banks, practices capital rationing is discussed in Chapter 9. Because of uncertainty in project performance, it may be rational for government to ration capital rather than to raise its target discount rate. Other aspects of uncertainty are discussed in Chapter 10.

2.5.   Externalities

The term *externalities* has been used so loosely and in so many different situations in the literature as to be nearly worthless for precise analytic use. The most general definition denotes that some effect external to the actor is somehow not properly taken into account. Interdependence exists in any situation of scarcity, because one person's choice and use of a resource affects the options open to others. So, far from being a special case for government investment, externalities are common to human interaction. To say that an effect on others is not properly taken into account is to presume who "owns" the opportunity to act when one person's use is incompatible with another person's use. In an economy of private property, government assigns ownership, and if another performance is wanted compared to that emanating from the present distribution of ownership, the rights can be reassigned. Governments sometimes prefer not to change openly all rights in a given category by legislative or judicial action, but prefer selective changes through the way inputs or outputs are accounted for in public investment.

For example, it is sometimes argued that private investment does not account for pollution effects of its industrial projects, but that a proper analysis of public investment would attach a value to any environmental costs. But if government wanted to, it could change private property rights in the environment so that private or public action requiring an input that diminished the opportunities of the owners of the environment could be the basis for the owner to sue. The threat of these suits is what makes people (or governments) who do not own a resource make a bid to its owners. It is the rights of others which make an action a cost for a new would-be user. These rights can, of course, be instituted by legislative or judicial choice, or selectively, by accounting in the context of government investment projects. The barriers to instituting new rights in some resources have already been noted in our discussion of high exclusion cost goods and other situations of high transaction costs.

Transaction costs of getting a large group of owners together may be high even where exclusion costs are low. For example, if a project involves the assemblage of land held by many small owners, there may be holdouts by owners of certain key parcels. Such action is often the rationale for the use of eminent domain to force sale at going market prices by the public authority. Of course, the right of eminent domain need not be exercised exclusively by public enterprise; it can be, and is, given to private firms building gas and electric lines. In any case, reducing or circumventing transaction costs alters the income of those whose interests are furthered by these costs.

Much of what is called externalities in the literature could be more clearly seen as a complete accounting of the multiple products of complex projects. For example, a dam may create downstream benefits as well as those on the dam site, or education may create benefits to others in the community as well as to the student. The conceptualization of these outputs will be discussed in Chapter 3.

2.6.   Market Imperfections

The existence of a monopoly may cause prices of inputs or outputs to differ from what would exist in a competitive market. In a first-best world the government could abolish the monopoly. But a second-best world raises the question of whether government should estimate what the competitive price would be and then use it to guide public sector investments. Modifying opportunities of a monopoly alters its rights and income distribution as much as any government subsidy would and thus it must be guided by a distributive objective.

In some cases government policy causes a divergence from competitive prices. Common examples are in prices of supported commodities, various taxes and tariffs, and foreign exchange regulation. These are the devices by which some people receive their income and to change them wholly or selectively in public investment projects is to change the distribution of income as surely as would be done by any redistribution of rights in factor ownership, such as land reform. Chapter 6 illustrates that the analyst cannot arbitrarily offset these policies with shadow prices without getting political input as to distributive objectives.

2.7.   Income Redistribution

Explicit income redistribution is often given as a rationale for public projects. According to this view, public spending for a specific good or service to a particular beneficiary is a substitute for other types of income and factor ownership redistribution that would permit the new owner to purchase these same or other goods and services in the market. But government may redistribute income in cash rather than in kind (specific goods and services). Such direct cash payment may be preferred by the recipient, because the good or service provided by government is not likely to be exactly what the beneficiaries would buy for themselves if they had an equivalent amount of money. But the issue is, who owns the money in the first place? Some people with money wish to escape the effects of specific consumption (or lack thereof) by others. People are offended by the slum housing and shabby clothing of others. Public projects providing housing and clothing are a device for meeting the preferences of people so offended. Thus, advice to substitute cash transfers for public projects as income redistribution methods is an expression of a value judgment.

The issue is not only which individuals are to have control over use of certain goods and resources but also whether these consumption decisions are to be made individually or collectively. For example, it is argued that people may express a different time preference rate and be subject to different risks when voting on a collective project where they know others will share in the effect than they express in capital markets (Arrow and Lind 1970). Of course, the capital market itself is influenced by collective decisions of the central bank. Government could change the rate occurring in the market to get a certain target investment rather than adopt a certain rate of discount for public projects.

Many countries have chosen to make sectoral allocations of resources among agriculture, heavy industry, energy, and consumer goods via the government budget. Within each of these, the government-owned enterprises may respond to the decentralized decisions of individual consumers. In a sense, this response is an expression of the distribution of ownership. A government can alter the distribution of income, which could produce a change in production in the various sectors of the economy, or it can give effect to these same preferences by its own budget allocations to public enterprises.

The institutional structure of an economy may be prized as an end in itself and not as a means to fulfill the preferences of selected persons. Public enterprise may be prized not to better produce a certain good or service but to create a certain social relationship among people. Although the evidence is not clear, a concern for avoiding human alienation may lead some people to prefer public production to market organization.

In Chapter 8, methods are explored whereby explicit income redistribution objectives can be systematically reflected in project ranking. The argument of this chapter, however, is that questions of income distribution enter into the analysis at many points. The conventional division between economists' recommendations of how to implement an efficiency objective separate from a distributive objective will be questioned throughout. We demonstrate that several analytic practices predominately treated in the literature as technical issues are really matters requiring political judgment. We believe that good analysis will point out these issues so that public officials and citizens can better understand them and predict the consequences of their choice of system rules for project analysis. But there is no guarantee of wise decisions.

2.8.   Inefficient Markets and Inefficient Government

The point has been made that many of the rationales for public investment to improve on "market failures" cannot be accepted as moving toward Pareto-better improvement in meeting the preferences of people as constrained by their initial distribution of income and rights. Pareto improvement would require an additional value judgment trading off the interests of free and unwilling riders; settling conflicts of interest over pricing, cost share, and tax incidence; settling conflicts over surpluses and externalities, and conflicts over time preference and other issues that we will explore. The resolution of these conflicts is a part of any so-called initial distribution of income.

In our approach we do not ask whether the market or government comes closest to achieving preferences *given* by some initial distribution of rights. Such achievement is impossible because the rules of BCA are themselves part of this initial (and evolving) distribution of rights. We often refer to the need for public choice, which is not a need for government to replace the market but for government to settle the conflicts over the initial distribution of rights. These rights include not only ownership of factors and the degree of market competition but also the "ownership" of rights in government's analytic and decision process (that is, ownership of the public treasury).

2.9.   Levels of Analysis and System Extent

Governments have made and continue to make expenditures without any analytic system. There may be cost estimates and some description of results, but the choice is essentially ad hoc, with no stated general principles applied to all instances. In this mode of decision, there is no basis for asking about consistency across projects. In contrast, some types of decisions involve choice and application of general principles across a range of projects. That is, the political choice is to select some system rules rather than treat each proposed project as a unique case. The ranking of projects is then deduced from application of the rules. This varies by degree from cost-effectiveness analysis to benefit-cost analysis.

2.9.1   Cost-Effectiveness Analysis

The public authority will often make an ad hoc decision to spend a given amount on a problem area. If output can be defined in some physical terms, it is possible to analyze alternative projects as to which produces the most for the given cost. The government chooses the amount of money but relies on analysis to suggest the means for achieving the highest possible output.

Conversely, there may be an ad hoc decision that a given level of output is needed, and the analyst is asked to find the cheapest means to obtain it. In the first instance, the question is how to get the most bang for the given buck, in the second, how to spend the fewest bucks for the given bang. In cost effectiveness, the choice of budget size or needed level of outputs is an ad hoc decision, whereas choice of projects (or regulatory alternatives) is left for application of a rule that says: choose the most effective means to maximize physical output per unit of cost, or minimize cost for a mandated level of output.

The government may not wish to commit itself to the application of any system rule, although it may ask that cost-effectiveness displays be made.

This is the U.S. practice in chemical regulation (pesticides and foods). The cost of establishing regulatory alternatives or tolerance levels is related to acceptable doses for humans and other organisms and perhaps to the carcinogenic activity or longevity of the chemical. No value is explicitly placed on human life, nor does any rule require that the regulation of one chemical achieve the same result per unit of cost as another. Still, to the extent that the output of one regulation or program is in the same physical terms as another, it is possible for the public to see how consistent the public decisions have been. Program budgets can be used for this. They display the effects of projects from different agencies in common output (performance) terms, as discussed in Chapter 3.

2.9.2. Benefit-Cost Analysis and the Second Best

When the public authority makes more decisions in terms of rules and fewer ad hoc piecemeal project choices, it moves toward BCA. It decides on policies and analytic rules that can be applied to various portions of the budget. Budget size and levels of outputs emerge as implications of the application of politically chosen objectives and associated analytic rules. Over some range, all inputs and outputs are priced, and these prices are consistently used over some specified planning period.

In practice, the use of rules is always a matter of degree. In the United States, BCA is used to minimally qualify a project in some segments of the budget (and for regulations in some instances), but it is almost never used to set explicit budget size in total or by agency. Governments never fund all of the available projects having net returns (capital rationing), which means that ultimately governments are not willing to live by their announced discounting and pricing rules. Governments are seldom willing to fund projects in the priority ranking suggested by application of its rules. Some inconsistencies are produced when the analysis is done as if the nominal rules were intended to be fully integrated but then are not. Suggestions are offered throughout this book on how a second-best and partial BCA can be utilized. Although in some make believe world of costless lump-sum transfers and commitment to a high degree of budgetwide systems analysis no second-best compromises would be necessary, it is a theme of this book that turning a blind eye to likely governmental uses of BCA produces faulty information. We believe that explicit incorporation of second-best requirements will make the analysis more useful. Economists can remain smug in their council of perfection, or they can incorporate second-best concepts to make analysis more relevant.

Notes

1. See Tresch (1981).

2.   For a contrasting view, see Sugden and Williams (1978, 97). Their conception of a decision-making approach has some similarities but is more constrained than that adopted here.

3.   For a more complete analysis, see Schmid (1987).

3

Program Information Structure

It is hard enough to change individuals, but it is even harder to change them to an unspecified state.

-- author unknown

3.1. Micro and Macro Perspectives

The micro view of public investment analysis is the project, whereas the macro view is the budget or plan. The way in which the project level analyses are done affects the way in which they can be aggregated into budgets and plans. One macro view is simply a list of projects of all types presented in rank order to decision makers. But, in fact, projects tend to be grouped by some organizational (agency) unit and involve some mix of micro and submacro views. Particular attention will be given in this text to preparing micro studies in a manner that permits them to be systematically aggregated for various purposes. The consequences of alternative taxonomies of effects and groupings of expenditures will be explored as they affect the ability of different groups to participate in public investment decisions (Carr-Hill 1984).

The benefit categories of some governmental programs are obvious. For example, if a flood control structure is built, the product is decreased flood damage to crops and buildings. The product of an irrigation project is increased tons of cotton. However, in many activities of government, the product category is not so obvious. What is the product of the office of civil rights or the state police? How can you tell if you have more of it than last year? A category of output that can be physically counted is necessary before analysts and politicians can proceed to place values on outputs and systematically set priorities among competing programs for the public budget. Total value is always a function of some price multiplied by quantity. But first we need a nominal category for the quantity.[1]

The purpose of this chapter is to provide some practical insight into the conceptualization and definition of categories for program outputs and impacts. The consequences of alternative formulations also will be explored in the broader context of alternative budget formats.

3.2.   Consequences of Input versus Impact Budget Formats

The operation of government can be seen as a causal sequenced flow system. Inputs of personnel, materials, and capital goods are combined by a government agency in certain operations and activities to produce outputs of various goods and services, which in turn have some impact on the lives of citizens (Mowitz 1980; CIDA 1980a, 1980b). The quantitative impact is rooted in a qualitative description of an objective or goal. The causal relationship between each link involves a set of external conditions (variables) that are outside the project manager's control. These conditions must be specified for the hypothesized relationship to be realized. In outline form, the flow can be depicted as:

Inputs------>Outputs------>Impacts------>Program Objective

Although there are no sharp distinctions between adjoining stages, this conception of the flow as a continuum is important, as we will see. An *input budget* consisting of line item inputs is the most common budget format. Budgets that add output data are often referred to as *performance budgets*, and those that add impact data and relate it to qualitative program objectives are called *program budgets*, particularly if all agencies contributing to a given type of impact are aggregated. Output and impact data are obtained from the analysis of individual projects.

As a result of the general lack of impact categories and counts, budget information is usually presented to political decision makers in terms of dollars attached to various inputs. When the production function is poorly understood, programs are evaluated primarily in terms of inputs such as money spent, people employed, and cases handled. Professional standards are developed that sanctify these inputs, often in terms of requirements per unit of population. The input budget does facilitate cost projections over time and the search for alternate suppliers to make sure the input is purchased at the lowest possible price.

Inputs are grouped by agency or government department. A typical example is the local school budget shown in Table 3.1. In this format, the political decision is focused on incremental changes in one particular input category versus another. For example, should there be an increase in spending for teachers and cutbacks in spending for texts and equipment? Teaching could be expressed as teacher days or student contact hours. These input categories have their own history of development. Some are related to the needs of professional managers of any governmental activity, who have developed certain categories for management control.[2] At some point, a check must be written for a particular good or service. In allocating funds, the legislature is interested in controlling the discretion of bureaucrats, and this is accomplished by making appropriations in input categories that can then be audited to ensure that the bureaucrat did only what was intended by

Table 3.1 Example of an Input Budget for Schools

Cost Category	Current Year Dollars (000)	Proposed Dollars (000)
Principals	197	200
Teachers	1,217	1,500
Secretaries	58	60
Safety patrol	1	2
Texts	10	9
Supplies	50	60
Audiovisual	15	18

the legislature. At least legislators know that the bureaucrats have not taken all the money and spent it to furnish their offices. Legislative oversight has traditionally focused on questions of fraud and misapplication of funds.

Input budget categories also reflect public concerns. Because taxpayers often lament that too much money is spent for administrative salaries or suspect that officials are taking recreational junkets at public expense, there are sometimes separate categories for administrative salaries and travel.

Whatever utility the input categories provide for budget control and accountability to taxpayers, input budgets do not provide much information on what government is trying to produce. The school budget is intended to fulfill an objective called education. But what are the units of measure? One that comes quickly to mind is number of graduates. This measure is certainly of interest to many people, but it leaves unanswered the question of what knowledge, skills, and behaviors these graduates possess as a result of the expenditures. In addition to the tough analytical and measurement problems raised by output categories, there are social and political reasons why output and impact category budgets are scarce. Although many may agree that administrative salaries are too high and travel by administrators is wasteful, there is less agreement on how to define an educated person. Input budgets allow political representatives to focus attention on categories of choice that are less likely to engender heated and divisive debate than would a program budget.

Not all interests are served by input budgets. A program budget serves different functions. First, it focuses the political decision on trade-offs among the ultimate effects on different groups of citizens, determining who will get what rather than who will have money nominally spent to their benefit. Of course, if you are an input supplier, you want to know which inputs are going to be purchased rather than who is going to receive a final consumer good or service or what it will do for different members of the public.

Second, the program budget focuses attention on the fact that several agencies and departments of government may provide the same final product. They may have different approaches, technologies, and intermediate outputs, but the impact on the citizen may be the same. A budget that is given in impact terms, facilitates comparisons among agencies and their respective abilities to produce more of a given impact for less money than another. This type of analysis is called *cost-effectiveness*. There is a large literature in which per capita costs of performing some given local function, such as police protection are compared. Middle management might be concerned with which kind of patrol car to buy or how to minimize cost per mile driven, but upper management may ask what miles driven has to do with crime rates. If crime rate is the category chosen, then not only can different patrol methods and equipment be compared, but police activity can be compared with penal corrections and social work. Even different police departments cannot be compared unless the product is carefully defined and held constant.

Third, the program budget facilitates calculation of changes in the rate of inputs compared to changes in the rate of output or impact. In many production relationships, an input threshold must be reached before any output is produced. At that point every 1 percent increase in input results in a more than proportional increase in output until output tapers off, eventually reaching the point at which no additional output is obtained, no matter what the input. Increasing or decreasing returns to size has important implications for budget choices. In a year of tight budgets, it is common to find governments asking for an across-the-board percentage cut in all agencies. This appears to be fair, and the politician does not have to explain to constituents why one program was cut and another not. However, this equal treatment may not produce equal results: output in one program may be significantly reduced, whereas there may be sufficient slack in another program to leave output unchanged. An input budget will not reveal these differences.

The program budget also highlights complementary relationships between or among agencies. Agency A may provide an input or complementary product for agency B. It makes no sense to cut agency A and expand agency B, the extra money for B will not result in any increased output without a corresponding expansion in A.

We can draw several implicit distinctions from the discussion thus far. The base unit is the *cost category*, which is a grouping of inputs by some physical or activity attribute, such as labor or travel. The level of aggregation for an input budget stops here. A *project* or *element* is a grouping of inputs by an agency (or set of agencies) to achieve a given effect. This discussion begins at the project level and moves upward. Alternative cost categories are of concern to project managers and are not extensively discussed. A *program* is a grouping of projects across agencies to achieve a given effect. A *budget* or *plan* displays investment allocation to all programs and may be for a national government or any subdivision thereof.

3.3.   Formulation of Output and Impact Categories for Projects, Programs, and Budgets

It is no easy task to conceive of useful categories or constructs for a program budget. In this section I will present some general principles of impact category conceptualization and illustrate their application. All measurement involves a nominal scale to classify objects, properties, or events, including quantity, quality, and time. The validity of these categorical constructs (nominal scales) cannot be tested by reference to a formula but can be probed by asking questions. It is easy to pass legislation and allocate money to agencies and programs; however, it takes the development of impact constructs to make politicians come to grips with what objectives they really had in mind.

3.3.1.   General Principles
The first step is to decide where the analysis is to be applied along the production function chain from inputs, through outputs (intermediate goods), to impacts (final goods). If there is to be broad participation of the public in decision making, the performance of projects must be described in terms of impacts--final goods and services that affect the lives of citizens. The problem is that as we move farther along this chain, categories aggregate, units become less distinct, and, increasingly, outside factors beyond the project manager's control affect results. Inputs are necessary and sufficient to produce outputs. However, although outputs are necessary to produce impacts, they are not sufficient; the outputs must interact with outside forces to produce impacts. Objectives are qualitative statements about impacts, so the link between the item that can be counted and the more qualitatively described objective needs to be forged.

In the case of national defense, for example, it is relatively easy to conceptualize the inputs of personnel, military hardware, and activities and outputs such as deployable missiles. But what do these produce? The common response would be national and personal security, yet this objective is highly abstract. Where is the dividing line between secure and insecure? Are we secure if we are not actually being attacked? Is security the same as peace or not being at war? How about appeasement or danger of nuclear accident? These are the types of questions the analyst must ask the political representatives to determine the construct validity of a quantitative impact category. The answers to these questions establish how valid it is to link a quantity such as the number of missiles with a certain destructive capacity to a qualitative concept such as security.

Any category of impact performance involves a purposeful distinction of qualities. For example, although there are many similarities between a horse and a cow, they can be distinguished according to human purpose: one is better for pulling loads and riding, and the other for giving milk. Whenever human purpose is part of classification, the interests of some people will be better served than those of others. In addition to nominal qualitative distinctions, we need to define the unit to be counted. Once we decide on what characteristics separate horses from cows, we need to determine what unit to measure. Is it to be individuals, families, or weight? In a manner of speaking, one dimension asks what characteristics constitute "horseness," whereas the unitary issue involves what constitutes more or fewer horses. What characteristics (and over what range of variance) constitute a horse as distinct from a cow, and is the quality of horseness important for the problem at hand or do we need, for example, grades of horses?

Take the case of a nutritional objective. What is the connection between qualitative objective and quantitative impact measure? It is common simply to regard the impact of an agricultural project as production of so many units of wheat or cattle. Yet, for some purposes, it may be more important to see the product as units of protein (in some countries, protein is the limiting factor in nutrition rather than calories). The basic property of a nominal or classificatory scale is that the properties of objects in one category must be equal to each other but not to anything else (Nachmias 1979, 85). Any category, however, is an aggregation of features. Not all units within a category are exactly the same. For example, not all bushels of wheat are the same; even all bushels of grade number one wheat are not identical. But if the analyst asks policy makers if the same value would likely be put on all units of number one wheat, the need for further subclasses can be established. It is human purpose that sets limits to the range of certain selected features, such as protein and moisture content. The problem for the project analyst is to decide when the variation of features is sufficient to distinguish a product qualitatively (such as grade number one wheat from grade number two), or one product from another (such as wheat from corn), or to select one feature over others and submerge other differences (for example, calories rather than type of grain). The object being measured is therefore equal with respect to chosen qualities and over a chosen range of allowed variance. The chosen range must be logically related to the choice of objective.

Impact can be conceived of as an index of production in which certain features are explicitly noted and summed according to some set of weights. For example, each unit of protein, fat, and calories can be assigned a weight, and then the food product can be expressed as an index number of summed nutrition features.[3] The choice of weights is a choice among competing interests.

The guiding principle in the choice of qualitative distinctions is to group impacts in such a way as to facilitate comparisons with other projects (or, in the case of budget level analysis, to facilitate comparisons among programs and agencies). The grouping of features or projects should raise questions of substitutes and complements. Since alternative groupings are possible, different interests are served by focusing attention on comparisons and trade-offs along certain dimensions.

Another consideration in choice of impact categories involves distribution over persons, geography, and time. Should the categories emphasize the general function being performed or the receiving clientele? For example, in documenting a housing project, should we note only the number of units, or should they be further divided into units in rural and urban areas, or units inhabited by rich or poor, or young or old?

This discussion may be restated more abstractly. The validation of a measure involves asking questions and gathering evidence to support the argument that the measure does measure what it appears (or is supposed) to measure. What it is supposed to measure is a matter of clarifying politically chosen objectives. The validation process involves construct, predictive, and content validity.

Construct validity refers to the relationship between the chosen quantitative impact measure and the underlying qualitative objectives of the project (see Cook and Campbell 1979, 59-70). It requires a theory to indicate expected relationships between the chosen measure and other included (and omitted) variables. If these do not hold, either the measure or the theory is poor. If the objective is vague, it provides no guidance as to choice among alternative quantitative physical measures. Furthermore, to say that quantitative measures fit the objective is not to say the objective is valid--that is a political question.

Choice of impact categories is antecedent to valuation (pricing). Yet, in many cases, the product categories seem to be given by the market. For example, everyone knows that rice is a certain kind of product and has a market price. There seems to be no issue of choosing the product category for an irrigation project, and it is easily multiplied by available prices. The program objective may also be expressed in quantitative terms, such as "raise farmer incomes." Then there is little issue of construct validity relating objectives and impact measures, as both are already in common quantitative terms. If analysis proceeds with these given product categories, which are bought and sold, government is in effect confirming these categories. But even market product categories are not simply natural phenomena. There are public choices of rules affecting grades and standards. For example, to be classified as milk and meat these products must have specified ingredients. Therefore what things are called affects demand and prices. The public could change these categories of commerce. However, in some cases it may want (or be able) to change them only for purposes of public project analysis.

In some cases, analysts do not seem to specify a unit of physical output/impact but just go directly from a project input to its associated change in income. For example, a health project might be measured in terms of changes in incomes (holding nonhealth inputs to income constant) without being explicit about the units of product, such as days of work missed because of illness. The calculation of days of work missed times the wage rate is implicit.

Although many government programs have the broad objective of raising people's incomes, some of the activities cannot be directly linked to income change. For example, police programs could have an income-enhancing effect, but one not empirically possible to specify. Prevention of theft and fraud enhances business income, but it may be difficult to determine by how much. Thus, the crime rate is chosen as an impact measure rather than a change in income. The construct validity linking crime rate and income objectives remains a qualitative judgmental issue. If the unit change in crime rate is explicitly priced later, it will be done administratively and not by any observed change in market incomes.

Closely related to construct validity is predictive validity. When some criterion measure is unavailable in the particular case being investigated, a proxy must be found. For example, does IQ score predict success in graduate school or on the job? Tests of correlation from other studies must be used as evidence.

In addition to conceptual problems, there are sampling problems. Content validity addresses the following question: Does the sample represent the total population of the variable being measured? Of all possible instances of a measure, what sample is sufficient? Content validity involves sampling from all possible examples of a chosen construct or concept.

To summarize, the project information system reflects choices of categories, which in turn reflect choices of where in the input-impact chain emphasis is given, what qualitative features are emphasized and how they are weighted, the degree of aggregation, and whether a functional or recipient focus is provided. The choice of the project information system then is the first place that value judgment enters into analysis.

Should the analyst include all effects in all dimensions? Too much information is not manageable by the public or its representatives; yet, if an effect is not listed, it is regarded as having zero value. Therefore the first analytic task is to determine what is important to individual groups so those items can be included. Any analyst is constrained by experience and the cultural bounds of learning, but interviews and hearings can help select the items to be included and the qualitative categories in which they are to be placed. Some guidance may also be available in statements of objectives contained in legislation or appropriation bills, budget messages of a chief executive, or national (or local) plans.

There is a debate in the evaluation literature concerning the appropriateness of qualitative versus quantitative analysis. Qualitative data "are collected as open-ended narrative without attempting to fit program activities or peoples' experiences into predetermined, standardized categories" (Patton 1980, 22).[4] But where do quantitative data collected in standardized categories, such as education test scores, come from? These categories come from qualitative experience, including other studies, theory, and preliminary interviews. Qualitative analysis is an input into quantitative model specification, into deciding what variables (both program input dimensions and nonprogram factors) are experimentally controlled, and into choosing the definition and specifications of performance categories. Therefore, the qualitative versus quantitative dichotomy might better be seen as a progressive and interacting continuum. Each analyst begins with some prior experience affecting his or her definition of categories. This is not to say that commonly used measures should not be questioned periodically through an inductive analysis of how persons affected by the project express its effect on them. The pragmatic analyst is willing to redefine categories as problems change but cannot afford to start with a blank slate each time or ignore relevant data previously collected by others.

The qualitative-quantitative dimension is a continuum. The results of a test, observation, or program participants' verbal response are shaped and limited by the defined features of output or impact categories. Even if the categories are recorded from open ended responses by program participants, the analyst must interpret them. A qualitative analysis must focus, aggregate, and suppress some information; the issue therefore becomes where some detail is lost, not whether it will be lost.

All data collection is limited in the sense that there is a limit to inclusion of more and more features that determine eligibility for inclusion of an item in a category. The definition of the category is standardized at that point and even though members of the category (class) may not be homogeneous in some features, these differences are ignored. The characteristics and boundaries of a category should be refined and elaborated up to the point that a member of the category would be similarly included or excluded by most observers (analysts and users) considering the objectives of the program. For example, suppose a program's purpose is to make juvenile criminals more mature. A descriptive, qualitative analysis would emphasize the client's verbal expression of program effects, including the direct assertion, "I am more mature." If anyone were willing to pay for a project whose output is people who make this statement, the data are sufficient. A qualitative analysis would probably collect further observations that the client and/or analyst would regard as reflecting maturity, such as punctuality and initiative beyond teacher or employer direction. Some informal judgment is made that indicates a client is more mature even if only one of the features were present or present at an intense enough level. Any category is a weighted index of features (qualities). When the summary statement is made that most clients increased in maturity, there is an implicit element of counting, both in the term "most" as well as in the aggregation of details contained in the concept "maturity." If the term "most" is made precise, we have explicit quantitative analysis. If the meaning of maturity is defined, then we might expect everyone to have the same image of what constitutes maturity and to place any given person in the same category. This is what is meant here by a standardized category or measure.

Definition of categories is a matter of degree. It might be asserted that rather than worrying about maturity as a factor affecting crime, the real test is whether the juvenile commits another crime. Leaving aside the question of availability of data, we can see that the concept of crime is also a definitional matter. Just as with maturity, we have to check occasionally to determine whether everyone (most) has the same image of crime and of the acts that are to be included in crime, that is, construct validity (and whether the recorded data include and are representative of all instances, that is, content validity).

To conclude, a category that can be counted is an aggregation of bounded features as is any nonnumerical qualitative category. It is possible to have meaningless counts of vague qualities, and it is possible to have only a sense of general quantity of rather precise and communicable qualities. To obtain a budget format that emphasizes comparisons of both input and output alternatives, it is desirable to move as far along the qualitative-quantitative continuum as resources and the importance of the problem allow. Many government projects probably warrant only a few impressionistic surveys; others exist that would benefit from both in-depth qualitative analysis and an intense development of precise standardized categories to facilitate meaningful quantification. Most projects probably lie in between. For further illustrations, see U.S. Department of Health, Education and Welfare (1966b), Kasl (1972), Kiene (1972), Schmid, et al. (1973), and Torrance (1986).

3.3.2. Application to Choice of Program Categories

The preceding discussion has involved the principles of choosing categories at the micro or project level. Some of the same principles are applicable at the macro level (where various projects are aggregated). Output and impact budgets, although rare, are not new, and reformers have long recommended them (Babunakis 1982). For a historical review, see Schick (1966) and Havens (1983). A major thrust in the application of program budgets came in the U.S. Department of Defense under Robert McNamara who brought to government some of his experience in private business with management by objective. In Washington, it was called the Planning, Programming, Budgeting System (PPBS) and was implemented in all departments by President Lyndon Johnson in 1965. PPBS was never firmly established in the habits of the Federal bureaucracy and only remnants remained after the Johnson administration. Another version, called zero-based budgeting, was added by President Jimmy Carter. It is perhaps ironic that, as the use of PPBS began to wane at the Federal level, it was picked up in a number of states (Schick 1971).

The substance of program budgeting in practice can be illustrated by reference to the system implemented in Michigan in the 1970s. The outputs of government and the proposed expenditures for each output were grouped into the following eight program categories that, when dollars of spending are attached, constitute a budget:

1. Protection of Persons and Property
2. Health--Physical and Mental Well-being
3. Intellectual Development and Education
4. Social Development
5. Economic Development and Income Maintenance
6. Transportation and Communication
7. Recreation and Cultural Enrichment
8. Direction and Support Services (administration and overhead)

The primary use of this level of aggregation is to summarize spending and examine trade-offs and priorities among large categories of programs. To indicate an alternative grouping, the above Michigan program categories can be compared to the functional categories used by the U.S. government in fiscal year 1977.

1. National defense
2. International affairs
3. General science, space, and technology
4. Natural resources, environment, and energy
5. Agriculture
6. Commerce and transportation
7. Community and regional development
8. Education, training, employment, and social science
9. Health
10. Income security
11. Veterans' benefits and services
12. Law enforcement and justice
13. General government
14. Revenue sharing and general purpose fiscal assistance
15. Interest on public debt

The establishment of the major program categories is not a key operational factor, as the real action is at the subcategory level at which output and impact quantification is made. Still, no categorization is politically neutral. Any aggregation tends to focus attention on certain trade-offs and submerge others.[5]

The program categories into which particular activities are placed can affect how a program is conceived and managed. For example, should Medicaid be placed in the health category or in the income security category?

Is the objective to improve health or to transfer income? The placement can affect political response. Do politicians think they can increase public support by reporting increased spending for health or poverty programs? The choice of category may also affect the determination of which agency should administer a program. If categorized as a health program, it can be argued that the program should be administered by the health department; however, if classified as an income transfer program, perhaps justification exists for having the program administered by the welfare department or building it into the tax system and having it administered by the treasury. The administrative assignment of such a program can affect its direction. For example, if a doctor is found to have made fraudulent claims for Medicaid payments, the welfare or treasury agencies may be inclined to immediately withdraw the payments and demand that the doctor's license be revoked. The health agency, however, may be more protective of medical resources and favor an educational approach.

The consequence of program categorization can be illustrated further by reference to Category 1 in the Michigan budget, "Protection of Persons and Property."[6] The budget display contained the following goal statement: "To provide an environment and social system in which the lives of individuals and the property of individuals and organizations are protected from natural and manmade disasters, and from illegal and unfair actions." The major categories were:

Protection from Crime
Consumer Protection
Personal Safety Protection
Protection from Disaster
Civil and Constitutional Rights Protection

Dollar amounts of spending for the previous year and that proposed for the next year were listed after the various items. If we select one of these categories and determine its structure in more detail, the hierarchy would be as follows:

Program: Protection of Persons and Property
Category: Protection from Disaster
Subcategory: Readiness and Recovery
Element: Readiness Force and Recovery Force

The program level is very general and although the items included have a common theme, they range in this case from ordinary crime to protection of consumer rights and civil rights. The specific category used for illustration has to do with protection against disasters. The most common type is natural disasters, such as tornado and flood. State government helps local government recover from such disasters by rescuing people and policing against looters.

The subcategory level is a major point of decision because it is associated with specific, measurable, time-related impacts. In this case, the objective was defined as "To undertake all necessary measures to anticipate the occurrence of catastrophic events for purposes of prevention or rapid recovery." The program structure is a hierarchy that concludes with elements or projects that are very specific tasks and activities performed by particular governmental bureaus or divisions thereof and to which dollar amounts are attached in the budget and in appropriation bills. Lower levels of management work with disaggregations, but the element (project) represents the decision unit chosen at the top executive and legislative level.

As previously noted, program budgets often reveal the fact that two different agencies produce the same or related outputs and impacts. In Michigan, readiness and recovery forces are provided by both the state police and the Michigan National Guard. In the usual input budget, the proposed expenditures for these two units would be listed in two different parts of the document under two different departments. It would not be readily apparent that they were producing related outputs. Performance budgets raise the immediate question of relative effectiveness of these two agencies.

The input budget lists dollars of expenditures but does not indicate what the agencies actually produce. Just what is meant by readiness and recovery? How would we know if we had more or less of it? The usual input budget categories list items such as salaries, equipment, and maintenance. The Michigan program budget went a bit further by listing output measures. The National Guard said it produced 6,000 personnel in immediate deployment positions in 1972-1973 and if given the proposed budget could produce the same next year. The number of deployable personnel supplies more information than the salary data, but still does not indicate what these deployable personnel actually accomplish. Information such as number of deployable personnel can be labeled "outputs" or intermediate products, but the citizens and their representatives need to have information on "impacts" or final products, expressed in terms of how government affects their lives.

The subprojects or inputs utilized by the state police differ from those of the National Guard. The police emphasize planning and training whereas the guard emphasize the direct supply of labor and service. The police help local governments and schools develop disaster plans. The output measures include the number of such plans for the current and next fiscal year, as well as the number of persons receiving first aid training and the number of hours that the police are engaged in actual recovery operations. Again, these workload measures contain more information than the input categories of salaries and equipment, but they are still intermediate products and not final results. People might like to know the consequences of these plans and recovery man-hours. A bureaucrat may believe that a beautiful plan is an end in itself, but the citizen with a broken leg under a pile of rubble wants to know what his chances are for getting out alive. Some possible impact indicators are annual dollar value of property loss avoided, time taken to restore a basic service such as electricity, and reduction in the injury rate per unit of population affected by disasters.

It may seem that the choice of output and impact categories is itself a make-work project for bureaucrats, with little substantive consequence. However, the choice of categories shapes the character of political debate. The budget display also contained data called "need-demand estimators." The data indicated that of 169 local jurisdictions eligible for disaster plans in 1972-1973 only 105 had such plans. Keeping track of governmental activity in these terms suggests that the gap between 105 and 169 should be closed. The focus of the debate then tends to be on how fast the gap should be closed, rather than what the plans accomplish, or whether the person caught under the rubble pile is better served by projects producing more deployable personnel of the National Guard or projects producing more man-hours of State Police recovery activity, more local people trained in first aid, or more disaster plans. It is not possible to determine how these various specified activities fit together unless there is some measure of a more final product. With an impact indicator, it is possible to determine what mix of projects ("elements" and "activities") from each agency can provide a given level of service to citizens at the least cost. The measure of percentage of jurisdictions with plans fails the test of construct validity when related to the qualitative objective of "protecting persons and property."

The level of aggregation represented by the element or decision unit is a policy choice, for it is the level at which top executives and legislators make dollar trade-off decisions. In the "readiness and recovery force" example, policy makers decide among increments in spending that achieve injury and property loss reductions. It is for lower level managers to determine the mix of military and police forces that is most cost-effective.

Simply observing changes in impacts over time is not enough to indicate that the program activities in question caused the change. Many things could be affecting property loss and injury rates other than the government programs. To determine causal relationships among levels (or mixes) of different inputs, outputs, and impacts that affect people requires careful testing and program evaluation studies, which is the subject of Chapter 4. One of the attractions of input or intermediate output category budgets is that the information needed to prepare them is readily available in agency files. For example, it is relatively easy to keep track of the number of plans prepared or personnel trained, but it is not as easy to determine if these caused a change in property loss or injury rate.

When impact data are unavailable, output measures from project analyses are still a worthwhile addition to the usual input budget. If an agency said that "X" dollars would produce "Y" outputs, it is possible in the context of next year's budget to ask if this level was achieved, or to see if some other agency did it more cheaply, or if an agency in another state used a different input mix at a lower cost per unit of output. None of this is possible if we keep track only of dollars spent for salaries and equipment.

3.3.3.   Application to Civil Rights Budget Component

Further understanding of the principles of construct validation can be obtained by looking at another example at both the micro and macro level. Impact or program budgets may be useful in analyzing physical impacts such as property damages and injury rates, but can they be applied to services? The fact that they can is validated by observing another "category" of the broad "program" of Protection of Persons and Property, namely, that of Protection of Civil Rights. The Department of Civil Rights has an "element," or project, called investigation and adjudication (Michigan 1975). This contains two components. The department receives complaints from individuals who believe their civil rights have been violated. Investigations are made and if the examiner believes the complaint is valid, an attempt at voluntary correction is attempted. If this fails, the case may be turned over to the attorney general for legal action. Another component of investigation is called contract compliance. State law requires that suppliers and contractors for the state meet equal employment opportunity standards. An investigation of each supplier is made and compliance with the standards determined. These two activities are quite different in technique and probably should be two separate "elements" so that their cost effectiveness might better be compared.

The 1974-1975 Executive Budget contained the following output measures:

Number of persons with formal complaints of unlawful discrimination
Number of formal complaints investigated
Number of contractors for whom certification to bid for state contracts has been requested
Number of certifications issued on awardability

Again, note how the budget categories themselves suggest a gap between the number of persons making complaints and the number of those investigated each year without any indication of just whose interests are being served. The backlog of univestigated complaints combined with the gap between the number of state suppliers requesting certification and the number that could be checked with current staff was the main argument presented by the department in its quest for funds. The data displayed showed the number of cases for the prior and current year and what could be expected in the following year if the requested funds were appropriated.

The existence of a backlog is often taken as justification for expansion of a particular government activity. However, there are several problems in interpreting such backlogs. For example, a service that is offered free of charge to the user will be used up to the point at which the product has no net value to the user. Sometimes free services are justified because some of the recipients cannot afford the cost. But even the poor might prefer that available resources be applied to other purposes and these preferences will not be discovered if program funding is directed to programs with existing backlogs.

There is another problem with defining program objectives in terms of backlogs and unanswered requests if these data are highly aggregative. It suggests that all types of complaints are of equal importance and priority. Some people may think adjudicating a housing or job-related complaint is more important than investing a complaint involving a barber's refusal to cut a person's hair or a slur against a homosexual. Others would disagree. Allocation of scarce funds by type of complaint is a political decision and will get made either consciously or by default and by either the legislature, governor, agency director, or some clerk deep in the bowels of the agency. If the legislature is given no data on number of incoming complaints by type, it cannot participate in the decision of how to allocate scarce funds and investigators among different complaint categories. Conversely, if the legislature provides no qualitative goals, the analysts do not know what to measure. If the executive or legislative branch does not give more content to program objectives than is contained in the reference to "Protection of Persons and Property," it will be impossible to determine construct validity and to decide whether the output measure should lump all kinds of complaints together.

Explicit resource allocation and clearly defined objectives are often risky for politicians.[7] They may complain bitterly about a particular usurpation of legislative prerogative by the executive but at the same time avoid responsibility for explicit allocation among contending groups. This is especially true where the competing groups are evenly balanced in numbers. No matter which choice politicians make, half of the constituents are upset. In this case, politicians who are accountable to voters may prefer to sidestep the issue and sympathize with both sides over the general scarcity of funds to meet all needs rather than to bite the bullet and make it clear that certain categories of complaints are to be investigated first. They will prefer an allocation of funds on a first-come, first-served basis or an arbitrary allocation made by some faceless clerk. Construct validity is tested by asking if all complaint cases are considered of equal value.

It was noted that budget categories are instruments of bureaucratic control. If the legislature appropriates money for salaries, the money cannot be used for travel unless officially transferred or reallocated. Related control consequences result from performance budgets. If an agency justifies its budget in terms of some intermediate output, then the agency will try to fulfill that output any way it can. Agencies will optimize performance to the measure of output rather than to the service criteria (impact) underlying it (Schon 1974, 157). For example, if the civil rights agency has promised to investigate 1,000 more complaints with its budget increase, it will have an incentive to accomplish that goal even if it means taking the easier cases first or taking cases that accomplish little even when settled. This is referred to in the trade as "creaming." A pathbreaking case that would set a precedent and thereby affect the lives of many people may be put aside as the agency fills its quota of cases with easy to settle, but minor, complaints. This is why it is important to move as far as possible toward accounting in terms of impact rather than output.

What do complaint investigations accomplish? One measure is a change in minority family average income as a percentage of majority family income, or minority unemployment compared to majority unemployment. As noted, it is not enough just to record the present state of these variables, it is necessary to determine whether these indicators changed as a result of a particular program or "element." It would then be possible in theory to compare the effectiveness of different approaches to achieving the objective associated with the "subcategory" Discriminatory Practices Control. In addition to the complaint investigation already discussed, the department offers preventative services. This "element" primarily involves education directed to changing attitudes and behavior. For example, employers are trained to be more sensitive in their relations with minorities. If the program element prevents a violation from occurring, it has the same impact as a corrective program element that obtains restitution for a civil rights violation. It would be desirable to determine whether the preventive approach or the corrective complaint investigation approach produced the greater change in minority income and employment per dollar spent on each.

It is also important to note the time flow of outputs. The same investment in preventive services may produce a greater output, but may take longer. The trade-off between products now and products later requires a political choice. The legislature or agency personnel face a dilemma. The public may demand that current complaints be resolved, although the agency may know that more could be accomplished in time with a preventative approach. Any system has to live with political realities, but it should be noted that what people demand is related to what they perceive. They will not be patient for results unless they have been given information on the magnitude and time flow of outputs associated with various approaches. The political reality is in part a function of what budget and performance information citizens have.

The more that final products or impacts of a service activity are influenced by the interaction of the intermediate good with the people being served, the more their perceptions, attitudes, and personal characteristics will affect what the activity actually accomplishes (Garn et al. 1976). The final result is often a joint product of the services of government and the consuming activity of the client or recipient. For example, the effect of complaint investigation on minority family income is influenced by the characteristics of the complainant and the person accused of civil rights discrimination. Again, this is why it is important to do accounting in terms of final rather than intermediate products and workloads.

The cause-effect relationships for some "elements" and delivery methods are easier to understand than for others. For example, it is possible to document the investigation of employment-related complaints that result in cash settlements. These impacts can also be counted in terms of number of people employed, reemployed, or promoted. It is relatively easy to relate program expenditures on certain classes of cases to the resulting impacts either in terms of dollar settlements or number of jobs, even though the budget makers have not done so. The same kind of cause-effect relationship can be established for the activity of contract compliance. The number of minority workers in various job categories can be counted for firms doing business with the state. We may be relatively confident that any change in number of minority employees was caused by the contract compliance investigation staff, which made loss of state business to these contractors real if they did not come up to standards. Causal relationships are never certain, but they are more clearly established here than in the link between preventative services and changes in employment. In the latter case, there are many possible intervening variables that could affect employment. Not everything that is poorly measured or uncertain is a bad investment. On the other hand, perhaps money should tend to flow to areas in which results are relatively certain. If money is so allocated it gives increased incentive to the bureaucrats to improve their impact measures. No budget format is neutral in its effect on appropriation decisions, though causal effects are hard to determine.

To summarize, the difference between an input and program budget can be seen by contrasting Table 3.1 with Table 3.2, which incorporates some of the ideas previously discussed. For each alternative project element there is an impact category and quantity at 2 budget dollar cost levels.

Table 3.2 Example of a Program Budget

Program: Protection of Persons and Property
Category: Civil Rights and Constitutional Rights Protection

Element (input)	Impact Category	Impact Quantity Each Element Has Budget Cost of	
		$1 million	$2 million
Employment compliance enforcement	Settlements after unlawful dismissal from employment	$2 million in cash settlement next year	$2.5 million in cash settlement next year
Housing compliance enforcement	Person obtained housing after discriminatory refusal	2,000 persons	3,000 persons
Prevention: to change attitued of employees	Reduction in claims for unlawful dismissal	$1 million in cash settlement 5 years from now	$2 million in cash settlement 5 years from now
Contract compliance	Minority employment income	$3 million in new wages	$6 million in new wages

3.4. Risk-Benefit Analysis

Choice of input and output categories is also central to a type of cost-physical output trade-off display that is misleadingly named *risk-benefit analysis* (Crouch and Wilson 1982; Haimes 1981). It is increasingly used in the United States as part of regulatory decisions on pesticides and food additives. The analysis is applied to costs of regulation borne by nongovernment entities instead of the public treasury costs previously analyzed but the principles are the same. An example of this type of analysis is that done by the National Research Council (1980) on the impact of chlorobenzilate used to control rust mites that harm citrus. Instead of alternative investment projects, the choice is between regulatory alternatives ranging from allowing use of the chemical without limit to various degrees of restriction in method or place of application including outright prohibition. Each degree of limitation reduces the amount of dose of the chemical to which different segments of the population are exposed, but at increasing cost in controlling crop damages. The forgone benefits of insect control or ameliorative practices to reduce exposure to the chemical are the costs of regulation. The cost and dose impact data are displayed in Figure 3.1. The cost and dose coordinates are shown as points but actually are a range of values because of uncertainty. Incorporation of judgments on uncertainty into analysis is the topic of Chapter 10.

The law requires the Environmental Protection Agency (EPA) only to weigh the costs and risk (benefit of reduced hazard to human and other life); it does not require systematic choice. In fact, the law requires a different standard for fresh as opposed to processed foods. Still, the cost-physical output trade-off display does create opportunities to make comparisons. The National Research Council made such a comparison with the formerly restricted pesticide heptachlor. The EPA reached its previous judgment that the risks outweighed the costs without actually measuring the costs. To make any comparison, the impact must be in similar physical terms and units. The EPA utilized a carcinogenic activity index. Each chemical is placed on this index, allowing development of the equivalent lifetime dose scale shown in Figure 3.1. The index is an intermediate output. There is some linkage to the final good, which is impact on life, but in the absence of tests of a lifetime of exposure to the chemical, the relationship remains uncertain. For a display in terms of rate of cancer per unit of population from food contamination, see U.S. Congress, Office of Technology Assessment (1970, 74).

Some cost-effectiveness comparisons of controlling different chemicals could be made.[8] For example, there could be a rule that says that because heptachlor was banned, any other chemical with the same dose-cost ratio should also be banned. This would not be of much use, however, if the new chemical being analyzed was more expensive to control or had less dose at the same cost. To make this trade-off systematic would require political choice and application of a trade-off function such as is drawn in Figure 3.1. The preferred alternative level of regulation then lies on (or nearest) the trade-off function. Any alternative to the right of the curve is too expensive and any to the left gives too little dose reduction (willing to pay for more if it is available).[9]

If the cost-dose axes are reversed, the cost-dose trade-off function is seen as a usual demand function in Figure 3.2. In drawing it, the government would place an administrative price on dose levels, and by implication, on the cancer index and human life. This choice of price and decision rule moves toward benefit-cost analysis.

This is not an easy move, however, because there is no single output. The dose is received in different intensities by different groups of people. Figure 3.1 shows the effects only on people who apply the pesticide on the

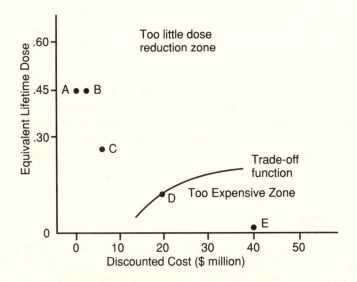

Figure 3.1 Cost-Dose Associated with Regulatory Alternatives and Trade-off Function (A is unregulated use and E is cancellation). Source of data: National Research Council (1980,227)

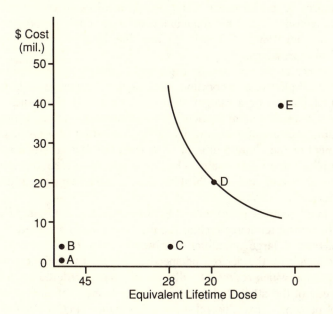

Figure 3.2 Cost-Dose Associated with Regulatory Alternatives and Dose Reduction Demand Curve (A is unregulated use and E is cancellation)

ground. The relationships are different for air applications or consumers or wildlife. Complete systematic analysis would require public choice of weights (prices) on each of these dimensions, which may exhaust analytic resources and political patience leaving the decision on an ad hoc basis. But a cost-physical output trade-off display, even if the outputs remain in multiple physical terms, is a good place to start and represents more information usefully organized than was available when the previous heptachlor decision was made by the government. For further discussion, see Graham and Vaupel (1981). Choice of a regulatory standard such as alternative D in Figure 3.2 implies a value for the effect on human life that is elaborated in Chapter 5, Section 5.8.

3.5.   Formulation of Units and Scales

The previous discussion has been in terms of choosing names with which to discuss performance. Implicit in the discussion is the attachment of numbers to these names. Nunnally (1978, 3) points out that "measurement consists of rules for assigning numbers to objects in such a way as to represent quantities of attributes." We do not measure objects as such, but rather through some process of abstraction we measure attributes. These attributes concern relations among objects on a particular selected dimension. When the analyst chooses a performance category, it involves a choice of what attributes to consider and this is done in a context of human purpose as these attributes are functional. This is no less the case in the selection of mathematical expressions.

Performance measures may be expressed as simple counts such as the number of unemployed, a proportion, such as the percentage of all people who are unemployed, or a rate of change in a stock or flow, such as the percentage change in unemployment per unit of time. Other expressions involving time are measure of severity, such as duration of a given state of unemployment or the elapsed time of shifts from one state to another. Each of these implies some relationship. The first is related to zero, the second to some selected whole, and the third to time. Each suggests a different perspective.

Other mathematical concepts are used to aggregate and simplify data. Measures of central tendency such as the mean and mode are used to give a selected picture of large quantities of observations. The choice of these measures depends on the desired perspective. Another technique is the use of fractile groups, which represent a division of persons ordered according to the magnitude of the attribute in question into a number of classes of equal numbers of persons. This is useful showing inequalities in the distribution of the attribute. The use of index numbers has already been discussed.

Implicit in all measurement is the choice of a scale. An ordinal scale ranks things from most to least. An interval scale is characterized by a common and constant unit of measurement that assigns a real number to all pairs of objects (properties, events) in the ordered set. A ratio scale not only indicates how far apart one project is from another, but how far each is from zero. The choice of scales and measurement models is a complex specialized field in itself and cannot be treated further here. See Nachmias (1979, Ch. 4) and application in Chapter 5, sections 5.7.2. and 5.7.3. It is important to understand in the context of this book that measurement is not only a technical issue, but also a political issue if it affects public discussion via choice and selection of perspective.

3.6.   Formulation of Cost Categories

Some of the same concepts previously outlined for impacts also apply to cost (input or causal) categories (Epp 1977). Grouping and naming costs involve selection and choice of perspective. For some purposes, it may be useful to simply name the project and sum the monetary costs. But, in other cases, this creates problems in interpretation. For example, although much research has been conducted on the relationship between total spending for education and educational impacts, in general, little correlation has been found (Coleman 1966; Hanushek 1986). Even selected categories of spending, such as teacher training and equipment, show little correlation. However, it is possible that the qualitative aspects of these inputs have been inadequately specified. It is also possible that the particular packaging of these inputs may make a difference. Although there are many educational models that combine inputs in particular ways, there is no well-developed classification of these groupings and no extensive records grouped in this fashion. This makes it difficult to collect a sample of schools (projects) of a similar input mix with which to determine impact in contrast to other input mixes. (This will be further explored in the next chapter on the production function.) It would be useful if we could speak of a type #1 school in contrast to a type #2 school, as is the case for some industrial processes such as the open-hearth or oxygen process in the manufacture of steel. Like any packages, however, the features selected for focus are related to human purpose.

As in the case for impact categories, analysts are sometimes implored to include all costs. Indeed, some authors argue that it is the completeness of cost accounting that distinguishes public from private analysis. First, there is a problem of information overload in the case of costs as in impacts. Some things have to be left out and aggregated if any picture is to emerge from the potential mountain of data. For example, U.S. agencies are now required to prepare environmental impact statements for all projects that might affect the natural environment. This requirement has produced much more data than before, but in some cases the long lists of detailed effects are indigestible. These "impacts," which represent alternate use of resources forgone if the project is built, are project inputs or opportunity costs. To be understandable, impacts that are costs must be categorized as are impacts that are project benefits and performance impacts, as the term was used in the previous sections.

As was noted in Chapter 2, governments have two broad methods to make a decision maker and entrepreneur take the foregone lost opportunities of other present or would-be users into account. They can change private property rights so that the opportunity to use a resource in a certain manner is owned by a particular individual or group. This owner then must be paid off and that expense thus becomes a cost to any new project that needs the resource. Alternatively, when government itself is the entrepreneur, it in effect assigns rights to others when it includes the lost opportunities in resource use in its cost accounts. As in the case of benefits, to omit a certain opportunity foregone from the information system is to assign it a zero value.

It is not helpful to state that a public project analysis includes externalities whereas a private accounting would not. The issue is more clearly seen if we begin with the facts of human interdependence in the face of incompatible uses of resources. It is property rights, whether in the form of legislative and court-made rules or in the form of rules for accounting in public projects, that cause the project manager (investor) to regard the resource as either already owned and at the manager's disposal or something that must be acquired from others at a price. Thus, the analyst, as a technician, cannot presume to tell government that it must account for a selected external effect on another party without having made a judgment of where the property right should lie. The analyst must ask the political authorities where they want the right to be vested, otherwise the analyst usurps the role of making value judgments. This issue will be clearer in Chapter 5 when values are attached to the items included in the information system developed here.

In summary, the issue of construct validity in the formulation of input, output, and impact categories is not to be established by formula, but by an interaction between analyst and politician. The objective of a program or project is developed and clarified by asking questions about alternative ways to specify and count its effects. This process shapes the character of competition among agencies and among its subunits.

Notes

1.   Bonnen (1975, 757) suggests that a data system is composed of three steps: conceptualization, operationalization of concept (definition of empirical variables), and measurement. Also see MacRae (1985). The same problems arise in national income accounting (Seers 1976).

2.   Some information is useful for several purposes, but sometimes different purposes require fundamentally different kinds of information. Data useful for judging employee performance as a basis for salary and

promotions may not be helpful to managers who wish to aid in the development of the skills of their subordinates.

3. An example is Total Digestible Nutrients. For an application to crime, see Sellin and Wolfgang (1964).

4. For a contrast in approaches, see Booth (1975), Hardin and Borus (1971), and Piore (1979).

5. For a discussion of the conflict over choice of program categories in the U.S. Department of Agriculture, see Nienaber and Wildavsky (1973, 121-125). Also see Lee and Johnson (1983, 110-116) and Hargrove (1980).

6. See Michigan, (1974). For definitions, see Michigan (1973).

7. For further discussion, see Chapter 11.

8. Where there are different mixes of options to achieve a given dose level for a given chemical, cost minimization can be computed. See National Research Council (1975 and 1977).

9. If the Delaney prohibition of any cancer exposure were applied, it would mean that the demand curve is above point E on Figure 3.2, which is the cost of cancellation (100 percent dose reduction). For further discussion, see Chapter 10, Section 10.7.8.

4

Estimating Project Effects

After choosing the classification of project inputs and impacts, the next step is to establish the causal relationship between the two. The question is, how do we know that the project made a difference in performance? In some cases, the public investment analyst works with production functions supplied by technical experts. For example, for an agricultural project, the input-output data may come from agronomists and engineers, for a health project, from physicians, and for an educational project, from educational psychologists. But in other cases these data are not available, and the budget analyst must participate in securing the required data. The analyst must at least know how to interpret production function data; this evaluation is the main purpose of this chapter.

Estimating project effects is usually referred to in the literature as evaluation research. The name is perhaps poorly chosen as it is not concerned with placing values on outputs, but rather in determining whether the project produced any observable output. When people refer to measurement problems, it is hard to tell whether they are referring to classifying units of product, or determining the production function, or placing relative values and priorities on the products. Each of these is considered as a separate step here.

4.1. Threats to Internal Validity

It is common to observe a change in performance sometime after a project has been initiated (time series data) or to contrast the performance of some area or political jurisdiction that has a project with one that does not. Under what conditions can these differences in performance be attributed to the project? What follows is a listing of other explanations of the change in performance. These are threats to the validity of attributing the difference to the project (see Cornbach 1982).

History: Some event may have occurred between the preproject observation and the postproject observation of the performance (impact) variable. In other words, something else may be different about the two periods in time other than the existence of the project.

Selection: In making cross-sectional comparisons, it is possible that there are nonproject variables affecting impact that differ between the groups being compared. This can be caused by the analyst selecting the comparison groups or by participants selecting themselves. In this case, the difference in performance may not result from the project but from initial differences in the population characteristics.

Maturation: Some differences in pre- and postproject observations may be caused by the passage of time. These differences would have occurred even without the project, for example, biological processes such as aging. There can also be an interaction between selection and maturation for comparison groups in which the groups being compared differ in the rate of maturation.

Instrumentation: There can be changes in the instruments used to make observations--for example, physical instruments, questionnaires, or the observer or scorer--that can make performance differences difficult to attribute.

Testing: Human subjects learn from experience and part of their experience is the testing device used to obtain the performance data. People may perform differently on a subsequent test not because of the presence of the project but as a result of learning from the preproject test.

Statistical Regression: Whenever subjects of a project are selected because they constitute an extreme expression of some characteristic, there is a chance that when performance is observed again, it will be closer to the mean of the universe from which the subjects were selected. This movement may not be the result of the project, but just the inherent instability of observations. Any time series with some instability will exhibit the tendency for successive observations to be closer to the mean of the series than the preceding extreme observation. This illustrates a regression artifact rather than the effect of the intervening project.

Experimental Mortality: Subjects may drop out between the preproject and postproject observations. Thus, the observations may differ because of changes in the sample being observed rather than because of the project.

All of these factors constitute alternative explanations of the apparent association between the project and a change or difference in performance. These threats to internal validity can be controlled in varying degrees by experimental design. Each design to be examined in the next section has its own strengths and weaknesses.

4.2.   Quasiexperimental Designs

The design of observations to determine whether a project made a difference involves timing of the observation relative to the initiation of the project and in comparison with other groups. This can be depicted with a notation following Campbell and Stanley (1963):

x = the occurrence of a treatment (project input) at or over a particular point or period in time.

o = an observation of project output (or impact) at or over a particular point or period in time. This observation may be a mean, and differences between them can be calculated cross-sectionally or over time. The usual statistical tests of instability apply. Observations occuring at different times are noted by subscripts.

The threats to validity from independent variables affecting output (o) other than the treatment (x) variable are controlled for in the design itself or by matching in control groups.

One-Shot Case Study: The simplest design is the posttest (project) only (x o). A project is followed by an observation at one point in time. The problem in interpretation arises because some comparison with other situations in which the project was not present is implicitly made by the reader. But it is impossible to rule out alternative explanations such as other historical events. Statisticians are united in their condemnation of this design, considering it of almost no scientific value (Boring 1954).

The design is mentioned only because it includes the first step in any analysis--namely the conceptual decisions that were discussed in Chapter 3. If this design is the best that can be done, at least the agency running the project has thought out its input and impact categories and has some indication of where it is now even if it cannot determine whether the project has made any difference. The design represents a social indicator that serves as the basis for problem diagnosis and further study decisions.

Before and After Design: The same group is observed before and after the occurrence of the project (o_1 x o_2). The problem is that performance could have been affected by other events or variables that occurred between the two time periods. The longer the time period, the greater is the chance of intervening historical events. Other threats to validity include maturation, testing, and possibly regression to the mean. Still, weak designs have some place in preliminary studies. If no change is indicated with this test, it probably is not worth the expense of a more complicated design, although this depends on the particular circumstances.

Static Group Comparison: Another pre-experimental design involves a two-group comparison. The first line of the following schematic shows an observation (o) for a group receiving treatment (x) compared to another observation at the same time for a group without treatment.

$$\underline{x \quad o}$$
$$o$$

Because both groups can be subject to the same extraneous events, history as a threat to interpretation can be ruled out. The same can be said of testing and instrumentation. The threat of maturation is problematic with the possibility of differential maturation of the two groups. There is also the possibility of differential mortality.

The most troublesome problem with this design is the threat of selection. There is no assurance that the group being treated did not select itself for exposure to the project. The characteristics of volunteers can cause differences in performance even without the project. The same problem arises when the agency selects subjects with a greater chance of success. In other words, the difference in performance can be the result of original differences in the two groups.

Perhaps these selection effects can be controlled by matching the two groups in terms of characteristics that from experience or theory are expected to influence performance. From all of those receiving and those not receiving the project, a sample is drawn to compare only those from the two groups that are similar on selected preproject attributes. This is sometimes referred to as the most similar group design, ad hoc comparison, or an ex post facto experiment (Chapin 1955).

Matching determines whether some particular factor other than the project's presence could have caused the difference in performance. But, to be satisfactory, this requires a complete knowledge of causal factors. The problem is to decide when to stop adding variables to be matched. Without it someone can always say, "I do not know what other factors that differ between the groups might be causing differences in performance, but your design cannot rule them out."

The above designs pose such severe threats to internal validity that they are often termed preexperimental designs. A group of designs that is significantly stronger follow. They are quasiexperimental in the sense that they do not utilize random assignment of the project to different subjects.

Time Series: The time series design extends the periods of analysis beyond those utilized in the before and after test previously outlined. Its notation can be shown as follows:

$$O_1 \ O_2 \ O_3 \ X \ O_4 \ O_5 \ O_6$$

By extending the period of observation, there is an opportunity to control for the effects of maturation and testing. If there is some long-run secular trend, it can be observed in the several observations preceding the project. Similarly, if there is an effect from testing, it will have already been established prior to the project. History as a rival explanation cannot be ruled out by the design itself, but some confidence can be gained in ruling it out in certain circumstances. The project effect is shown by some discontinuity in the series of observations. If the entire series of performance observations changes in level after the project and stays at its new level, there is some support for the interpretation that the project had an effect. This effect may be further supported if there is a change in the slope (rate of change) in the series. In the case of a project that is expected to be short-lived after its removal, we could infer project effect if the series of observations changes level after project initiation but returns to its old level after project cessation. Similarly, some effect can be inferred if the rate of change in the performance variable is the same pre- and postproject but there is a sharp discontinuity in the before and after trend lines (different intercept).

In some cases, where there is a discontinuity at the point of project introduction, it may be impossible to determine the impact of treatment if it is preceded and followed by great variability in observations. There is a similar problem in interpretation if the postproject series is too short to establish a trend. This is particularly troublesome when the public demands quick evaluation immediately after a project begins. The interpretation of this time series is greatly enhanced after repeated replications produce the same results.

Dynamic Control Group: Where data permit, it is possible to achieve a relatively strong design by contrasting the change in performance before and after the project between those exposed to the project and a control group. The notation is as follows:

$$O_1 \qquad X \qquad O_2$$
$$\overline{}$$
$$O_1 \qquad\qquad O_2$$

In this quasiexperimental design, the group receiving the project and the control group constitute naturally occurring collectivities rather than having their members drawn from some preexisting universe and assigned randomly to the two groups, as is the case with true experimental designs. Examples of naturally occurring groups might be classrooms and, in some circumstances, political subdivisions. The project is then randomly assigned by the experimenter to one of the two selected groups. Some support for the effect of the project can be obtained if there is no obvious bias in the selection method used by the agency.

This design helps control for history, maturation, testing, and instrumentation as these should affect the project and control groups in the same manner.

There is a matter of judgment involved as to whether the project and control groups are similar enough to rule out selection threats. This is where the preproject performance measures are important. The more similar the two groups are in preproject scores, the more effective is the control.[1] But this design is much more difficult than the static group comparison because the evaluator is often called in after the project is underway and there is no opportunity to obtain preproject scores.

Some information can be obtained from a control group even if it differs from the project group on preproject performance. But when these scores differ, there is an opportunity for differential regression. If either of the comparison groups represents an extreme preproject performance score, retesting will show its score regressing to the mean of the larger universe from which the group was selected at a different rate than the other group. Some of these problems can be solved by replacing a matching procedure with a statistical technique.   The matching variables could be used as covariates in a multiple-covariate analysis of covariance (Johnson and Jackson 1959). However, whether matching or analysis of covariance is used, there remains the problem of making sure that some unexamined variable is not causing the difference in performance (as was the case for the static group comparison as well). This latter problem can be fully solved only by the use of true experimental designs.

Regression Models: In the previous design, variables that might explain the performance output other than the project (treatment) variable are unnamed and controlled by the choice of design or by selecting variables for matching when groups are compared. Regression models use statistical control by including other explanatory variables explicitly in a functional model of the form $O = f(X,Y)$, where Y is any other variable believed to be related to output (O) other than the project variable (X), which is often a dummy variable. The coefficient on the project variable indicates how output changes with changes in X with Y held constant. The same data obtained for a time series or dynamic control group can be analyzed by a regression model. They are therefore subject to the same threats to validity, namely, that some variable not matched for in a comparison or not included in the regression equation may be causing the change in output.

Preproject-Postproject Control Group: True experiments are marked by random assignment of subjects to the group receiving the effects of the project and the control group. The presence of randomization is noted by the symbol R. One such design can be diagramed as follows:

$$R \quad \frac{O_1 \qquad X \qquad O_2}{O_1 \qquad\qquad O_2}$$

This design controls for all the threats to internal validity that have been noted. The problems of history, maturation, testing, and mortality are controlled by the use of the control group. Random selection controls for selection bias as factors that might affect performance other than the project X are equally present in both groups and thus, in effect, cancel each other. The great advantage of experimental over quasiexperimental designs is that complete knowledge of causal factors is not needed. It is not necessary to understand what they are to control for their effect.

There are many more designs than those highlighted here. For further discussion, see Achen (1987), Cook and Campbell (1979), Campbell (1969), and Caporaso and Roos (1973). It should be emphasized that problems of interpretation are complex and situation specific. Although a certain design does not in itself control for a particular threat to validity, that particular threat can still be ruled out by circumstances present in the particular case.

Specification Search: Model specification is the major problem in all of these designs. In the various comparison group designs, the analyst asks what variables to match for and how good the match has to be. In a regression model, the question is what variables to include in the equation. The decision is guided by theory and experience. Omission of variables reveals something about the prior probabilities attached--namely, that they are zero, or small, and therefore can be ignored. But because these beliefs are not certain it is difficult to be sure what to include or omit.

Data analysis and study of anomalies can help with this uncertainty. Leamer (1983) suggests that analysts report the results of trying different specifications. In a regression model, the range in the size of the dependent variable (or the coefficient of the treatment variable) can be noted as other variables are added or deleted. The same can be done for the difference in output between groups by adding variables for matching in a comparison group design. The sensitivity of the output to different specifications can be noted. If the results are sensitive, the inference as to the effect of treatment is fragile and must be discounted. No formal rule for the discounting is practical and judgment is inescapable (Leamer 1978, 306).

In a regression, the number of variables that can be included is limited by the degrees of freedom and judgment on the appropriateness of any interpolations or extrapolations. In a group comparison design, it is limited by the naturally occurring examples in which a given set of variables can be found to be similar. Up to these points, what is the stopping rule for ending the specification search? It is tempting to stop the search when one is comfortable with the results, which is to say, when the results fit prior beliefs. Leamer (1978, 311) suggests that we search our experiences for possible variables to add that we would expect to make small differences, because our selective memories are unlikely to have retained any greatly inconsistent data. The latter is probably best provided by our critics, and over time, theory and experience evolve to produce different models. While some search rules are better than others, one is still left with judgment based on qualitative and rhetorical argument (McCloskey 1985).

Common Threats: There are two further threats to internal validity. They are listed separately because they are not controlled by choice of experimental design and are treated the same in most designs.

Proxy Selection: The linkage between project inputs and output is confounded by the difference between variables used in a theoretical statement and the actual observable variables and available data, i.e. the proxy for the theoretical variables (Leamer 1978, Ch. 7). This is related to the problem of construct validity discussed in the previous chapter.

Instability: One further threat to internal validity must be noted. It is listed separately because it is not controlled by choice of experimental design. Its presence is established by statistical test. All measurement is subject to inherent variation, fluctuation, and lack of reliability. Any series of observations of the exact same universe will not be identical. The fact that one measure differs from the next--independent of the project--is a potential source of misinterpretation of pre- and postproject observations. Thus, the question is whether the observed difference in performance associated with the project is the result of chance variation alone. These tests of significance appropriate for quasiexperimental designs are reviewed in Galtung (1967, 358-389).

Instability is the only threat to internal validity for which statistical tests of significance are relevant. Good survey methods emphasize taking a sufficiently large random sample of those who received the effects of a project and those who did not. But this is not the same as randomly assigning subjects to the project. If the experimental design does not control for self-selection or history, securing a large and significant statistic of correlation between the project and the performance variable is meaningless. It is easy to be overly impressed with a highly significant treatment variable from one study when confidence might be more deserved with replication of results (Carver 1978; Morrison and Henkel 1970).

4.3.   Threats to External Validity

If the results of evaluations of previous projects are to be used in determining a budget for future projects, these results must be generalized and applied to other settings. In doing so, there are threats to external validity. In certain cases, the previous results may not be replicated. One common type of problem arises from inadequate specification of the project inputs and the subjects to which these inputs are applied. This brings us back to the previous chapter's discussion of cost categories. The project's inputs are grouped and classified for ease in description, but when the project is repeated, it may be difficult to precisely duplicate the ingredients and their mix. Often a project combines a number of features that might have been separated. When an agency is short of funds, it may simplify the project and eliminate features. If it does, it cannot be certain how present performance will differ from performance in the past. In addition, project managers want to show their creativity and to differentiate themselves by adding project innovations.[2]

Another class of external threats might be labeled *reactive effects*. The conditions of the experimental or pilot project may have a degree of artificiality compared to the conditions occurring when the full-scale program is implemented in the field. This occurs, for example, when the results of agricultural trials are taken from the experiment station to the farmers' fields. Various kinds of *Hawthorne effects* may have occurred along with the evaluated project--people who participate in a pilot project know they have been singled out for something special and they may react differently than they will react when the project is applied generally. People may also react differently when they know the project is a trial and may not be continued, than when they regard it as permanent.

One of the practical problems in evaluation is that people want quick judgments after a program is started. But many processes involve growth or decay. The benefit produced in the first year after the project may erode in subsequent years. When the trial project is adopted on a large scale after only one or two years of performance observations have been made, there may be great disillusionment when the project fails to maintain output in subsequent years.

Although several other external threats are discussed in the literature (Campbell 1969, 411), one more will be noted here because of its frequency of occurrence. As discussed in the Chapter 3, any performance variable is an aggregation and selection of features. Because human purpose is usually changing, budget analysts often have to use the performance categories of past evaluations even though the thing they would now like to emphasize may be slightly different. When existing records of program performance are utilized, the analyst is in effect utilizing a variable that is a proxy for the ideally desired variable. The usefulness of these proxies is always a matter of judgment. It creates the possibility that the performance of new projects will be disappointing, not because the new project did not perform as effectively as the previously evaluated project, but because the performance measure used in the past really did not capture the performance features most wanted today. This argues for the use of multiple measures of performance whose imperfections are independent of each other (Webb et al. 1966).

4.4.   Choice and Weight of the Evidence

There is a large literature of individual project evaluations. For a review of notable evaluation studies and their methodological problems, see Rossi and Wright (1977). However, there is little literature on bringing this information together in the context of budget formulation. For example, most of the evaluation studies are for a single mix and level of inputs. The evaluation is concerned only with whether this particular project made a difference. This is only one point on a production function. In days of budget stringency, it is common for agencies to be asked what they could accomplish if the budget were the same as last year's level, were 10 percent less, or were 10 percent more. To answer this question evaluations of multiple project levels are required. Although determining that a past project did not make a difference might be a reflection on the agency involved, it rarely affects the determination of project continuance or discontinuance. If the project were aimed at an important political problem, the government cannot afford to discontinue it in spite of poor performance. The agency needs to know not only whether the project made a difference, but what factors might be changed to increase performance. This again suggests multiple pilot projects.

But, in many cases, experimental control is not possible and we try to learn from naturally occurring events. The treatment variable is mixed with many other complementary inputs whose proportions cannot be varied. It is easy to mistakenly attribute output to the current project when in fact it is a joint (undifferentiable) product of many inputs (some occurring at an earlier date).

One observer has noted that "no evaluation can be expected to be unassailable in terms of its methodological and field development." There will always be some degree of doubt associated with the various threats to internal and external validity. In addition, the world has a large random element. For example, econometric equations used to evaluate returns to education can explain only 20 to 30 percent of the variance in earnings in a random population sample (Eckhouse 1973). Prediction with such a large random component is difficult. Compared to the ideal, most evaluations fall short. The practical problem is not a dichotomous belief or disbelief in a particular inference. The name of the budget game is choice among competing projects so that the relevant comparisons are not between one project and the ideal but between one project and another. If it is necessary to choose between two competing projects, it is better to select the one that (1) has been tested (and hopefully replicated) and found incapable of being rejected with respect to some alternative explanations of its performance than to choose one that has not been exposed to disconfirmation at all or overcome fewer threats to interpretation,[3] (2) has the strongest quasiexperimental design, and (3) has results that are not sensitive to small changes in model specification. Therefore, choice involves judgment of the comparative weight of the evidence.[4] No government can wait to act until evaluators are certain that the project produces the desired impact. A project with some plausible causal hypothesis and the absence of a plausible non-project-related hypothesis is likely to be implemented even though the evaluation design cannot ensure that alternative hypotheses can be ruled out.

There is no formula to convert the weight of the evidence into a summary, subjective estimate of the probability of the project output occurring. Depending on the evidence available, a person may be unwilling to state the probability of different outputs in mathematical terms and can indicate only rank order.

Evaluations are subject to benefit-cost analysis as are other spending projects. The evaluation design that controls for more threats to validity probably costs more than a less powerful design. But at some point the extra assurance of causal impact costs more than it is worth. Evaluation resources are scarce and not all projects are worth systematic study at the same level. Usually some hierarchy of design is in order. A simple design may first be utilized to determine whether the project shows any of the desired impact. Then if the decision is deemed very important, a more costly design can be used to eliminate some other explanations for the changed performance.

A continuing theme of this text is to examine the points in analysis at which it is necessary to consider the political choice of whose interests are to count. This is to clarify what the analyst and the politician must contribute and how they can interact. Choice of projects is influenced by the relative weight of the evidence supporting confidence in achieving results with different projects competing for public monies. Suppose, for example, that two projects with identical projected rates of net return differ in the degree of validity attached to their results. This difference may not be expressible as a matter of mathematical probability; it may only be possible to rank the projects based on the number and kind of threats to validity that have been controlled (and to what degree). Because people can be expected to differ in their weighing of the evidence, they will differ in their subjective probabilities, however expressed. Further discussion of incorporating judgments concerning uncertainty is contained in Chapter 10. The evaluation resources allocated to different projects and the choice of experimental design will influence political outcomes in the allocation of the budget. This will be discussed further in Chapter 12 on the political economy of budgeting.

Notes

1.   Campbell (1969, 417) says that it is a mistake to match on pretest scores because of the possibility of regression artifacts. Also see Miller (1977).

2.   Provus (1971) argues that the needs of ongoing management make the usual fixed evaluation methods impractical. He advocates an interactive evaluation process that will reflect the fact that evaluation and corrective managerial action are intertwined and must resolve continuing conflicts among clients, practicioners, and evaluation.

3.   This is not to say that all quantitative analyses are superior to qualitative analyses. When there are multiple, complex causal factors at work, a qualitative analysis of participant reports may be more useful than a statistical analysis of alternative programs. See McCloskey (1985).

4.   For an example of an application of the weight of the evidence concept, see National Research Council (1980, 79).

5

Valuation of Direct Effects

A classification of project effects will indicate the relationship of this chapter and the several to follow. The subject of this chapter is valuation of *direct* effects, which are the benefits (or costs) to direct users of the project output. This is in contrast to *indirect* effects, which accrue to people one or more steps removed from the users of the project output. In this chapter, prices do not vary as a result of the quantity of project output, but in Chapter 7 the effect of the project on direct output prices is considered.

Opportunity cost adjustments to market prices are the subject of Chapter 6; included are considerations of nominal versus real opportunity cost in the context of unemployment, both for direct input suppliers and subsequent indirect effects such as processing of the project output as appropriate. Then, in Chapter 8, the problems of summing up all of these effects for the gainers and the losers are considered. Particular attention is paid to cost (tax) distribution and how a redistribution objective might be implemented.

What is the value of a project output to its users? For goods sold in the market, value is expressed by the bids that buyers offer. These bids are a function of individual preferences constrained by the distribution of wealth, which is in turn a function of human endowments and property ownership. These bids express willingness to pay or effective demand, which is distinguished from wishes and wants not supported by command over wealth. In Chapter 2, we explored some of the product characteristics in which the public authority may not wish to utilize the market to register willingness to pay even though it does not want to redistribute income. In other words, it wants to serve the preferences of those who now have income and wealth, but it does not wish or is unable to use the market institution. This is sometimes referred to as the *objective of allocative efficiency*. The task for analysis then becomes estimating willingness to pay even though project output is not sold.

By utilizing the methods to be described in this chapter, the analyst essentially tries to estimate what persons would or could pay if they could be motivated to reveal the bases for these valuations. For project outputs that are utilized in further production (producer goods), the analyst duplicates the computations that an entrepreneur would make in deciding how much could be paid to acquire an input. For consumer goods, the analyst tries to secure any evidence of what the person would pay to acquire the product. The same product (e.g., the value of life) can be valued by more than one method. The method chosen depends on the available data.

The same methods can be used to value costs when project inputs have no direct market prices to indicate their opportunity cost. For example, environmental costs of project construction are direct costs. No separate treatment of so-called externalities is needed as per Section 2.4.

At any given time only a part of the rights system is considered for confirmation. Therefore, willingness to pay (WTP) and willingness to sell (WTS) based on existing rights are useful references. But it will be seen that WTP and WTS are ambiguous in many instances and must be interpreted-- which really means that rights are not fully determined until project analysis rules are specified and the money is taxed and spent.

In a market transaction, the analyst accepts the price outcome as a reflection of the owners' rights that were exchanged. Without agreement as to rights there would have been a court suit or the police would have been called. The analyst does not have to have an inventory of the respective rights. However, when the analyst does not have price information and is trying to deduce price from other data such as time or other costs saved, changes in income, or responses to hypothetical questions, the inference of rights becomes all important. An assumption of rights is implicitly part of the deductive chain from some limited economic data to price and value. In some cases it is straightforward to infer rights to the income behind willingness to pay--for example, in evaluation of projects that save previously incurred costs. But in other cases, even if decision makers instruct analysts to accept the present distribution of rights, it is not always clear what these rights are. Since the analysis infers rather than observes a market value, the analyst cannot determine whether one of the parties would have sued or otherwise challenged the assumed right. In these instances, the analyst must request some political input.

5.1.   Market Analogy (Substitute Products) Method

In some cases, government projects produce outputs similar to those produced in the private market, although the government may not wish to sell the good. In that case, the market price of the marketed product that is similar indicates the value of the project's product in comparable supply and demand situations. An example is the production of campsites at a water reservoir. Similar campsites may be provided by private entrepreneurs on natural lakes, and these give an indication of the value of the camping product of the public project even if it is not sold or is sold at less than cost. Another example is public housing. The problem of application is to make the judgment that the products are substitutes, that is, similar in all characteristics that might affect willingness to pay. Not only must the products being compared be the same, but demand conditions, incomes, and preferences of the users of the two products must be the same. This might be estimated by data on socioeconomic characteristics. Further, the availability and price of complementary and substitute goods must be similar (or independent in the utility and demand functions). This requires comparison of an inventory of goods in the area served by the marketed product and the public project product.

When government projects produce marketable goods that were formerly imported, there may be a savings to consumers and input purchasers because of import substitution. The previous purchases show effective demand and if the domestic project can replace the formerly imported product, the old price becomes a measure of value even if the domestic product is sold for less. In this case, where effective demand for a given quantity is proven, the price of the alternative product is a measure of value. Unless demand is inelastic, the price of the previously purchased quantity cannot be accepted as a measure of value for an additional supply.

The market analogy method utilizes output price data of substitute products that are comparable to those of the public project. The method is conceptually similar to the alternate cost method described in Section 5.6., which utilizes production cost data of substitute products. Use of the method requires a judgment on what constitutes a substitute product. It is the same question as was explored in Chapter 3 relative to program budgets and cost effectiveness. Judgments can differ as to whether slightly different products are substitutes and this presents a problem in deducing willingness to pay.

Another application of the analogous good method, the essence of which is the observation of purchases of a marketed product similar to that produced by the project, is in the valuation of projects that improve human longevity. Where people can be observed buying products that reduce risk or trading reduced income for increased longevity, they are in effect purchasing longevity.[1] The analyst can then inquire whether the product obtained in this fashion, such as seat belts (Blomquist 1979) or smoke detectors (Dardis 1980), is analogous to products produced by a public project that increase longevity such as pollution control, safety projects, and regulations.

The labor market application requires data on the risk associated with various jobs and the incomes from these jobs. The difference in income between jobs is the inferred bid for the reduced risk and improved longevity.[2] The major interpretive problem is to control for other factors affecting income differences such as age, education, and race. This method has been applied by Thaler and Rosen (1975), Olson (1981), and Smith (1976). Freeman (1979, 186) points out that the value of a statistical life derived from these data indicates only the marginal value of a change in the probability of death, whereas the choice may be nonmarginal. He further argues that those who accept risky jobs may not be representative of the general population. They may be less risk averse than the total population. In other words, it is difficult to control for differences in preferences from usually available socioeconomic characteristics.

5.2.   Intermediate Good Method

The output of a government project may not be sold, but where the output is used as an input in the production of a final product that is sold, the value of the public project product may be inferred. The analysis requires the preparation of a complete enterprise budget with and without the project involving knowledge of the production function, a list of all enterprise inputs for the user of the project product, and the prices of these inputs and the market price of the final product of the user's enterprise. Input prices must be in competitive equilibrium with marginal cost equaling average cost. Project gross benefit equals the change in net income (NY). NY = (with project gross income minus with project cost of nonproject inputs) minus (without project gross income minus without project cost of nonproject inputs). The difference in the with and without project net income is the implicit value of the project output. It is what the project user could afford to pay to obtain the project product for use in the user's enterprise.

The intermediate good method is widely used. One example is a project in which irrigation water is provided or drainage is improved. The change in farm incomes with and without the project is a measure of the value of the public water project. Note that both physical output and inputs may be different with and without the project.

Another example is education and training. The lifetime net income of people with and without a given level of education or training is compared. As noted in Chapter 3, all other factors affecting income must be held constant. It should be emphasized that we are measuring the change in net income. All costs of participation by individuals must be netted out. This includes out-of-pocket costs as well as any opportunity costs of income that otherwise might have been earned during the training period (see Hardin and Borus 1971).

In the case of projects such as those in agriculture, we may estimate enterprise physical output with and without the project and then multiply this output by some appropriate expected price. In other cases such as education, we may not estimate the change in skill levels or adaptive behavior but can go directly to changes in net income. Care must be taken to determine whether there are some physical effects that are not reflected in net market determined income.

How are these data used in budget planning? When the physical production function is available from previous similar, pilot, or experimental projects and the degree of external validity threats has been determined, it is possible to do a preproject estimate of expected returns by applying expected prices of the final marketed product. A postproject evaluation is useful in determining accountability, but for budget planning, preproject analysis is needed. Therefore, the value of the postproject analysis is its use in predicting the performance of a similar project being considered for future funding or determining whether an existing project should be continued.

When a postproject analysis of change in net income (without any estimate of the production function) is utilized as a basis for predicting the returns to a future investment, care must be taken to consider not only the external validity of the implicit production function, but also the replication of the implicit prices of the final products.

In Chapter 9, the summation of effects over time will be considered. But some note of the relationship of a flow of value over time and its equivalent present lump-sum value is in order here. If there is a fixed factor of production such as land that is combined with other inputs including the input obtained from the project, the change in net income over time will be capitalized into the land value. Thus, it is possible to compare land values with and without the project for an alternative measure of the change in net income.[3] The analyst can use either the net income change or its capitalized value as a measure of project benefit, depending on the type of data available; the two cannot be added together for they are two measures of the same thing. When both types of data are available from independent sources, one can be used as a check and confirmation of the other. For further discussion of the rent method, see Section 5.5.

Anything said concerning the context of benefits can also be applied to cost as the cost of a project is the output that could have been obtained if the resources had been used elsewhere. If the foregone alternative has no market price, then its value can be estimated by these various methods. For example, suppose the construction of a government project involves use of the air for waste disposal. The value of alternative uses of the air can be estimated by the intermediate good method in those cases in which the air is used in an enterprise whose final output is sold.

The intermediate good method utilizes the computation of the change in net income. The method has previously been applied to project outputs that are inputs into another production process. Some projects, however, do not produce a good but rather remove a bad, for example, flood control and some health and safety programs. The removal of a bad input from the production environment can also increase net income.

In the case of flood control on agricultural land, calculations similar to those for irrigation are made to obtain the costs of all other inputs and thus obtain the change in net income with and without floods. Production costs and type of crop may vary between the two cases.

Various health, safety, and environmental regulatory programs reduce the risk of early death. One measure of the effects of these programs is the change in the flow of net income. Application of the intermediate good method in this area follows a human capital conception with life as an intermediate good. The present value of the future flow of income is gained if death is prevented.[4] For an application, see U.S. Department of Health, Education and Welfare (1966a), U.S. Department of Transportation (1976b), and, for the United Kingdom, Dawson (1971).[5] The output is a change in the probability of death. Use of the approach requires the value judgment that the worth of an individual is equal to the individual's net contribution to market-valued output.[6] Future consumption could be treated as a production cost and subtracted from future income (Jones-Lee 1976, 46). This raises several policy questions. If consumption is regarded as a measure of the utility of life, it should not be netted out (Arthur 1981). There is also the issue of whether objective historical loss or subjective estimates of risk should be used (Akehurst and Culyer 1974; Dreze 1962).[7] In addition, the flow of future income must be converted to a present value by a discount rate. These are not technical matters, but a property rights and policy judgment.

The value of longer life and avoidance of lost earnings is job related. This means that different values are obtained as a function of age, sex, race, and market institutions (Cooper and Rice 1976; Sagan 1972). This approach does not measure the value of nonmarket production such as production in the home or give any weight to the infirmed who produce no material goods, nor does it measure what others might pay who care for the person at risk. These same problems exist in using the intermediate good approach for valuation of regulatory programs as well as investment projects such as education.

Many people reject using BCA to value human life because of unacceptable moral implications (Kelman 1981). If the method determines a proxy for willingness to pay, it reflects the current distribution of income and job opportunities and more would be invested to save the lives of the rich than the poor. It should be noted that many societies prohibit the trading of some goods such as purchase of avoidance of military service. The rich are not allowed to fully exercise the implications of their wealth and there are some areas in which we reject the implications of lack of wealth (Kelman 1987, 144). One of these is in the health area, in which we do not let consumption fall below a certain level even where there is no effective demand. Shall we then reject all BCA analysis in the value of life area? No; these conflicts just suggest the policy choices that must be made before BCA can be applied. It maximizes wealth, but the prior decision is what and whose wealth counts (i.e., how wealth is defined). Whether the analysis uses a human capital approach, willingness to pay, or assigns an equal value to everyone is a question of property rights that is then implemented by BCA. The right that is chosen will determine the wealth maximization.

The U.S. Supreme Court in *American Textile Manufacturers Institute v. Donovan* (1981) ruled that the Department of Labor's promulgation of workplace health standards did not have to meet a benefit-cost standard that had been ordered by the president (Karpf 1982). The Court seemed to say that just because the income lost by poor workers if the health standards were not implemented would not equal the cost of protection, the workers could not be denied their health. In a sense, the court said that the workers own their health and cannot or would not sell it for the cost of protection. The Court implemented this property right by restricting the application of benefit-cost analysis. Alternatively, it could have insisted that a certain value of life be systematically used in all project evaluations. The Court seemed to act to further humane values against what might be regarded as narrow economic values. But by not insisting on reform of systematic analysis, it cannot be certain that with limited budgets, the greatest number of lives will be saved.

The intermediate good method and many others to follow are a measure of capacity to pay rather than an observation or prediction of actual behavior. The distinction turns on uncertainty and the cost of information. The method assumes perfect knowledge, but actual behavior is based on imperfect knowledge. Do people know the risks associated with different occupations and environments? This is discussed in detail later in the chapter. People spend more to insure themselves against low-valued hazards with which they have had some experience than against catastrophic losses with low probabilities (Kunreuther and Slovic 1978). Less is spent on the latter than is justified by actuarial studies. This behavior is the result of the level of actual knowledge and individual differences in risk aversion. The intermediate good or capacity to pay method requires the analyst to select a discount rate whereas the market analogy method has an implicit rate chosen by those observed. Because these factors are present to some degree in all consumer purchases, Freeman (1979, 171-73) prefers the method that has been described as the analogous good method or what he refers to as the willingness to pay method. Freeman and this author would emphasize that the choice of method is a value judgment and not simply a technical matter when methods differ on their perspective of calculations of advantage (capacity) or of behavior. Available empirical studies using the two methods differ by a factor of two or three and suggest that model specification within a method affects results as much as choice of method.

In the previous discussion, the intermediate good method is implemented by use of enterprise budgets. Another technique is linear programming that derives the marginal value product for any input whose use is constrained below the optimal level. For example, there may be a government project (rule) to improve water quality by reducing plant growth in lakes caused by phosphorus runoff from agricultural fields. The problem is to estimate the cost of this project. If farmers cannot put on the optimum level of phosphorus and therefore have to change their cropping patterns, a linear programming model can impute the loss to farmers of not being able to use preferred inputs (see Jacobs and Casler 1979). This benefit lost by farmers is the opportunity cost of environmental improvement implemented by regulation of private activity or public investment.

In summary, the intermediate good method of computing change in net income is applicable to projects that:

1. Add a productive input (e.g., irrigation, education)
2. Remove a bad (e.g., flood control, disease control)

3. Remove a productive input, usually in the context of regulation (e.g., pesticides)

All affect a change in net income.

5.3.   Cost Saving Method

Even when the project output is not sold, in some cases it substitutes for a product that has a market-valued opportunity cost. Where the project output is a perfect substitute for some formerly necessary expenditure, this saving of the former expenditure is a measure of gross benefit. A reduced opportunity cost is a benefit. Data are needed only on the costs saved rather than calculating net income. It is not necessary in this case to inventory all costs, price the final product, and calculate a residual; but if this were done, the change in net income would be equal to the cost saving. This illustrates the relationship between the cost saving and the intermediate product method.

A common application of the cost savings approach is in transportation projects. Improvement of a mode of transportation or substitution of one mode for another can save fuel, time, wages of drivers, repairs to equipment, and capital cost of goods in transit. Each of these will be generalized and examined and illustrated not only for transportation but for other kinds of projects where applicable.

A relatively straightforward example of cost saving is the project that substitutes one mode of transportation for another, such as barge navigation for trucks or railroads (see Schmid and Ward 1970). The data used are price paid for a given volume of goods previously shipped. The difference between the cost of truck or rail shipping and the costs of barge shipment is a measure of net benefits for public navigation projects. (If the barge takes more time, the cost of time must be added to the other project costs to make them comparable).[8] This assumes that the alternate mode is priced at marginal opportunity cost.

As in all methods, care must be taken to determine effective demand. For the previous volume of traffic, demand is proven. But the cost saving may encourage additional traffic that did not previously move by any mode. The willingness of this new traffic to pay can be expected to be less than the average cost saving for the existing traffic. It is necessary to estimate net returns for the added traffic rather than the difference in costs of alternative modes. The marginal new traffic may not add to net benefits.[9]

One variety of potential cost savings is associated with reduction in losses resulting from the adverse effects of some phenomena. For example, projects are built to reduce flood damage. The cost saving differences with and without flood damages and repairs are the project benefits for existing firms (U.S. Army Corps of Engineers 1980). For new construction expected to be built in the newly protected floodplain, the benefit equals the difference in net income between the protected site and the alternate upland sites, which is not the same as the damage that would occur if it were in a location subject to flooding (see Section 5.5). Other cost savings involve regulation resulting in water or air pollution damage reduction (Feenberg and Mills 1980; Freeman 1982; Halvorsen and Ruby 1981), including that to human health (Lave and Seskin 1970; Raucher 1986) and reduced household cleaning and repair (Watson and Jaksch 1982).

Another class of possible cost saving involves reparative expenditures. These are the costs of restoring the usefulness of something after it has been damaged. This includes medical treatment. For example, if a public project to improve auto safety reduces accidents, the difference in hospitalization costs is a benefit (U.S. Department of Health, Education and Welfare 1966a). This is in addition to any loss of income estimated by the intermediate good method previously discussed. An improved highway may reduce damages to vehicles and cargo (Adler 1971, 37). The reduction of pollution may also increase the life of industrial parts. In this case, the benefit of a pollution reduction project is the difference in the stream of replacement costs with and without the project (Maler and Wyzga 1976). If the adverse effects are reduced, the cost saving method can be used. If the adverse effects are completely eliminated, the alternate cost method of Section 5.6 may be applicable.

The last group of cost savings involves instances in which the output of the project is a substitute for a former expenditure of time. The most common example of this savings is transportation projects such as improvements of road beds or reductions in congestion that save travel time (Tucker and Thompson 1979).

Care must be taken to distinguish cost savings in national income terms from changes in transfers. A program may make a group productive that was formerly receiving a transfer payment (grant). This "cost saving" of the no longer necessary transfer is not a gain in national income as the size of the resource remains the same when its use is returned to the donors.

5.3.1. Value of Time Saved

Implementing the cost saving method for transport projects requires an estimate of the value of the time saved. For reduction in working time in which the time or the product of work is valued in the market, the calculation is relatively straightforward. For example, if a faster route saves wages of truck drivers, this is a measure of the cost savings benefit. Similarly, if transit time is reduced, there is a capital savings when goods are turned over more rapidly when shipment time is reduced.[10] This may be particularly important in poorer countries. For an application of this approach, see Fleischer (1962), Harrison (1974), and van der Tak and de Weille (1969).

One of the problems in applying a cost savings approach is to determine whether the resource saved can and actually will be utilized in some other productive way. There may be various market imperfections that keep the saved resources from being reallocated. At best, there may be some time delay involved until other components in the shipping and handling system can be altered to take advantage of the reduced transit time. For further discussion, see Chapter 6 and Harrison and Quarmby (1974, 175-79).

The calculation of the value of leisure time saved is more difficult. One approach is to examine the trade-off made by people between leisure and work earnings (see Cesario 1976). Utilizing the theory of labor supply, it can be reasoned that people use their time for work up to the point at which the marginal utility of another unit of time used to gain income is equal to the marginal utility of leisure. Therefore, the wage rate should give an estimate of the value of leisure time saved by faster commuting trips. For example, Adler (1971) reports on a study of a new expressway in Japan. Travelers were divided into two classes, those with incomes sufficient to afford private cars and those who rode the bus. Thus, the value of time differed as a function of the average income of the two groups.

This approach has been criticized on theoretical grounds by Moses and Williamson (1963). They observe that the length of the work week is often institutionally fixed. Although some workers may choose to work overtime, for many the work period is offered on a take it or leave it basis; therefore, no indication of people's marginal valuation of leisure can be given. Another problem with the approach is that it ignores differences in the marginal disutility of work for different people, in different jobs, and in various transport modes. The marginal utility of leisure time is equal to the wage rate (marginal utility of money earned in work) less the marginal disutility of work. If the change in utility relative to a change in work time is negative at the margin, we would expect the value of leisure time to be below the average wage rate. The extent of this divergence is an empirical matter for which no data are available. The value of time saved will further differ from the wage rate depending on the disutility of travel. In some cases, such as reading and socializing, the trip may have some intrinsic value that can be lost at some threshold as the trip is shortened.

These shortcomings have caused researchers to use other methods to infer the value of time from consumer choices. The analyst searches for situations in which people make a trade-off between time saved and the cost of doing so. These arise in the context of choice of mode of travel, of route, of speed to drive, of locations for housing and work, and of travel destination and frequency of trips to a given destination. This is often referred to in the literature as the behavioral or revealed preference approach (Watson 1974).

Travelers often can choose between alternate modes of travel that differ in time consumed and price. A current example might be the difference in speed between the conventional jet airplane and the Concorde supersonic. The latter saves time, but the tickets cost more. The value of time can be inferred from people's choices. To make the inference possible, we must assume that the users of both modes place the same value on time. In this case, it might be necessary to draw our conclusions only with respect to the income class of the users of the Concorde. In that case, the costs of the two alternatives can be expressed as:

$$C_o = a_o + bT_o + M_o \text{ and } C_s = a_s + bT_s + M_s$$

where C_o is the cost of the ordinary airplane, and C_s is the cost of the supersonic, a_o and a_s are parameters indicating the intrinsic utility of ordinary and supersonic travel, respectively, T and M are the time spent in minutes and ticket money cost, and b = value of unit of T. The difference in costs (dC) then equals the net difference in intrinsic utility of the two modes plus the change in time (dT) and money cost (dM) involved, or

$$dC = a_o - a_s + b \, dT + dM$$

If the two modes have the same intrinsic utility, the value of one unit of time is then given by the ratio b dT/M which is b = dM/dT.

A more usual application of this approach is the comparison of bus and subway modes. In this case, the change in costs is largely a function of where a person lives and is thus a good predictor of choice of mode. In many transportation planning studies, this prediction is the main interest, but the same type of model can be used to estimate the value of time saved.

It should be noted that in the labor supply approach discussed previously it was necessary to "estimate the disutility of work," whereas in the behavioral mode it is necessary to estimate the inherent utility of the transport modes (e.g., differences in comfort while in transit). Both problems are hard to ignore, but perhaps it is easier to make some qualitative judgment that two modes are roughly equivalent in their inherent utilities than it is to deal with the question of the disutility of work. Thus, most studies are of the behavioral type (for example, Beesley 1965).

The logic of this approach can be further demonstrated by a graphic analysis that is sometimes called the Beesley method after its originator. In the previous example, all of the observations involved people who are similarly situated and face the same costs and time savings. The following graphic analysis utilizes observations of choices by people with different costs and savings such as in the case of a bus-subway comparison. Each person's choice is plotted on a four-quadrant diagram (such as shown in Figure 5.1) as the difference in time and cost between the preferred and alternate modes. There are four possibilities corresponding to each of the quadrants:

1. Travelers choose cheaper, but slower modes.
2. Travelers choose cheaper and faster modes.
3. Travelers choose more expensive, but faster modes.
4. Travelers choose more expensive and slower modes.

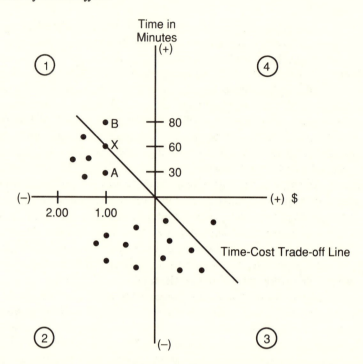

Figure 5.1 Derivation of Time-Cost Trade-off Rate Arising from Selection between Two Modes

For example, individual A in quadrant 1 has chosen a mode that is 30 minutes slower and $1.00 cheaper than the alternative mode available to that individual. No observations would be expected in quadrant 4 as it would be irrational to seek a more expensive and slower mode (other qualitative features being similar). After the observations are plotted, the analyst draws a downward sloping line from quadrant 1 to quadrant 3 through the point of origin so that the number of observations above the line is minimized. The line will represent the rate of trade-off between time and money. If this is the correct representation of the trade-off, and 60 minutes is worth $1.00, then person A is quite rational to choose a mode that uses 30 minutes more time but saves $1.00. On the other hand, person B is made to look irrational for choosing a mode that requires 80 minutes more time but saves only a dollar. Thus, the line is drawn to minimize the number of apparent irrational choices.

The slope of the chosen line then represents the rate of money and time trade-off. It is the usual run over rise or change in cost divided by minutes. Selecting point X on the trade-off line, each minute of time is worth $.016 ($1.00 divided by 60 minutes).

The graphic method can accommodate only two variables, provides no statistical test of significance, and must assume the modes are perfect substitutes (given by the trade-off line going through the point of origin at which the traveler is indifferent as to which of the two modes is selected when the cost and time differences are zero). Still, it provides a quick and dirty estimate. Where data and other resources permit, more complex models can be used that can accommodate more variables such as difference in quality of the modes. For specification of these econometric models, see Goodwin (1976), Howe (1976), Vickerman (1972), and Harrison and Quarmby (1974, 193 and 198) who suggest the use of discriminant analysis.

Many of these studies suggest that the value of time saved is between 25 and 50 percent of the wage rate. On the basis of this, Anderson and Settle (1977, 64) suggest that for a quick and dirty analysis, the simple wage rate analysis previously noted be used by reducing the values by 50 to 75 percent.

Another opportunity to observe time and cost trade-offs is provided by the availability of toll roads and slower multiple access public roads, or a toll bridge or ferry across a bay versus a longer route over land. The same methodology used for modal choice is applicable here for choice of route. Some of the problems in application include (1) little variation in variables in which most people are faced with the same time and cost differences and everyone does the same thing; (2) the cost differences involve much more than time, for example vehicle operation costs that may be imperfectly perceived by the driver; and (3) statistical analysis requires some observations of choice of cheap and faster modes, cheaper but slower modes, and expensive but faster modes. However, in the choice of route situation, the time and cost variables are often highly correlated. For an application of this method, see Thomas (1968).

Another similar situation is provided by choice of speed at which to travel a given route when a trade-off is available between increased operation costs at the higher speed and time saved. From this relationship, Mohring (1965) reasoned that cars with more passengers would drive faster because of the lower per unit cost of the extra speed. All of these factors presume that drivers are aware of these cost differences and that no other factors, such as preferences for safety, affect the choice.

The number of trips to alternate locations from the same zone of origin provides another opportunity to observe time and cost trade-offs. This is appropriate for nonwork trips such as trips to shopping centers. The destinations must have some degree of substitutability and the differences in attractiveness must be quantified. There must be variations in speed between routes to different places so that the time and cost variables will not be so highly correlated as to make regression coefficients meaningless. For details on the construction of these so-called gravity distribution models, see Harrison and Quarmby (1974). An alternative version of this approach uses data on trip making to one destination from several origins. This method introduces many other possible variables that may influence the visitors' choices, all of which may be difficult to control. A judgment must be made as to the availability of substitutes to the people at the various origins. This will be discussed further in Section 5.4 on the price-quantity behavior method. For an application of this method, see Mansfield (1969).

The final example of time and cost trade-offs is reflected in decisions as to where to live and work. People often pay a location rent for lower cost accessibility to work centers. Application of this concept is difficult, however, because all other rent-creating factors must be separated out. In additon, accessibility to non-work related areas may be a factor. These will be discussed further in Section 5.5 on using rents to derive values of direct benefits. For a review of empirical studies using various methods to determine the value of time, see Cesario (1976).

Several general precautions in interpreting time savings are in order. Is 5 minutes saved by each of 1,000 people worth the same as 10 minutes saved by each of 500 people, even if the total minutes saved is the same? Do individual savings below a certain amount have any value at all? Mishan (1976, Ch. 41) argues that the proportion of time saved counts as much as the absolute time saved. In a long journey saving of a few minutes even by many people may be worth very little and not even be perceived by the travelers. Small bits of time saved here and there may not be used for anything else. Harrison and Quarmby (1974, 185), however, point out a number of cases in which small bits of time are very important. Traffic management plans in cities are often made up of many individually small projects, but, in total, they add up to a considerable impact. Often, the value of time saved is not in the time itself but in correlated factors such as reduced tension and discomfort. To argue that these small bits of time saved are worthless is not consistent with consumer purchases of many convenience appliances and foods that are individually of small impact. This is an area in which there may be differences in judgment.

Care must be taken to differentiate types of time that may have different value when saved. Walking time is different from driving time and both may be different from waiting time. Most transportation improvements seem to be concentrated on the time between two points rather than the accompanying functions. Thus, we have faster and faster airplanes but still aggravating delays in baggage handling and ground transportation to the final destination.

Finally, a reduction in the time variance for a journey is important. A reduction in variance without any corresponding reduction in mean journey time may be a benefit to those for whom precise planning of departure and arrival is critically coordinated with other events.

This section has been detailed because it is suggestive of the need for creativity in finding situations in which value can be inferred from human choices that can perhaps be applied to other areas. Elaboration of the cost saving associated with the saving of time is justified by the fact that transportation is a major public sector in most countries and the results of these studies are used in decision making as witnessed by the use of such estimates in guidelines published by the American Association of State Highway Officials (1960).

This text is organized by analytic method rather than by commodity so as to facilitate generalization and widespread application. The reader who wishes to look at the full range of methods applicable to transportation may consult several general texts, in addition to those previously cited, such as Kuhn (1962), Adler (1971), and Meyer and Straszheim (1971).

Studies to estimate the value of time raise a set of issues concerning the use of subjective versus objective measures. These issues are not unique to time value studies, but they are particularly important there. The analyst can either objectively measure the amount of time saved, the vehicle operating costs, and miles reduced, or the users can be interviewed and their perceptions of these quantities can be used in estimating the value of time saved. One study reported values of time as being twice as large when perceived differences in travel time were used instead of the actual measured time (Thomas 1968).

Objective and subjective measures can differ because of information cost (travelers not aware of actual vehicle operating expense), because the objective measure is an average and different people actually have different experiences, and because people tend to rationalize whatever choice they have made and overestimate the time involved in the rejected mode of travel. Most analysts such as Harrison and Quarmby (1974, 205-06) prefer the perceived quantities because for them the issue is which is a better predictor of actual choice. From the perspective of this book, the issue is seen as one of public policy. Some believe that the economy should be devised so that people get the products they want (given their budget constraints) regardless of how well informed their choices might be. But another value position is that projects should be built to save the most resources regardless of how they are perceived. This is particularly relevant in the context of current energy supply concerns. Some groups would like the government to make investments to save energy even if the traveler does not perceive areas in which this can be most efficiently accomplished. The point of view is not simply a technical issue; it involves a conflict of interests that requires a political input and the label "merit goods" does not help.

5.4. Access Cost-Quantity Demanded Method

The analyst who wishes to estimate the value of nonmarketed goods is constantly looking for situations in which consumers are faced with some related trade-off between costs and use. Another opportunity to infer the value of a public project output arises when consumers face different market-valued costs of access to a nonmarketed good. The good itself is not sold, but expenditures in time or money are made to get access to it. The method has been widely applied to recreation projects and is sometimes called the travel cost or Clawson approach after its originator (see Clawson and Knetsch 1966). The method is here called the access cost-quantity demanded method as any type of access cost will do.

To make use of a national park, for example, visitors must incur the expense of getting there. It is not the sum of these costs that determines value, but rather the inferences that can be drawn from observing the number of visitations of people encountering different access (travel) costs.[11] The method has some similarities to the gravity models used in the preceding section to value time saving in transportation projects. Here the project is not designed to save time, but the differences in time (travel cost) facing different users gives a variation in cost of access.

The method is best applied to a specific site that is the main purpose of the trip. If the site is not the primary destination, some of the cost must be allocated to other products (Beardsley 1971). This inserts an obtrusive element into the measures as the respondent may never have consciously allocated total trip costs before. The first step is to divide the area surrounding the site to be evaluated into a series of zones.[12] All residents within a zone are to have equal costs of access to the project output (costs of travel). For convenience, concentric circular zones are often drawn, but these could be modified to reflect availability of roadways and speeds. The population of these zones is then estimated. Next, a sample of visitors to the site is taken to estimate their zones of origin and number of visitor days from each zone. From these data the number of visitor days and a percentage of the population of each zone (or the visitor days per capita) can be estimated. Travel time in hours may be added to the estimating equation, keeping in mind that there is a statistical problem because of correlation between time cost and money travel costs (Stoevener et al. 1972).

Next the cost of access from each zone is estimated. The value of time for the round trip can be estimated using the methods described in the previous section (see Cesario and Knetsch 1970; Brown and Nawas 1973). To this is added the costs of vehicular travel from each zone to the site. These time and vehicle operating costs are usually expressed as some rate per mile distance from the site. This gives the data for the hypothetical case shown in Table 5.1.

From these data it is possible to observe how behavior (number of visitations) corresponds to access cost. People in zone A have a higher rate of visitation than those in other zones with higher access costs. From this, some inferences can be made about the character of the demand curve. When there is no entry fee for use of the park, there are 9,500 visits (the sum of visits from all zones). This is the point on the demand curve corresponding to a price of zero. But what would be the quantity demanded if the entry fee were $20? We can ask this question in relation to the people in each zone. Those in zone A would now have travel costs of $20 plus

Table 5.1 National Park Visits

	Population of Zone	Distance from Park (miles)	Visitor Days (% of Population)	Number of Visitors	Travel Cost per Day $
A	10,000	100	50	5,000	20
B	20,000	300	15	3,000	40
C	30,000	500	5	1,500	60
D	n	>500	0	0	80
				Sum 9,500	

an entry fee of $20 for a total of $40. The data for the people in zone B indicate visitation behavior when total costs are $40.

Use of the method is based on the assumption that people respond to the total cost regardless of its composition. This is problematic, particularly for local facilities in which travel cost is submerged in total car costs. Differences in consumer awareness of masked travel costs versus visible entry fees may lead to errors in predicting behavior. Further, it must be assumed that the people in all the zones have the same distribution of demand for the site, which means they have the same preferences and availability of substitutes. The people in zone B have a visitation rate of 15 percent. If this rate were applied to the population of zone A, it would suggest 15 percent of 10,000 people or 1,500 visitor days from zone A at an entry price of $20. The people from zone B now have a travel cost of $40 plus an entry fee of $20. It is assumed that they will respond as do people who are now faced with a total cost of $60. This is given by the behavior of people in zone C, who have a visitation rate of 5 percent. If the 20,000 people in zone B come at this rate, there will be 1,000 visitor days from that zone at an entry fee of $20. The analysis is continued for all zones. The total cost of travel plus entry fee for the people in zone C is high enough that no one from this zone visits the park. If the visits are summed from all zones at the $20 entry fee, we have a point on the demand curve of the quantity demanded at $20 and shown in Figure 5.2 as 2,500 visitor days. A similar process of computation can be used for other entry fees.

The previous numerical example is designed to indicate the logic of the method. In practice, it is seldom possible to assume that all zones have the same preferences and this variable must be controlled in a statistical model that includes variables not only for travel cost, but also income and other socioeconomic variables thought to affect demand (Brown et al. 1964).[13] The availability of substitute sites in the various zones may also be controlled in this manner (Gum and Martin, 1975; Cicchetti et al. 1976). For unique sites

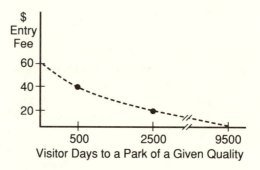

Figure 5.2 Demand Curve Derived from Cost-Behavior Data

such as Yosemite National Park this is not a problem, but it is for a local fishing lake.

Use of individual survey data allows separate variables for travel cost and time cost (monetized or not), whereas aggregation by distance zone or cost requires summation into a single variable. It also allows use of a dependent variable reflecting duration of use rather than merely crossing the entrance gate (for example, half days of use rather than number of visits).

Another complication is introduced by possible differences between close and far zone residents. The income and other socioeconomic variables included can only approximate differences in preferences. Further, they cannot control for differences in preferences that are a function of distance. There is an old adage that says, "familiarity breeds contempt." Those who are close to a recreational site may not be as impressed with it as the more distant resident. Thus, the nearby residents may not have the same visitation rate as a more distant resident when faced with the same total costs.

Mention has already been made of time costs spent in traveling. What about time spent on the site? McConnell (1975) argues that time on the site is part of the cost of a visit (also Cesario 1976; Freeman 1979, 206). This follows from a household production function or utility maximization model where choice is constrained by a time and money budget. Since travel time may have a positive, zero, or negative marginal utility, the allocation of time to the site and on the road is part of utility maximization. The opportunity cost of time on site and time in travel need not be the same. If time on the site is independent of the zone of origin, then including on-site cost has no effect on site value as it does not affect the marginal relationships. But if the residents of the closer zones spend more time on site, then ignoring on-site time will result in the site benefits being overestimated. Also, it might be expected that as admission prices rise, users from a long distance will reduce the number of trips but expand user-days per trip more than local users. Whether site time is a fixed or marginal cost depends on the consumer decision process and may differ for different goods and for different people (cf. Knetsch and Cesario 1976; McConnell 1976). There is little research to indicate the importance of this in practice.

There is a large variation in the way time is incorporated into empirical studies. Some studies ignore time altogether, some include travel time in hours and some in dollar amounts imputed from wage data, and some include time on site. The conversion of hours to dollars is a problem because of disequilibrium in labor markets. Some people have flexible work hours and can trade leisure hours for money at a constant rate. Others have fixed hours and thus a discontinuity in their budget constraint. This means that the marginal utility of time is higher than for money. The value of time is greater than the wage rate. This suggests that the person who has more dollars than they want relative to time would prefer to pay for projects in dollars and be compensated for any resources they own (project costs) in terms of time. The unemployed prefer the opposite. Those with flexible work hours do not care how they pay, but are affected if the choice affects project ranks with limited government budgets (Bockstael and Strand 1985, 168-69).

When markets are in disequilibrium, the wage rate does not indicate the marginal value of time or money. Bockstael, Strand, and Hanemann (1987, 301) conclude, "for individuals with fixed work hours, the arguments of demand functions and the computation of welfare are different from people whose labor/leisure choice is at an 'interior' and whose opportunity cost of time is reflected by the wage rate."

In the context of second-best labor market disequilibria, a government that is trying to achieve a given welfare distribution has to specify not only money income, but also the standard of payment and compensation. This has practical implications for the design of projects that can either save time or money (such as equipment costs for users).

It is common practice to relate price to an aggregation of visitor days. For some products such as a national park, visitors stay different lengths of time and thus may consume and regard each length as quite different products. The more distant user often stays longer. So if this behavior is used as a proxy for the behavior of the nearby user, it may overestimate demand. It might be better to compute separate demand schedules for each length of stay, keeping in mind that we are looking for guides to allocation in an imperfect world in which even private goods markets do not exploit all possible differentiations in consumer demand.

All ex post studies of output value have their utility in budget planning for proposed similar projects (analogous goods). This raises problems of external validity. When is the proposed project similar enough to the old project for which data are available? There is also the problem of predicting future demand over the life of the proposed project. The number of visits at some future date for a specific population can be estimated with a reduced form equation inserting values for various socioeconomic variables expected to be operative at the future date. For further discussion, see Cicchetti

(1973). For a discussion of learning over time, see Munley and Smith (1976). These problems apply to all of the value estimating approaches.

The estimation of recreation benefits can be used to estimate the value of projects that improve the quality of the environment and thereby the availability of recreation. An environmental quality variable can be added to an equation estimating use of a recreational product. If the quality variable shifts the demand curve, then the difference between the two curves is a measure of the benefit of quality improvement. A major problem is to control for other factors affecting use across sites or time. For further discussion of this application, see Freeman (1979, Ch. 8).

After a demand schedule is derived from the approach just described, the next question is how to use it in project appraisal. Many writers advocate estimating the total area under the demand curve (consumer surplus) (see Mansfield 1971). Other approaches would be to utilize the curve to select a single price that would maximize total or net revenue if fees were charged. This is discussed in Chapter 7.

The method is site specific and can be applied to evaluate future projects only if they are similar in quality and relative quantity. One of the features of quality is the degree of congestion (Bouma 1976; Knetsch 1963). Two recreation sites differing in quality are really two different products, each with its own demand curve. Quality concerns not only the available resource and original design of the recreational development, but also its subsequent management including pricing, which affects the number of visits and thus congestion. This means that if there is congestion, the demand curve estimated from the results of the cost-quantity demanded method shown in Figure 5.1 cannot be projected onto the proposed facility if it is managed in such a way as to reduce the number of visits observed previously at zero price (see Freeman, 1979; Freeman and Haveman, 1977). Charging an entrance fee at an otherwise similar project reduces visitors and congestion, and thus the willingness to pay for a given number of visits increases. This means that the analyst must find a cost-quantity demanded study of a previous project that has the same quality as the project to be built. For analyses of the effects of congestion on wilderness recreation use and benefits, see Fisher and Krutilla (1972), Cicchetti and Smith (1976), and Cesario (1980).

The application of the cost-quantity demanded method to public recreation projects has produced an immense literature. For further examples see Brown et al. (1964), Stoevener et al. (1972), Cicchetti et al. (1976), and Knetsch et al. (1976). This approach is widely used by the U.S. Park Service and water resources development agencies such as the U.S. Army Corps of Engineers. Prices for visitor days for different types of water recreation are given in the manual of procedures issued by the U.S. Water Resources Council (1979a, 30233). It is not clear, however, whether these unit values are based on studies of representative projects and can therefore be used for similar projects, or whether the prices represent a direct political and administrative pricing. Application of these prices would be more meaningful if they were in the form of a price schedule for different quantities at the site and of substitutes.

5.5.   Rent and Hedonic Price Methods

In the cost-quantity method discussed in the previous section, the value of an unmarketed product was derived from observations of behavior in response to the existence of a complementary market-valued factor controlling access to the publicly provided good in question. The method to be discussed now is based on the idea of a marketed factor controlling access to a publicly provided good. For example, to benefit from a governmental investment in irrigation, flood control, or transportation, you must have access to land served by these outputs. Similarly, to benefit from a project that improves the quality of the air or provides other amenities, you must live in the area in which these benefits occur. In the cost-quantity method, the cost of travel, for example, is given to the consumer and is determined in a broader market for cars and petroleum. The summed cost of access is itself not the value of the project because there is no evidence that consumers would pay any more than the access cost for the project. In the rent method, the cost of access to the governmental product is uniquely determined as people bid to obtain access and this access cost is itself a measure of project value. People bid up the price of land where irrigation water is available or the air is clean relative to land in lower quality sites. This produces an economic rent that can be observed and is direct evidence of willingness to pay for the project. For a producer's good, the rent is directly related to the net income change obtained by using the project output as an input. The rent is the capitalized present value of the flow of expected future net income. As noted in Section 5.2, the rent method can be used as a substitute for, or a check on, the accuracy of the intermediate good method, which estimates change in net income. Note, the rent or land value method estimate cannot be added to the value obtained by the intermediate good method as they measure the same thing. Where both types of data are available, however, the one can be used as a check on the other.

Suppose the price of land subject to flooding in the project area is $200 per acre and that similar land in the area that is flood-free sells for $600 per acre. The cross-sectional difference in land values (rents) is a measure of benefits ($400) (see Vondruska 1969). Alternatively, the change in land values in an area in which a similar project was constructed could be observed. The price of the flooded land was $200 before the project and $600 afterward. The time series change in land value associated with a previous project of $400 is then the expected benefit of another project. In either case, a change in land value of $400 is predicted and can eventually be tested by observation. Some adjustment in land value differences must be made where the land is taxed (Niskanen and Hanke 1977). In this case, some of the increase in value created by the project goes directly to the government. This increase in tax revenue must be added to the change in private land value as it is deducted from the estimated income flow when a private buyer bids for land (see Section 6.2).

The basic rationale for the rent method has been sketched. But to answer some of the questions of interpretation, economic theory must be explored in greater depth. The essence of rent theory is that any utility created by the project is reflected in economic rent, so that utility or nonland factor return is equalized on all qualities of land as people bid to secure access to it. If any surplus (difference in factor returns or utility) remains, then differences in land values do not measure the total benefits of the project (but only the value to the marginal buyer). If the reaction of producers to a change in productivity caused by the project is observed, we might find that the previous equilibrium in locations of each activity is disturbed. Some activities relocate to the enhanced site, some may move away, and still other changes may occur off the site. It would be costly to trace and estimate all of these changes. As the value of the improved site is bid up, rents on the previous locations of the relocated industry might fall, and rents on other land similar to the enhanced site might fall if the project increased total supply.

Two key assumptions emerge from the theoretical land value literature.[14] The market must be competitive and buyers must be mobile. This will mean that no user surpluses will exist after a new equilibrium is reached. The role of these assumptions can be intuitively understood by examining several of the indicated changes. If a producer moves from an existing location to the area enhanced by the project, there is no loss of rent in the old location if there previously was no rent or if someone else moves in to take the vacated site. The perfect and costless mobility assumption guarantees that any project-induced increase in supply of land with a given characteristic will be marginal. For example, although the supply of housing sites with pure air may be increased enough to drive down the price of such sites in a metropolitan area, this will still be marginal in terms of national supply. As people from other areas move to take advantage of the increased supply of clean sites in the project city, the other clean land in that city retains its rental value. These assumptions allow Lind (1973) to conclude that analysts need measure only the change in value of the enhanced land and can ignore changes in off-site land values.

The perfect mobility assumption (sometimes referred to as the open-city assumption) also serves another function. It ensures that any increase in utility or factor returns gets translated into observable changes in rents. If there were no new migrants who want the enhanced land, there is no evidence of willingness to pay. We might suspect that utility is enhanced, but since utility can not be estimated directly, there is no market evidence of the increased utility. Housing markets are often segregated by income. If air quality in a slum is improved, it would change residents' utility but may not be reflected in housing value change if there is no migration into the area (Freeman 1979, 116.) Note again that if there is no remaining surplus, then the net utility of users is unchanged after land enhancement, and only the wealth of the land owner increases. But if there is a surplus, then the utility of users increases although there is no easily observed evidence for this.

The value of land in high air quality areas is not an indicator of the willingness to pay by slum residents of low quality areas. WTP will be less than the rent differential unless there are higher income people waiting to move in and redevelop the slum. Brookshire et al. (1982) found that a bidding game survey of existing residents' WTP for an air quality improvement was less than the existing rent differential between housing occupied by these existing residents and the next-best air quality area.

When might we expect these open-city assumptions to be met so that we can focus only on land value changes on the project-enhanced sites? Not all rents are the result of differential access to natural resources. Nodes of economic activity can create their own agglomeration or associational rents even if there are many substitute sites for these nodes. For example, rents will be paid to be near a small city serving an agricultural area. Still, this center might be located at many points within the agricultural area. This means that within the general area if businesses and residences move to a project-enhanced site and vacate an old site, the owners of the former site will lose rent whereas the new project-enhanced land owners will gain. If the analyst measures only the gain in the project site, the national income value of the project will be incorrectly estimated (Lind 1973, 199-200). In this case, the correct concept is that of net locational advantage (Bromley et al. 1971; Mills 1972).

There is a project benefit only if there is a net rent increase, which would suggest that returns are higher in the new location than in the old and the sites are not perfect substitutes if developed for whole towns. Note that the agricultural area is served as before, so it is not possible for incoming migrants to maintain the old service center and its land values after its former occupants have moved to the enhanced site (perfect mobility assumption not met). Part of the gain in land values at the new site represents a transfer from the old sites and not a national income gain (Anas 1984).

This situation is a source of error in current practice by some agencies. For example, some analysts claim large benefits for navigation projects that open up new areas to ocean ports. By documenting the increase in land rents (employment and income earned are also often added) in towns along the route, the project benefit is overestimated. Some of the businesses now located on the river were in the region before, only on some off-river location. The extra rent arising from the transportation savings is the appropriate measure (net locational advantage), not the before and after land values (rents) on the riverside land. It is easier to determine when the land value change of the project enhanced area is incorrect than it is to replace it with the estimate of net locational advantage.

The perfect mobility assumption seems difficult to fulfill in many cases. We all probably imagine some idyllic spot where we would prefer to live. However, we can not duplicate our jobs and income at that location. If the supply of these idyllic environments were increased, we cannot expect the utility of those already in the area to be bid away by new incoming migrants. This means that differences in land value will underestimate project benefits because some surplus remains unobservable. On the other hand, if the enhanced site is isolated and the market for its land is unaffected by intercity migration, then the increase in supply will be nonmarginal to the local market, and other local land of similar quality may be expected to decline in value as supply is increased. This results in an overestimate of benefits if the loss of rent in similar local land is not considered. This discussion is best summarized by Freeman's (1979, 151) conclusion that, "in general, property value changes can be interpreted as benefits only when there is some mechanism to assure that there are no economic surpluses accruing to households, and when there are no changes in wages or other factor prices." In fact, some of the surplus may be absorbed in wage decreases (Rosen 1974; Hoehn et al. 1987).

In the rent method, the observation is land rent, and benefit is predicted land rent change. However, this is generally possible only for bare farm land. In other cases, the land rent is embedded in the price for a multiattribute product. A model can be constructed that regards property value as a function of a set of product characteristics. If the effects of these other non-project-affected independent variables can be controlled, then it is possible to estimate how the total property value changes with the project-enhanced variable. This is referred to as the *hedonic* or implicit price method (see Freeman 1979, 78-82; Harrison and Rubinfeld 1978b; Mendelsohn 1983), also sometimes called the characteristic or multiple regression approach.   A related technique called conjoint analysis is used in marketing research to determine the importance of various features of a multiattribute product (Green and Wind 1973).

To estimate the price of a product of public spending or regulation such as air quality if it is not itself sold, we reason that the value of a product class (X) such as housing is related to air quality (Q_j) and perhaps other environmental quality dimensions such as quality of schools (Q_k). Housing price is also related to other housing characteristics such as number of rooms (C_k), lot size (C_i), and so on.

This relationship can be expressed by saying that price of a particular house and lot Px_1 is a general function of its characteristics including air quality. This housing value equation is as follows:

$$Px_1 = Px(C_{1k},...,C_{1i},...,C_{1n},Q_{1k},...,Q_{1j},...,Q_{1m}) \tag{1}$$

The price of a particular unit of X, say house X_1, equals a general function (Px) of that unit's number of rooms C_{1k}, lot size C_{1i}, school quality in the area Q_{1k}, air quality Q_{1j}, and some other environmental factors. This function Px is the hedonic or implicit price function for housing (X). If equation (1) can be estimated by observation of selling prices and characteristics of a sample of houses, then the equation can be used to calculate the price of any given house with known characteristics. But to estimate benefits of achieving a particular air quality level, it is necessary to calculate the implicit price of that characteristic. The implicit price of a characteristic can be found by differentiating the implicit price function with respect to that characteristic.

$$dPx/dQ_j = P_{Qj}(C_{1k},...,C_{1i},...,C_{1n},Q_{1k},...,Q_{1j},...,Q_{1m}) \tag{2}$$

This marginal willingness to pay equation gives the increase in expenditure on X that is required to obtain a house model with one more unit of Q_j, *ceteris paribus*. For an empirical estimation, see Harrison and Rubinfeld (1978a). For estimates of other environmental variables, see Blomquist and Worley (1979), Nelson (1980), Freeman (1974 and 1979), Wabe (1971), Anderson and Crocker (1971), and David (1968).

If the public project is nonmarginal and changes the price of the project-created characteristic, the estimation of benefit is more complex. Freeman (1979, 80-82 and 121-29) reviews several methods for obtaining a demand function (from the above implicit price function) that can be used to calculate consumer surplus associated with the price decreasing nonmarginal output. Some questions concerning interpretation of the nonmarginal case are raised in Chapter 7.

Equation (1) could be estimated with an ordinary least squares regression. To understand the relation between the implicit price function and regression statistics, note that if the function were linear and the characteristics were independent of each other, the beta weight for the air quality variable is the same as the partial derivative of Px with respect to air quality. In other words, the beta weight represents the change in the dependent variable (price) with a standard unit of change in air quality with the other variables held statistically constant . This is also what the partial derivative expresses, though it is the correct measure even if the function is nonlinear, which would make interpretation of the beta weight difficult.

Freeman (1979, 152) argues that the hedonic price technique does not require assumptions about interurban mobility or factor price equalization as does the rent method. It requires only a competitive local market to produce price differentials for goods with different qualities at a moment in time. These cross-sectional differences between land qualities observed before the change in supply can be used to estimate the value (benefits) of a good of a particular kind if its supply were increased. However, the marginal willingness to pay equation could not be used to predict actual prices over time after the supply is increased unless the perfect mobility (open-city) assumptions are expected to hold. These assumptions ensure that the supply change is marginal. A rent model could be used to estimate the value of a quality improvement from time series data, and the mobility assumptions must hold to interpret the observed and predicted change in price. But, a hedonic willingness to pay model interprets cross-sectional differences without the assumptions, as we are not trying to predict what the price will be after the project, but only to deduce what it would be in a perfect market.

The hedonic method provides willingness to pay, but the net change in welfare as a result of the project is another matter in which some gain and some lose. Without perfect mobility, an increase in supply results in a decrease in the price of the formerly available high-quality goods, with a consequent reduction in the wealth of its owner. The problem of interpersonal utility comparison cannot be avoided by declaring that the owner had only been receiving a rent that is now transferred to consumers and that cancels out in national income accounting. It will be necessary for the analyst to document the price changes off the site of the project so that the distributive changes can be judged by policy makers (see Chapters 7 and 8).

5.6.   Alternate Cost Method

The alternate cost method is valid in limited instances, but it is frequently misused. Its appeal comes from the mistaken belief that if a public project with a certain output costs less than the next-best public or private project with the same output, then the cost of that alternate next-best project becomes the value of the output of the public project under consideration. The problem is to establish that the higher cost alternative would actually have been constructed in the absence of the project under consideration; that is to say, effective demand for the alternate project must be established (Randall 1981, 301).

Evidence of effective demand is what is missing in nonmarketed outputs. Can we infer effective demand from legislative mandate that a certain output be achieved? This explicit political pricing is valid, but if it is accepted, then no further economic estimation of benefits is appropriate. The existence of a more expensive alternative does not further legitimize the legislative mandate. The only economic consideration is to construct the cheapest possible alternative producing the mandated output. This is a straightforward exercise in cost-effectiveness analysis and should not be confused with benefit-cost analysis, which is directed at illuminating the original decision to obtain the output. For further discussion, see Steiner (1966).

The alternative cost method is widely used in practice in spite of its limitations. It is used by U.S. water resource development agencies to estimate the value of urban water supply and hydropower. Note in this case that the output does have a market price. The common practice is to project per capita use trends or population growth trends. Projection of continuing growth in per capita use can be dangerous when past observations are based on prices that are lower than those necessary to cover the new project costs. The problem is to estimate a demand curve that will estimate quantity demanded at an increased price. If these prices are beyond the range of past experience, there is little support for projecting effective demand. Consumers may decide substitutes for water, including conservation, are better than paying more for water.

Where effective demand is indicated by market bids for the product, then if the output of the public project is a perfect substitute for the alternative output that would be produced in the absence of the public project, it is valid to use the cost of the alternative project as a measure of benefit. In perfect competition, the cost of the alternative project would also be the market price of the output. For example, if private electric utilities are planning to build a new thermal plant to meet expected demand at today's market price, this price becomes the value of the new capacity. If the public hydroplant can produce electricity more cheaply, it should be built. Another example is import substitution. If the output of a domestic project can substitute for currently imported goods, the value of the project's input is the border price.

Any currently borne cost that can be averted becomes a benefit . This is true not only for production of substitute goods, but for any actually made defensive expenditure that reduces the effect of some undesirable feature of the environment, such as disease, air, or water pollution.

These defensive expenditures may be less than perfect and some of the problems may remain. In this case, the alternate cost is not a full measure of the benefit of a project that entirely rectifies the problem. In other words, the project may be better than its alternate substitute. Another practical problem in using this method is that individuals may use a variety of defensive devices, some of which are purchases and some of which are time and other nonmarketed resources. All of these need to be considered as part of the alternative opportunity costs. For a theoretical discussion of substitution relationships, see Maler (1974, 116-18).

The alternative cost method is the same concept as the cost saving method described in Section 5.3 and the market analogy method described in Section 5.1. A project that substitutes for a known expenditure creates a saving that is the measure of benefit. The different methods just use different data, such as output prices, production costs, or alternative cost.

The differences and similarities between the cost saving and alternate cost methods can perhaps be made clearer in Table 5.2. The cost saving method is applicable when there are still private user costs after the project is built. The difference in costs is the measure of gross benefits. In cases in which all costs are eliminated and the output of the project is a perfect substitute for the alternative project expenditure, the alternate cost method can be used. The alternate cost itself is the measure of gross benefit, if and only if effective demand can be proven. Both methods estimate gross benefit,

Table 5.2   Cost Saving versus Alternate Cost Methods

Cost Saving Method	$	Alternate Cost Method	$
Private cost of truck transport (now being made)	100	Cost of alternative project (e.g., thermal power)	100
Private cost of barge transport	75		
Cost saving (gross benefit)	25	Cost of alternative (gross benefit)	100
Cost of barge project	20	Cost of project being evaluated	75
Net benefit	5	Net benefit	25

that is, the *cost saving* in the cost saving method and the *cost of the next-best alternative project* in the alternate cost method.

5.7.   Bidding Games and Surveys[15]

The previously described methods all infer willingness to pay as revealed in consumer (producer) behavior. Alternatively, it is possible to directly ask people to indicate what value they place on different goods. Some of this information can be used in systematic analysis of projects and some could be used by public authorities in establishing budget size by agency or program.

There is a common belief that public opinion surveys are able to indicate "what the public wants" on a wide range of subjects. Survey results are often quoted uncritically in support of, or in opposition to, various public policy options, with the implicit belief that a democratic society should be aware of and act on the preferences and opinions of its citizens. Policy makers, it is felt, should not have the right to ignore what "the public" says it wants or does not want. Whether or not we accept this normative position, we must examine more carefully the contention that good survey techniques are capable of reflecting *the* public's opinion.

An analogy can be drawn between the selection of voting rules and the selection of survey techniques. Voting is a common method of preference aggregation in which the determination of results is influenced by the selection of procedural rules. Political rules determine how issues are worded and grouped, who is eligible to vote, how voters will be grouped, what degree of unanimity will be required; in turn, these factors determine how differing preferences are weighted. In a similar way, the selection of public opinion survey techniques will differentially weight different preferences. The selection of survey samples, the type of questions used, the explicitness of trade-offs, and the methods of aggregation of results, for example, all influence which public opinion counts. It is incorrect to conceive of a single measure as representing what the public wants and therefore what a democratic government must grant. As a result of analyst-politician dialogue choices are made as to which public, and hence which preferences, to consider.

5.7.1. Statistical Bias and Whose Preferences Count

A statistical bias occurs when an inference is made based on data that do not accurately describe the relevant universe. For example, a nonrandom sample of a given target population will lead to descriptive statements about the population that are not true. Other problems of this type related to experimental designs will be noted.

There is another variety of error that is not based on falsehood, but is derived from implicitly choosing whose preferences to describe. For example, if a person with an intense preference for program A over program B is grouped with a person who has a mild preference for B, this is reported as one-half of the population favors A and one-half favors B. This is not a falsehood; it is a subtle device for weighting preferences and deciding how conflicting preferences are counted. If this conclusion is uncritically accepted as public opinion by the political process, the analyst, by selecting a particular question format has in effect decided a political issue while perhaps pretending it is only a technical issue and without telling anyone that a political choice had been made. These issues of political choice are not a matter of bias or no bias. There is no single truth to be approached and verified. The question is whose point of view is to be taken and how different points of view are to be aggregated. In some cases, the questions of statistical bias and political choice are confounded.

5.7.2. Experimental and Survey Design

Several problems of survey design will be discussed, including problems of internal, external, construct, and policy validity. As noted in Chapter 4, internal validity is the term applied to the possibility that there is an alternative explanation for a hypothesized relationship. In terms of the methodology of experimental design, the central proposition of a preference survey is that preferences cause the responses recorded in terms of spending priorities. As in any causal hypothesis, there are alternative explanations for the recorded observations. The ranking of spending categories may be an expression of something in addition to the respondent's preferences.

One threat to internal validity is the problem of simulating a real choice situation. Can the hypothetical situation create the same sense of choice the respondent experiences when buying something or voting?   Will the respondent answer the question any way just to get rid of the interviewer? There is a literature on how question format and technique affect the survey results compared to actual choice (Hochstim 1967). For example, does a phone or personal interviewer affect how the survey results compare to actual choice behavior such as voting? In some cases, such as a preelection survey, the survey results are verifiable by comparing the results of the survey and the actual election. But in other cases, no specific verification is possible because the question does not involve the prediction of any future action on the part of the respondent.

People find it very difficult to evaluate low probability situations with the potential for catastrophic loss. If people are pressed, they may respond to a question such as how much are you willing to pay to reduce the chance of dying from one in 1,000 to one in 100,000 (Acton 1973), but the respondent may attach little meaning to the response and supplies it only out of politeness.   To summarize, the problem is attributing a response to preferences when in reality it is an expression of something else.

Strategic or gaming behavior, in which the respondent believes there is a purpose behind the questions, presents another threat to internal validity (Bohm 1972). The response may be biased, for example, by the fact that the respondent wishes to avoid some tax or other means of payment implied in the question or feels that the question implies being asked to pay more than a fair share.

In the case of goods with high exclusion costs, the respondent may not take the question of willingness to pay seriously because of the knowledge that no one can be excluded regardless of the bid. Or conversely, the response to a question of willingness to receive may be biased if it is a joint impact good in which a fixed quantity is available to all users and no one user can sell without jeopardizing its availability to other common users. Several empirical studies suggest that strategic bias may be of little consequence (see, for example, Schulze et al. 1981).

External validity is the degree to which results from a particular survey or experiment may be generalized to other situations. A factor that strongly affects external validity is sample selection (see Lansing and Morgan 1971, Ch. 3; and Sudman 1976). Are respondents truly representative of a larger population from which they were drawn? Sampling procedure also has important consequences for preference weighting, as will be discussed.

Questions of construct validity arise from potential misinterpretation of the categories of choice (Cornbach 1982; House 1983; Oppenheim 1966). Information bias may be induced by the test instrument, interviewee, or process. The responses may represent preferences, but it may be a preference for a good other than that seen by the analyst. Abstractly, a person is asked to rank two situations. But the respondent's images of them may differ from the images of the interpreter. Moser and Kalton (1972, 318-325) discuss the problems of interpretation caused by question wording: nonspecificity, incomprehensibility, ambiguity, vagueness, leading questions, and presumptiveness (also, see Payne 1951). Reference points, question sequencing, and the introduction of questions may influence survey results (Carpenter and Blackwood 1977; Rowe et al. 1980).

Policy validity refers to the application of survey results to policy. A distinction has been made between statistical bias and implicit choice of whose preferences count. This latter will be referred to here as questions of policy validity. A major question already noted is the matter of reflecting the intensity of preferences when results are aggregated. Another issue is whether the survey question can ever approach political reality when choices are grouped, compromised, and traded off. The usual survey question presents choices as if each choice were to be decided on its own merits. Many political decisions are compromises among sets of programs. For example, a group supporting farm programs may support a nonfarm item to obtain the votes of other groups for farm programs. These groupings of issues are greatly influenced by events and would be difficult to capture in a survey. Policy validity is compromised when survey questions are not presented in terms of trade-offs.

It appears that there has been no systematic investigation of the limitations and capabilities of different types of survey questions in terms of the voting rule analogy, that is, whose preferences are promoted or given expression by each set of rules and techniques. There is a large literature on internal and external threats to validity and these will not be further noted here. The balance of this discussion will focus primarily on questions of policy validity and construct validity that are particularly relevant in the political interpretation of survey results. A classification of some of the major questionnaire techniques will be proposed to suggest what limitations and preference weighting might be expected under the different categories.

The techniques involve two major groups of surveys, each with a different purpose. The first involves attitudinal surveys. They are aimed at the program or agency level and are used by lobby groups to argue for larger budget allocations for a particular area. The second involves willingness to pay surveys producing product prices. They could be used by government agencies for systematic analysis of projects in the same way as any of the methods previously discussed in this chapter. Either technique may or may not contain explicit budget constraints.

5.7.3. Attitudinal and Rank Order Surveys

Perhaps the most common type of survey question involves the use of scales (or indexes). Points on such scales may represent degrees of concern, of agreement or disagreement, or of some other attitude or preference attribute. Respondents are asked to select some point along the scale that indicates, or most closely corresponds to, their feelings on the subject, for example, to rank their perceptions of the seriousness of various community problems or to rank their preference for more or less money to be spent by a public agency on various budget categories or programs. Ordinal or internal scales offer the advantage over open-ended questions of providing easily quantifiable measures that are amenable to statistical manipulation and interpretation. Commonly a series of questions will be used to measure the attitudes of respondents from different angles. Statistical manipulations may then be used in an attempt to achieve greater internal validity and confidence in the conclusions reached. Care must be taken to ensure an isomorphic structure between the chosen numerical system and the entity being measured.

Scaled questions are well adapted to the discovery of general attitudes and perceptions.[16] Scales devised for use in psychological and sociological research are not as useful, however, in the discovery of respondents' specific marginal preferences. Care must be taken to avoid construct invalidity. It is important to distinguish, for example, between respondents' perceptions of the seriousness of a problem and their preferences for additional budget expenditure. Although a problem may be considered serious, some solution other than government spending may be favored.

Most attitude surveys contain no limitations that would prevent people from saying that they feel all problems are serious or taking some other consistently extreme position (cf. Carlson 1976; Clark 1976). The Louis Harris (1977) organization conducted a survey in which people were asked "how serious a loss would it be if federal programs in certain areas were cut by one-third?" A high percentage rated the loss as very serious for social security, health programs, education, law enforcement, employment, and defense. Would respondents also have rated these areas as "serious problems?" Would they favor additional expenditure in these areas (even if taxes had to be raised)? Did the questions measure people's attitudes about the program or about the general tax level? When this is not specified in a question, the respondent may answer a question that is different from the question the analyst thought was asked. Responses are then confounded by attitudes to the particular vehicle and pattern of cost incidence. Respondents may favor additional expenditures for a particular program as long as they are not required to pay much toward its cost or as long as they are satisfied that others are paying their "fair" share. Randall et al. (1974) showed different responses when payment was via sales tax, user fee, or added to an electricity bill (see also Sinden 1974; Walsh et al. 1978). Willingness to pay may be confounded with judgments of fairness.

5.7.4.   Willingness to Pay (Sell) Surveys

The willingness to pay technique (or bidding game) involves an interview or questionnaire in which persons are asked to state their maximum willingness to pay money for various quantities of a good (Knetsch and Davis 1972; Cocheba and Langford 1978; Hammack and Brown 1974).[17] The individual data may be summed to indicate a demand curve in the usual way. This is sometimes referred to as the *contingent valuation method* because the values obtained are contingent on the interpretation of hypothetical markets and products (Cummings, et al. 1986; Hoehn and Randall 1987).

These surveys often make a presumption of property rights. Significantly different results will be obtained if people are asked how much they would be willing to pay (WTP or equivalent variation) to enjoy clean air rather than if they are asked how much they would be willing to sell (WTS or compensating variation) their right to clean air for (Randall et al. 1974).

Gordon and Knetsch (1979, 4) reviewed seven studies in which users of publicly provided goods were asked to state willingness to pay and to receive. WTP was less than WTS by 350 to 2,000 percent (also see Meyer 1979, 226, and Knetsch and Sinden 1984). Bishop and Heberlein's (1979, 929) study of goose hunting showed WTS higher by 481 percent. The difference between WTP and WTS is a difference in the distribution of property (income) affecting demand (bid) and supply prices, and this requires a value judgment and public choice. In terms of welfare economics, it is the difference between the equivalent and compensating variations and indicates an income effect. Meade (1972) objected to Mishan's failure to recognize the property rights implication and Mishan (1981, 163, n. 9) now says that "in the absence of radical legislation on amenity rights which would decide who owns (who is buyer and who seller) . . . any project should be able to meet two tests; aggregate compensating variations positive and aggregate equivalent variations negative." (See Chapter 7 for discussion of these concepts.)

An entitlement to a national pattern of income distribution including exposure to mental and bodily harm is valued in a social context. The end states so secured have their value in part because they are property entitlements. Kelman (1987, 147) makes the point by saying that people "may value the thing they are declared to be entitled to because these things are sanctified by the entitlement." There may be a difference between values placed on commodities by people acting as individuals and values worked out by interacting with others. Some preferences are developed in a social and legal setting. A person might decide to give to charity in a wholly private calculation. But if that same person is an owner (whole or part) of a shared state of the world collectively arrived at, this may affect that person's valuation. This is the setting if I am asked the price at which I would give up (sell) an interest in some national pattern of income distribution, exposure of others to bodily or mental harm, or environmental quality. This is different than a decision made noncollectively to give to charity or buy a person relief from what I consider to be an unjust low level of living or exposure to harm. One difference is what Kelman (1987, 148) refers to when he notes that we may pay less to secure our moral concerns than we would accept to relinquish established states "in part because we might feel that we had caused the victim harm, rather than simply failed to prevent it." The value of some states of the world results in part from their being socially and politically approved, just as some goods are valuable because a movie star endorses them.   The social setting and reference point are different depending on whether the person is a buyer or seller.

Behavioral science offers an explanation of the difference between WTP and WTS. Prospect theory suggests that decisions are framed by a reference point and individuals exhibit loss aversion. Losses are valued more than increases from this point. Empirical studies support this interpretation and further indicate that the difference between WTP and WTS is less for a Smith auction process than for a contingent valuation format (Brookshire and Coursey 1987). The Smith auction process puts the bidder in a context of what other individuals are doing and presents information on the cost of alternative levels of the good in question.

The results of contingent valuation willingness to pay surveys are also affected by survey format (Boyle and Bishop 1988). The iterative format begins with a price and asks if the described product would be purchased at that price. If the answer is yes, the price is raised until the response is no. If the initial answer is no, the price is lowered until the response is yes. The resulting bid is sensitive to the analyst's selection of the starting bid (Samples 1985).

The use of payment cards employs a different format. The card indicates per capita spending for various public services (similar to and different from the product in question) for people in the respondent's income bracket. The respondent is asked to state a value for the product in question. This format becomes part of the respondent's learning and invites comparisons with other public products as well as general opportunity costs. The budget constraint could be made explicit if the respondent also had to indicate what items of expenditures would be decreased so that the bid for the new public product could be made.

A simpler question format may involve dichotomous choice.   A respondent is given a specific value and asked whether this is acceptable. Other respondents are given another value. Each accepts or rejects the single take it or leave it value. The frequency of response to the different bids is used to estimate a logit function. The results of this approach are affected by choice of functional form (Hanemann 1984). Again, format affects learning. Also, a person who may have stopped bidding in an iterative format may accept the higher single offered value because rejection may suggest that the product has no value.

Political choice of budget allocations may be influenced by who has the resources to do a single item survey and call attention to a particular item (put it on the decision agenda).

In answering willingness to pay survey questions the respondent may not have to make choices and trade-offs in stating their preferences. This can be seen, for example, in questions that involve items that are very small in terms of per capita costs. It might be pointed out that a new program would cost only 50 cents per person. This might be followed by the question, "Would you support this program at the cost of 50 cents?" It is reasonable to expect that many programs of such magnitude would get a positive response to a single item survey, yet they could not all be adopted without resistance to a great increase in the public budget. For example, we would expect different responses to the question, "Would you be willing to pay 50 cents more for a mosquito-free park?" as against "Would you be willing to pay 50 cents more for a mosquito-free park, and 50 cents more for increased garbage collection in the park, and 50 cents more for improvements in other park facilities?"

Still different results might be obtained if the question were "Would you pay 50 cents more for a mosquito-free park when the same money would prevent X children from dying of lead poisoning in slum housing?" If the questions are asked serially, the bids may be affected by the sequence (Randall et al. 1981).

The choice of sequence in willingness to pay questions involves both visibility and competition. Because public attention is limited, how visible a particular product is and how well it is advertised affect its demand. The same is true in politics. Politicians strive to control the agenda--literally giving attention to selected items and the sequence of voting on budget and other items in an attempt to place their favored projects in a position of best comparison with substitutes and complements. The rules of the game influence demand and whose demand counts. Value does not exist independently of its measurement when it impacts on learning.

Some survey questions are designed to evaluate respondents' allocative preferences under some explicit form of constraint at which the level of complements and substitutes is explicit. One type of approach utilizes what is called a budget pie (McIver and Ostrom 1976; Clark 1974). A respondent is presented with a circle representing the budget and is asked to "cut the pie" into segments that represent the preferred mix of budget allocations to some set of goods or services. The question does not normally allow the respondent to propose increases in all categories and thus a more restricted decision setting is involved. The information is gained only with regards to average allocation preference.

Another type of restricted question involves the use of a display in which stacks of tokens such as poker chips are used to represent current budget allocations (Beardsley et al. 1974). The respondent is allowed to move chips from one stack to another to reflect preferences. Attitudes toward total budget size may be determined by allowing the respondent to add to or subtract from the total number of chips to represent additions to or reductions in tax burden. This latter approach has greater scope for more realistic and more probing investigation, but involves greater conceptual complexity and often greater survey cost. This factor weights the question in favor of those with higher education or greater capacity to comprehend the ideas. For questions that investigate willingness to pay or allocative preferences, there must either be a presumption of prior knowledge or some more or less explicit educational aspect to the questions. Either of these will influence the weighting of preferences. If knowledge is assumed, then those who actually are informed will possess a greater ability to effectively communicate their desires. If the survey includes an explicit instructional element, then a different set of preferences will be favored as learning occurs. There are differences in budget allocation by citizens with and without provision of information on present budget allocation.

The language used to describe alternatives is particularly important when selecting the names used for categories in an allocation game. How are spending items to be grouped and labeled? People may have a different attitude, for example, toward programs called "welfare" and programs called "investment in human capital." It will make a difference, therefore, if aid to the aged for health care is included under a welfare or a health program category.

Choice of the relevant target population to survey is highly important. Dwyer et al. (1977, 76) state, "It is best to survey actual beneficiaries only, in order to reduce the hypothetical nature of the questioning." This ignores the fact that there are opposing interests for whom these questions are not hypothetical. The choice of a sample frame or boundary will have great consequence in determining whose attitudes and opinions are registered. No selection will please all interests and none can be said to be neutral, just as the drawing of boundaries of congressional districts favor some interests and frustrate others.

5.7.5. Survey Formats and Politics

Ultimately, the election of political representatives and their budget votes determine whose preferences count. A number of objections have been raised about adding polls or even special referenda to the system of representative democracy. However this issue is judged, there is no right or wrong way to measure or assess the public's point of view. Analysts must be aware not only of the statistical biases that survey techniques involve but also the necessity of choosing which public opinion will be surveyed, which attitudes and preferences will be given expression, and the extent to which the respondent is reminded of substitutes and complements. To decide that the major opinion (or the one with the most adherents) is the relevant one does not avoid the necessity of further normative choice. Surveys are as much a part of the process of learning and political representation as are elections and referenda. Just as we have political debates on constitutions and election laws that determine whose preferences affect public choice, so we can have public awareness and debates on survey formats and techniques, the results of which are increasingly used to supplement the elective process.

5.8. Systematic Choice among Multiple Outputs of Public Projects without Prices[18]

Systematic choice in the preparation of government budgets is rare. The same trade-off between outputs is not consistently made and projects ostensibly chosen to achieve a stated objective either do not produce that output or other alternatives would produce the output with less input. This is convenient for some politicians who can take credit for nominally doing one thing while in fact doing another (serving a hidden clientele). The politician's preference for nonsystematic decision making is aided by some intellectual confusion over decision making in the absence of market prices to indicate relative value of some or all outputs (and/or inputs). Some reformers feel that benefit-cost analysis as currently applied unjustly weights decisions in favor of market-valued outputs (goods and services) at the expense of non-market-related outputs. In their reaction to this, they fail to see the role of any kind of systematic relative value weights. It is the purpose of this section to demonstrate how systematic weights can be generated by the political process and applied by analysts. These administrative prices are as valid as any price inferred from market behavior.

The procedure will be explained in terms of all outputs having no market prices and all inputs having market prices. See Schmid (1975) for a parallel discussion of mixed situations.

Step 1: Output Categories

The political process (administrative, legislative, or both) must decide what inputs and outputs are relevant. This is a political value judgment that determines objectives as discussed in Chapter 3. For purposes of illustration, consider outputs. Analysts can provide information on alternative outputs and their consequences to help politicians in their selection. It is preferable if analysts can present each output in terms of quantifiable physical units and mental states. These products can be anything from endangered species and job satisfaction to math test scores. For example, the politicians may suggest that they want a children's program and that improved health and skills for future adult roles are the important outputs. A unit of each is needed that allows an objective count of what is achieved. Health is too general to be measured. A measure such as disease rate or days missed of normal play or school is needed. It is the analyst's job to suggest such taxonomies from which the politicians can choose.[19]

Step 2: Importance Weights

Units of output must be ranked by politicians.[20] This might begin by asking politicians to put their selected units of output in rank order. For example: First--Days of play missed. Second--One point on math achievement test score. Third--Etc. Analysts can help politicians select meaningful aggregates of units for comparison. For example, it may be difficult to determine whether a day of school missed is worth more than a point on a math test. Salient aggregates might be units of a week for school missed and 10 points on a math test (keeping in mind that a particular math test represents an aggregate of specific math skills).

The process continues by asking politicians to place importance weights on a given quantity of the selected outputs. This is an increment in addition to the do-nothing alternative. They can ask, for example, whether avoidance of a week of play missed for children 2 to 5 years old is twice as important as an increase in math achievement scores of 10 points for children 10 years old. Suppose this is agreed to by political process. For ease of comparison, the math achievement unit can be given a value of 1; then if the health unit is twice as important, it would have a value of 2.[21] The process continues for other outputs. Suppose there is a third output that we shall here call "Z" and suppose the political compromise decision is that it is half as important as the math achievement unit. The value weight of Z is then .5, which reflects the chosen comparative value ratio. The value judgments now can be recorded as follows:

Output	Importance Weight
X (health)	2.0
Y (education)	1.0
Z (etc.)	.5
Sum	3.5

Step 3: Importance Weights Standardized

Sum the importance weights, divide each by the sum. For example,

(X) health output 2.0/3.5	=	.57
(Y) education output 1.0/3.5	=	.29
(Z) etc. .5/3.5	=	.14
Sum		1.00

This is a purely mechanical step done by the analyst. The assumption is that projects are marginal and do not change value weights as outputs increase.

Step 4: Determine Project Outputs

The next step is for the analyst to determine the amount of output of alternative public projects. This is based on experimental designs, evaluation of pilot projects, and prior experience as described in Chapter 4. How many units of each selected output will project 1 produce, how many for project 2, and so on.? For example, project 1 may produce a 10-week reduction in days

Table 5.3 Method A Using Physical Output Units

Project	Output (units)		
Number	X	Y	Z
1	10	20	5
2	30	10	0
3	30	15	0

Table 5.4 Method B Using Index of Relative Outputs

Project	Output (scale)		
Number	X	Y	Z
1	250	500	125
2	750	250	250
3	750	375	0

missed due to illness (output X). These outputs could be displayed as shown in Table 5.3.

In some cases, this process is necessarily subjective, in which case an alternative, equivalent method can be used. For example, consider choice among research projects. Experts could be asked to rank the project on an imaginary scale of one to 1,000 for each of the output variables. This means that although they cannot count units of output, they may be able to reach some consensus on each project's expected relative contribution to a given output.

For example, the outputs of projects are ranked by analysts on each output scale as shown in Table 5.4.

Note that regardless of whether method A or B is used, the relative magnitude among outputs is the same for each project and the relative size is the same for a given output among different projects. The only difference is that the latter may help analysts represent relative project output when physical units are not available.

Step 5: Compute Utilities

The value weighted outputs for each project are now summed into an aggregate utility (U_j). The output magnitude (O_{ij}) computed in Step 4 is multiplied by the value weight (W_i) computed in Step 3 and summed for all outputs for each project as follows[22]: $U_j = \Sigma_i W_i O_{ij}$, remembering that $\Sigma_i W_i = 1.00$. The specific computations for these data using the two alternate methods of indicating output magnitudes are shown as follows:

Project 1

Method A $(10 \times .57 = 5.7) + (20 \times .29 = 5.8) + (5 \times .14 = .7) = 12.2$
Method B $(250 \times .57 = 142.5) + (500 \times .29 = 145) + (125 \times .14 = 17.5) = 305$

Project 2

Method A $(30 \times .57 = 17.1) + (10 \times .29 = 2.9) + (10 \times .14 = 1.4) = 21.4$
Method B $(750 \times .57 = 427.5) + (250 \times .29 = 72.5) + (250 \times .14 = 35) = 535$

Project 3

Method A $(30 \times. 57 = 17.1) + (15 \times .29 = 4.35) + (0 \times .14 = 0) = 21.45$
Method B $(750 \times .57 = 427.5) + (375 \times .29 = 108.75) + (0 \times 14 = 0) = 536.2$

In this example, projects 2 and 3 are nearly equal and both are superior to 1. (Both methods give the same ranking.)

Step 6: Benefit-Cost Ratios
Projects differ not only in the mix of outputs, but also in cost. Thus, it will be convenient to rank projects according to the ratio of the summed utilities (benefits) to costs. For example, assume the following costs:

Project	Cost ($)
1	500
2	1,500
3	1,000

The benefit-cost ratios are as follows using the benefits (U_i) from Step 5 and the above cost data:

Method	Project 1	Project 2	Project 3
A	12.2/$500 = .024	21.4/1500 = .01	21.45/1000 = .021
B	305/$500 = .61	535/1500 = .36	536.2/1000 = .53

The benefit-cost ranking is as follows:

Rank	Project	Cumulative Cost ($)
First	1	500
Second	3	1,500
Third	2	3,000

Although projects 2 and 3 produced more benefits (utilities), their costs are proportionately much higher, so that 1 is more cost effective. For example, project 3 costs twice as much as project 1 (i.e., the ratio of their costs is 1,000/500 = 2), but because its importance weighted outputs (benefits) are not twice as much (21.45/12.2 = 1.75), project 1 is preferred. If the budget were limited to $1,500, projects 1 and 3 would be chosen. Because the benefits and costs are not in comparable terms, the absolute size of the benefit-cost ratio has no implication for choosing the size of the budget. The budget size is an independent political decision that must be given to the analyst. If this is combined with a political decision on the weights given to each of the various output categories (X, Y, and Z in this example), the analyst can complete the systematic analysis. After examining the results, the political process may want to reevaluate its earlier political decision on budget size and output weights. This method makes all value judgments visible for everyone to see.

Step 7: Compute Implied Prices

It is a small step from explicit value weighting to monetary prices. These prices are politically chosen. The value weights as applied here perform one of the same functions as monetary market prices--namely, to reflect desired rates of output trade-offs. If costs are in money terms and the budget level is set, the outputs are in effect minimally priced.

The standardized importance weights (from Step 3) allow computation of an index of output (also see Sugden and Williams 1978, 185). The different physical units of output can be summed when weights are applied.[23] The index of output = $(40X \times .57) + (35Y \times .29) + (5Z \times .4) = 33.65$. When the budget is allocated to these projects, it implies the total value of the outputs. Thus, the index of output (33.65) has a total value of ($1,500). The value of one unit of the index value can be calculated by dividing the total value by the index number ($1,500/33.65 = 44.58). Because Step 3 standardizes the importance weights in terms of one unit, the contribution of each project output to that unit is obtained by multiplying the standardized importance weight by the value of one index unit as follows:

Price of X = .57 × 44.58 = $25.41
Price of Y = .29 × 44.58 = $12.93
Price of Z = .14 × 44.58 = $ 6.24
$44.58

This procedure prices a variety of outputs (with their chosen relative values) as surely as if the political process had attached an initial monetary value to them. Only in this case the political decision on budget size determines the prices, rather than price indicating the budget size as is the case in monetary benefit-cost analysis. Explicit value weighting of public project outputs is related to explicit attachment of monetary prices by the political process. Step 7 performs no essential role in systematic choice. It does, however, facilitate comparison with market-valued products. People can interact with their political representatives and ask themselves if they want to support a politician who says that a unit of education is worth only as much as two seats at a professional football game.

Choice of a budget level plus choice of importance weights implies a summed benefit-cost ratio for the systematically chosen group of projects of at least unity.[24] The choice of a regulatory standard with its associated cost has similar implications in risk benefit analysis discussed in Chapter 3. Application of this principle can be seen in Figure 3.2. If regulatory option D is chosen, it implies that the associated dose reduction that is translatable into a risk of cancer is minimally priced at $20 million for the 700 pesticide applicators. The opportunity cost of a chosen regulation or a chosen project and budget is conceptually similar, and to choose is to price the output.

This format for analyst-politician dialogue requires the politician to think in terms of importance weights and budget size. Because this combination is equivalent to pricing, politicians can be asked to directly express themselves in terms of administrative prices.[25] This would be equivalent to the direct bidding games outlined in Section 5.7. As already noted, a bidding response for a given quantity has meaning only with respect to an income constraint. The decision maker can be made aware of this necessary trade-off by asking what private or public consumption item will be reduced as more is bid and paid for the project item in question. The same thing is accomplished by first asking the decision maker for an importance weight for a given quantity and then an explicit allocation of the budget to a set of projects, followed by a reexamination of the derived prices (i.e., the analyst asks the decision makers, who have now seen the prices implied by choice of importance, weights, and budget size, whether they want to change their original choices).

In a bidding game, the prices are interpreted by the analyst with the hope that the bidders were aware of their income constraints (otherwise the bid is a wish and not effective demand). The analyst then applies the prices to projects and the budget size is derived by seeing how many positive return projects are available. Then the bidder can again be asked if the former bid seems appropriate now that the implied budget is seen. In the importance weighting *cum* budget size format, the budget size is explicitly chosen and the prices are derived. Both approaches are equivalent if carefully done, but the latter assures that the income constraint is not ignored.

This method produces a price for a given quantity (only one point on a demand schedule). It would be clumsy to repeat the dialogue for various quantities. It would seem more straight forward to request an administratively specified demand schedule. The exercise outlined here might help policy makers to think about their prices. A similar analysis could be applied to regulations. In that case, the cost is the public cost of administration plus the private opportunity costs of complying with the regulation. A life saved by instituting industrial safety practices can be evaluated the same way as a life saved by an investment in medical care. To choose is to price.

5.9. Conclusion

Conceptually, all of the methods discussed in this chapter are measures of willingness to pay by people with effective demand. Choice of which method to use often depends on data availability. At the same time, choice of method (and analytic choices within each method) can involve some choice of who has what effective demand.

Benefit-cost analysis is sometimes seen as guiding resource allocation as it would be if the market worked for all goods. But government decisions on property rights affect market prices. Thus, if governments ask their analysts to infer prices for nonmarketed goods from market behavior by any of the methods discussed in this chapter, government is affirming and adding to its previous property rights decisions. Occasionally, it may make changes in particular prices without changing private property rights that are the economy's general systems rules. And, in some cases, market inferences are impossible and direct administrative pricing is done (either directly or inferred as in the previous section). The project analyst can systematically apply prices from any of these sources as directed. There is no technical basis for preferring one source to another. They all represent interpersonal comparisons of utility that is a political decision.

BCA is a systematic method for maximizing wealth and is, thus, a guide to public investment and regulations. In reaching these decisions, however, some implicit determination is made of whose interests and which interests are to be recognized. These decisions are a function of policy perspective and are separate from the logic of wealth maximization. Wealth maximization follows from decisions or property rights rather than being a guide to these rights. Property rights are involved in decisions such as to whether to use a human capital approach, intermediate good method, or an explicit administrative price, whether to use objective agency statistics or people's subjective estimates, whether to adopt a willingness to pay or sell mode as well as the sequence of questions in a bidding survey, and how to treat loss of rents. It is not a question of replacing individuals' valuations with government decisions. Public decisions are always present in the distribution of rights that lies behind market price inferences or administrative prices.

Notes

1. The approach potentially could be applied to price data for consumer products that are differentiated by riskiness in use, for example, airlines with different accident records. Labor market studies of wage premiums have estimated value of life between $300,000 and $3.5 million (Graham and Vaupel 1981, 179; also see Conley 1976).

2. Then if the production function (relation of the pollution or safety control project to probability of death) is known, these quantities can be multiplied by the prices obtained in these studies.

3. The data could come from a cross-sectional comparison of the value of land that is of similar quality except for the project-produced quality. See Section 5.5 for potential problems in interpreting time series data.

4. Jones-Lee (1976, 50) argues that the present value of anticipated future output is conceptually wrong because it is not the subjective marginal value of the probable decrease in risk. He prefers the survey method of Section 5.7 in which people are asked, for example, to trade off hypothetical differences in cost and safety of alternative transportation modes. Also see Jones-Lee (1982).

5. Government agencies use a variety of value-of-life estimates in their decisions on safety regulations. For example, the U.S. Consumer Product Safety Commission uses values ranging from $200,000 to $2 million (see Baram 1980, 485; Graham and Vaupel 1981; Hartunian et al. 1981). An Environmental Protection Agency (1985) study used a value of $1 million. See Hapgood (1979).

6. This concept is related to claimed benefits of birth control projects as value of consumption avoided (Zaidan 1971; Simon 1970). In poor countries, birth control causes a net benefit to national income if people are expected to produce less than they consume. The prevention of the birth of a poor, unproductive person would be more valuable than that of a productive person. It follows that health projects preventing the death of an unproductive living person would have negative benefits, but this is objectionable on moral grounds. Note, however, that in private damage suits a young high-income doctor will be given more damages than a low-income worker.

7. This is an example of the general question of the significance of market prices that represent mistakes. As there is always a degree of

uncertainty in many decisions, this is not a minor matter unique to health projects.

8. Or an appropriate adjustment of cost or benefits can be made to reflect differences in quality.

9. One applied study used a general rule of valuing the new traffic volume at one-half the cost saving for old traffic because net income of the new firm was not available (Stanford Research Institute 1966, 45). This is a rough approximation of consumer surplus. Also see Sugden and Williams (1978, 258).

10. In this and the other methods to follow, the number of trips (and travelers) is assumed to be constant. Chapter 6 discusses evaluation in which the cost saving results in additional trips.

11. Total expenditures for access give a lower bound for the value of the total recreational experience, but what is needed is the value of the park itself, which is not indicated by spending on travel or equipment.

12. It is also possible to work with individual disaggregated data or data aggregated in different ways (see Wetzstein and McNeely 1980). Disaggregated data require a product that is used more than once per year.

13. Algebraically the steps are as follows:

a. Estimate visits for each travel cost zone z: $V_z = V(M_z, S_z, C_z)$ where z = $(1, \ldots, n)$ is the index of the zone, M_z is the average income in the zone, S_z represents other socioeconomic variables, C_z is travel cost, and V_z is the number of visitor days from the zone. Other possible variables are hours of paid vacation and hourly wage for discretionary work time.

b. Given no entry fee, find total visits: $V = \Sigma V_z$.

c. Let increments of travel cost (dC) be proxies for entry fees. Compute $V_j = \Sigma V[M_z, S_z, (C_z + jdC)]$ for successive j. The demand function for visits is V_j as a function of jdC.

14. For some of the relevant theoretical literature outlining the conditions that must be met before differences in land values can be used as a measure of project benefits, see Anderson and Crocker (1971), Freeman (1974 and 1975), Lind (1973 and 1975), Maler (1974, 192-95), Polinsky and Shavell (1975), Small (1975), Harrison and Rubinfeld (1978a), Nelson (1980), and Anas (1984).

15. This section is based in part on Birch and Schmid (1980).

16. For discussion of Likert scales, see Nachmias (1979, 88-93) and Oppenheim (1966). Also, see Section 3.4. For application see U.S. Congress (1977).

17. For studies of willingness to pay for reductions of the risk of death, see Acton (1973) and Landefeld and Seskin (1982).

18. Portions of this evaluation method are loosely based on Guttentag and Snapper (1974). Some other relevant literature is reviewed in Freeman (1977), Sugden and Williams (1978, 181-86), Dasgupta et al. (1972, 247-55), and Izac (1981).

19. For a discussion of this methodology see Schmid et al. (1973).

20. It should be emphasized that this step involves a political choice among the conflicting interests of members of the public who have different views of importance weights.

21. Alternatively, the first ranked output can be given a value of 1. If the importance weight is expected to change with the size of the added output, the weight might change at a designated threshold.

22. U_i is the aggregate utility for the ith project, W_j is the normalized importance (value) weight for the jth output category, O_{ij} is the output magnitude (or position) of the ith project on the jth output dimension.

23. See Step 4 for outputs of projects 1 and 3.

24. A parallel conception to that developed here has been worked out for government rule making instead of government spending. See Thomas (1963, 143-48) who states, "To set a criterion is to impute a benefit:cost ratio." Also see Schmid (1969b, 579-91).

25. Only occasionally is that done, as noted at the conclusion of Section 5.4.

6

Opportunity Cost Adjustments

6.1. Introduction

In Chapter 5, the objective was to obtain prices for project outputs (inputs) when no market prices exist. If these nonmarketed goods were not accounted for, the allocation of investment funds to maximize the value of net output for the economy would not be achieved. Similarly, even if market prices are available, if they do not reflect opportunity cost, net output will not be maximized and the wrong investments will be made. In certain cases, available market prices may not be appropriate and some adjustments are necessary. The adjusted prices are sometimes referred to as *shadow prices*. Adjustment issues arise in the context of taxation, monopoly, subsidies, foreign exchange, and labor policies. The adjustments also suggest indirect project beneficiaries other than direct producers or consumers and also costs not otherwise reimbursed.

The cost of a project is the forgone benefits lost from not using the resources elsewhere. Opportunity cost is benefits sacrificed and renounced. But not all possible sacrifices are relevant (Dasgupta et al. 1972, 53). A person could have a physical opportunity, but not a legal one. The illegal alternative is not an opportunity cost that the government wants to consider further as an alternative to a government project, that is, constitute a cost of that project. Project evaluation can be treated as an integral part of the implementation of an overall policy objective. It should then be consistent with this objective and with the other complementary policy instruments. Analysts cannot shadow price without ascertaining the government's intent in formulating policies such as taxes, exchange controls, and employment. A theme of this chapter is that although opportunity cost is the relevant guide, some policy questions must be asked to determine whose opportunity cost counts. Opportunity cost is not a single thing to be technically measured.

6.1.1. Numeraire

Price adjustments are necessary to systematically change one price relative to another. This gives the analyst a choice. The price of good A can be raised relative to B, or B can be lowered to achieve the same relationship. The price to be regarded as the fixed base is called the *numeraire*. Different authors may choose a different base, which at first may appear as a fundamental difference in approach, although it is not. For example, the adjustment for foreign exchange might be to increase border prices to the domestic market level by the premium on foreign exchange, or domestic prices might be decreased to border price levels by a conversion factor. Choice of numeraire is largely a matter of convenience and will not affect the size of net benefits, but it can affect project ranking if benefit-cost ratios are used (see Sections 6.5.9 and 9.3.6).

6.2.   Taxation and Tariffs

If government wants only to raise revenues and not affect resource allocation by driving a wedge between demand and supply prices, the first-best tax is a lump sum. But this tax is not feasible and government must live with some tax-caused price distortion in the private sector, although shadow pricing can compensate for this unwanted distortion at least in the public sector. When price is determined only by supply and demand, the marginal cost of production (supply price) equals the marginal value of consumption (demand price). But with a tax (tariff) on goods, these prices are not equal and BCA must utilize the information in each as appropriate in pricing project inputs and outputs. The divergence in supply and demand prices means that the opportunity cost (and thus the appropriate accounting price) of an input or output depends on whether the project affects the total amount supplied or displaces a previously available unit.

First, consider project output sold to consumers. If project output adds marginally to total supply, the appropriate accounting value is gross of indirect taxes (i.e., includes the tax).[1] The correct value is what consumers are willing to pay (demand price).[2] But if the project output displaces a previously produced unit, the appropriate accounting value is the marginal cost of production, which is the market price net of taxes. Consumer spending is constant, but the economy saves the former marginal cost of production (supply price) if resources are mobile.

For example, the output of a transport project may be saving of fuel. The value of the saving is net of any fuel tax. It is the marginal production cost of the diverted fuel that is saved. But if the project increases traffic because of time savings, the net increase in taxation is a measure of value to consumers (benefit). This logic was followed by Coburn et al. (1960) in an evaluation of London motorways. The U.S. Water Resources Council (1973, 87) advises that "Taxes forgone on the proposed Federal plans and taxes paid on the nonfederal alternative will be excluded". Thus, output such as electricity is valued at market prices which include income taxes paid by private utilities.

Little and Mirrlees (1974, 223-25) disagree with this analysis. They regard indirect taxes as correcting income distribution and thus net of tax price is a better measure for value of new production (also see Pearce and Nash 1981, 110; Weckstein 1972). The corrective may reflect rejection of the demand of people with unjustified income or an estimate of what the price would be if new owners were questioned about their willingness to sell (rather than pay). Government may place a tax on a good to reduce consumption (willingness to pay) to the level that would exist if property rights were changed. If desired income distribution cannot be achieved by costless lump-sum redistribution, taxes may be a corrective and not a distortion. In this case, Little and Mirrlees (1974, 224) state that "taxation and subsidization of consumer purchases is a useful and socially desirable weapon of policy. Project planners and economic advisors have no general warrant to attempt to nullify the effects of that tax system." The point would seem more relevant for excise taxes and tariffs that differ for different goods than for general sales and value added taxes that have the same rate for all goods. However, if the purpose of a sales tax is to reduce consumption of market goods and increase investment or production of government goods, it is a corrective measure that cannot be ignored. The point is that treatment of taxes is not simply a technical issue. It depends on public choice involved in the purpose of taxation.

Second, consider inputs purchased for the project. If the needed input results in added input supply, the value is net of tax.[3] The opportunity cost is the marginal cost of production.[4] But if the project requires an additional input in which the tax represents someone's right to be free of an externality, the value is gross of tax. It reflects the opportunity cost of the owners. If the input is in fixed supply and would have been used by others, the value is gross of taxes. The diverted input is worth what others would have paid for it including taxes, and not what government actually pays--since government does not have to pay taxes to itself (see Brown and Jackson 1978, 166). However, the questions of tax policy intent again apply. Was the government just raising revenue or did the government have any reason to restrict private sector use of the input in question and thus reject the demand price? For example, the government may not be able (or wish to) find other ways to encourage use of substitutes.

The analysis just presented requires knowledge of the relevant supply and demand elasticities to calculate what proportion of inputs and outputs represents added output or diversion. This is a formidable task and leads to adoption of rules of thumb, the most popular of which in practice is to ignore taxes altogether.

Direct income taxes are a tax on labor and their effects can be the same as previously noted for sales taxes on inputs. If the project causes a reallocation of labor, its value is the gross of tax market wage. This reflects the value of the alternative output not realized. If the project brings unemployed new labor to use, the value is net of tax if the intent of the tax is

Table 6.1 Adjustment of Market Prices with Taxes, Tariffs and Foreign Exchange Controls

	I. Noncorrective Intent	II. Regarded as Corrective
Indirect (Sales) Tax or Tariff:		
1. Output		
Added (new supply)	Gross of tax	Net of tax
Diverted (replacing)	Net	
2. Input		
Added	Net	Gross
Diverted	Gross	
Direct Income Tax:		
3. Labor		
Added	Net	Gross, but intent to increase leisure seems unlikely
Consumption Subsidy:		
4. Output		
Added	Net of subsidy	Gross
Foreign Exchange Controls and Quotas:		
5. Imports		
"Added" -- amount. of foreign exchange flexible	Cost of production foreign exchange (net)	
"Diverted" -- amount. of foreign exchange fixed	c. i. f. price plus premium (gross)	
6. Exports	f. o. b. price plus premium (gross)	c. i. f. at official exchange rate

only to raise revenue and if the tax produces no utility to the payer. The opportunity cost is the value the worker puts on leisure, which is no more than the accepted net of tax wage.[5] This analysis is summarized in Table 6.1. The effect of taxes on labor supply is difficult to assess conclusively and is subject to much debate among economists. Because of this uncertainty, most agency and academic analyses ignore income taxes and use gross market wages (if there is no involuntary unemployment). This is correct if the utility of both private and public consumption is in equilibrium.

An element of arbitrariness is introduced by the need for tax allocation (Foster 1973, 66-68). The previous discussion involved taxes of all kinds that do not represent payment for government services rendered. A tax for a publicly provided input, such as a special assessment for drainage, is an opportunity cost as for any production input. But where do payments for production inputs stop and payments to finance public consumption begin? A local sales tax might be used to provide fire and police protection inputs for business and industry and also for household protection. What part of a sales or income tax pays for public education and research, which is an input into the firm's production function? It would simplify price analysis if public and private firms received separate itemized bills for these things, but this is not possible. Adjustment for taxes is not just a technical issue. The relevant opportunity cost is that chosen by public policy. For further discussion of taxes and tax allocation effects on income distribution see Sections 8.10.3 and 8.10.7.

6.3.   Monopoly, Subsidy, and Economies of Scale

Public projects may produce output that competes with that of private output produced in noncompetitive markets. The general principle of how to adjust observed market prices is similar to that for indirect taxes because, in a sense, a monopolist's price is a private tax (see Table 6.1). If the public output adds marginally to total supply, the value is the gross monopoly market price. If it replaces former monopoly output, the value is the marginal cost of production (net of "tax"), which is the long run competitive market equilibrium price if the public output is large enough to force competition.

In practice, a price between the market monopoly price and estimated marginal cost may be appropriate. New public projects, if large enough, will depress prices with some output adding to supply and some replacing previous production. Instantaneous adjustment cannot be expected and short run profit signals the attractiveness of competitive investment, as would be true if private firms could break the barriers to entry. The analysis for pricing monopsonistic inputs also follows that of input taxes.

Policies such as price supports or subsidies that directly affect market prices are common and affect income distribution (see Section 8.2). These observed prices may indicate willingness to pay for any marginal added supply from a public project. But it is necessary to determine the public purpose behind these policies. For example, if the subsidy to consumers is to increase consumption, the gross of subsidy price could be the price that would prevail if consumers had higher incomes, and it signals higher production by the cheapest means. On the other hand, if the subsidy is paid to increase producer income, no extra public output is wanted; it would not make sense to increase public output, thereby canceling out the performance desired by the producer subsidy.

The usual counsel for goods traded internationally is to price potential project output at border prices--f.o.b. for exports and c.i.f. for imports (Little and Mirrlees 1974, Ch. 12). This represents the opportunity marginal cost of production when imports are a substitute (an application of the alternate cost valuation method). Yet, if more output would lower prices to intentionally favored producers, it would not make sense to increase output even if the public could produce the product domestically at less than border prices. The analyst must again ascertain the distributive objective (Bates 1983; FitzGerald 1977).

In practice, many agricultural project analyses in less developed countries (LDCs) use border prices when evaluating output. In the United States, however, little attention is paid to world prices, though in the process of projecting future prices it is difficult to determine what factors agencies actually include in the calculation (see Section 10.7.5).

Where marginal cost data are deemed relevant, they are not always easy to obtain or interpret when the good in question is produced under decreasing costs to scale. Unsubsidized private producers will not be able to price at marginal cost because it will not cover total costs. Take the case of a public navigation project that replaces traffic on a privately owned railroad. The usual counsel is to value the public output at marginal cost rather than the observed market price, which probably is closer to average cost. In practice the issue is confused by oligopolistic pricing strategies in which railroads charge all the traffic will bear. Nevertheless, if it priced at marginal cost, it would have to be subsidized to cover its fixed costs.

Some economists advocate public ownership of decreasing cost industries so that the difference between marginal and average costs can be covered by taxes. Any practical (second-best) tax, however, carries its own potential distortions. So governments frequently leave ownership in private hands and regulate to obtain average cost pricing. When the public is the owner, some economists advocate that the value used for evaluating the desirability of the project be based on total consumer surplus even though the output is priced at marginal cost. The concept of consumer surplus is discussed in Chapter 7 and some of the distributive issues are noted in Section 8.2.1. Suffice it to note here that any tax scheme to pay for public output is unlikely to have the same incidence as people's differential willingness to pay even if it could be measured.

In summary, in a second-best world even the opportunity cost principle requires public choice to settle distributive conflicts. By United States law, navigation project benefits from diverted traffic are valued at the prices charged on alternative modes of transport rather than at marginal cost (U.S. Water Resources Council 1980b, 64449). Congress may be trying to be consistent with a policy judgment to leave some decreasing cost industries (such as river barges) in private hands. Thus, it uses average cost pricing in applying the cost savings method to valuation of navigation channel projects; or it may just want higher benefits so it can build more public projects.

6.4. Foreign Exchange

In the previous section, adjustments in observed market prices were made because of taxes and monopoly. Further adjustments may be necessary because of foreign trade policies. The value of exports and cost of imports for public projects are influenced by foreign currency exchange rates. The value of a country's currency can be market determined, as can be done for any commodity.

In theory, the market for currency should adjust in value so that the value of exports tends to balance imports in the long run. If one country's rate of inflation increases relative to another then its currency depreciates relative to the other. If one country imports more than it exports, its currency depreciates, causing a reduction in imports (which then cost more) and an increase in exports (which cost other countries less). If this worked perfectly, no adjustment to observed market prices at market exchange rates would be necessary. Investment (based on domestic saving or foreign borrowing) will maximize consumption when evaluated at these market prices.

In practice, some governments do not accept these market prices. They set official exchange rates and require their citizens to exchange money at the official rate. If the official rate requires less local currency per unit of foreign currency than the market rate (overvaluation), the policy is equivalent to an import subsidy and importers will demand more foreign currency than can be supplied. The government then sets quotas to ration the supply or borrows or begs for foreign currency. An overvalued currency is equivalent to an export tax. This may mean that market prices do not reflect opportunity costs, though again the issue is whose opportunity costs are to be considered.

Why do governments set official rates and quotas instead of allowing the international market exchange rate to be used? An undervalued currency functions as an import tax and allows a government to raise revenue for public spending or protect domestic industry from competition. In the process of development, poor countries require increased imports to modernize industry and to meet the consumption demands of a population with rising incomes, and this increase in imports outraces its growth of exports (Dasgupta et al. 1972, 214).   Such governments continuously have balance of payments deficits in their capital accounts if not in their commodity accounts.   Why not let the market exchange rate function to control deficits?   Governments often have conflicting objectives.   They want to increase consumption but they care about whose consumption.   Currency devaluation in poor countries helps rural and hurts urban workers.   Farmers receive more in local currency for the crops they export, but urban workers pay more for imports, of which they consume more.   On the other hand, an overvalued currency discourages food export which keeps the supply in the country and causes lower prices to the benefit of urban consumers.

Removal of official rates works to devalue currencies of trade deficit countries, thus making all imports proportionally more expensive. Government may, however, want to discourage some imports more than others.   Just as it places excise taxes or tariffs on some goods to discourage their use, it can place import quotas on some goods while offering low cost foreign currency to favored importers.   The favored importer, including the government itself, may be seen as contributing more to future development than meeting the demands of those citizens who now have money. Government rejects the willingness to pay of current wealth holders.

The same result might be obtained by taxation and redistribution of wealth from one group to another via payments or subsidies.   But this is very visible and often unacceptable.   Also, allocation of available foreign exchange is a patronage benefit available to help the government's friends.   A quota that restricts the supply of an import causes the domestic price of the import to exceed the domestic currency cost of importing it, thus giving a profit that the government has the power to allocate.   Even if a government does not care about its trade deficit, it may want to allocate foreign currency benefits.

Why should a government care about trade deficits?   The United States has had deficits for years even with floating exchange rates.   Countries send real goods to the United Staes and instead of getting real goods in return, accumulate United States paper IOUs.   This is fine for the United States as long as it lasts, though it complicates monetary policy and introduces an instability.   The fear of panic selling of dollars at some future date reduces the utility of these deficit causing gifts.   Fear of domestic job loss (if not made up by other policies) is more likely to stimulate policies to restrict imports than any direct balance of payment effects.

For poor countries, the fear of instability is greater, though not often great enough to cause policies sufficient for deficit removal.   If a country wants to develop based on foreign borrowing, it has to hope that it can grow fast enough so that it can export enough to pay interest and principle on the loan in the future.   A trade deficit is accepted today in hopes of a surplus tomorrow.   If growth is not sufficient or terms of trade worsen, the gamble will have failed and when devaluation occurs it will be even harder for the country to pay off its foreign loans (take even more real goods than when the loan was made).   This is the downward spiral that many poor countries now face. The balance of payments and the market exchange rate are thus not necessarily indicative of the future. The wisdom of deficits is based on uncertain projections. A country may simply not accept the speculative judgments of international financial markets. A country's reputation is subject to mass psychology. Others may dump (or acquire) a country's currency in a frenzy of short run speculation and the country may not wish to make long run investment plans on the market's current signals.

But suppose a poor country is concerned about its trade deficits and wants to decrease imports. If the amount of available foreign currency is relatively fixed, how shall it adjust observed market prices, given its implementation of selective quotas (or tariffs) rather than general devaluation? If the objective is to maximize the value of consumption given current income distribution, then the project's imported inputs diverted from other uses must be valued not at the c.i.f.[6] import price at official exchange rates, but at what the good would sell for in the domestic market in domestic currency.[7] For example, consider an imported product that because of quotas or tariffs is limited in supply and sells for a domestic price (e.g., 45 rupees) higher than the domestic currency cost (c.i.f.) of importation (30 rupees). The domestic price (45) is the marginal value to those with purchasing power and is the accounting price. In practice, instead of obtaining values by multiplying physical quantities by the estimated accounting prices, it is common to use an accounting price ratio (APR = accounting price/c.i.f.) to adjust total c.i.f. rupee cost paid by the government for the imported input.[8] In this case, 45/30 = 1.5. The APR × total c.i.f. rupee cost = total opportunity cost in rupees. This is convenient when the APR is computed as a weighted average for a whole sector of commodities, avoiding the need to disaggregate total costs into individual prices and quantities (for detail see Ward 1976; Irvin 1978, Ch. 5; Powers 1981).

The APR is used to express foreign purchases in domestic currency so that cost of imports can be added to inputs produced locally (called nontraded goods). However, nontraded goods such as labor may have foreign exchange implications, for example, if wages are used to buy foreign goods. Thus, the opportunity cost of wages may also be adjusted by the APR.

Whatever the government might pay for the imported input, its cost for accounting purposes is the domestic value if it were a private import. The quota accomplishes the reduction in imports, and the allocation between private and public use depends on a comparison of private and public investment returns.

Use of the weighted average accounting price ratio assumes that the shadow price for foreign currency and the foreign exchange content of goods are constant over time and, further, assumes that the government wanted to achieve the results it would have obtained with a general devaluation to unsupported market exchange rates. This raises the question of why it used the quota and fixed rate route in the first place. It might have been an accident that it is now too embarrassed to change. More realistically, governments choose quotas to achieve a distributive impact that they do not wish to achieve by more direct redistribution of wealth. The government may not regard the 45 rupee price as an indicator of the opportunity cost of public use of the input. If income were redistributed, this price could be lower even with quotas. Thus, it regards the quota as a "corrective," just as noted in the case of excise taxes. To ignore this corrective signal is to make the BCA adjustments contrary to other policies. The government wants to do more than reduce trade deficits, it wants to shape the allocation of access to available foreign currency. If the exchange policy is corrective, then the accounting input price is the unadjusted c.i.f. price. (This is summarized in Table 6.1.) The international lending agencies prefer the more innocent sounding term *accounting price ratio* to the concept of a *shadow exchange rate* because the latter clearly indicates that the government's foreign trade policies are wrong. If this is honestly asserted, it may be rejected. As stated by Dasgupta et al. (1972, 218): "The shadow price of foreign exchange thus depends on how increments of foreign exchange will be divided among alternative uses, not on the wishful thinking of the project analyst who perceived (or misperceives) the irrationality of the overall policy framework in which he operates."

The government can experiment with its quotas to reduce total imports and achieve a desired trade balance. If the government continues to run a deficit, it may be because it does not assume a constant shadow price over time or simply because it wishes to increase current consumption by foreign borrowing, leaving it to the next government or generation to pay. Governments have been known to run trade deficits and borrow for current consumption rather than investment, and even borrow more to pay current interest obligations on old debt, but this cannot continue for long.

Some governments such as China have not previously wanted to play this exposed game. Even when foreign borrowing is profitable, it is not acceptable because of the dependence on foreigners. A government may shadow price so that trade deficits never occur. The shadow price here is an administrative price placed on independence even at the expense of reduced consumption over time. It is not to be derived from any other set of prices.

In the case of exports, a fixed rate below probable market exchange rates is similar to an export tax. The government sells the output of its projects at world prices but pays any domestic producers less at official rates. Still, the accounting price is the higher world price if the recipients of the tax (trading profit) count.[9]

If a country is trying to reduce imports by devaluation or quotas, these policies will raise import prices. People will object and try to increase their incomes to maintain consumption. If output is not growing, the government may comply by increasing the money supply. If so, there will be inflation and imports will not be reduced as expected. Foreign exchange policy can be defeated by monetary policy and BCA cannot proceed independently of macro policy.

In summary, foreign trade policies are quite similar to taxes and subsidies as discussed and the same points apply to both. These policies represent a compromise among conflicting groups concerning growth and income distribution and freedom from foreign influence and the analyst must be careful that the compromise is not presumed by making foreign exchange adjustments in public projects inconsistent with the performance intent of other policies. The key point of this discussion can be summed up by reference to the popular policy of quotas and official rates by noting that such policies may produce the same effective average exchange rate that international markets and devaluation would achieve for deficit countries, but its domestic income distribution impacts would be quite different. There are major differences among economists on this topic. For a review see Bacha and Taylor (1971). In application, it is common in World Bank projects to use either border prices multiplied by a foreign exchange premium for traded goods or a standard conversion factor to lower the price of nontraded goods. The conceptual and measurement uncertainties are such that the World Bank will not share its conversion factors with other lenders (Gittinger et al. 1982, 4).

6.5.   Labor and Capital Goods

6.5.1.   Whose Opportunity Cost?

To maximize the net value of output in an economy, inputs and outputs must be valued at opportunity cost. In the case of labor, it may mean that as a result of opportunity cost pricing, some projects will be built that otherwise would not have been. As a result, unemployment can be reduced. Reduction in unemployment need not be a separate investment objective but can be achieved as a result of maximizing net output. The critical policy issue is whose opportunity cost will define the value of output.

There are reasons to suspect that the price paid for labor used in a public project may not indicate the value of its alternate use (opportunity cost). If workers were able to work or not work at the prevailing wage, there would be no involuntary unemployment. Unemployment would indicate that a person's reservation price for leisure time is greater than the wage. But if workers cannot offer to work for less than the going wage, their valuation of leisure may be less than the prevailing wage. Labor has characteristics that do not produce an equilibrium in a price-auction market (Thurow 1983, Ch. 7). Wages do not fall to remove excess supply. Information costs prevent employers from hiring labor even when its marginal value product (MVP) exceeds the wage (Stiglitz 1987a). Lowering wages may decrease the average quality of labor and thus is not in the employer's best interests.

If the project uses some of this involuntary unemployed labor, how shall it be priced? The general principle is that labor should be valued at its opportunity cost, but, as always, the problem is to decide whose perspective of opportunity cost is to be counted. Different perspectives arise in the context of persistent disequilibrium.

This section on labor (and capital goods) will first raise policy issues in government spending guided by use of accounting prices in the context of cyclic and sectoral unemployment. The next step will be to discuss the principles involved in estimating (choosing) the opportunity cost of redirecting the use of a given class of workers. This is followed by a discussion of sectoral interdependence and multipliers to determine which classes of workers throughout the economy might be affected by a project. The final question is whether a given project will actually impact on a given class of underused workers or whether it just reallocates fully utilized workers.

6.5.2.   Cyclic Unemployment

In the case of general cyclic unemployment, one policy prescription is to let wages decline to a new full employment equilibrium. Hopefully lower costs lead to lower output prices so that quantity demanded is maintained. In most countries, unions and other institutions keep wages up even when demand falls. Other than sheer power politics, there are reasons why policies are not implemented to force wages down. The new equilibrium wage may well be unacceptable or even below subsistence. It also sets in motion the social trap of a downward spiral in which lower wages cause output demand to fall again, thus lowering the equilibrium wage, and so on. Falling demand is not a good climate for investment, so labor for new plants is not wanted, further decreasing income and aggregate demand (Minsky 1978). Keynes sought to avoid this trap by trying to increase aggregate demand. Before discussing this policy, the distributive conflict should be noted. If wages and output prices fall, those with accumulated currency get a larger share of output.

If government prefers the results of deflation, then for its own investments the cost of using unemployed labor is still the nominal market wage. It does not want to build more projects and increase the demand for labor; rather, it wants the wage to fall so that everyone who wants to work at the new wage is employed in the private sector.

Employers who enjoy sustained demand for their products prefer the deflationary approach because of the downward pressure on wage costs. Those who object to higher taxes and borrowing also benefit if government projects fail when unemployed labor is priced at nominal wages (Gramlich 1981, 63). From this perspective if labor will not work at lower wages, then it values leisure highly and deserves what it gets and there is no involuntary unemployment. The opportunity cost of unemployed labor (less than nominal wage) may be closer to the new equilibrium wage that would be achieved by deflation. But if it is used too soon to evaluate public projects, the desired deflation may not occur.

During periods of large structural changes in an economy, there can be unemployment, but this can signal the need for retraining and occupational shifts. Public projects designed to utilize labor in the old job categories may frustrate this restructuring within the private sector.

In summary, if government chooses to trade-off full use of the economy's labor for the pursuit of other objectives (such as reducing redistributive inflation, increasing corporate profits, or being more competitive with foreign goods) it would not make sense to have public inputs priced below nominal costs. Even if a lower shadow price were used, the implied increase in public spending for projects and aggregate demand might just be offset by restrictive monetary policies or other budget cuts (Pearce and Nash 1981, 109).

An alternative to deflation is Keynesian stimulation of aggregate demand, which has a quite different implication. One approach is to borrow and implement a tax cut or increase benefits paid to citizens. Another approach is to increase government spending in areas in which BCA is little used in deciding spending levels, such as the military. The distributive implications of these policies are quite different and different still from the deflationary approach. The tax cut goes to those who have income, benefits go as designed, and particular kinds of spending go to capital and labor owners in those industries.

If increased government spending goes for projects chosen systematically by BCA, a policy to stimulate aggregate demand is implemented by the shadow pricing of labor (and capital) at less than nominal wage. This is the link between macro policy and project level analysis. The impact of public investment on employment is quite slow compared to tax cuts and spending for current social benefits. High technology military spending is also relatively slow and employment effects less than general consumer spending (DeGrasse 1983).

Government could not only use a shadow price in evaluating relative investment returns, but also could actually pay this less than market wage to the formerly unemployed. The discipline of the market's marginal calculus means that if the unemployed marginal workers accept lower wages, the currently employed (intramarginal) get less as well. To follow deflationary policies is to deny the presently employed the right to maintain their wages. In fact, in the United States, the Davis-Bacon Act prohibits paying employees on Federal construction projects less than the union standard (Raphaelson 1983). New York State law prohibits public works programs that draw from the unemployed from performing any work ordinarily and actually performed by regular employees.

Property rights in the United States are such that although a shadow wage can be used in choosing public projects, it cannot be used as the basis for actual wage payments. If unemployed workers could be paid more than opportunity cost, but only up to the net benefits remaining when all other inputs are first paid their opportunity cost, projects could be built that would use all available labor (if the accounting price is the opportunity cost and if there is no budget constraint). Benefit-cost ratios are forced toward unity. In this case the actual wage affects only the distribution of the project net income. But if all workers must be paid a higher going wage, then those workers adding less than this wage to output require a transfer of income not only from those who otherwise would have received the project's net benefits, but also from the general taxpayer. The unemployed worker then gets a claim on consumption greater than what is added to output. This is fine if the government wants the unemployed to have it; however, all may not agree on the consequences for growth.

Whose opportunity cost counts--that of the donor or the recipient? If the amount transferred would have been saved and invested, the transfer may reduce growth. Little and Mirrlees (1974, 169-76) advocate a shadow price greater than the opportunity cost of the unemployed, the amount being determined by a policy judgment on the trade-off between transfer and growth objectives. This is contradicted by Chervel (1977, 341) who says "Raising the problem of the loss of savings at project level seems to us both illogical and erroneous: illogical, because it amounts to assuming that the authorities lack the means of increasing savings directly...and erroneous because no empirical observation proves that a more equal distribution of income would reduce savings."

Growth is ambiguous when people have different time preferences. It will be seen in Chapter 9, Section 9.4.4, that benefits have different values over time depending on whose time preferences count--so that projects otherwise equal have different ranks depending on who receives the benefits. The wage paid to the unemployed, although a nominal project cost, is a net benefit gain for those unemployed and thus the question concerns whose time preference and thus growth perspective counts. Second-best reality requires compromises.

If the shadow price is set at more than labor's opportunity cost, fewer projects will be built and some unemployed will remain unemployed. Minimum wage laws in the public sector force transfers tied to the decision to use unemployed labor. There is a conflict among the opportunities of the unemployed, the already employed, and those with different views of the optimal growth rate that must be resolved by public choice.

When payment of the going wage can be covered by net project output it is critical that this payment be financed by credit creation; otherwise the output of the formerly unemployed just replaces former consumption by the already employed taxpayers. It makes no sense to put the unemployed to work by reducing the consumption, savings, or investment of the employed (Schmid 1982). Monetary policy can cancel the intended effect of fiscal policy projects.

All writers agree in principle that labor should be priced at opportunity cost, but this requires an interpretation of which data reflect opportunity cost. If there is more than one view of the opportunity cost, then there must be a political judgment. One policy choice is to regard the market wage for comparable skills as the opportunity cost of the unemployed because it is interpreted as the value of leisure and the unemployment regarded as voluntary. If wages are inflexible, this policy would force them down. Government would not want to reduce the downward pressure by using an accounting price below the going wage and building more public projects, which increases the demand for labor. With this policy, the opportunity of employed workers to keep their wages up is lost.

The contrasting alternative is to regard the existence of surplus labor as prima facie evidence of its zero marginal product and thus to use a shadow wage of zero. But what is the value of what these people formerly did? If they were not employed in the market, they still did something. Some may have done subsistence agriculture, home improvement, or child care. Is this opportunity cost to be valued at the unskilled market wage that these people supposedly rejected? Or is this lost output to be valued at what the unemployed would be willing to pay (sell) or what others would pay? A person with no income and savings has no willingness to pay for home improvement or child care, implying work on the project would have no opportunity cost (but unemployed laborers may have a reservation price higher than the alternative product's market value). Or shall the lost output (opportunity cost of labor) be valued at what unemployed workers would pay if they had positive incomes, that is, the market price, or at what third parties might pay to avoid external effects of the unemployed person's behavior? For example, some might pay to maintain child care for other's children to avoid the possibility of juvenile delinquency. It requires a policy decision to decide whose willingness to pay is the relevant opportunity cost. (This is further discussed in the context of valuing in-kind transfers in Section 8.7). The decision makes a difference if shadow pricing is systematically applied. For example, if the opportunity cost of child care is set high reflecting third party concerns, public projects that would use parents may not have net accounting returns and few unemployed parents would be hired.

6.5.3. Structural and Regional Unemployment

Even when the general economy is fully employed there may be sectors of unemployment. The pricing of these resources is problematic. One interpretation is that unemployment is temporary or voluntary requiring no shadow pricing, because if people do not change occupations or location, it is because of transaction costs and the value of leisure or place. The policy that follows keeps the pressure on in terms of wage differentials, assuming that the sensible will move and the rest will deserve what they get.

But what about immobile assets? If people move to a new location for a job, they may suffer an asset loss to the value of their house, whose price falls if the region in which it is located is being depopulated. The wage elsewhere must be great enough to overcome this loss. People stay even though local wages are less than wages elsewhere as long as net assets including present value of wage flow elsewhere and salvage value are less than depreciated acquisition costs plus local wage flow. New private capital is mobile, however, and might move to the location of immobile labor, particularly if the private firm could pay wages equal to opportunity costs and less than going national wages. If property rights of unions require the national wage in all locations, then the second-best may be for public investment to price and use unemployed labor at the shadow opportunity cost. Public jobs are moved to the immobile labor.

One problem with persistent regional unemployment is that economies of scale may not be reachable by marginal investments (Chenery and Westphal 1969). At low output levels, nonlabor inputs may be so costly in a region that it offsets the attraction of low cost labor. If input suppliers had a larger regional market they would offer lower prices, but the input user is not there. Each is waiting for the other. Public projects per se do not solve this problem and may suffer losses while private and public complementary investments are made. Planning and contracting for simultaneous construction could reduce the problem.

Diseconomies of scale may also be a problem. Sometimes firms do not pay for the congestion costs created by further investment in developed areas. Again in the second-best world, it may be easier to shadow price labor or even subsidize it to locate in depressed areas than to make firms pay for their congestion elsewhere.

If a policy judgment is made to reject the thesis of voluntary unemployment market equilibrium, and there are valid reasons for government intervention to utilize unused localized resources, the question becomes one of choosing the appropriate shadow price (opportunity cost). Some analysts (Haveman 1977) and many U.S. agencies use a zero opportunity cost for use of unemployed labor. For a critique see Young and Gray (1985). Alternatively, MVP could be estimated from an aggregate production function or a linear programming model. These are rarely used in practice, perhaps because they have their own interpretative problems including adjustments for seasonal and peak load situations (Bruce 1976; Powers 1981, 35-37).

Adjustment for opportunity cost of labor is particularly relevant in developing countries. Many LDCs exhibit persistent disequilibria with urban unemployment, differentials between urban and rural wages, and differences in unemployment rates among different groups. There are many causes of disequilibria, including minimum wage laws (Harris and Todaro 1970), information cost (Stiglitz 1987b), and mistakes by labor and investors. In the case of subsistence agriculture, Lewis (1972, 80) argues that it would be possible to move agricultural labor to public projects with no reduction in agricultural output. Also see Prou and Chervel (1970, 191). The remaining labor would work more hours or with greater intensity. But if use of the unemployed on urban public projects results in additional migration, then the aggregate loss of agricultural output may approach or exceed the equivalent loss of the urban wage. This would occur, for example, if one new urban job results in the migration of two people from agriculture who have positive marginal products. Stiglitz (1987b) thus recommends a price above the agricultural wage approaching the urban wage. Harris and Todaro (1970) suggest a shadow price below the urban wage if combined with regulation of migration.

Disequilibria expose several conflicts. If the opportunity cost of the present urban unemployed is considered as equal to the urban wage to prevent migration, these persons are disadvantaged because fewer public projects demand their labor. If a shadow price less that the urban wage is used, it may result in migration and loss of agricultural output. It also means that those urban employers who enjoy the surplus may face higher labor prices. If the formerly unemployed are paid the going wage, the necessary non-lump-sum taxes affect resource allocation. In addition, the government cannot ignore new unemployed migrants who are politically explosive. In response, the government often pursues a cheap urban food policy that lowers agricultural incomes and creates even more surplus labor in agriculture. The migrants also strain urban public services. If, in this context, governments restrict migration, there are objections to the loss of freedom of movement. Because of these conflicting views and uncertainties as to labor behavior, some public choice is necessary to guide the analysts' selection among competing opportunity costs existing in disequilibrium. Use of opportunity cost is a valid principle in pricing inputs to public projects, but the policy question is whose view defines the relevant margin when several views are present.

6.5.4.   Intersectoral Interdependence

If there is a concern about the possibility of using underemployed or unemployed labor as a result of a project, it will be necessary to look beyond project construction, operation, and direct utilization. A project causes *indirect effects* on suppliers of inputs to the project and to its users and on the further processing of project outputs. An illustration of these linkages backward and forward from a particular public project being evaluated is outlined in Figure 6.1. The construction of a public navigation project might use unemployed labor. Going backward, there were machines that were used to make the project machines and these might have been made by the unemployed and so on. Going forward from the project, the steel maker that uses the project employs people and the steel is used to make other goods

Figure 6.1 Types of Indirect Benefits Illustrated with Navigation Project

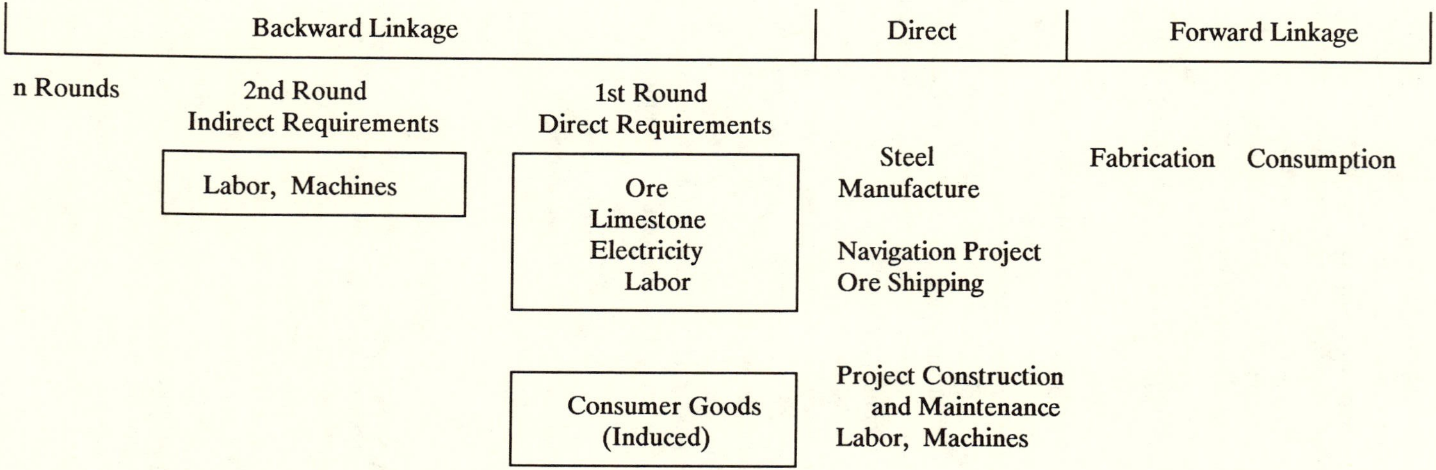

	Backward Linkage		Direct	Forward Linkage
n Rounds	2nd Round Indirect Requirements	1st Round Direct Requirements		
	Labor, Machines	Ore Limestone Electricity Labor	Steel Manufacture Navigation Project Ore Shipping	Fabrication Consumption
		Consumer Goods (Induced)	Project Construction and Maintenance Labor, Machines	

that are eventually consumed. All along the chain there are opportunities for using unemployed resources.

A model of these flows would be helpful and its elements come from Keynes and macroeconomics. Keynes was interested in the failure of aggregate demand to support full employment. He postulated a relationship between any increment in government spending and the increment in aggregate demand. Aggregate demand rose by some multiple of increased government spending. Thus, the concept of the Keynesian multiplier is defined as 1/1 - MPC. The change in national income equals the change in aggregate demand multiplied by the multiplier. The marginal propensity to consume (MPC) is the key variable that affects how a dollar of increased government spending is in turn and in part respent by its recipients to create additional demand a step removed (indirect) from the spending of the original dollar. Put into employment equivalents, this relationship suggests that eventually a given number of unemployed can be put to work by initially creating new demand for the output of some proportion of these unemployed. National income increases as aggregate demand increases via government spending until full employment is reached.

6.5.5. Economic Base Multiplier[10]

If demand for a region's exports can be increased as the result of a project, the region's change in total income (and employment) increases by some multiple. The export sales multiplier is 1/(1 - propensity to consume locally). The key variable is the marginal propensity to consume locally, which is (total expenditures - imports)/total income. To the extent that income from regional export sales is respent locally, local income is increased by some multiple of the original sales. Respending is for locally produced inputs necessary to produce exports and for locally produced consumption. The unit of analysis can also be employment so that the export employment multiplier is 1/(1 - nonbasic employment/total employment). Nonbasic employment provides inputs to the export industry. Total increased employment equals the increased employment necessary to meet an increase in export sales multiplied by the employment multiplier. The key variable is the marginal propensity to consume locally (i.e., locally oriented nonbasic employment/total employment).

Data can be collected from regional firms either assuming that certain industries are wholly export oriented or wholly produce for local markets, or firms can be asked to list employees according to where their output is sold. This is a very general picture as we might expect the ability of a region to locally produce inputs for export sales to differ by the variety of sale.

These employment or income multipliers can be used to estimate the indirect impact of a public investment project. If the project makes an expansion of export sales possible (by an industry using the project output), then these sales can be converted to an equivalent number of jobs. The total new jobs created in the region is some multiple of the initial employment expansion in the export industry. The net effect of this on the economy is discussed in what follows.

There are several problems in the application of economic base multipliers. For further discussion see Isard (1960).

1. It is often difficult to accurately obtain data on what portion of local income (or employment) is oriented to local or export markets.

2. The multiplier does not account for interregional effects where extra income in region A increases sales in region B, which in turn increases demand and sales in region A.

3. The predicted new employment assumes a short run perspective with prices unable to change. In the longer run, increased export sales may be converted to price increases for currently employed resources rather than utilizing the unemployed. This is the problem of many economies in which increased money supply or public spending may cause inflation rather than utilize pockets of unused resources.

4. If the unit of analysis is number of jobs, differences in wage levels among industries are not distinguished. All jobs are not the same. Further, the analysis ignores possible change in labor productivity.

5. The theory of economic base analysis assumes marginal data (marginal propensity to consume locally), but available data are usually average. This is troublesome if a region produces more of its own inputs and consumption items as it grows. If should not be inferred that external leakage is bad. It depends on the region's comparative advantage.

6. The economic base multiplier reflects all rounds of indirect effects (inputs into export sales, inputs into the inputs, and so on) including respending for consumption.[11] It is assumed that the rounds occur instantaneously. If resources were as mobile as these assumptions imply, there would be no need to shadow price labor in the first place.

6.5.6.   Input-Output Analysis

Some of the problems of highly aggregative economic base analysis are avoided in input-output (I-O) analysis, which builds on the economic base concepts. Because it is a more elaborate version, it is more costly to make. I-O reflects the interindustry flows in a region. It is based on surveys of who sells to whom. These data can be displayed in matrix form as in Table 6.2. Producing sectors are shown in the left-hand column (from) and the sales of these producing firms to various purchasing sectors (to) are shown in their respective rows labeled along the top of the table. Varying degrees of aggregation are possible. A relatively simple aggregation is shown in the table. The section labeled purchasing sectors are the purchases of locally supplied inputs by local industry. The next section labeled local final demand is broken down into local consumer (C) purchases from local firms,

Table 6.2 Gross Flows Table

From	Intermediate Demand Purchasing Sectors X_1	X_2	Final Demand Local C	I	G	Exports	Total Gross Output
Producing sectors							
X_1	25	40	40	1	2	2	110
X_2	35	20	30	15	10	15	125
Households (labor)	30	50	10	3	5	2	100
Other value added	10	15	10	--	--	--	35
Imports	10	15	20	--	--	--	45
Total gross outlays	110	140	110	19	17	19	415

investment (I), and government purchases (G). The final aggregation of purchases is by firms and consumers outside the region (export). This sums to total gross output for each producing sector.

For example, reading across the first row, we could see that firms in producing sector X_1 sell their output to other X_1 firms, X_2 firms, local consumers (C), investment (I), government (G), and exports (E). This sums to total sales or gross output.

The same phenomenon can be viewed in terms of purchases by sector (instead of sales by a given producing sector) by examining the column under X_1. This column shows that for X_1 to produce its output, it buys from other firms in X_1 and X_2. It also hires labor (sometimes called the household sector) and additional other types of value added (interest, net rent, before tax profit, depreciation, and taxes) and imports. The sum of this equals gross outlays.

The relationships between the columns and rows are related to some familiar Keynesian macro variables:

(row) Gross output = intermediate demand + final demand = sales to local industry + C + I + G + E

(column) Gross outlay = intermediate demand + value added + imports = purchases from local industry + value added + imports

The people of the region get their income from the value-added component. Because intermediate demand cancels in the two sets of equations, and subtracting imports from exports we have,

Total value added = C + I + G + net exports = final demand

Keynes was interested in how change in final demand (subject to fiscal and monetary policy) affected income. For impact on the regional economy of a public investment, we are interested in how a project-stimulated increase in output (assuming effective demand for that output) affects total regional income. To see this, the following equation can be derived from the previous relationships:

Final demand = gross output - purchases

For convenience in working with these data, the relationship of purchases to output can be expressed as a direct input or requirement coefficient, that is, the purchases (outlay) per unit of gross output. Matrix tables of these coefficients are usually computed. These indicate that for every $1 of sales (output) from industry X_1, it buys so many cents of inputs from other X_1 firms, X_2 firms, labor, and so on. A table of *direct requirement*[12] coefficients is similar to a recipe to produce a dollar of output of a given product.

There is more to intersector flows than the first round or direct requirements, however. Inputs are needed in turn to produce these direct requirements and so on. In input-output terminology these subsequent rounds are called *indirect requirements*. This can be derived from the table data by a series of computations that determine the magnitude of local purchases required to produce a dollar of sales to support a direct requirement and so on. The sum of the direct and indirect requirements is typically referred to as *interdependency coefficients* and is displayed in what is called the *Leontief Inverse* or *B matrix*. This is obtained by application of matrix algebra.[13]

To predict the change in total economic activity created by a given expansion of one industry, it is useful to derive a total output multiplier. The *output multiplier* for a given industry is the sum of the interdependency coefficients[14] and thus includes the direct and indirect effects from all sectors needed to produce the output of the given industry. For example, to produce $1 of output from X_1 the inverse matrix table might indicate that $2 will be generated in additional output. Hence the output multiplier is 2. It represents total requirements per unit of final demand. How is this related to indirect benefit? This is a change of economic activity, but not all of it is new income as part of this activity reflects imports.[15] Although it shows the extent of structural interdependence between each sector and the rest of the economy, it is of little value for project benefit analysis. What is needed is an income (or employment) multiplier. Household sector data are needed to separate local income from total purchases.

The *income multiplier* is the ratio of total direct and indirect income change to the direct income change resulting from a dollar increase in the final demand for a given sector. It is obtained by summing the products of the column entry coefficients in the inverse matrix and multiplying by the supply sector's household coefficients. The product of this multiplication is the direct and indirect income change from a dollar of new labor income. The ratio of this product to the direct income change is called a *Type I multiplier*. It indicates the direct and indirect income changes emanating from a dollar of increased sales of each producing sector.

This income in turn is respent and its consumption further stimulates local income. These consumption respendings and local inputs to produce for local consumption are called induced effects. To calculate this, the household sector is added and the inverse matrix recomputed.

An income multiplier is now computed combining the direct, indirect, and induced requirements. This is called a *Type II multiplier* and is defined as the ratio of the summation of direct, indirect, and induced coefficient (from the expanded inverse matrix) to the direct income change resulting from a unit increase in final demand. The household row in the expanded inverted matrix shows the direct, indirect, and induced coefficients for each sector. By adding the consumption respending, the income multiplier is greatly increased. The Type II income multiplier from input-output analysis is similar in concept to the economic base income multiplier. For both the household sector is endogenous.

6.5.7. Steps in Estimating National Income: Adjusting for Frictions and Complementary Investments

The first step is to specify the initial increase in demand caused by the project. This is clear in the case of project construction if construction is financed by credit expansion. It is not as clear whether the uses of the project output add anything to final demand that has not already been included in the regular project benefits. For example, in the case of Figure 6.1, the steel company using the transportation project has a cost saving already counted at this point; there are no added indirect benefits if it produces the same amount of steel as before and employs the same amount of labor. Even if the company expands as its costs decrease, it may be at the expense of other steel companies.

The next step is to estimate the on site construction labor from direct requirements data. To illustrate the process, the steps use data from a study by Haveman and Krutilla (1968) and Haveman (1977) for large multipurpose water projects in a southern U.S. region. For every $1,000 of construction cost, $416 was for on-site labor and $514 for materials, and $70 was unallocated.

Next an output multiplier for the $514 of new demand for materials is computed. Gross output was $1,032 including the many rounds of inputs to produce the projects materials (backward linkage). The labor component of this was $719 which is a product of the Type I income multiplier. Data are usually unavailable to determine what percentage of this gross output will be purchased in the project region. Are there regional producers of the needed output and can they increase their present production at competitive prices? Because of lack of information on these matters, some rough estimates are made by relating some economic or social variable in the region to the nation and then by assuming the proportion supplied of a given output is the same relationship. This is called the coefficient of localization.[16] For example, a region might have 10 percent of the output of a given industry and then it might be assumed that it would supply 10 percent of any gross output required. In the case Haveman analyzed, the project region was allocated 29 percent or $300 out of the total $1,032 gross output.

The next question is how much of the $300 gross output purchased in the project region is composed of labor costs. This is obtained from the regionally disaggregated Type I income multiplier and totals $111. If this is added to on-site labor construction costs of $416, this means a total of $527 of new labor income is paid to people in the region. If the taxes had not been paid to build the project, a similar amount of income would have been distributed differently between this and other regions. If resources are fully employed, the $527 is only an indication of how resources move around in response to changes in the composition of demand.

Thus, the last question is how much of the labor cost by occupation is paid to the formerly unemployed? Because no data are available an estimate must be made. Haveman guesses that the probability of a project actually drawing from the idle pool is some increasing S-shaped function of the unemployment rate.[17] For example, when there is 9 percent unemployment about 20 percent of the labor comes from the unemployed. Haveman assumes the opportunity cost of this unemployed labor is zero.

So if 20 percent of the $527 labor income new to the region is paid to labor with no opportunity cost, then $105 is a benefit to the unemployed.[18] If this is related to the market cost of project labor to the government of $416, only $311 or 74 percent is opportunity cost for the total economy (the accounting price ratio is .74). The accounting cost of the project labor is $311, although the government wrote a check for $416 (all per thousand of total cost).[19]

A similar process is applied to the use of idle capital. Remember, however, that when capital goods are storable, the use of an idle machine in one year has an opportunity cost (measured by its annual depreciation) in terms of forgone future output. For this reason, Haveman found that shadow pricing for the opportunity cost of capital adds only 2 percent to the adjustment in nominal project costs.

The labor and capital adjustments vary by type of project and region of construction. Haveman (1977, 238) summarizes by saying that "the level of social costs typically falls only about 10 to 15 percent--at most 25 percent-- even when the rate of unemployment is 8 to 9 percent."

Note that in this analysis the unemployed labor component was always allocated to the project region only. If the problem is that of a poor country or cyclical general unemployment, there would be less interest in disaggregation. But most economists think the start up time for public works in developed countries is too great and thus advocate adjusting for unemployment only in depressed regions when unemployment may be expected to persist. Also for this reason, future operating labor costs are adjusted only for the period unemployment might be expected to remain.

There are two problems of accounting for unemployed labor benefits that are often treated only implicitly. The first is our understanding of the process of economic development and the second is a matter of credit and causality in an interacting system. Input-output data show a static picture of sectoral interdependence. But for development the dynamics are the key. If economists could easily predict supply responses to new demand, much of the development problem would have been solved long ago. There would be no dual economies in which a modern high-wage sector seems to exist independently of more traditional low-wage sectors. This whole analysis of shadow pricing labor arises because labor is immobile, yet for the input-output analysis to predict the effects of change, mobility is assumed. Thus it seems realistic to allow for frictions and bottlenecks even where economies of scale might work in the opposite way. But how much?

Because of lack of information of possible frictions, analysts usually adopt some conventions that scale down the multiplier effect present if everything worked smoothly for all rounds of interdependence. One common convention is to omit the induced effects of household respending for consumption. This was done by Haveman, who used only the Type I and not the Type II multiplier. Further, he applied the analysis only to project construction costs and not to users of the project output. As already noted, the users may not be adding to supply, but even if they are, the forward linkages to final consumer goods are uncertain (cf. Bell and Hazell 1980).

The general rule is simple in concept, but difficult in application. The forward and backward linkages as pictured in Figure 6.1 should be traced until it seems that friction will reduce the multiplication of the original stimulus of new demand. Lacking concrete data, analysts restrict their projection by limiting the number of rounds, omitting induced effects, and/or limiting analysis to backward links. My own preference is to try to estimate the first two rounds both forward and backward from the project construction omitting induced effects altogether. After that, the data in most cases become too uncertain.

The second problem is one of how to give credit to the necessary complements to any initial stimulus of public spending. Carried to an extreme, the input-output link can make the whole world the product of a key public investment. Part of the problem of friction is that complementary investments do not get made. If they do get made, then they may deserve part of the credit for the ensuing growth. Perhaps a concrete example can be used for illustration. If the Corps of Engineers builds a flood prevention dam allowing expansion of industry it becomes necessary also to make complementary investments in roads, education, health, and so on. These are some of the direct and indirect inputs that, if using unemployed resources, get credited to the Corps project. Yet, in turn, each of the other government bureaus regards its own input as the key constraint that once in place creates the demand for flood-free building sites. Not everyone can count the same multiplier effects. It is essentially a problem of interdependence and if there is coordination, there is growth. If this were easy, any new investment would be as good as any other to start, everything else would follow automatically, and there would be no underdevelopment.

Perhaps some closely related investments can be evaluated only as a package and thus credit for the multiplier would not have to be allocated. It does not make sense to raise the budget ranking of a project because of its multiplier effects, if the other implied private and public complementary projects never get built because of having a lower priority. The necessity to credit complementary private investment is recognized by many programs that combine public projects with subsidies to achieve related private investment. There is no technical answer to the question of allocating credit for employment multipliers. Allocation of jointly caused effects is necessarily partly political, but in any case some cutting off of the input-output linkages seems in order to at least acknowledge friction and the crediting problem.

6.5.8. National Income versus Distribution Effects

The input-output tables describe the interconnecting recipes of ingredients for the goods of an economy. If its linkages hold, it indicates how resources must be allocated to produce more of any one good. There is a multiplier effect of these linked recipes for any given ordinary shift in consumer demand. Projects generally are in response to shifts in demand and then their benefits are generally already measured in the direct benefits of Chapter 5. The multiplier links are of interest only in emphasizing possible bottlenecks in supplying inputs or further processing of outputs. If there is full employment, then the multiple of jobs reallocated because of the project was just shifted from some other activity.[20] Any income increase to the owner of these factors is just marginally necessary to entice movement and does not represent anything available to help pay project costs. If a multiplier analysis were done on the spending that would have taken place with the taxes for the project left in the private sector, the same employment and incomes would have occurred although different goods would have been produced and different amounts of inputs would be moved around. A tax cut has a multiplier also. This is why the analysis given focused on the possibility of using unemployed resources.

The project can increase aggregate demand without any necessary offset of a multiple of taxes withdrawn from the private sector (if financed by new credit). Although the analysis given determines whether there is a net change in national income as opposed to only shifts in occupation and location of economic activity, there may be distributional effects that need to be carried forward to Chapter 8 (see Section 8.5). Mobile resources are unconcerned about what they do as long as they are paid as before. However, immobile resources create problems. People create rents depending on what they buy and where they live. For example, if there is a shift in demand in the private sector, labor moves, destroying land rents in the old location and creating them in the new location. This shift cancels out in national income accounting, but makes a big difference to the owners of the fixed assets involved.

The convention of deleting induced consumption effects to adjust for frictions was previously suggested. But the profits (rents) of local business are involved in that Type II multiplier. If these effects are deemed to be distributionally important, they must be identified by group and documented in the distributive displays of pecuniary externalities of Chapter 8. It will be easier for merchants in the project area to see what increased sales volume will do for them than for the dispersed losers in the various places in which the resources were formerly used. This is why project supporters are always touting the project's indirect effects. Economists know there are offsetting effects elsewhere, but these are diffuse and do not call forth a countervailing organized interest group.

6.5.9. Labor Pricing in Practice

The accounting principle as regards labor effects is to visualize labor as owning all of the activity linked to a project. If this integrated firm would have any benefits (paid in wages or dividends) in addition to the direct benefits already enumerated in Chapter 5, then there are additional parties who benefit and could help pay for the project. Underemployed labor (or capital) that is immobile could attract new private (or public) employers by agreeing to wages below the going wage, thereby more nearly reflecting its own opportunity cost. A more popular approach is to obtain the going wage and instead pay the taxes that the employer usually would pay or subsidize credit or services to the employer. Some countries get in trouble by borrowing to subsidize new industry, but its people get used to the higher incomes and refuse to support politicians who try to raise taxes to pay the debt.

In practice, one of the common applications of indirect benefit analysis is in subsidies that local governments give to private investment to locate in certain places (Morse and Hushak 1979). Tax reduction is given by many governments in the hopes that its taxpayers who make up the lost tax revenue get enough in extra income above their opportunity cost to make it worthwhile. Another common application is in government subsidies to tourism (Bryden 1973). Private hotel development is subsidized, tourism is promoted, and parks, convention facilities, stadiums, and world fairs are subsidized, all in the name of new or better jobs. The fact that many of the studies (e.g., McKillop 1974) tend to show inflated benefits by referring to gross output multipliers rather than income multipliers with and without the program often leads to disappointment, but has not dimmed the continued extension of these projects. Even the building of new universities is justified not only on its direct product of education but on its indirect effects on employment (Brownrigg 1974). Much of this is a zero sum game that does not increase overall employment, but just shifts it among regions (Goodman 1982). Still, even if the local benefits are at the expense of other regions, the benefits should be accurate and ignore the gross output multiplier that is not a measure of benefit to anyone.

If analysts say there are indirect benefits, the beneficiaries may be liable for cost sharing and extra taxes. This is not just some abstract exercise that makes certain projects look better, but raises questions about who pays the bill. It is incumbent on analysts to make some adjustments for uncertainty about frictions between sectors. In the face of ignorance about supply response, some conventions are necessary. My own preference is not to use any of the multipliers that account for all rounds of respending, but rather to look at the change in net income associated with direct requirements tables, including the first round of subsequent processing of project output, and the first round of induced consumption. The analysis is carried only to the point at which there is confidence that the potential linkages are likely to occur. This modest approach should satisfy both those who might thereby be made liable to help pay for the project and those public and private managers of complementary inputs who would also like some of the credit if the multiplier actually works (need some of the credit to make the potential multiplier work). It is more important to consider opportunities to realize net economies of scale (not offset by diseconomies in contraction elsewhere) than to worry about all rounds of respending. This requires the analyst to make detailed enterprise studies rather than to rely on the I-O data whose use assumes constant returns.

In the guidelines for U.S. government water projects evaluation, the Haveman and Krutilla method was specifically rejected as too complex and uncertain (U.S. Water Resource Council 1979b, 72908). Instead employment benefits are restricted to the use of unemployed labor for on-site project construction in those areas designated as having substantial and persistent unemployment. Where specific data are lacking, the guidelines (p. 72970) require a convention that multiplies the wage bill by a percentage factor for three categories of labor: skilled--30, unskilled--47, and other--35. This combines the probability of drawing from the unemployed pool and the opportunity cost in one number. The numeraire here is benefits and the wage payment above opportunity costs is considered an added benefit. This is in contrast to computing a shadow wage to reduce nominal costs. Choice of numeraire will affect project ranking if ranked by benefit-cost ratios even though absolute net benefits are not affected.

It is the author's observation that all of this is more window-dressing than part of project choice. Projects in high unemployment areas of the United States seem to be of the same design as ones in labor-deficient areas. It may occasionally make a project eligible for funding that would otherwise have negative net returns, but it otherwise has little impact on budget choice or project design.

Some LDCs do not use shadow prices at all (Birgegard 1975). International lending agencies such as the World Bank do utilize shadow pricing for wages of unskilled workers used in project construction and operation, such as labor on irrigation project farms (Gittinger et al. 1982). The impact of labor availability in agricultural project design is illustrated by an irrigation project designed to permit cropping in the dry season when there is a surplus of labor. Calculation of multipliers is not done. However, it is common to shadow price the direct input requirements of project construction and use (such as fertilizer on an irrigation project). So in effect, indirect impacts are largely limited to first round inputs. Shadow pricing is infrequently used for industrial projects. In industry, perhaps fewer unemployed people are used and there is a tendency to want to use the latest technology even in labor surplus ares.

One of the most common errors in application of indirect benefit analysis to policy is failure to apply a with and without analysis and to consider alternatives. For example, local politicians often call attention to the new jobs that would be linked to an expanded public highway program, but ignore the fact that the program was paid for by state taxes whose alternative spending would also have a multiplier effect. The same experimental design point applies to national tax cuts as a device to increase aggregate demand. Multiplier effects are not the exclusive domain of the spending side of fiscal policy. Use of multiplier analysis in the United States to justify state projects or subsidies is usually nonsystematic and ignores alternatives.

6.6.   Conclusion

Most economists agree that to choose investments to maximize national income, market prices may need adjustment to more accurately reflect opportunity costs because of policies causing a divergence. There are a number of technical problems in estimating these opportunity costs, particularly in the case of labor in which there are great gaps in our knowledge of mobility over time and supply response. In addition, there are some areas here for public choice. Where there are conflicts there is not a single opportunity cost. Politicians must answer the question of whose opportunity costs count. It cannot be assumed that the divergence causing policies are arbitrary and not part of a design to achieve a particular income distribution and effective demand pattern. Thus, project spending (fiscal) analysis cannot arbitrarily cancel an intended distribution effort by pretending that shadow pricing is purely a technical matter of discovering the one true opportunity cost. Analyst and politician must be involved in an interactive, iterative process which resolves conflicting points of view and illustrates the consequences of systematic implementation of rules relecting these political choices.

Notes

1.   These are second-best prices and not the ones that would exist if resources were allocated optimally throughout the economy (no tax "distortion"). Note the parallel to consumer surplus in Chapter 7.

2.   The development literature (Little and Mirrlees 1974, 68) makes a distinction between traded and nontraded goods (refer to international trade). A project output such as electricity may not be traded internationally because of prohibitive transmission costs. The value of increased output is gross of taxes.

3.   Again, the development literature distinguishes traded and nontraded inputs (Powers 1981, Ch. 2). The value of increased supply is net of tax production cost. Similarly, if a tradeable good is nevertheless not freely traded because of import quotas or prohibitive tariffs, the value is production opportunity cost.

4.   If an input-output table is available (see Section 6.5.6), production cost is estimated by deleting the tax portion of value added from the list of direct requirements (to take account of taxes on the indirect requirements, the tax sector of the inverse matrix can be subtracted).

5. The development literature advises that labor's reservation wage be reduced by a consumption conversion factor (CCF) that reflects a weighted average of indirect taxes incorporated into the prices of a typical market basket of consumer goods (Powers 1981, 34-35). This advice assumes that government wastes the taxes and provides no utility to the taxpayers.

6. c.i.f. = import cost, insurance, and freight to the entry port. The f.o.b. (free on board) is export price at point of origin before insurance and freight to destination are added.

7. If the objective is to protect domestic industry against foreign competition, the shadow price is also the gross domestic market price caused by quotas or tariffs.

8. If a domestic consumption numeraire is chosen, then the APR is used to adjust local currency (c.i.f.) cost of the import to its domestic consumption equivalent. If a foreign exchange numeraire is chosen, then a consumption conversion factor (CCF) is used to adjust domestic income to its foreign exchange equivalent. CCF = 1/APR. (See Ray 1984 and Squire and van der Tak 1975.)

9. One of the reasons devaluation is often resisted is because the government does not want to increase the profits of its export sector when it is primarily foreign owned.

10. For an elementary discussion and suggested format for empirical study, see Tiebout (1962).

11. In this regard the economic base multiplier is conceptually similar to the Type II multiplier in input-output analysis.

12. Note that in input-output terminology the term *direct requirements* has a different meaning than the term direct or primary benefits used elsewhere to denote the benefits received by users of project output.

13. An explanation of the mathematics of the inverse matrix is contained in Isard (1960, 363-71).

14. For this reason it is sometimes called the *column multiplier*. Another common term is *sales multiplier*.

15. There can be much sectoral interdependence but little payment to households output so that the output multiplier will be larger than the income multiplier. The reverse is also possible. Expansion of a particular sector creates much payment to households, but is not linked to other sectors. Thus, the income multiplier may exceed the total output multiplier (as it does in the case that follows).

16. See Sasaki and Shibata (1984).

17. For an empirical test of this relationship see Epp (1979). Also see Bruce (1976) and Westley (1981, 175-76).

18. If the unemployed were paid only their opportunity cost, net project benefits would be $105 higher and no shadow price adjustment would be necessary.

19. Other adjustments to the total labor cost (and materials) could be made for taxes, tariffs, and other items not reflecting opportunity costs in a fashion similar to that noted in Section 6.2.

20. An exception is where economies of scale are available in the activities linked to the project and not to its private alternative, as noted in Section 6.5.3.

7

Valuation of Nonmarginal Projects

When a public project output is marginal, added supply has no effect on the price of that output. In this case, profit of the project agency and/or the profit (changed net income--net of associated costs of production and project costs) of the project beneficiaries is a measure of the relative merit of the project. These profits measure the capacity of the beneficiaries to pay for the project. But what if the project is nonmarginal and the increased output lowers price? This can happen in many kinds of projects ranging from large agricultural projects to education, in which an increase in the number of college graduates affects the differential between the earnings of college and high school graduates. Although the additional output may cost less than the cost (and price) of the previous supply, in certain situations the after-project price may fall to the level of the cost of production (including project cost), so that no profit or net income is earned. This is very disconcerting since there is no net project revenue and the benefit-cost (B/C) ratio is 1:1. This does not make the project attractive relative to other investments.

In this case, profit is not a good measure of what the project accomplishes. Total supply of a useful commodity of positive value has increased but its price and money value have decreased. Common sense suggests that a price drop with other things being equal can increase utility as more income is left over for other things.

The value paradox is related to a classic conundrum in economics when it was observed that diamonds sold for much more than water. Yet, water is a necessity of life. Although it might be suspected that people would pay more for water even if it meant no money left for diamonds, given an abundant water supply, they do not have to. This led to the concept that price indicates value at the margin and not total value. Consumers of water get a product for less than what they might pay if required. Thus, the idea of a consumer surplus is defined as the difference between what is actually paid and the maximum that would be paid if required. If the user of the project output earns no profit in producing final goods, perhaps the ultimate consumers could help pay for the project.

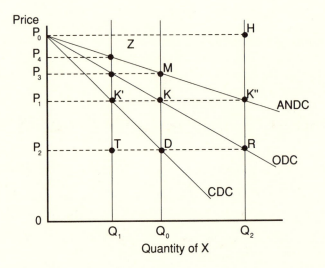

Figure 7.1a Relationship of Ordinary, Compensated, and All-or-Nothing Demand Curves

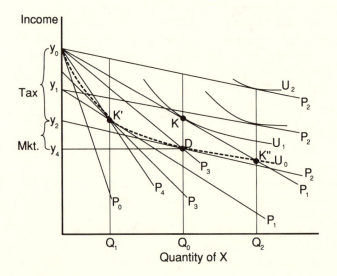

Figure 7.1b Measures of Price Change Effects

7.1.   Conceptualizing a Welfare Measure of Change in Price

If the producer net income does not change, perhaps the consumer utility does. There is a need for a money measure of the extra utility made possible by a price fall. Conceptually, the maximum that a person could pay for a price reducing project is an amount of income which would keep the person on the same utility level obtained before the price fall. This would be the maximum willingness to pay (WTP) or compensating variation (CV). These terms may be used interchangeably.

Imagine a person at Y_0 income on Figure 7.1b. At price P_0 for a good, none is purchased and the person achieves utility U_0. If the average price were P_4, that price radius from Y_0 would intersect the original utility curve at K' which is quantity Q_1. This is the maximum price that the person could pay for that quantity and not be worse off. Similarly, P_3 intersects with the indifference curve U_0 at Q_0, and P_1 intersects U_0 at Q_2. So the intersections of a series of price radii from Y_0 with the same indifference curve at different quantities indicate the maximum amount that could be collected from the person on an all-or-none basis for each of these quantities.

This schedule is called the all-or-nothing demand curve (ANDC) shown in Figure 7.1a. For example, the ANDC shows that P_3 could be charged for Q_0 and the area P_30Q_0M is a measure of maximum willingness to pay (WTP). It may be collected by either a lump-sum charge or an average price of P_3 for each unit. Point M on Figure 7.1a for P_3 corresponds to intersection D on Figure 7.1b for price line P_3Y_0.

Another way to conceptualize total WTP for a price drop is in terms of income on Figure 7.1b. Total WTP is the income paid at the intersection of the price radius with the indifference curve. For example, if a person has Q_0 of the good, it is possible to still be on utility curve U_0 with Y_4 income. So if the amount of income equal to Y_0Y_4 is paid, the person has the same utility as before the price drop. Therefore, Y_0Y_4 on Figure 7.1b is equal to P_30Q_0M on Figure 7.1a. It is the maximum that can be paid and remain on the original indifference curve.

An alternate conception of the change in income associated with a price change is to return to income Y_0, price P_0, and utility U_0 and ask a different question. In the previous case we chose a quantity and asked the buyer for an all-or-nothing bid (expressed as an average price per unit). Instead we might let the buyer choose the quantity for a given market price. To implement the same constraint as before, keeping the person on the original utility curve, it will be necessary to require an additional payment of income outside of the market. Given a price (e.g., P_2), the total payment necessary to keep the person on the original utility is given by moving a price line with a slope indicated by P_2 down the income axis until it is tangent with the original utility curve (i.e., at D on Figure 7.1b). The total payment keeping the person on U_0 is Y_0Y_4. It is composed of a market payment of Y_2Y_4 income plus a nonmarket payment of $Y_0 Y_2$ which in total keeps the person on U_0.

(If the extra nonmarket payment were not extracted, the person would move to a higher utility curve U_2 as the price drops from P_0 to P_2.) If this exercise is repeated with a series of prices, the price line tangencies with U_0(e.g., P_2 at D and P_1 at K') trace out a schedule of quantity demanded at various prices with an accompanying series of extra payments extracted to keep the person on the original utility (no matter what the market price). This schedule is called the compensated demand curve (CDC). Point D on Figure 7.1a for P_2 corresponds to tangency D on Figure 7.1b for price line P_2Y_2.

The CDC indicates a two-part way to show total WTP. A market price of P_2 collects area P_20Q_0D on Fig. 7.1a. and a tax could collect area P_0P_2D. The area under the CDC is total WTP and is equivalent to P_30Q_0M which equals income Y_0Y_2 on Figure 7.1b. as previously noted. The WTP in excess of the market price for a price drop from P_0 to P_2 equals P_0P_2D and is equal to Y_0Y_2 on Figure 7.1b. Given a market payment of P_2 covering other production costs, then Y_0Y_2 is the compensating variation and the maximum amount available to pay for the price-reducing project. This is the dollar amount needed to estimate willingness to pay for a project that lowers price from P_0 to P_2.

To summarize, the *tangencies* of a series of price lines to the indifference curve U_0 at different quantities indicate the CDC. The *intersection* of price lines from Y_0 with U_0 indicate the ANDC. The relationship of ANDC and CDC is that of an average to a marginal curve (Patinkin 1963). Thus, if ANDC is declining, CDC will be below it.

If the analyst could observe either the ANDC or CDC, it would be easy to calculate the compensating variation, which is WTP for the price-reducing project. Unfortunately these needed curves are not observable. In principle, they could be obtained by a bidding game such as described in Section 5.7 with instructions to the bidders to pretend that it is an all-or-nothing game or to indicate in sequence their maximum WTP for each unit purchased remembering what was bid for the previous units. The results of such a game would not be creditable.

What can be observed as a result of the other methods of Chapter 5 is the Marshallian ordinary demand curve (ODC) along with the quantity change resulting from the public project (e.g., Q_0Q_2). Can this ODC be used?

First, it is possible to calculate bounds to the compensating variation. The lower bound is computed by application of the Laspeyres price index, which is the change in price multiplied by the original quantity. So the lower bound of WTP for a price change of P_0 to P_2 can be seen in Figure 7.1a. The index is zero since the original Q is zero.[1] From the previous logic we know that this is an underestimate of the compensating variation P_0P_2D which is the substitution effect of the price change. Second, the upper bound is given by the Paasche price index, which is the price change multiplied by the new quantity P_0P_2RH. It is an overestimate of the compensating variation by P_0DRH.

A better estimate is possible if the ODC is available. The area under the ODC is intermediate between the Laspeyres and Paasche measures.[2] It is an overestimate of the true compensating variation by area P_0DR which is the income effect. The ODC is observed when buyers got the benefit of a lower price and are not asked to give up a payment to keep the buyers at a constant utility. The project costs were in effect ignored by consumers and thus quantities demanded are not optimal (see Tresch 1981, 528-530). Thus, the area under the ODC, although better than the upper bound measure, still overestimates compensating variation. Various other approximations have been developed in the literature (e.g., Willig 1976). But the exact measure requires a logic to go from the observed ODC to the needed CDC. This logic is supplied by duality theory, which has long utilized the quasiindirect utility function and expenditure function. For a theoretical discussion see Hausman (1981) and for a detailed guide to application, see Cooke (1985).

7.1.1. Partial Equilibrium Problems

The usual empirical estimate of a demand curve makes the fundamental assumption that real income and the prices of complements and substitutes are fixed.[3] Where goods are interdependent, the quantity demanded of good A is a function of the price of good B. If the price of B is changing, the demand curve for A is changing. If the maximum that people will pay for the first unit of good A is collected, it may affect their real income and thus the price they are willing to pay for B. If the market price of B changes (it will unless MC is constant), the demand curve for A must be redrawn. And now the demand curve for B is wrong because it was drawn for a given price of A, and so on.

If the price of good A changes, the demand curve for other commodities begins to shift at a certain rate. However, if good B's price changes, the demand for commodity A may change at another rate. If these rates are not equal, the way in which the price of A and price of B changed, for example first A then B or vice versa, will affect the area under the demand curve for A. Unless the rates are equal, the order of change (path) affects the results. In order for path independence to exist, some severe restrictions on the character of the utility functions are required--preferences must be homothetic (all income elasticities of demand equal 1) or preference functions must be parallel with respect to the numeraire good (Chipman and Moore 1980). Silberberg (1972, 950) illustrates the implications of the commonly occurring path dependence as follows:

> Suppose a dam is constructed which lowers the marginal costs of electricity, local recreation, and irrigation. In evaluating what benefit consumers would place on this project, some assumption must be made about the price adjustment path. Curiously paradoxical is the fact that a given consumer will impute a different

shadow price to the project if first the price of electricity is lowered, then that of irrigation, and then of recreation, than if prices were lowered in some other sequence; yet the nagging truth remains that nothing can be done to correct such an inconsistency. It is therefore time, at long last, for economists to abandon the term "welfare loss" in their discussions...the phrase simply has no meaning at all.

Hausman's theory does not solve the problem of multiple price changes.[4] He says the formulas "cannot be used to analyze the welfare change when more than one price changes (except proportionately) without further analysis" (Hausman 1981, 670). Willig's (1976) simpler estimate of an individual's consumer surplus (CS) using ordinary demand curves and an estimate of the degree of approximation to the exact CV measure is also for a single price change and linear technologies. It cannot be applied in the aggregate to the many-consumer economy where the first-best assumption of optimal income distribution does not hold (Tresch 1981, 198). Just et al. (1982, 374-86) have proposed a formulation to compute error bounds for multiple changes but still with restrictive assumptions.

Most empirical studies have ignored the indirect price and income interdependencies among markets (Diewert 1983). But a computable general equilibrium model specified by Kokoski and Smith (1987) suggests that proportionality in price movements as a result of a nonmarginal project is questionable. Partial equilibrium estimates are subject to large errors and fail to reveal the nonuniform effect on the rich and poor.

Morey (1984) has suggested that some of the apparent conflicts in the literature are the result of imprecise language. He interprets Silberberg (1972), Richter (1977), and Burns (1973) as saying that when the marginal utility of money is not constant, dollar measures of utility changes do not exist. Morey (1984, 169) concludes, "One can never determine the cardinal properties of the individual's cardinal preference ordering (i.e., the individual's intensity of preferences) solely on the basis of the individual's behavior in the market." He further details problems in deducing demand functions from market data. The essence is that it is not possible to entirely avoid imposing a priori restrictions on preference ordering when working with utility functions and demand equations.

Most theorists seem to agree that there is no money measure of the utility of a price change, but that the compensating variation can be interpreted as a willingness to pay measure. Recall that the CV is obtained by varying price along a given utility function so there are none of the problems that arise when movement from one function to another is to be cardinally measured. This still avoids the policy question of whether willingness to pay or sell is appropriate. These two measures are different under realistic conditions as noted in Section 5.7.4.

The partial equilibrium character of consumer surplus creates further problems. It seems plausible that more revenue could be collected for any given product by price differentiation. But this is impossible for all products. The area under the demand curve for all products would greatly exceed the GNP.[5] Such a measure of wealth is not actually available to cover project costs. Even with a compensated demand curve, consumer surplus is a partial measure of what can be collected only if other producers do not try to capture their consumer surplus as well. Satisfaction and utility are not just some abstractions that affect project rankings. The question of liability for paying project costs is therefore raised. If it is claimed that some people have greater utility, should they then pay more for the project?

It is physically impossible for consumers to pay the asserted consumer surplus for all products for which it can be computed. The area below the demand curve and above the single price line is not an extra wealth available to cover project cost. Such areas are simply a part of the income spent for other goods. You do not have ordinary price multiplied by quantity for all goods plus consumer surplus (CS), but only price multiplied by quantity which equals the GNP. You can collect CS for one good, but only by reducing the sales of another good (perhaps via a tax increase).

If the consumer surplus makes sense on the benefit side, it must be considered on the cost side. Cost is simply the value of goods that might have been produced if the resources were used elsewhere. Some of these forgone goods had inelastic demand and CS even if the individual producers of the forgone goods, if purely competitive, may not have been able to see any CS as each produces a marginal amount. But just as the unseen consumer surplus is credited to public projects, must it not also be credited to forgone private projects that constitute the public project's costs? But as we have seen, it is impossible to count CS for all commodities and thus it cannot be done simultaneously on the benefit and cost side.

Some welfare theorists calculate consumer surplus losses for taxes that reduce private production of a given good and refer to it presumptively as a "deadweight loss." This conception suffers from being a partial equilibrium analysis. In practice, taxes cannot be evaluated independently of their distribution effects. As Tresch (1981, 351) states, "it may not be very useful to think of the effects of distorting taxes in terms of deadweight loss. Unambiguous notions of efficiency loss involve the use of the expenditure function, which is best suited to one-consumer economies."

Whatever its generalization and method of computation, there are problems with using CS as a measure of willingness to pay. The empirical measure depends on policy decisions regarding what else is happening in the economy. With many market goods, everyone pays the same price, but CS implies price differentiation. The political authority may or may not have affirmed the rights leading to the usual market prices, but it will certainly have to act if the analyst's partial use of CS on publicly provided goods, but not on private goods, is to be anything but value presumptive. If price differentiation is allowed for some private goods, it will affect the empirical estimates of CS for public goods. Willingness to pay for a given product depends on the property rights of other producers to also collect consumer surplus.

7.2. Policy Problems

7.2.1. Price Differentiation Equity

Suppose these empirical problems are solved. What are the policy implications? Can economists advise government to count consumer surplus and remain neutral with respect to conflicting interests? Consumer surplus implies price (tax) differentiation. In the private sector, public policy sometimes attempts to prevent price differentiation. People do not readily accept the idea of paying a price different from that paid by another. There are surely firms and products that would be in business if more price differentiation were practical or allowed (Samuelson 1963, 197). It takes a value judgment to label price differentiation as discriminatory or desirable. Of all projects and firms that would otherwise fail, there is no evidence to indicate which ones consumers want to save when the demand for any one product is a function of whether maximum willingness to pay is extracted for others.

7.2.2. Rents and Income Distribution

The distribution of rents (producer surplus) is another problem that arises out of the interdependence occurring with nonmarginal projects. When consumer surplus is extracted in payment for project good A or its price drops, it affects the demand for and the price of good B substitutes and complements. The producer of good B having formerly earned a rent (payment above the cost of production) may find that rent eliminated or reduced. If there are immobile assets, there may be capital losses. Price interaction between A and B occurs unless good B is produced under conditions of constant marginal cost, in which case a shift in demand for B causes only a shift in quantity demanded and not a change in price. A further problem occurs unless price is everywhere equal to marginal cost. If it is not, a reduction in output causes a loss in profit, even if price remains unchanged. This loss in profit is not offset by a gain to consumers if price is unchanged (Little 1957, 175-179). Harberger (1971, 785) has suggested the following convention be adopted by all applied project analysts to gloss over the problem: "when evaluating the net benefits or costs of a given action (project, program or policy), the costs and benefits accruing to each member of the relevant group (e.g., a nation) should normally be added without regard to individuals to whom they accrue."

This means that if consumers gained $2 and producers lost $1 of rent, there would be a $1 net gain. But such a convention surely requires a value judgment and is not neutral with respect to conflicting interests. The economist as scientist who hesitates to advocate a tax transfer or land redistribution must also be uneasy about Harberger's convention.[6]

There is an interaction between policy and empirical problems. Gramlich (1981, 84) advocates that the rent loss in nonproject goods be subtracted from consumer surplus in project goods. But unless the real income effect of collecting consumer surplus on prices of other goods is concentrated on one or a few substitutes, the effect will be a small change in price for many goods. This will be impossible to estimate empirically and, thus, it will be impossible to know if the gain in consumer surplus is large enough to compensate the losers (Little 1957, 178). Politically, this large group of small losers is unlikely to be active and provides no check on any estimate the analyst wishes to attach to these losses. If consumer surplus suggests an interest group to help pay for a project, the loss of producer surplus suggests an interest group that might pay to prevent a project, if only they could estimate its impact. Most of the literature seems addressed to the question of whether the cross elasticities are small enough for feedback on the demand for the project good to be ignored. But if the asserted CS is collected, it will affect the producers of other goods even if it is so diffuse that no one is aware of it. Problems of interpretation are further confounded by the existence of uncertainty (Graham-Tomasi and Myers 1986).

However the analyst hopes to sum costs and benefits, this conceptualization of pecuniary externalities does suggest that project documentation include a display of distributive impacts (see Chapter 8) so that, in so far as possible, the resource owners may be apprised of expected changes in factor and product prices (even if they are asked to bear it in the name of enhanced net national income).[7]

7.2.3.   Aggregation over Individuals

Much of the theoretical welfare analysis has been at the level of the individual's demand curve.[8]   As Tresch (1981, 525) points out, "The aggregation problem is sticky, one which researchers typically avoid by assuming identical individuals (or a few subsets of identical individuals), with homothetic preferences."   With ordinary measures, a dollar's worth of product counts the same, whether bought by rich or poor. But with CS, the measure of compensating variation can be greater for the rich than for the poor. So projects producing normal goods with income effects benefiting the rich will show a larger value, even if preference structures of rich and poor are identical (Bockstael and Strand 1985). The implementation of projects favoring the rich continually modifies the distribution of welfare. And, for a given project, if both rich and poor are charged the same tax capturing the estimated average compensating variation to pay for the project, the poor are overcharged. The tax collector is not sure whom to charge anymore than a firm is sure or able to price differentiate and segment markets.

Currie et al. (1971, 753) say that Marshall

> felt justified in equating the triangle under the market demand curve for a commodity with collective consumer's surplus on the ground that "by far the greater number of events with which economics deals, affects in about equal proportions all the different classes of society." However Hicks denied the necessity for such a questionable assumption. He claimed that the amount of money which consumers would have to lose in order to make them each as badly off as prior to the introduction of a commodity has a clear meaning, even though it says nothing about how this loss would be distributed among individual consumers.

Policy makers interested in income distribution cannot ignore who pays the compensating variation if costless lump-sum distributions are not available. As Boadway and Bruce (1984, 271) state, "The use of the unweighted sum of household compensating or equivalent variations as a necessary and sufficient indicator of potential Pareto improvement is rife with difficulties." Also see Boadway (1974).

7.3.   Resource Savings and Asset Mobility

The venerable lasting power of the consumer surplus concept is in part the result of its consonance with the common sense rejection of the idea that total wealth can decrease with increased nonmarginal supply. Perhaps it can be dispensed with if another solution to the value paradox can be found. To illustrate, consider the empirical study of investment in hybrid corn research. Griliches (1958) estimates that the new seed resulted in a 15 percent increase in yield. He argues that the appropriate measure of the benefit is "the loss in 'consumer surplus' that would occur if hybrid corn were to 'disappear'" (p. 373). The situation is portrayed in Figure 7.2. The available data were the price and output with hybrid corn (area P_1bQ_20), demand elasticity of -.5 from which the demand curve ab is derived, and the yield change (13 percent less than the new output Q_2). The slope of the supply curve is less well understood, so Griliches chose to bracket the results by comparing the estimates obtained by the polar extremes of perfectly elastic and inelastic supply.[9] The infinitely elastic assumption is shown in Figure 7.2. Griliches does not investigate the particular cost functions of firms in the industry, but it will be seen later that this is critical to evaluation. Assume initially that all firms have the same costs (representative firms are shown in Figure 7.2) along S_1. Hybrid corn is a technology that can be adopted by almost all firms and should reduce costs for all firms (shown on S_2 in Figure 7.2).

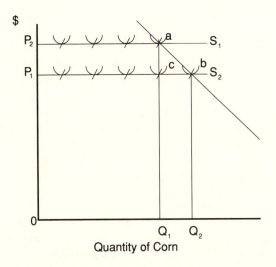

Figure 7.2 Impact of a Project Reducing Costs of All Firms Equally (firms have equal costs and input prices are constant)

A reduction in costs for the old level of output for the sum of firms in the industry is inferred from the estimated price change by P_2acP_1. It is the value of inputs needed given that they now produce 15 percent more (at former input prices). Although in competition this cost reduction will not be captured by producers in the long run as price falls, it does represent resources saved that are potentially available to increase the national income elsewhere. This is another application of the cost saving method of valuation discussed in Section 5.3. The cost saved is a gain to consumers and is thus related to the consumer surplus concept, but this part of the gain in consumer surplus that is resources saved can be estimated from the preproject output and cost data without any entanglement in the empirical problem of partial equilibrium analysis involved in estimating P_2abP_1. The net gains to consumers and producers and input suppliers are not necessarily equal to resources saved and depend on supply and demand and the effect on rents.

The focus on resources saved helps to show the gain to a project such as hybrid corn that we intuitively feel has benefits even if the total value of the crop declines. This focus has other uses as well. A saved resource cannot increase national product if it cannot be moved to the production of alternate goods.[10] If the saved resource is wasted, there is no more output than before. Analysts must inquire into the mobility of the saved resources (cost reduction). Griliches (1958) did not consider this problem. However, some subsequent studies of technological development projects have examined resource mobility.   Schmitz and Seckler (1970) in their study of the mechanical tomato harvester were concerned about where the released migrant pickers could go.   Data are not good, but clearly not all of the released resource will be used for production elsewhere.   Immobile resources cause a reduction in the area P_2acP_1, which is converted into national income.   As a matter of income distribution, the released workers have a stake in these estimates.   If they had a property right in their former income,[11] project beneficiaries (growers/or consumers) would have to pay the workers any losses and thus costs of production do not fall by as much as the previously estimated "potential" resource savings rectangle.   The workers former income is in effect an acquisition price, whereas subsequent income is a salvage value.   It can be seen that many conflicts emerge when we show some firm and household level data rather than the innocent looking total supply curves.

Griliches did not know the shape of the historical supply curve.   Even when these data are available, they may have no relevance for welfare analysis.   To estimate rent change it is necessary to know the marginal cost (w/o rent) at acquisition prices of all firms (representative groups) in the industry with and without the supply shift (Mishan 1968, 1277).   The historical expansion path and discontinuous supply curve do not necessarily indicate the current rents with and without the supply shift.   For example, it is possible that at the old and new supply points all firms have identical costs and earn no rents (such as in Figure 7.2) even when the long run supply curve is upward sloping (or the firms may have different costs as in Figure 7.3). Viner (1932, 44) referred to the needed data as the "particular expense curve."   Unfortunately for welfare and distribution analysis, the necessary firm level production data are costly to obtain and various guesses and bracketed estimates must be made (see Cooke 1985).

The resource saved concept may be clarified by reference to a simplified numerical example.   Suppose two factors of production.   A particular expense estimate for a group of firms in the industry prior to the project may indicate a cost of $100 for a given output as follows:[12]

	Total Cost	= Factor 1	+	Factor 2
W/O project	100	= 10 units × $5	+	10 units × $5
With project	90	= 8 units × $5	+	10 units × $5
Nominal change in "costs"	10			

The cost of production at acquisition prices without the project is $100. The project can save two units of Factor 1.   Suppose these two units acquired at a cost of $10 have a total salvage value in other uses of $6.   The acquisition value minus the salvage value of the saved resource is therefore $4, which is a capital loss that must be deducted from the nominal change in cost.   Because

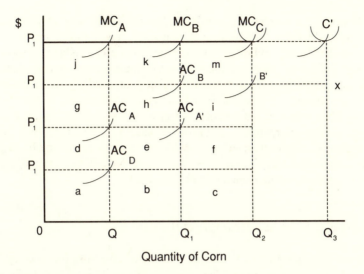

Figure 7.3   Impact of a Project Whose Costs Are Lower than Previous Marginal Firms (but does not affect costs of previous firms)

the saved resource did not have an equally productive alternative use, the resource saving is only 6 rather than the nominal 10. Lesson: It is better to save durable inputs whose acquisition value equals salvage value. Nondurables used in one production period have equal acquisition and salvage value. The same analysis for another group of firms may show a profit equal to the nominal change in cost when salvage and acquisition prices are equal and the MVP of the factor exceeds its acquisition price.

There is a further problem if the analyst can observe only the resulting price and quantity plus the magnitude of the supply shift from engineering or biological data (i.e., how much less production would have been if the "project" had not occurred). Some rent may be paid to input suppliers that will not be accounted for in producer rents. If the product demand at the new price causes more total inputs to be used in this industry, these have to be bid away from other users at higher prices (pecuniary externality). The amount paid to the marginal input must also be paid to the intramarginal inputs creating rents for them (see Just and Hueth 1979, 951-52). In that case, resource saving and rent cannot be measured in the goods market and must include the input market.

What about the remaining consumer surplus triangle abc (assuming we ignore the empirical problem in its estimation)? Does this represent additional wealth available to finance the project? An earlier negative answer can be further supported by focusing on resource savings $P_2 ac P_1$ of Figure 7.2. These can be used in further corn production or in other goods depending on demand. Just for purposes of illustration assume the saved resources are shifted and combined with reallocated resources from elsewhere to an equivalent area cbQ_2Q_1, which is the cost of producing Q_1Q_2. Can we increase this area by adding abc? The national income can increase only by P_2acP_1 and this is the only new resource available to pay for the project. If price differentiation is used, some old resources can be captured as profits by project managers. But that capacity is available to many resource owners if price differentiation were permitted.

It might be assumed that because resource savings is the major part of the change in consumer surplus that how the triangle abc is interpreted is of little consequence. However, in some cases the project costs may be larger than the mobile resources saved and the project would have negative net benefits unless the triangle is included in benefits.

7.4.   Project Firm as Intramarginal Firm

The previous analysis applies to a project in which the cost functions of all firms in the industry are reduced. The analysis differs if the project adds only new firms (or the particular expense curve shift is not parallel and alters costs of a portion of the existing firms). For example, a large-scale irrigation project may lower the industry average and total cost, but not affect costs of existing dryland firms. The increased output should not be conceptualized in the same way as for new technologies shown in Figure 7.2. If other firms are not affected, price does not come down to the costs of the irrigation firms. The irrigated firms should be shown as intramarginal (rather than the last increment). Price is determined by the marginal cost of whatever becomes the new marginal dryland firm. Figure 7.3 shows a case in which the particular expense curve shift is convergent at point C (or alternatively at C' or X).

It is necessary to know the cost structure of the industry, that is, the cost curves (at acquisition prices) of groups of firms in the industry obtained from economy of size studies (not from econometric supply estimation). Suppose a group of firms producing 0Q with costs shown by representative average total and marginal costs designated by the subscript A. The amount of land with these costs is fixed. Another group of firms on less fertile land is similarly shown with subscript B. Yet another group is shown at C and contains the marginal firms whose costs interact with demand to determine price P_1. Marginal cost (MC) does not include any rents paid to land inputs. Now assume that the irrigation project creates a new group of firms whose average costs for 0Q output are P_2. It would be erroneous to assume that these firms are the marginal producers determining price in the long run. Rather the new firms are an intramarginal group that can be conceptualized as taking the place of former group A as the lowest cost group. The new project firms' costs are shown with the subscript D in the figure. Group A remains in the industry producing output QQ_1 (shifts location in the figure) and group B also remains in the industry.

What happens to group C is problematic. Unless demand is perfectly elastic at P_1, the price of output (Q_2Q_3) of group C won't cover the nonland production costs at acquisition prices. If any rent had been capitalized into land values, there will be a capital loss based on acquisition prices.[13] Nevertheless, if these firms have nonland fixed assets some may stay in the industry and the supply curve may run through C′ although price will decline from P_1 to the benefit of consumers. (If all firms stay, the supply curve intersects at X with a price of P_3.) If only one firm in this group stays in the industry, then the new supply curve converges with the old one at C and the price remains at P_1. The rest of the old C group's resources are available to increase national output elsewhere.

A similar case of a convergent supply shift occurs if firms A and B adopt a new cost saving technology (but C cannot). Then resource saving is d and h. Firm C remains as the marginal firm and price is unchanged.

Returning to the case in which the project does not affect the costs of previous firms, although price and output may remain unchanged and consumers derive no benefit, the resource savings approach measures the change in national income. In this situation it is equal to the project firm's profits (shown as areas d, g, and j for group D). Measured as resource savings it is a saving of resource block d for output 0Q, block h for output Q_1 and block m for output Q_1Q_2 (i.e., the shift in the particular expense curve). Or, alternatively, the four resource blocks m, i, f, and c of group C minus the one new resource block (cost = a) utilized by new firms in group D is a measure of resources saved and potentially available for use elsewhere. Profits of the project firm and resources saved are identical. The resource saved concept works equally well whether gain is captured by producers or consumers.

In the previous discussion, the impact of collecting consumer surplus on the demand for other goods and thus on rents accruing to producers of those goods was noted. Consumers of project output may gain at the expense of these producers of other goods. Similar income transfers may occur among producers in the project industry. If price falls to P_3 in Figure 7.3, producer group A, which formerly enjoyed a rent of area g plus j, now gets only h and asset values are reduced. Group B, which formerly had a rent of k, now gets nothing. These transfers from resource owners and producer to consumers need a value judgment for legitimation. The producer may well be the poorer of the two groups.

The previous discussion portrays a discontinuous particular expense curve to emphasize the position of firms with different costs. The more familiar continuous supply functions with a shift from PEC_1 to PEC_2 and a decrease in product price from P_1 to P_2 are shown in Figure 7.4. The shaded area between the expense curves for the original output Q_1 is resources saved and a potential national income gain. The slightly larger cross hatched

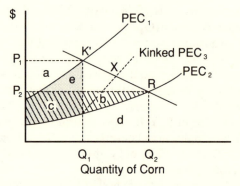

Quantity of Corn

Figure 7.4 Impact of a Project Reducing Costs of All Firms Differentially

area is rent paid to producers when input prices are unchanged. Consumers gain some of the former rents of area "a" as a result of a fall in price and also some of the resource saving (area "e"). Whatever happens to prices, it does not affect resources saved on the initial output.

If some inputs are less than perfectly elastic in supply, the resulting particular expense curve (PEC_3) may be kinked upward and result in an output less than Q_2 and a different output price.[14] If inputs get bid up and receive transfer rents, this affects the distribution of resource saved and rents among consumers, producers, and input suppliers.

7.5.   Regulatory Applications

Regulation can also have nonmarginal impacts. For example, if the sale of a product is limited, prohibited, or taxed, its price rises, the quantity demanded falls, and the price of substitutes may increase (Bullock and Ward 1981). Reduced output loses consumer surplus which some economists prejudicially term "deadweight loss" (Just et al. 1982, 160). The same measurement and policy problems previously noted apply to regulation.

7.6.   What Governments Do

U.S. Government guides for project evaluation are increasingly providing for the use of consumer surplus measures. It is not clear, however, that this has had much effect on project choice to date. For example, the U.S. Water Resources Council (1982, 12303) allows use of consumer surplus for projects affecting price. Nevertheless, the agencies have only partially implemented it.

A U.S. Forest Service (1987) guideline for preparation of its 1990 planning studies provides for the display of consumer surplus measures along with other "accounting stances." It does not specify which one is to be used in recommending investment and management alternatives. Also see U.S. Department of Agriculture (1987) and U.S. Department of Interior (1986, 27749).

The U.S. Environmental Protection Agency (1988) guidelines for regulatory impact analysis refer to consumer and producer surplus. The document warns that "it is necessary to take account of income and multiple price changes that can have a significant effect on benefit computations." No method for doing so is described.

7.7.   Conclusion

The nonpresumptive and unambiguous measure of national income change of a nonmarginal project is that of resource savings (even when producer profits are zero). Both projects that do and do not affect the cost curve of all individual firms in an industry can be analyzed with this concept. Data required for the analysis include the quantity of preproject output (or that subject to cost reduction) and the old and new cost of production (particular expense curves). The analysis requires explicit attention to resource mobility, for a resource saved is wasted and cannot increase national income if it has nowhere to go. This suggests that technological research should be directed toward areas in which resources are mobile or tied to programs to facilitate mobility. If the cost of production data are collected by groups of typical firms, income transfer within the industry may be identified.

The consumer surplus concept is excess baggage as far as empirical estimates are concerned. It remains a useful heuristic device, however. It supports the common sense conclusion that real wealth (as distinct from market value) cannot be increased by destroying resources or otherwise reducing supply. It also suggests that benefits of a project that would prevent loss of an existing resource with relatively inelastic demand are greater than suggested by existing total revenues. For example, a research project to prevent insect damage, which could cut wheat and corn output in half, may be worth more than a project to expand output of the same crops even if the outputs valued at current prices were the same. The politician's sense of this from sampling public opinion is probably as good as any demand curve artifact of consumer surplus. There is no general theoretical argument that can be applied to the real world, either for or against the consumer surplus criterion or any other. Any criterion embodies value judgments.

The concept suggests that price decrease does increase utility. Some of the new intramarginal users may be willing to pay higher differential prices (more than marginal cost) for the output of a nonmarginal project so that the project will have more positive net return and look better when competing with other investments. But some other projects (private and public) would also look better if they utilized price differentiation. Which among many should price differentiate?   Existing demand curves (even derived compensated ones) cannot provide the answer.   Consumers with different preferences conflict over whose projects should have price differentiation rights.   The measure of aggregate welfare increase of a price change coupled with tax incidence relative to different people's consumers' surplus requires political choice.   A political judgment is surely needed to decide if the consumer gains are larger than the many small losses to producers of competing products.[15]   As Little (1957, 184) states, "The best criteria for investment decision must, within wide limits, be determined at dynamic and administrative levels--and not at the level of static welfare theory."

The concept further suggests that the pricing rule is a potent device affecting income distribution (see Chapter 8).   The market can be as effective in distributing income as any land reform or transfer program.   If exclusion cost is relatively cheap, then a seller practicing selective price differentiation can affect the distribution of income.   The piecemeal extraction of total willingness to pay for any one product can be used to show a large net revenue that can be returned to the public treasury for other purposes or can be used to provide extra project output to additional users who otherwise could not be served.   For example, in U.S. water projects, differential charges are made to municipal water users and irrigators (Bain et al. 1966).   The municipal users pay more and irrigation users pay less than the price that would exist if a single price were charged to all users.   Whether this is fair or not requires a value judgment and public choice.   Where exclusion costs prevent market transactions, the tax price incidence may or may not fit the distribution of benefits or someone's sense of fairness.   The government can tax equivalent to the technical estimate of total consumer gain and build those projects in which total benefits exceed costs, but government has no magic meter to perfectly discern individual differences in willingness to pay when designing tax incidence.   Can it ignore the unwilling rider in the name of increasing net national income without a value judgment?

Notes

1.   In the more usual case when the original price is not zero, the Laspeyres index is positive.

2.   A quick and dirty approximation of this ODC area is the average of the Laspeyres and Paasche measures (one-half the price change multiplied by the new market equilibrium quantity).   It is exact only when the ODC is linear.

3.   The   discussion of a general equilibrium input-output model in Chapter 6 provides insight into possible intersectoral interdependencies.

4.   For further discussion of the implications of multiple price change see Tresch (1981, 197-198) and Richter (1977).   Vartia's (1983) numerical method was not extended to the multiple good case.

5. The point is made by Viner and Bishop, but disputed by Patinkin (1963, 95). See also Tresch (1981, 75).

6. Harberger (1971, 785) says income distribution is "not a part of the package of expertise that distinguishes the professional economist from the rest of humanity." Yet, he inconsistently advocates an analytic rule that has income distribution implications.

7. For a hypothetical numerical example, see Sugden and Williams (1978, 259).

8. For a general discussion see Tresch (1981, 198).

9. For a discussion of the consequences of alternative supply shifts, see Linder and Jarrett (1978) and Rose (1980). Griliches (1958) implicitly assumes salvage and acquisition prices are equal, prices affecting resource use decisions and cost savings are the same, and supply functions are continuous and reversible.

10. A saved immobile resource adds nothing to national income but is the occasion for a transfer from the resource owner to the former resource user. Thus, capital losses occasioned by price shifts caused by the project (technological change) must be netted out. The preproject production cost is computed at acquisition prices less any depreciation to date.

11. Even if cash income in new employment were the same, a property right by workers might require the stress of moving to be counted as a cost by tomato growers.

12. At this time there already may have been a capital loss, but if salvage price < MVP < acquisition price, the internal opportunity cost (shadow price) is controlling the resource use decision. The capital loss may increase as a result of the project even if a durable remains fixed in use.

13. Price may be less than the historical costs at acquisition prices of the marginal firms, that is, the firms may continue to produce although suffering capital losses (Johnson and Quance 1972, 185-96). If assets are valued at acquisition prices then group C firms were breaking even, and if price falls, they suffer capital losses. But it is possible to view the immobile assets of firms in group C (formerly producing output Q_1Q_2) as formerly earning rents if assets are revalued at salvage values. If the value of the input in available alternative uses is P_3, then resource block m was a rent, and the project then results in a destruction of this rent and an income transfer from producers to consumers. How that is viewed depends on property rights.

14. For discussion of kinked supply curves, see Rose (1980).

15. A related problem of rent transfers was discussed in Section 5.5 when estimating benefits from changes in rents--a project may destroy rents in one area and create them in another. The concept of *net locational advantage* is similar to that of *resources saved*.

8

Distribution Effects

It would be well to be quite sure
Just who are the deserving poor
Or else the state-supported ditch
May serve the undeserving rich.
                    -- Kenneth Boulding

8.1.   Introduction: Alternative Means for Distribution

If distributional issues are at the heart of project analysis, a methodology is needed to compare the effectiveness of alternative projects in meeting a politically chosen income distribution and to identify and compare alternative means for achieving a given distribution, including project designs and management. The purpose here is not to engage in moral debate, but rather to make sure the function of this debate is neither usurped nor poorly implemented.

In this chapter a display of the distribution of project benefits to selected groups is discussed that incorporates the results of applying the publicly chosen property rights called for in the previous chapters. The most obvious variable influencing distribution is the project design that determines the beneficiaries of the project's direct output.   Additional conduits for distributive effects will be noted.   Some outputs of public projects are marketed, and pricing to different groups affects income distribution. Similarly, where costs are shared among different levels of government (and/or between taxes and charges) different groups then pay different amounts.   Where outputs of multiple product projects are priced in the market or in tax shares, the allocation of joint costs affects relative prices and thus affects real income. Further, projects can affect prices of inputs and outputs facing other suppliers and producers.   These pecuniary effects, including regional relocations of production, affect income distribution. Some projects use inputs that although previously accounted for as part of the total benefit-cost analysis, may not actually be paid for or subsidized. Finally, the effectiveness of projects versus direct cash transfers must be evaluated. An aggregative transfer or grants account will be developed to compare these alternative means for redirecting the flow of income.

This chapter is designed to take distributive objectives seriously, which means to treat distributive alternatives systematically. In practice this is seldom done. Often some of the benefits of a project are noted by groups of recipients on a piecemeal basis and used to further legitimize support for a project, perhaps chosen for another reason. Projects can be ranked in terms of their comparative ability to transfer resources to politically chosen worthy groups. Grants efficiency analysis aggregates the effects of different transfer sources and asks how to deliver the most from a grant of a given size.

It is fundamental to distinguish between changed distribution of income and redistribution (Schmid 1972). Beginning with an existing distribution of income, the change in the proportion of total income going to a given group may be noted. This indicates nothing of the source of the change. It may be the result of superior productivity of investments available to that group or it may be the result of a transfer of income from another group, leaving total national income unaffected.[1] Redistribution implies a change in ownership over time. It suggests a movement from one person's pocket to another's. Project choice can cause redistribution as surely as can changes in the constitution or court-made liability laws. It is not possible to speak of redistribution unless there is a property rights reference point, which establishes who would have had the money without the project. Where rights are not clear, the measurement of redistribution is difficult. In what follows, the various sources or instruments of income transfers are noted in turn and then combined into a single grants account display.

8.2.   Pricing of Marketed Output

The output of state enterprise is sold in the market, and some other products are financed in part by user fees. For the competitive firm, products are priced to cover marginal cost and total revenues cover total costs. In such a system all units of output have the same price. If the state enterprise sells to one group at a lower price, it will have to be financed by higher prices to other groups or by a tax transfer. The same applies to paying higher than market prices for inputs. Redistribution is conventionally defined with reference to the usual practices of pricing to maximize profits (or at least cover costs). A subsidy is the difference between long-run marginal cost and the price actually charged.

It is quite common for governments to charge less than cost for a publicly provided product to some or all customers. For example, the charges of the U.S. Postal Service sometimes do not cover costs. In other countries, many of the state owned basic industries such as steel pay wages such that losses occur. In many socialist countries, price policy is the major distributive instrument (Szakolczai 1980). However, any flow labeled as a subsidy must be interpreted by reference to some property right. For example, if steel workers have a right in their jobs or the right to expect orderly adjustments in employment, then the payments are for services rendered according to contract and must be built into the long-term cost of steel via taxes or other means. For example, in Japan where large private firms have an obligation to maintain their work force over the business cycle, the wage of cyclically redundant workers would not be regarded as a redistribution, but rather covered by the long-run pricing strategy of the firm.

Terminology reveals much about public attitudes. In the United States when a former tax-financed service is now subject to charges, such as for libraries or garbage pick-up, it is referred to as a "user fee." In areas in which services have long been charged for, such as use of buses, it is referred to as a "product price." In any case, these are frequently provided at different prices to different classes of people. For example, senior citizens are charged lower bus fares. When first implemented, such a system is a redistribution. But after long standing it may become the equivalent of a property right that if changed would constitute redistribution.

8.2.1. Pricing under Decreasing Cost to Scale

The conventional prescription of first-best welfare economic theory is that all products should be priced at marginal cost even when produced under decreasing cost to scale. In that case, total receipts will not cover total costs. There are several alternative pricing rules that imply quite different rights and income distribution. One alternative advocated by Bain et al. (1966, Ch. 10) is to charge fees related to the amount of use based on marginal cost and then to cover the fixed cost by lump-sum taxes. Another option is the practice of a single price monopolist who chooses the output level to equate marginal cost and marginal revenue and then prices to more than cover total costs. A variant is the regulated discriminating monopolist. Here the market is segmented and subgroups are charged different prices. This can be done to maximize profits or to give relatively low prices to favored groups and still pay for the whole project via market pricing. Bain illustrates this with respect to U.S. public water projects in which irrigation water users pay a lower price than municipal users. This is an ability to pay concept of pricing.

Goods could be priced in such a way as to equalize the incomes of project beneficiaries who may differ in their resource base (Bain et al. 1966, 336). This is sometimes done in LDC projects in which farmers are necessarily settled on land with differing fertility but are compensated by paying different prices for water. On the other hand, if the government priced to maximize project income, any profit could be used to lower everyone's taxes. It all depends on whose property rights are implemented.

This analysis applies to any situation in which building or management of the project has an effect on price. In Chapter 7 on nonmarginal projects it was noted that the discovery of a downward sloping demand curve, even if not precisely measurable, provided the opportunity for differential pricing. A rule requiring the same price for all users or one allowing differentiation affects income distribution.

Differential pricing is common in transportation systems. Rush hour passengers have more inelastic demand than the off-peak user and can be and often are charged a higher price because they have fewer substitutes. It makes sense to provide an incentive to the person who has a choice of travel times for shopping to go at off-peak hours and reduce the cost of total system peak capacity. However, it requires a judgment of fairness to take advantage of the person with no substitutes. Another example is the differential pricing of air tickets. The person who makes short duration trips and makes last minute plans has more inelastic demand, so U.S. fares are higher for this class of rider than for people who make advance reservations for trips between 7 and 30 days. It requires a value judgment to sanction charging a person who must make an emergency trip to visit a sick relative more than a person going for a two week holiday on the same route. It is insufficient to say that no one pays more than one's own consumer surplus.

In summary, Ruggles (1949, 123) says, "Every pricing system results in some sort of income distribution. . . . In choosing a pricing system, it thus becomes necessary to make specific assumptions about interpersonal comparison of utility and then to judge the pricing system in relation to these assumptions as well as in relation to the marginal conditions." See also Little (1957, Ch. 11). The right to expect use of a pricing rule by public firms (as well as private) is part of one's wealth as surely as is a claim on the public treasury, tax incidence, or ownership of land. Pricing rules are part of one's property rights and not just a theoretically derived rule for maximizing output from a set of predetermined rights. Departures from the "normative rule" can then (and only then) be defined as redistribution.

However much of the total cost is covered by user fees (as opposed to general taxes), if the effect of the fee is to be neutral, the same price would be charged for each unit rather that charging some users only the marginal cost. The difference between the amount paid by a target group and what it would have paid if every user of that kind of output had paid the same price alters distribution.

8.2.2.   Are Cost Savings Passed On?

Some projects reduce the cost of an input into a private production process. For example, a research project may develop a new technology. Market structure (and elasticities of supply and demand) may affect who the ultimate recipient of benefits may be. It could mean higher profit for producers or lower product prices for consumers as discussed for nonmarginal projects in Chapter 7. In general, because of the competitive structure, the benefits of research are passed on to consumers frequently in the agricultural sector but somewhat less so in other industries. If a saved resource is immobile, it occasions an income transfer between the resource owner and user.

8.3.   Cost Sharing

The cost of some projects such as highways, urban mass transit, and water resource development is shared by different levels of government in the United States, as well as between general taxes and user fees. These shares can be chosen to achieve a given distribution objective since tax incidence varies by level of government. The distribution objective is seldom stated and it is difficult to raise questions as to consistency.

Some understanding of the complexity of the problem can be seen by reference to a special study made by the U.S. Water Resources Council (1975). It surveyed 25 agencies that produce water-related goods and found 185 different cost sharing rules relating to 32 types of products. For some agencies each project may have a specific or unique cost sharing policy for all or some outputs and even different project technologies. There are also variations based on the type of financing--whether by direct Federal or local funding, intergovernmental grants, or loans. There are additional variations in the non-Federal payment terms. Some non-Federal parties pay in advance or during construction whereas others pay their share on the installment plan with and without interest. Some contribute cash and others provide lands or personnel for the project or contribute to the future operating costs. This welter of different rules and methods of participation makes it very difficult to determine in the aggregate how costs of different projects and different agencies compare. The study put all of these variations of participation on a common cost basis and computed the mean effective composite non-Federal cost share by project output and agency. The variation was large as illustrated by rural flood damage reduction, which varied from a low of 7 percent by the Army Corps of Engineers to a high of 60 percent by the Tennessee Valley Authority. Other outputs showed as large or larger differences. This was the first time this information was available and nothing like it exists by income group as opposed to product user category.

The distribution of cost shares between Federal and non-Federal parties affects project design (see Milliman 1969; Loughlin 1970). Local beneficiaries lobby the agencies to design projects in such a way that the Federal cost is maximized because tax incidence differs between local and national taxes.

Many public projects are administered by state or local governments and part or all of the cost is funded by intergovernmental grants from the national level. For example, states in the United States construct highways and the percentage cost share paid by the national government differs according to type of highway. Public higher education in the United States is cost shared between students (tuition) and the states, with limited contribution by the national government, whereas United Kingdom university costs are primarily funded at the national level. Many social services in the United States such as job training are state administered, but Federally funded in part or whole.

The same is true for many cash or in-kind transfer programs such as aid to dependent children (ACIR 1988; Break 1980; Gramlich 1985).

8.4.   Allocation of Joint Cost

Many projects have multiple products that are received and paid for by different people or levels of government. The total costs of these projects must be allocated to the various products. This allocation is straightforward when costs vary by addition of a marginal product (or group of users). But in some cases, there is a portion of the facility that is common to more than one output. Joint cost is defined as cost not attributable to a particular unit or kind of output (Eckstein 1965, Ch. 9). It is inherent in goods in which over some range of use the marginal cost of another use or user is zero. The commonly cited example is multiple purpose water resource projects, but it applies equally to programs such as education where schooling inputs produce both benefits captured by students and a general population benefiting from an educated society.

Joint costs occur in private enterprise as well. The private firm may select the prices of the multiple outputs in such a manner as to maximize profits and let the implicit cost shares (relative prices) fall as they may. Eckstein (1965, 261) suggests that the private firm computes the revenue from some arbitrary set of prices given the intersection of these prices with the demand curves giving quantities demanded. The total cost of producing these quantities is also computed. Then a different set of prices is selected and the process is repeated. From such a calculation it is possible to determine whether the increased revenue of the new set of prices is greater than the increased cost. The process is repeated until the familiar point of marginal revenue equal marginal cost is reached. Profits are then maximized and, if positive, total costs are covered including the joint costs. In practice, it is probable that information cost saving rules of thumb are used. A department store with thousands of items may assign a constant percentage to each product's purchase price to cover joint costs of overhead in administration. However, by tradition certain items carry no overhead, and marketing strategy often involves selling at (or below) cost to attract traffic through the store. In any case, the private firm probably is not trying to achieve a certain income distribution by manipulating relative prices through allocation of the joint costs.

The public firm, however, may not try to maximize profits and can use the opportunity of distributing joint costs to help one group of consumers versus another. The various methods that will be outlined have all been used by some public agency at some time. Each differs according to the concept of its allocation base, that is, the source of the inputs used to relate the parts of the whole.

Engineering Capacity: The physical capacity of the jointly used facilities is computed and the allocation base is the percentage of capacity utilized by each of the multiple outputs. For example, if a reservoir is used for both flood control and hydroelectric power generation, some proportion of the storage capacity is allocated to each. This is rather arbitrary where the stored floor water is released through the electric turbines. Another example from the private sector would be the determination of floor space used by each line of goods in a store, and then allocating joint costs in a similar fashion.

Priority of Use: One of the multiple outputs is chosen as the priority use.[2] This use is then allocated an amount of the joint cost up to the cost of a single purpose project for the priority use. Assume a project that cost $100,000 for the jointly used facilities and produces two products, flood control and power. The single purpose of flood control is chosen as the priority use (usually by technicians rather than policy makers) and a project that only produced flood control costs $80,000. In effect, flood control pays 80 percent of the cost of what it would have paid acting alone. The power outputs are considered marginal and pay the difference only between the single purpose flood control project and the total cost of the multiple purpose project. With this method, the purpose given "priority" gets no benefit from the joint participation.

The allocation of costs depends on which output is designated as the intramarginal and which the extramarginal use. It is the same issue as appeared in Section 8.2.1 on marginal cost pricing. In that case, the output is the same, but is used by different people, such as seats on an airplane. Everyone wants to be designated as the last one on who pays none of the fixed costs of the flight, but only the costs associated with occupancy of one more seat after the prior (priority) passengers have paid fares sufficient to cover the fixed costs. How the marginal passenger is defined, for example, senior citizens, is a policy question. The passenger charged the full fare gets no help in paying the fixed costs just as the use designated as the priority use in a multiple purpose project gets no help toward the joint costs of the project. The other methods to be outlined are less severe in allocating costs but no less demanding of a policy judgment.

Single Purpose Net Benefit: Instead of focusing on costs alone, the allocation base may be related to benefits (when benefits are known). In this method allocation is based on the degree to which benefits exceed single purpose cost (or alternatively separable cost). To illustrate, assume the following data:

Power benefit	100,000	Flood control benefit	120,000
Single purpose cost	35,000	Single purpose cost	53,000
Allocation base	65,000		67,000

Table 8.1 Allocation of Costs by Separable Costs-Remaining Benefits Method (in thousands of dollars)

Item	Flood Control	Power	Irrigation	Navigation	Total
1. Benefits	500	1,500	350	100	2,450
2. Alternative cost	400	1,000	600	80	2,080
3. Benefits limited by alternative cost	400	1,000	350	80	1,830
4. Separable costs	380	600	150	50	1,180
5. Remaining benefits	20	400	200	30	650
6. Residual cost*	18	360	180	27	585
7. Total Allocation (items 4 and 6)	398	960	330	77	1,765

*In this example, the total residual costs to be allocated ($585,000 in line 6) are 90 percent of the total remaining benefits ($65,000 in line 5). Therefore each purpose is charged with residual cost equal to 90 percent of its remaining benefits. The same results will be obtained by using distribution ratios (percentage of each item in line 5 to their total).

Source: U.S. Inter-Agency Committee on Water Resources (1958, 49).

Total allocation base (net benefit) = 65,000 + 67,000 = 132,000. The cost allocated to any purpose is its own allocation base divided by the total, or in the case of power it is 65,000 divided by 132,000 = 49 percent. With this method, no allowance is made for any part of the total multiple use project cost that might be uniquely related to only one kind of output. The methods that follow do make such allowances.

Separable Costs-Remaining Benefits (SCRB): The SCRB allocation base is benefits remaining after subtraction of separable costs. This net figure for any given user cannot exceed the alternative cost of a single purpose project or the users would not join the multiple purpose project. Separable cost is defined as the difference in the cost of the entire project with and without the given purpose. The method is illustrated in Table 8.1 as used by U.S. water resources agencies.

Alternative Justifiable Expenditure (AJE): The AJE allocation base is equal to the lesser of either (1) the benefit or (2) the cost of a single purpose alternative project, each net of *direct costs* defined as cost uniquely necessary to provide the given purpose. In the case of a multiple purpose water project, the cost of the lock would be unique to navigation and the cost of the turbines unique to power. The assignment of items to unique uses requires some judgment in contrast to the straightforward calculation of separable costs in the SCRB method. The contrasting concepts and results of the two methods are illustrated by the following data:

1. Cost of single purpose navigation project, $85,000: low dam ($35,000) plus locks ($50,000).
2. Cost of single purpose flood control project, $48,000: high dam. A dam with the same height with locks incorporated within it is only $45,000.
3. Cost of a multipurpose flood and navigation project, $95,000.

For the *SCRB method* it is necessary to calculate separable costs for each use as follows:

$95,000 cost of multipurpose project
$48,000 cost of single purpose flood project
$47,000 separable cost of navigation

$95,000 cost of multipurpose project
$85,000 cost of single purpose navigation project)
$10,000 separable cost of flood control

For the *AJE method* it is necessary to calculate direct costs as follows:

$50,000 direct costs uniquely assigned to navigation (locks)
$10,000 direct costs uniquely assigned to flood control (cost of higher dam with more flood retention capacity but locks incorporated within it, $45,000, less the cost of the low dam, $35,000)

In some cases the separable costs and direct costs may be the same, but they may often differ because the margin is defined in a different way. In the preceding case, the separable cost concept defines the margin as $48,000 to $95,000 whereas direct costs are $95,000 to $45,000. The SCRB method continues as follows (recall that the allocation base is remaining benefits):

	Navigation		Flood Control		Total
Benefits*	$100,000		$80,000		
Separable cost	$47,000		$10,000		$57,000
Remaining benefits	$53,000	plus	$70,000	=	$123,000
	43%	plus	57%	=	100%

*Note that benefits are limited by the size of alternative costs.

In contrast the AJE method is primarily related to costs. It relates only indirectly to benefits that serve only to justify cost.

	Navigation		Flood Control		
Single purpose cost	$85,000		$48,000		
Direct cost	$50,000		$10,000		
	$35,000	plus	$38,000	=	$73,000
	48%	plus	52%	=	100%

Note that the percentage paid by each purpose differs in the two methods. The joint costs to be allocated also differ as follows:

	SCRB		AJE
Total cost	$95,000	Total cost	$95,000
Total separable cost	$57,000	Total direct cost	$60,000
Total cost to be allocated	$38,000		$35,000

The end result of the two methods can be contrasted:

AJE: Navigation pays 48 percent of $35,000 = $16,000 + direct costs of $50,000 = $66,800

SCRB: Navigation pays 43 percent of $38,000 = $16,340 + separable costs of $47,000 = $63,340

All of these methods have attracted debate as to which one is correct. Eckstein (1965) rejects certain methods (such as engineering capacity) that according to marginal principles might cause the unjustified rejection of a particular purpose (use) when its benefits could not cover its assigned costs. Within broad ranges acceptable methods produce widely different income distributions. The issue is not one of who subsidizes whom, as the definition of subsidy requires an initial policy judgment of initial rights distribution. The issue is how to allocate the advantages of joint action, and it is reduced to who is considered the marginal use (or user). The rules for allocating joint costs are part of the wealth of persons just as are their land titles or stock certificates. The question can be submerged and made to appear technical with complicated formulas and definitions, but it can only be resolved by reference to a public choice of distributive objectives. If the general character of the end results is specified, the analyst can select a formula to achieve it.

Projects that are similar except for the amount of joint costs and the relative size of such costs to single purpose and separable costs, benefits, and so on will have their ranking affected by the joint cost allocation rule applied. It will also affect the charge to the grants budget and thus the grants efficiency ratio. It is advantageous for a group to be declared the owner of the major share of the advantages of joint production because this lowers the group's assigned cost, which has to be covered by its own payments or tax transfers. In other words, as in the computation of direct national income benefits, it is better to get yours before any subsequent flows get labeled as transfers and redistributions.

8.5.   Pecuniary Interdependencies (Externalities)

The building of a sizable project or a series of projects can often affect both input and output prices (the same is true of the necessary taxes, see Break 1974). These effects on people's wealth via market exchange and prices are called *pecuniary externalities*. In general, the conventional prescription in economic theory is to ignore these effects for several reasons (McKean 1958, 139).

These changes in relative prices are the signals of a market economy for a reallocation of resources. If these incentives for mobility are modified, then some other signaling device is needed. Further, it is generally argued that wage reductions (increases) and asset losses (gains) are short lived in competitive markets and as the resources move to new uses, normal returns are again earned. This, however, is true only in the absence of fixed assets (see Schmid 1987, 115-19). Whereas resources have unique uses or are otherwise fixed, the change in price results in permanent losses and income change. For example, public investments in irrigation in the southwestern United States resulted in the loss of income for former producers of cotton in the South (Tolley 1959) and an increase in wages and rents in the southwest. The land and immobile machinery in the old South were reduced in value and though many farmers moved to northern industrial areas, they created costly social problems. For an estimate of the displacement effects of a new recreation project on prices at old substitute sites, see Mansfield (1971).

It is generally argued that although a project may reduce input prices in one area, it creates new rents in another so that national income is not changed.[3] This may be true for national income accounting, but it does not avoid the distributive question. This was explored in Section 6.5.8 on indirect and employment effects.

In summary, the size, performance, and incidence of pecuniary effects must be noted. If these effects are negative and inconsistent with income distribution objectives, the affected individuals can be afforded rights, and compensation paid as for any other unrightful diminution of property rights. Suffice it to say that it is surely inconsistent to have an explicit transfer program favoring a certain group and then reduce that group's income by building projects that reduce their wages and destroy their asset values (including human capital) via price change. On the other hand, new demand for inputs may create rents that may or may not contribute to distribution objectives.

8.6.   Technological Interdependencies

A public project may utilize inputs whose ownership is unclear, or at least a particular party's interest in the resource is made effective only by an accounting in the context of a benefit-cost analysis.   Technological externalities are the essence of the physical interdependence caused by incompatible uses and users in the context of scarcity (see Section 2.4. and Schmid 1987, 44). For example, a public as well as a private project may put wastes into the air or water. A resource is consumed (clean air or water) as surely as the land input used for a government building. In the case of land, the government will have to pay market value (by negotiation or eminent domain) or be sued for theft. If it uses someone's clean air or quiet street, the court may not listen to claims of theft if the government has not previously given such a right to groups or individuals. If those affected acknowledge their lack of ownership, their only option is to make a bid to avoid the effect. This bid whether accepted or not is an opportunity cost of the project.

What if the analyst suspects that the bid recorded is much less than willingness to pay because of transaction costs (such as those involved in free rider behavior)? The government may want to act as the agent for those making the bid. To reduce transaction costs, it could collect taxes from those affected. If the bid is high enough, the government may refrain from using the input in question in its project. What would the government do with the taxes so collected? Distribute them as a dividend to all citizens deemed owners of the right to use clean air and water for public purposes? This sounds incredulous even if conceptually logical. In practice, governments place constraints on their own projects. For example, the United States may not build a water development project if a required input involves the extinction of a natural species. The original Endangered Species Act in effect puts an infinite price on this input (at least larger than any conceivable project benefit). It assumes that the owners of the opportunity to enjoy snail darters (Tellico Dam) would reject any offer of money in exchange for their resource (Gramlich 1981, 146).

Conceptually, analysts might urge government to be more flexible and put some finite price on resources for which they act as agents in the name of the "owners." If this were done and the resource were used in a project, it would raise the question of compensation of those who formerly enjoyed the use of the resource. The philosophical and practical problem of doing this is probably why governments prefer to use absolute constraints rather than administrative pricing and exchange.

It is difficult for the analyst to construct a systematic display of distributive effects when property rights are not clear. It is possible for government to order the owner of a resource to give up its use (forfeit the use right) for a public project, the beneficiaries of which may be other people. This is conceptually the same as a transfer of income via taxes. But it is rather easier to account for a direct money income transfer than it is to account for the transfer of use rights, particularly when the initial allocation of the use right was vague. But to say something is difficult is no reason to ignore it, even if the best that can be done is to chart qualitative shifts in direction. Otherwise governments may find themselves in the position of taxing use rights away from the very poor to whom they are otherwise making money transfers. But if an administrative price is put on inputs provided by nontarget groups, there may be a temptation to inflate values to make it appear as if large grants are being made to the targets.

8.7. Cash versus In-Kind Transfers

What is the value of in-kind goods consumed by project beneficiaries who would otherwise be too poor to purchase them? For example, what is the value of public housing or parks to those too poor to have effective demand? The opportunity cost of these resources is easy to compute, but what is the value of the transfer received? (See Prescott 1974.) In the case of cash transfers, the usual convention is to regard the B/C ratio as unity. Even if this is explicitly accepted by policy makers, how shall in-kind transfers be conceived? If it is valued as the willingness to sell after it is received (compensating variation) it is different from willingness to pay, if it creates an income effect (which is common in the case of the poorest people).

If the efficiency of transfers is to be evaluated, then a system for comparing alternatives is needed including those of cash and in-kind consumer goods. If the output is valued at its general market value (not willingness to pay of the recipient),[4] the B/C ratio could be positive, but misleading in the sense that the recipients might have preferred cash or another good because of their particular income level and preferences. If public choice decides that the cash inputs were just temporarily in the hands of "donors" but really belong to some other ultimate recipient, then it is the recipient's preferences that count. A stigma may attach to cash transfers, but should be checked rather than assumed. On the other hand, from the point of view of the giver of the transfer, the transfer may have been intended to remove an externality caused by the particular consumption of the recipient. An example is public housing removal of slums as an eyesore. In this case the value to the giver may exceed the market value. Alternatively, housing codes may be enforced that may cause tenants to allocate more of their income to housing if landlords raise rents (Ackerman 1971). It would be difficult to chart whether the resulting transfer was from landlords or tenants to others in the community.

The question can be resolved only by a public choice of the property rights allocation of the resource in question. If the input costs are owned by the "donor" then it is their point of view that should count rather than the preferences of the recipient (Friedman 1984, 65). If the donors derive utility from changing the specific consumption of the recipients, then cash transfers are removed from consideration. It is difficult to see how further systematic comparison of alternative in-kind goods might proceed. Relative market prices do not indicate the relative utility obtained by donors from changing one specific consumption pattern to another. It is a property rights conflict between the poor and those claiming the public treasury to reduce the negative externalities caused by the specific consumption patterns of the poor.

Cash transfers can also be made in the form of wage subsidies for those employed in public project construction and operation. A rule requiring government to pay going wages for unemployed labor has distributive implications (recall Section 6.5.1). If returns do not cover the nominal wage, the wage paid above opportunity cost is a transfer. This grant tied inadvertently to projects may not have been the transfer that would have been explicitly chosen in the absence of the project. If returns cover nominal wages, then the issue is whether labor or users of project output get the gain above opportunity cost. In other words, who owns the production made possible by increasing aggregate demand to the full employment level?

Public choice must decide whether the formerly unemployed have an income claim or if any wage payment is a transfer from other rightful claimants. A transfer is equivalent to saying that unemployment is the fault of the unemployed rather than a macro policy failure. When aggregate demand is lacking, the unemployed person who is newly employed on a public project may be just as skilled and hard working as the already employed. Who is intramarginal and who is extramarginal is often highly arbitrary in disequilibrium.

Alternatively, if aggregate demand had been increased by expanded money supply and a tax cut, the subsequent increase in private spending would put the unemployed to work at the going wage. The wage would then be regarded as rightful and not a transfer. Public choice must decide whether the relevant opportunity cost defining transfers is what the labor could get in the present economy or in a fully employed economy.

An adequate distributional display should be able to compare productive investments, provision of specific consumption, cash grants, input or consumption subsidies, as well as regulatory approaches such as code enforcement and rent control.[5] Regulation redirects resources as surely as any taxation and spending program, though often with different incidence (see Schmid 1969b; Gramlich 1981, Ch. 11). The grants display does not settle the rights issues, but it does indicate the trade-offs for political choice.

8.8.   Distributive Weights

The most commonly advocated method of implementing distributive objectives is to weight benefits received by targeted groups (Marglin 1967, 25;

Helmers 1979; Sugden and Williams 1978, 201). Two approaches to deriving weights have been suggested. One infers weights from past project choice decisions (Weisbrod 1968) or tax incidence decisions (Eckstein 1961, 448; Christiansen and Jansen 1978) or from a more active and explicit interaction of analyst and decision makers (Dasgupta et al. 1972). Weisbrod computes a solution to a series of simultaneous equations that include data on benefit-cost ratios, order undertaken, and distribution of benefits. The solution is then used to derive a weight on the benefits to different groups consistent with the choices made. The mathematics of the model requires the same number of projects and groups. This undesirable constraint could be avoided by the use of discriminant analysis (Pearce and Nash 1981, 36), which is conceptually similar. Haveman (1968) has critiqued the preference revelation model by noting that the weights are sensitive to the number of projects included and thus the entire budget must be included, which creates prohibitive data and computational requirements. In addition, the use of the results requires an assumption of decision maker awareness of their distributive objectives and results. If decision makers were clear about their distributive objectives, there would be no need for the analyst to describe what they had already done.

The approach of Dasgupta et al. (1972, 139-48) insures distributive awareness of decision makers by preparing distributive information and then asking for explicit project choices. The analyst displays the benefits of two alternative projects to two groups and calculates a distributive weight called a switching value that would make the total benefits of the two alternatives equal. Then the decision makers are asked to make a project choice, and from that choice it can be inferred that the weight is greater or lesser than the switching value. Theoretically if decision makers were consistent, a large number of these pairwise choices would reveal a unique weight that could then be used for future project evaluations.

The assumptions necessary to derive weights stretch one's credulity. But there are other shortcomings of the concept. Weighting can mask an inefficient transfer unless cash grants are also displayed and weighted. A monetary unit of input can produce less than a unit of output, in which case the cash transfer would be a more efficient transfer instrument. Champions of the cause of the poor may rejoice when a large weight is attached to benefits received by the poor. But the same weight multiplied by cash would produce a larger B/C ratio. Bish (1969) indicated that it takes $109 per unit expenditure of U.S. public housing to produce a unit having a market value of $75. If this benefit to a poor target group were weighted by 1.5 it would look good in absolute terms, but not relative to cash grants. If a cutoff B/C ratio of unity is used to suggest budget size, a positive weight on project benefits and cash grants would suggest no limit on the amount of money to be transferred as no cash grant would ever have a ratio of less than unity.

Weighting benefits can have little explicit meaning to politicians or the public. Whether weights were chosen directly or derived from project choices, the total size of the resulting transfer would not be explicit. The size of the actual transfer would be clear only when the weights were actually applied to the total supply of available projects.[6]

Alternatively, the decision can focus on how much is to be transferred to a certain group rather than the size of the weight. This argues for a two-step public decision making process. First, the public decides on the extent and recipients of an annual grants (transfer) budget. Amounts are specified for each group. Then the analysts can display the effectiveness of alternative transfer instruments in terms of the recipients gaining the most from the amount to be transferred. It is equivalent to an objective function of maximizing net aggregate consumption gains (national income) subject to the constraint that various target groups receive the maximum consumption gains associated with exhausting their grants budgets. In this formulation, the *size of the grant* is explicitly chosen and the *size of the consumption gain* for target groups is a derivation; alternatively, when the minimum consumption gain for the target is explicitly chosen, the size of the grant is a derivation (Marglin 1967, 25). Donor groups whose objective is a minimum consumption gain for the target will grant more than donors whose charity is influenced by actual grants efficiency opportunities. However, if the decision focuses on weights, the size of the grant is not clear.

Use of the grants budget method implies a certain weighting of benefits to recipients that could be derived from the process, but it is more meaningful as a derivative summary of results than as a subject of explicit choice. For example, derivation of weights can compare grants budgets over time to determine whether changes are the result of changes in donor's utility function or only of changes in size of income. In comparing alternatives, it should be remembered that cash grants can be made as direct payments or by increased cost sharing for a project received by the target group. The latter reduces the group's taxes or user fees.

Entitlement programs make it difficult to choose explicitly the size of the grant budget and to compare transfer instruments. The U.S. Congress specifies that individuals meeting certain criteria of physical or family status are entitled to cash grants. Since the environment affects the number of people in a given status category, the amount of the grant budget is not fully known in advance. Politicians adjust the budget indirectly by adjusting eligibility requirements. There is some iterative process between donors' general desire to help others in certain categories and the size of the donation. Entitlements have elements of a property right and are stronger than a fixed appropriation (Wildavsky 1988).

8.9.   Grants Account Display

The challenge is to construct a display of the distributive effects of alternative projects so that alternative transfer instruments can be compared after the size of the transfer is explicitly decided. As a practical matter, national income budget size will be constrained so that not all national income efficient projects are built. The following steps are suggested:

1. Ask the political authority to set the amount of the grants budget to be given to each target group they wish to identify (including intergovernmental grants that eventually reach the target). The origin of the grant (donor) should also be chosen. The problem of cash benefits versus in-kind consumption changes is discussed later.

2. A display such as shown in Table 8.2 could be developed for each project and each selected target indicating the size of the distributive effect for each of the categories previously noted. The central budget agency would (1) aggregate the various transfer sources incidentally embodied in projects already selected to maximize returns to the national income budget as charges against the grants budget for each target group and determine if any of the budget remains, and (2) rank the remaining projects including cash grants[7] by the grant efficiency ratio and select those projects to utilize any remaining grants budget. If there were no national income budget size constraint, there would be no more available efficient projects. The grants efficiency of line 17 is not the same concept as the national income accounts efficiency shown in line 1. The size of the grants budget is explicitly chosen by public choice and is not obtained by application of some grant efficiency calculations or weights.

Each line in the table is now summarized and further issues noted:

Line 1 contains the results of applying property rights rules called for in previous chapters, including any politically priced nonmarketed outputs. Note that if project costs are reduced to reflect opportunity costs of unemployed resources and the treasury still pays going wages, there is already a transfer (recorded in line 8 if received by a targeted group).

Line 2 shows the part of the line 1 national income benefits that goes to a selected target.

Line 3 reflects a policy choice to accept or modify the national income values to accept the point of view of grant donors or of recipient's preferences (Section 8.7).

Line 4 is that part of the gross benefits of line 1 that accrues to those other than the target. It may include cost savings accruing to consumers as price reductions. Where the benefits in line 1 are from a cash grant (project E), line 4 shows a negative transfer of national income from others to the target. For a cash grant, the negative benefit of line 4 is equal to the tax transfer of line 10. The gains to others can be subdivided into as many groups as data permit and distributive objectives require.

Line 5 is the target group's share of separable costs, which are those costs uniquely necessary to produce the benefits going to the target. In project A, because all project benefits accrue to the target group they should pay all of the project cost of 50. In project B, assuming the separable cost is

Table 8.2 Hypothetical Display of Grants Budget Performance for a Target Group

				Project		
	Distributive Factors	A	B	C	D	E (cash grants)
1.	B/C ratio national income all groups	100/50	100/50	9/10	18/10	10/10
2.	National income gain to target (selective productivity)	100	50	9	18	10
3.	Willingness to pay by target group?	-	-	-	-	-
4.	National income benefit to others	0	50	0	0	-10
5.	Target group's share of separable cost	50	10	10	10	10
6.	Joint cost allocation to target	0	10	0	0	0
7.	Result of departure from flat price user fees to other buyers in favor of target	0	2	0	0	0
8.	Result of departure from opportunity cost wages if paid to target	0	0	0	0	0
9.	Gain to target net of all projects costs (2 - 5 - 6)	50	30	-1	8	0
10.	Gross tax transfer (5 + 6 + 8 - 7)	50	18	10	10	10
11.	Actual cost to target (user fees and identfiable taxes)	0	2	0	0	0
12.	Net potential tax transfer (10 - 11)	50	16	10	10	10
13.	Technical and pecuniary grants	8	0	0	0	0
14.	Technical and pecuniary transfers received by target	8	-10	0	0	0
15.	Grant total (from donors) (7 + 8 + 12 + 13)	58	8	10	10	10
16.	Total net potential gain to target (2 + 14 - 11)	108	38	9	18	10
17.	Grantor B/C (grant efficiency) (16 / 15)	108/58 1.8	36/8 4.5	9/10 0.9	18/10 1.8	10/10 1.0

10, the remaining 40 is a joint cost to be allocated by some publicly chosen rule (perhaps the separable cost-remaining benefit rule as discussed in Section 8.4). The table shows the total allocated cost (line 5 plus 6) to be 20 for the target group. As will be explained further, it is not possible at the project level to determine what percentage of this assigned cost is actually paid by the target.

Line 7 indicates when there is some differential output pricing being applied in the context of decreasing cost to scale as discussed in Section 8.2.1 or in the context of nonmarginal projects discussed in Sections 7.2.1 and 7.6.

There is none in project A, but in B some other groups pay more than the target group for the same good or service, which may reduce the amount in lines 5 and 6 that has to be covered by taxes. An example would be target group irrigators who pay less for a cubic meter of water from a multiple purpose reservoir than municipal or industrial users pay. Some other group loses some net benefit and pays for the fixed costs whereas the target group pays only the marginal cost. The allocation of *joint costs* among uses (products) in line 6, the allocation of *fixed costs* among users of the same kind of product produced under economies of scale, and *price differentiation* for nonmarginal projects (both in line 7), all involve similar distributive issues (Schmid 1987, Chs. 5 and 6).

Line 8 indicates the results of public choice on whether project wage payments to unemployed target workers above opportunity cost are transfers or not as discussed in Section 6.5.1.

Line 9 is gain to target net of all allocated project costs (national income gain to target minus target's share of costs). It indicates the net productivity obtainable by incurring the project's costs. It is negative for inefficient projects such as C with respect to national income benefits and costs, and zero for cash grants

Line 10 is the potential tax transfer if the target paid none of its costs. It is included only as a computational step. The potential net tax transfer of line 12 is the gross tax transfer minus any user charges or special identifiable taxes levied against the target group (line 11). The term "potential" tax transfer is used because there is no way of knowing what general taxes (e.g., income taxes) are paid by the target at the project level. Lines 10 and 12 are not descriptions of what exists, but a synthetic conceptual reference point to give all project alternatives a common base. If this were a national project the national taxpayers would be the source of the potential grant unless the states were required to contribute. If this were a state or municipal level project the state or municipal taxpayers would not be the whole source of the transfer if there were intergovernmental grants as discussed in Section 8.3 on cost sharing.

Line 11 is actual cost paid by the target in user fees and any special taxes that are directly incurred by individuals as a result of the project, including tuition, entrance fees to parks, gas taxes for boats, or special property taxes as discussed in Section 8.3.

Line 13 includes technological and pecuniary externalities. Technological grants involve the administratively priced value of nonmarketed inputs to the project as discussed in Section 8.6. An example would be an airport that creates noise although no compensation is paid from the public treasury. In some cases there may be market reference values, but in other cases it may be a non-market-related consumption good (such as destruction of an ancient burial ground by a highway). In project A, line 13 suggests that the national income cost of 50 in line 1 is wrong. The cost is really 58 but the target group or treasury pays only 50 with 8 paid outside of the government. Line 13 also includes pecuniary transfers (implicit grants)-- for example, employers paying wages bid up as a result of the project (Sections 6.5.8 and 8.5) and losses in the value of nontarget group assets (such as rent losses noted in Sections 5.5 and 7.4 because of nonmarginal increase in supply). That part of the transfer received by the target is included in line 14.

Line 14 is the project-caused change in prices for goods and services sold or bought by the target. As noted, the project may increase the market price of labor sold by the target group to project and nonproject buyers. Or it may cause a decrease in the price of output sold by the target, such as a decrease in the price of cotton for all cotton farmers caused by an increased cotton supply from new irrigation projects, giving a negative number as in project B. This incorporates the indirect wage transfers calculated in Chapter 6 and the rents of Sections 5.5 and 7.4. Increases in direct wage payments to targeted project construction workers are already included in line 8. The source of these transfers includes the implicit grants shown in lines 7, 8, and 13, although some does not reach the target.

Line 15 is the total grant given by donors summing line 12 potential net tax transfer, line 7 differential pricing effect, line 8 project wage above opportunity cost, and line 13 technological and pecuniary externalities. This total is charged to the grants budget. If distributive objectives were already met by lump-sum transfers, there would be no need of a grants budget.

Line 16 is the potential net gain to the target group that comes from the productivity of the project and transfers. It is the sum of line 2 gain to target, plus technological and pecuniary gains in line 14, minus any actual payments made by the target in line 11. This potential net gain assumes the target group pays no general taxes.

Line 17 expresses the efficiency of each alternative as a vehicle for making a grant. It is the ratio of the target group's net gain to the grant cost incurred to achieve the target's gain. The grantor B/C ratio is a synthetic concept to guide project choice in the right direction and not a description of what will happen, since description of net effects is impossible at the individual project level.

If the table included all spending alternatives in the national budget that impact the target, then the sum of line 16 net gain (omitting line 12) could be compared with actual taxes and fees paid by the target. The difference is made up of the productivity of investment projects plus grants. Therefore the actual grant could be computed as follows: net gain line 16 minus net productivity of the project line 9 minus actual taxes and fees equals the actual grant from others to the target. However, if the budget is unbalanced, some of the gain to the target is financed by borrowing and perhaps credit creation rather than taxes (see Peacock, 1974).

Whatever the size of the grants budget, choosing projects according to their grant efficiency ratio would maximize the gain to the target. For ease in demonstration, assume that B, C, D, and E are available and that the grant total is the same for each. If the grants budget were 20 then B and D would be chosen with total potential net gain (38 and 18) = 56, which is larger than for any other combination of available projects. It is possible that the actual aggregative taxes and fees are larger than 20 so that no grant is actually made (although positive returns may be earned on the target's investment). The best vehicles for transfer have been chosen, but the tax structure has defeated the intended grant. This ultimate systems test melding aggregate spending and taxation seems to require more information than can be produced and can be approached only with the macro studies noted in Section 8.10.1.

8.9.1. Tax Transfers

Musgrave (1969, 804-05) suggests that "if distributional effects of expenditures are included in the objective function, this would seem to call for a similar inclusion of the distributional effects of the financing mechanism." This is impossible to do on a project-by-project basis and must be done in the aggregate by a central agency that can then provide guidance to each project agency consistent with the overall distributive objectives.

In Table 8.2 the target group's share of costs is noted (separable plus joint cost allocation lines 5 and 6). It is easy to compute any of these costs that might be paid as user fees or as direct benefit taxes (such as assessments against property for improvement line 11). But how shall contributions to general taxation be considered? Haveman (1965, 89) in a distributive analysis of the U.S. Army Corps of Engineers water projects assumed that the target group (in his case a geographical region) paid for projects in the same proportion as their payment toward total tax financed spending (also see Shabman and Kalter 1969). But this is quite artificial. Groups pay into a common pool but can benefit only from certain governmental expenditures. The fact that they receive a higher percentage of a given program than their percentage of the total Federal taxes paid just indicates what projects are relevant to them; it indicates nothing about net distribution, which must consider the other programs they did not use (but in Haveman's analysis are assumed to have benefited from in proportion to their contribution of total taxes). Although it is impossible to allocate general taxes to a project, it is conceptually possible to sum up benefits of all projects to a group and compare it to their taxes. This macro net description has its uses (see Section 8.10) but not for comparative project grants efficiency analysis.

What this means operationally is that line 12 is equal to the unpaid part of the costs (net of user fees and direct taxes) assigned to the target group. To examine the efficiency of each project alternative as a transfer vehicle, each is treated as if all of its remaining tax costs were paid by others. So the potential tax transfer equals the net cost of the project assigned to the target group and appears in the grants budget display.

The total potentially granted is summed from all sources (line 15) and compared to the net benefits received by the target for each transfer instrument or project (line 16). A grants efficiency ratio may be calculated (line 17) and projects chosen accordingly to exhaust the grants budget. If in fact a group pays more in total taxes than it gets in total public projects, at least the choice of efficient grants instruments implementing its grants budget has minimized the loss. The aggregative analysis that could help government decide on the size of the grants budget is the subject of Section 8.10. Productive investment will be favored over cash grants and cash grants will be favored over unproductive projects. However from the recipients' point of view, they may prefer to receive wages and products from an uneconomic project rather than more money in the form of a cash grant which is labeled a hand out. Administrative costs should be netted out. Any "deadweight" losses associated with certain types of taxes can make the transfer (line 10) greater than nominal tax payments (see Gramlich 1981, 24; Okun 1975, Ch. 4). This is qualified and discussed further below in section 8.10.7. Existing transfer programs can be put in the same budget system to see if they should be continued. As long as the net cost to the target is assumed to be zero, all transfer alternatives are judged on an equal basis and can be compared in terms of their efficiency in delivering the grant to the intended target.

If the pecuniary transfers are negative for the target, the net total grant is reduced. If a chosen group is disadvantaged by price changes, it must be made up to them (as if it were added to their grant budget). This is conceptually superior to constraining national income project selection if it disadvantaged a group.

A distributive accounting broadened to include pecuniary effects is difficult and costly and could be done only on a limited scale. Yet its conceptual impact on policy can be substantial. The presently available analyses focus on the size of public expenditures for different income groups. Donors may believe that they help the poor with spending, but the poor may receive no net benefit because of declining prices for what they have to sell (or rising prices for what they have to buy). The poor are threatened by shifts in demand for their services occasioned by both public and private spending. Some would prefer property rights in a job rather than public spending and transfers.

8.9.2. Intergroup and Interaccount Conflicts

A grants display could be made for all projects considered for the national income accounts (nongrants budget). Any transfers incidental to those projects selected are charged against the grant budget. For these national income projects, line 15 indicates the amount to be charged.[8] But the recipients may have preferred that the grant be used in another project that has a more productive grant efficiency ratio rather than being incidental to projects chosen in the national income budget. This is a question of property rights and who controls inputs. If the "donor" is in control, the fact that the receiver would prefer a different producer (or consumer) good is irrelevant. A similar issue arose in the discussion of in-kind projects in Section 8.7.

The problem of multiple groups of beneficiaries with different degrees of enthusiasm for a project based on differences in their net return rates is submerged if only total net returns are considered. There are always conflicts in group projects and it is a property right decision as to which group dominates. In fact, no country builds projects in order of their total rate of return ranking, and some dominant groups get projects that favor them even at the cost of a higher overall B/C ratio project, which is forgone under budget constraints.

A project with a higher national income (line 1) that does not benefit the target may have been passed over in the national income accounts competition because of budget constraints. This project is not built, whereas a poorer national income project benefiting the target group gets built to meet the grants budget objective. Why not build the better project and use the net returns to make cash grants to the target? This trade-off can be noted in the previously suggested framework and is a data input into public decisions on grants budget size. But as a practical measure, it is not so easy to convince the intermediary recipients of the "better" project benefits that they are just a vehicle to aid some other target group and must pass on their net benefit in taxes. Taxing systems do not work that smoothly from either an administrative or psychological view.

If there is more than one target group there may be conflicts between grant objectives. The most efficient transfer instrument for one target group may have pecuniary and technological externalities for another target group. This conflict would require a political choice of the trade-off between target groups.

8.10. What Governments Do

8.10.1 Macro Distribution Studies

If first-best costless income transfers are not available to achieve income distribution objectives, government needs to consider the net aggregate effect of transfers, taxes, pricing, cost allocations, and so on. If grants budget displays such as the one presented in Table 8.2 were available, the micro level project data could be periodically aggregated to determine the total net grant or transfer (line 15) and resulting income gain for different groups (line 16, net potential gain to target minus actual total tax paid). In the absence of these data, ex post macro level net expenditure studies are possible to provide background for public decisions on transfer objectives. Reference will be made below to analytic practices used in both ex post macro country studies describing the results governments have achieved and to current practices used by governments in their preproject micro project studies. The study of the methodology of the macro distribution studies also illuminates many of the issues raised by construction of the grants budget performance table.

Macro studies are of two types: (1) redistribution studies that allocate all spending and taxes, and then by reference to some original income concept (without government intervention) define the extent of redistribution (expressed as mean benefit as a percentage of mean original income for specified groups), and (2) distribution studies that allocate spending but not taxes, and are content to describe the distribution of expenditure by groups. Although the term benefit is sometimes used, these macro country studies do not try to compute benefits but only allocate expenditures. Benefit studies will not be possible until such data are built up by micro studies, which place values on the outputs of government projects.

Redistribution studies such as O'Higgins and Ruggles (1981) utilize census or other official surveys to indicate program use and taxes paid (see also Bird and DeWulf 1973; Musgrave, et al. 1974; Gillespie 1976; Ruggles and O'Higgins 1981). Where the specific data are lacking, allocating routines are used to assign taxes and expenditures according to proxies for use such as income or family characteristics. Some of these proxies are supported by research and others are largely based on hunch and convention. The data of O'Higgins and Ruggles (1981) for the United States and United Kingdom show that expenditures varied only slightly with income whereas taxes increased with income indicating substantial redistribution toward lower income groups. Expenditures made to provide goods and services to a group net of the group's taxes can be computed without accounting for the level of government at which the taxes are collected and the money transferred (intergovernmental grants) to the level of government managing the expenditures.

Distribution studies such as Meerman (1979) and Selowsky (1979) utilize household consumption surveys to reduce the need for proxies in allocating expenditures. They focus on health, education, and public utilities. Goods with high exclusion costs such as national defense are not included. Meerman's (1979, 320) data for Malaysia show similar expenditures for the middle income quintiles with a lower amount for the lowest quintile and a higher amount for the richest group. It should also be noted that some studies are confined to the tax side alone, such as Pechman and Okner (1974).

Many of the same issues arise in both types of macro country studies and will be discussed in the following section according to the topic headings used earlier in the chapter. In general these studies treat these issues as technical questions, deciding the issue on the basis of theory or data availability. This is in contrast to the theme of this book that many of the issues are a matter of property rights choice, which must be given by the political representative.

8.10.2. Starting Place (Original Income)

To define redistribution there must be a reference point as to the income that would have prevailed without the government activity in question. The previous redistribution studies utilize income before taxes and spending, including transfers. No one believes that this represents what would occur in the absence of government (Prest 1968, 88). O'Higgins (1980, 41-42) uses the before tax and transfer income in empirical work, but has expressed grave doubts because it does not acknowledge possible private substitutes for public programs. He prefers the concept of disposable income as it contains no explicit pretensions to be the without government situation. Whether it is explicit or not does not satisfy Meerman (1979, Ch. 2), who states categorically that estimating budget incidence for an economy without government is impossible because of the difficulty of measuring the general equilibrium effects of spending and taxes including subsequent changes in the price structure (more on this in Section 8.10.6. on indirect effects). This is why he eschews redistribution measures and addresses only the distribution of expenditures in a partial equilibrium analysis holding prices, production functions, and asset endowments constant and independent of budget activity.

This debate is largely in technical terms with only a suggestion that the issue is a matter of public policy. There certainly are formidable technical measurement problems. However, defining redistribution is not only a technical problem, it requires a public choice to legitimize the reference point. A given level of transfer payment can become a property right as much as owning land, inheriting a dividend-producing stock certificate, or income enhanced by publicly provided inputs (including social overhead costs).[9] Whatever is included in "original income" becomes rightful property and thus involves a political, not a technical decision. Other sources of income then get defined as transfers from the property of others. The distinction between corporate dividend payments to stockholders and "welfare payments" financed from corporate profits is a social one. Stockholders are regarded as rightful claimants in profits whereas welfare recipients may or may not be rightful. The fact that government acts as trustee for the recipients (and participates in setting the size of the "dividend" as an owner might otherwise be expected to do) does not alter its similar functional character. The difference is that welfare recipients are often regarded as benefiting from someone else's property rather than the corporation being regarded as the temporary holder of revenues that must be paid to the revenues' ultimate owners. Any cost is paid from gross revenues only because a claim is owned. Ownership should be determineed by government explicitly, not by analysts theoretically or as a matter of measurement convenience.

Under the usual concept of original income used in redistribution studies, any revenue from publicly owned resources (and trading profits from state enterprise) paid as cash benefits is labeled a transfer payment. Then a group who pays taxes but receives a citizen's per capita share of the receipts would be regarded as benefiting from a redistribution. Yet, it is surely not from the property of others. If a private corporation uses the public's air and water, any general tax payment is often seen as tribute rather than payment for a productive input, and its distribution to public owners is often labeled a transfer. But this depends on whether the general public is the chosen rightful owner of these natural resources.

Many old-age benefit recipients receive more than they paid into the program. Yet much of the investments they made publicly and privately in their children can be repaid only by a tax on current incomes. Are the aged pensioners living off the property of others or off of their own property collectively invested and turned over to a collective trustee for repayment (perhaps with a variable rate of interest)? The point is that the definition of earned and transfer income is a matter of property rights and not a technical matter.

The life cycle presents another starting point conceptual problem. Most of the current social programs are oriented toward identifiable groups, for example, the old, those with children in school, or patients in hospitals. Public sympathy with these groups is affected by whether their needs are temporary or are locked in for generations. It would be useful to compute net income (or consumption) distribution over the life cycle.

To determine the amount of spending going to any group, it is necessary to allocate capital expenditures (O'Higgins and Ruggles 1981, 299; O'Higgins 1980, 32-33). Because of lack of data Selowsky (1979) omits capital expenditure altogether, and Meerman (1979, 64) estimates that replacement costs are 14 percent of capital expenditures (a kind of annual depreciation charge). Peacock (1974, 157-58) disagrees with these attempts to allocate expenditures when received rather than when made. These procedures reduce the amount allocated to a group at a given time, but still do not solve the problem of movement into and out of groups over the life cycle or account for changes and use of capital stocks.

The problem is partly one of data and partly a question of property rights, and the data problem confounds the rights choice. The rights issue is based on the objectives of distribution. Some donors do not care about life cycle consequences. They are interested in removing the negative externalities associated with a specific kind of consumer. Membership in the group may change, but it is only the current members who create the externality and the fact that some members move on to better things is of no interest to this class of donor. On the other hand, other donors may be primarily motivated by the net life cycle consequences and the size of their grant and sympathy is a function of expected lifetime net flows. Neither group wants capital costs ignored because they want to compare the efficiency of capital versus current expenditures. But one group wants the annual capital equivalent charged against the grants account established for a group with shifting membership whereas the other wants it charged to the grants objective set for individuals over the life cycle. It is a question of choosing the target group eligible for the grant.

Choice of target groups can have a large effect on distribution conclusions. If groups with changing members are used, the amount of redistribution may be illusory. The higher income groups tend to be mature (no children at home), so it appears that these groups are redistributing money to others (those with children at school and the elderly). But, to a significant extent, they are just paying for benefits they received in the past when they had school children and will receive in the future when they are old. The amount of money actually going from the richer lifetime to the poorer lifetime groups is much less than what gets termed redistribution (Hansen and Weisbrod, 1969; comment by McGuire, 1978; Hight and Pollock 1973).

The grants display in Section 8.9. differs fundamentally in that it is in terms of value of benefits, but it does allocate an annual amount of spending (probably best seen as more or less constant) that can be spent on a target group's current consumption (or let them decide on their own consumption investments) or invested, in which case the present value of the benefits can be compared to the present value of the grant cost.

8.10.3. Joint Cost

Macro country studies acknowledge that some programs benefit different groups simultaneously. An example is education, which benefits both students and the general public. This is the same problem as allocating the joint costs of a multiple purpose reservoir. Most macro studies allocate a program's costs wholly to specific groups (typically education is so included). O'Higgins and Ruggles (1981, 323), for example, determine on whose behalf an expenditure is primarily made and then allocate funds based on this determination, for example, all current spending on education is regarded as benefiting households with children. They fudge a bit with capital costs, leaving some unallocated. Meerman (1979, 10) ignores externalities and allocates education costs wholly to students.

It is difficult to allocate the cost of goods with a high exclusion cost such as national defense policy paid for by general taxes. It is typically done on various arbitrary bases such as by family or by income (Gillespie 1976).

Aaron and McGuire (1970) point out that cost allocation on per capita cost of service basis implicitly assumes that the marginal utility of income is constant across all income classes. They suggest allocation in inverse proportion to the household's marginal utility of income. But this again necessitates a political choice of interpersonal utility objectives. When it is judged that marginal utility more than proportionally falls with income, country studies show redistribution from middle-income families toward both richer and poorer families.

Preproject micro studies made by the U.S. water resources agencies use the separable cost-remaining benefit (SCRB) method to allocate joint cost of multiple purpose projects. In other areas such as education or health projects in which there is the problem of allocating costs between individuals and general public beneficiaries, there are few agency analyses. The SCRB method would not be applicable when all costs are joint and the public benefits have never been explicitly priced. The joint impact character of education, for example, might be used to justify public subsidies to private education, or conversely, it might be used to justify requiring childless people to contribute to public education. In practice, joint costs do get allocated but in an ad hoc manner with no systematic analysis. It has been argued (Section 8.4.) that joint cost allocation is a policy matter rather than a technical decision. It is part of the distributive judgment to be made, not a prior fact.

8.10.4. Pricing Rules

Distribution studies largely avoid the issue of pricing rules. To the extent that they are able to net out user fees, they tend to assume the same price to all consumers for all units of consumption even under decreasing cost. An exception is Selowsky (1979, 138-42) who does examine public utility rate structures (e.g., mix of fixed charges and variable rates depending on blocks of use). Governments do commonly charge different rates for different uses. They may take advantage of the inelastic demand (consumer surplus) of some groups to charge lower prices to others (see Section 8.2.1.). Again redistribution cannot be defined without a judgment on the pricing system property right.   The problem becomes even more complex when governments use price controls on private goods as a distributive instrument (Szakolczai 1980). There is a technical measurement problem in determining who benefits from subsidized inputs and controlled prices (Harberger 1978, 597-80). Agricultural programs are particularly troublesome (Meerman 1979, Ch. 7). The elasticity of supply and demand can affect incidence of input and product price directives. For example, an input subsidy for a product with inelastic supply will benefit consumers more than producers.

8.10.5. Nonmarket Inputs

Government projects often utilize nonmarket inputs. Macro distribution studies are concerned only with actual treasury costs and ignore unpaid inputs. This assumes that there are no rights in these inputs. Preproject micro studies made by the U.S. water resources agencies generally note nonmarket inputs in a footnote or an environmental impact statement in physical terms with no systematic analysis (U.S. Water Resources Council 1980a, 25329). For a perspective on the distribution of environmental services, see Freeman (1972).

8.10.6. Indirect (Pecuniary) Effects

Public projects can indirectly affect the income and employment of people who do not use the project. The same is true of tax effects (to be discussed in the next section). Project output or a project-caused shift in location of input demand or output processing may create and destroy local rents, although consumers may gain. Macro studies ignore these indirect effects and it is for this reason that Meerman (1979) rejects redistribution studies and will countenance only admittedly partial equilibrium distribution studies. Public projects that represent collective reallocation of consumption can alter relative prices affecting both other producers and consumers. But the same is true of any private reallocation of demand. As noted in Section 8.5, most governments accept these effects as the cost of flexibility in fulfilling changing tastes. Because of the cost and difficulty of measuring indirect efforts, it was suggested in Chapter 7 that this be attempted only when there is expected to be sizable potential for picking up unemployed labor from the direct project construction and first round of inputs and subsequent processing of output if relevant. Here in the context of documenting distribution, it can be added that the studies should be made only if it is suspected that there are major income-reducing effects on the poorest groups as directed by political authorities. For example, it might include migrant agricultural workers and apply to mechanization projects. This means that in Table 8.2, lines 10 and 14 would be estimated only when selected target groups are involved in a major way. The same applies to the source of transfer grants in line 10.

8.10.7. Transfer Costs (Tax Effects)

Transfers (grants) are not costless. Some of what is given does not get to the targeted recipient and this reduces the amount available for transfer over time. This is caused by administrative costs, inability to fully differentiate the target from others, and effects of taxation.

Tax theorists have put forward the concept of deadweight tax loss or excess burden (Harberger 1978). Any tax other than a lump-sum causes indirect effects on relative prices and thus on consumption and resource use. The concept involves the measurement of consumer surplus, which was questioned in Chapter 7.[10] It is illustrated by a reduction in the equilibrium consumption and output of a given good representing the amount of the tax. The total area under the demand curve is regarded as its total value, which is larger than the total area under the supply curve, which is regarded as its opportunity cost of production. The familiar surplus triangle is then declared to be a loss of producer and consumer surplus, which is lost to the economy, and thus part of the donors' transfer that is not received by recipients. Harberger would regard this as a transfer cost and notes that if gains and losses to different parties (consumer and producer) were to be weighted differently, it would make the conventional Kaldor-Hicks tests of welfare gains of projects impossible as the producer and consumer welfare change on intramarginal units could not be easily netted. Also see Sugden and Williams (1978, 203).

There are many problems with empirical measures of consumer surplus in general equilibrium as noted in Chapter 7. Tresch (1981, 352) summarizes the theoretical work of Boadway (1976), Diamond (1975), Feldstein (1972b), Green (1975), Hartwick (1978), and Mirrlees (1975) by saying "it is painfully obvious just how hopelessly intertwined distributional and efficiency terms become in many second-best tax (and expenditure) decision rules." Tresch notes several conditions that must exist for the dead weight tax loss to be regarded as an efficiency loss measure. These conditions include some method of lump-sum redistribution so that social marginal utility of income is always equal for all consumers and consumers have identical and homothetic tastes. Because this is unreal, he argues that a social welfare function is needed. Public choice is the only source of social welfare functions.

Consumer surplus cannot be used without a property rights decision on who will be subject to differential pricing. A consumer who loses surplus because of taxes can also lose it to differential pricing. Reallocation of demand by collective choice is not different from private shifts in consumer demand (including private charity). All shifts in demand, whether implemented by private buying or taxation and collective buying, can cause a shift in surplus.[11] Why do we speak only of dead weight tax loss and not of dead weight private consumption shift loss? This biases governmental versus private choice. In the dead weight analysis, the amount taxed away for transfer is valued as the area under the supply curve that is market determined opportunity cost. But wouldn't the transfer once in the hands of the recipients also show a consumer surplus as well? Are we then to compare the recipient and donor surpluses? It is curious that some who normally abhor interpersonal utility comparisons are quite willing to net producer and consumer surplus with the value judgment of equal weights and then give recipient surplus a zero weight. Some citizens are concerned not only with the cost of raising revenue, but also with the government's use of the revenue and receive a "charitable donor surplus" that is obtained by making a loving grant rather than selfish consumption?

The earlier theory of optimal taxation suggested that there is less deadweight if taxes are placed on products with inelastic demand so quantities are unaffected (Harberger 1978). But this is in conflict with the usual transfer objectives as the payers of such taxes may not be the groups desiring to make a transfer. "Optimal taxation" produces its own deadweight.

Taxation can affect hours worked and output available for redistribution in the next period. Government may choose limits to the reduced output it would accept to accomplish redistribution. The value of the output lost can be valued in the usual national income sense without reference to consumer surplus. The work hours of the recipient may also be affected. It would be less value presumptuous if we dispensed with the words deadweight and distortion.

There are some tough measurement problems in tracing the incidence of taxes. The effect of elasticities of demand plays a role in affecting incidence parallel to that noted in the discussion of pricing subsidies in Section 8.10.4. For example, when a taxed item has infinitely elastic demand, suppliers pay the tax, not consumers. If this is not traced through, the transfer may come from an unintended source.

One of the costs of transfer is the cost of lobbying the government decisions (Rausser 1982). These costs cannot be labeled as wasteful as is done by so-called "rent seeking" analysis without a value judgment on the desirability of the transfer. The existence of transfer costs cannot be a conclusive defense of the status quo. Market exchange has costs, but less than the net advantage of trade. So to find that government transfers have costs is not to condemn transfers, but to raise the political question of whether there are practical and acceptable alternative transfer instruments and whether the result of the transfer is worth the cost.

8.10.8. Grants Budgets and Constraints

Some agencies do have constraints that function much like a grants budget. With different degrees of formality, a certain percentage of the budget is allocated to certain regions or groups. For example, the World Bank has favored projects aiding small farmers. There is no announced percentage of loans that might be given to such projects, but it becomes known in effect that there is money available for projects benefiting small farmers. The U.S. Army Corps of Engineers (1980) proposed a project in which houses in a low income section of a city would be relocated out of the flood plain even though the value of the flood damage to the low valued housing was not enough to pay for either a structural project or the relocation. The project display, however, did not include a grant efficiency ratio showing the cash equivalent of the transfer, which the poor families might have preferred to a relocated, dry, but still shabby house. The relocation portion of the project just lowered the B/C ratio on the total project, which primarily aided higher income flood plain occupants.

In building political coalitions to support a grants budget, the grant can be constrained. These constraints include the availability of cash versus in-kind grants (Section 8.9). The political decision not only creates rights to a grant, but also determines whether its spending serves only the recipients' interests or also the noncharitable interests of the giver in removing the externalities of others' consumption. If the time preference of the donors has little to do with the charitable demands determining the size of the grant, the donor may wish to accept the time preference of the recipients in the design of grants projects.

8.11.   Conclusion

Many governments neither regard the present distribution of income as optimal, nor can achieve that optimality wholly via lump-sum transfers. This means governments are using many instruments to affect distribution, ranging from transfers in money and in-kind, taxes, pricing, to cost allocation. To determine government progress toward meeting its distribution goals, there must be some way to aggregate the net effects of these instruments. This chapter has provided heuristic tools with which to consider this aggregation. Pending further development, government will have to proceed by iteration using macro distribution studies to check its progress.

There has been a debate in the literature (Mishan 1982; Azzi and Cox 1973) between those who advocate as a condition for project acceptance a potential Pareto-improvement and those who want to implement distribution objectives by applying weights to costs and benefits according to who receives them. The latter approach involves a trade-off between efficiency and distribution. The potential Paretian approach can ignore who received and who pays by focusing only on the change in national income that creates the capacity for the winners to compensate the losers, whether or not they actually do.

The argument of this chapter finds these approaches unsatisfactory both in theory and practice. The following interactive, iterative process is therefore suggested.

First, the government can choose its distributive objective and set out to implement it with whatever means are available. It cannot be certain how much of the objective can be achieved by selective productivity and how much has to be supplemented by other means. So it can set some tentative grants budget. Envisaging the total amount to be transferred is the only practical way for distributive objectives to be explicitly chosen in a meaningful way. Analysts can provide background input in the form of descriptions of macro income distribution and recent changes induced by private and public action to inform the choice of distributive objectives.

Second, projects are selected to maximize national income. The distributive consequences of this public investment for a few selected groups can be noted in a grants account display such as presented in Table 8.2. and all types of transfers engendered are charged to the grants budget (line 15). It is not sufficient to focus on direct benefits received or the size of tax spending on projects benefiting a certain group and ignore the other distribution dimensions of projects such as joint cost allocation, pricing of marketed output, and pecuniary and in-kind transfers. Systematic analysis requires a display of the net effect of all these factors after obtaining a policy decision on the rights involved.

Third, if the grants budget is not exhausted, remaining investment projects and transfers can compete and be ranked in terms of grants efficiency. If there were no national income budget constraint, only cash transfers would be left.

By using macro studies of changes in distribution, the government could appraise its progress toward distributional objectives and alter its grants budget accordingly. The grants budget is not wholly a treasury outlay since some of the transfers occur in the market.

It is not practical to do a grants performance budget for all projects and for all the distribution factors. Not all transfers incidental to national income project choice will get noted and charged to the grants budget, but the major ones could be. On a selected and manageable basis the information in Table 8.2 can be used to choose efficient transfer instruments according to their major dimensions.

This procedure moves in the direction of making transfers explicit and efficiently delivered. That is to say it clearly defines what is meant by efficient transfers. It links public choice for national income maximization to distribution objectives and lets alternative transfer instruments compete systematically. The key is to require explicit judgment on the amount of transfer to be aimed at specific target groups, so that the alternative projects and other policies can be compared as to their efficiency in delivering the grant and in turn achieving the politically chosen distributive goal.

Notes

1. This is why it is unsatisfactory to define redistribution as "the difference between their willingness to pay and the actual charges levied upon them" (Marglin 1967, 44). See also Kalter and Stevens (1971)

2. A variant of this is to look at legislative intent as to the intended primary user in whose name the project was built; Ruggles and O'Higgins (1981, 140) say "expenditure on schooling would be allocated to families with children in school, on the grounds that these expenditures are costs incurred on behalf of those children," even if society as a whole benefits from an educated population.

3. The resulting change in relative product prices (locally or nationally) has implications for welfare change even for those whose money income remains unchanged (Scitovsky 1941).

4. Foster (1966) suggests using a price equal to the willingness to pay of people with average incomes. Apart from the empirical problem of this measure, it is a statement of a distribution objective, not a guide to choosing it.

5.   For an illustration along these lines, see the comparison of the negative income tax, minimum wage, and public employment by Gramlich and Wolkoff (1979). Cf. Hylland and Zeckhauser (1979). For an analysis of general price control see Miller and Yandle (1979).

6.   This is an example of the difference in marginal and average values. Theoretically, a weighting could be stated as a function of the donor's income and changes in recipients income, but this places great demands on analysts and politicians.

7.   Ideally it would also include "tax expenditures." These tax breaks or departures from generally applicable taxes are hard to define. Conceptually it is equivalent to departure from flat price user fees. The alternative should also include price controls.

8.   The distribution display plays no part in the choice of alternative national income budget projects. It is used only to determine the size of the remaining grants budget.

9.   For this reason if Table 8.2 were used to describe total redistribution, the whole of cash grants (e.g., project E) is not necessarily to be added to other entries in the grant total line

10.   It is also questioned in this context by Maital (1973) and Aaron and McGuire (1970), who point out that national income accounting ignores consumer surplus.

11.   It would also apply to any shifts in rights to factors made by courts or legislature.

9

Valuation over Time and Selection Criteria

9.1.   Introduction to Time Preference

Different projects have different cash flows over time. Some projects have early returns, and others may have larger and more distant returns. How shall projects that differ widely in size and length of life be compared systematically? This chapter explores possible conflicts among individuals as to valuation over time, and how the resolution of these conflicts may be systematically displayed and projects ranked.

It is essential to begin with the actual expected cash flows of the alternatives considered. Consider the cash flow opportunities shown in Table 9.1. A reference trade-off rate is needed to compare projects that have different values occurring at different times. This is called the rate of time preference and it is obtained by observing people's choices.

Choice of trade-offs between size and time of receipt of cash depends on one's values and opportunities. A unit of monetary value can be consumed now or invested. If it is consumed, it may be inferred that the utility of the present consumption is greater than the utility of later consumption of the future returns of the investment, even though the number of future units is greater.

To illustrate how choice reveals time preference, assume the decision maker has a choice between project B or C in the use of a newly available unit of money as shown in Table 9.1. Project C is current private or public consumption of the unit and project B is an investment of one unit today that will grow into 1.46 units in 4 years. What can be inferred if the decision maker acting personally or as agent for others decides to consume? It implies that the utility of the current consumption is greater than the utility of 1.46 received in the fourth year. In a manner of speaking the future 1.46 has been discounted and from the present perspective is not regarded as being as large as the present 1.00. A trade-off has been made between present and future consumption. Any trade-off can be expressed systematically as a rate-- so much of this (present consumption) for so much of that (future) or vice versa. This rate of trade off is referred to as time preference (TP).

Table 9.1 Alternative Projects Cash Flow

Project	Time Periods				
	t_0	t_1	t_2	t_3	t_4
A	-1.00	0	0	1.33	0
B	-1.00	0	0		1.46
C	-1.00	0	0	0	0
D	-1.33	1.46	0	0	0

The deduction of TP from peoples' choices among the alternatives of Table 9.1 can be shown graphically as in Figure 9.1 using utility indifference curves (all points of equal utility). The greater utility of 1.00 present consumption relative to 1.46 future consumption is shown by the fact that the utility curve U_2 (dashed line) going through 1.00 in period one being higher than the curve U_1 going through 1.46 in period two. The slope of the line connecting the two available choices (1.46 and 1.00) indicates the given rate of trade-off available (marginal rate of substitution) in the two periods (assumed here to be 10 percent).

The indifference curve implies a rate of trade-off of income in the two periods such that the chooser is indifferent as to which is selected. It follows that if the highest curve that originates at the observed chosen income does not also intersect the alternate amount, the preferred rate of time preference is greater or less than the available rate of trade-off, depending on whether the higher or lower absolute valued alternative is chosen. When the lower absolute valued project is chosen it indicates that the rate of trade-off that would make the chooser indifferent is greater than the rate available (greater than 10 percent in this case). The curve U_2 indicates that it would take more than 1.46 in year 4 to have the same utility as 1.00 now. The 1.46 is thus being discounted more than the available rate of trade-off.

If 1.46 in year 4 were preferred over 1.00 at present it implies a different preference map such as U_1^* and U_2^* (solid line) where 1.46 lies on U_1^* and is higher in utility than U_2^* on which 1.00 presently lies. When the higher absolute valued project (1.46) is chosen, it implies that the chooser has a rate of trade-off less than 10 percent. If there are two individuals with the two preference maps shown, they will have conflicting attitudes toward the two projects. The consequences of this is explored in Section 9.2.1.

To understand time preference better, consider the concept of present value (PV) obtained by *discounting* the future backward to the present. The rate or speed at which the future consumption is discounted backward can be expressed as $1/(1+r)^t$ where r is the rate of discount (interest) and the

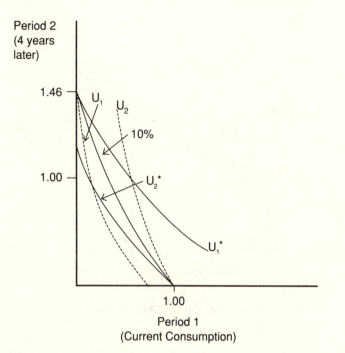

Figure 9.1 Consumption in Two Periods with Two Choices

exponent t is the year the income is received. There is some value of r that makes the discounted future value equal to the present consumption of 1.00. This is the marginal rate of transformation of present to future income or vice versa. Therefore in the present example of 1.46 in year 4 the calculation is $1.46/(1+r)^4 = 1.00$ such that the future income is just equal to the present consumption of 1.00. The expression is satisfied when r = 10 percent. (Note this is the same rate as shown in Figure 9.1 inferred by the slope of the line of available trade-off of the two choices.) When 1.46 is discounted at a rate of 10 percent, the future income is reduced to a PV of just 1.00. If this alternative of 1.46 is rejected, we can infer that the rate of trade-off or TP discount exceeds 10 percent. Because present consumption is always worth unity (1.00), the rate of discount implied by the choice of consumption must be such that it makes the present value of 1.46 less than 1.00.

Alternatively, if we observe the choice of investment project B, we can assume that the discounting is less than 10 percent and the present value of the future 1.46 is more than present consumption of 1.00. Note that investment in your own project or lending with a promised flow of cash return is equivalent, so project B might be the expected return from a savings account or bond.

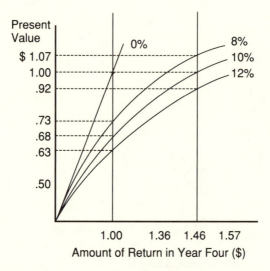

Figure 9.2 Relation of Present and Future Value to the Rate of Discount

This relationship is shown graphically in Figure 9.2 which shows the PV of the sum of 1.46 received in year 4. At 10 percent time preference, the PV is 1.00; but if the chooser is very impatient or has better investment opportunities available, then time preference might be 12 percent and the corresponding present value of 1.46 would be less than 1.00. Conversely, if the time preference were 8 percent, the PV is greater than 1 and investment is preferred to current consumption.

Now to complicate the comparisons, assume an added alternative of project A in Table 9.1. It stops producing one year sooner than B. The question is whether this is the literal end (forced consumption) or whether this project can be combined with some investment external to the project to produce income in the fourth year. Could the 1.33 in the third year be invested in another public project such a D that would become 1.46 after another year? If so, projects A and B are identical. If the chooser is indifferent between A and B (over C) then we deduce something of the expected growth of the 1.33 of year 3 to year 4. From the previous choice of B over C, we know that TP is <10 percent, so we know the value of the private opportunity cost of consumption is <10 percent and thus the implied income lost in year 4 by consumption in year 3 is <1.46. Then why was the chooser indifferent between A and B? It must be because the chooser sees another public investment possible that grows at 10 percent to produce a value in year 4 of 1.46. So it is not enough to know the private cost of consumption, we also need to know all of the public reinvestment (transformation) possibilities. Therefore indifference between A and B does not change our deduction of TP, it just indicates that public reinvestment growth opportunities are better. (Alternatively, if B is chosen it means there is no better reinvestment opportunity available than that reflected in the TP of <10 percent.

Consumption is always in effect compared against the generally available future cash flow forgone. This makes short lived projects that otherwise force consumption comparable to longer lived projects. Implicit in this discussion is the concept of a terminal value (TV) obtained by *compounding* the present forward into the future. The rate of interest is the speed at which income in any given year increases. It is expressed as $1(1+r)^t$. The exponent t is the number of years until the terminal year is reached. The concept is demonstrated in Figure 9.2 by following a line from the present value of 1 across to intersection at different interest rates. At 8 percent, the present 1.00 is compounded to become 1.36 in year 4. At 10 percent it becomes 1.46. If the chooser expects 1.46 from project A in year 4, then the rate of growth (compounding) is 1.33 $(1+r)^1$ and r is found to be 10 percent. (The exponent is 1 because there is 1 year of growth from year 3 to 4.) We either consume, in which case a value equivalent to the compounded value of the opportunity forgone is implied,[1] or the short-lived returns are reinvested and compounded at the rate of the opportunity available. This is the logic implied by rational consistent choice. The primary question then becomes whose opportunities are to be counted.

9.2.   Time Preference Determinants

9.2.1.   Differences among Individuals

What factors affect a person's time preference? At any point in time it would be a function of the person's existing wealth, expected flow and degree of uncertainty of future real income, age, impatience, and concern for future generations. It might also be related to expectations of future needs, such as change in one's family situation or health. This may or not be correlated with age. The poor (people and nations) might be expected to have higher time preference rates than the rich. And if the poor expect real growth, they might have higher rates initially than later in their lives (or planning period). These differences among individuals present a problem for public choice. Whose time preference is to be used in comparing projects such as illustrated in Figure 9.1?

If everyone has access to capital markets and a common rate of interest for lending and borrowing, they will all have the same marginal rate of time preference (MRTP). This can be demonstrated by first assuming that a person has an MRTP of 8 percent but can lend (invest) or borrow at 10 percent. Ten percent is the marginal rate of transformation (MRT) at which present income can be transformed into future income, as illustrated in Figure 9.1 by the curve connecting 1.46 and 1.00, which is now regarded as the borrowing-lending possibility line. The person with an MRTP of 8 percent will lend until the value of the last dollar consumed (MRTP) has risen to the MRT represented by the market rate. MRTP can never remain less than the available market rate of interest. On the other hand, if MRTP is 12 percent, the person will borrow at 10 percent to increase present consumption at the expense of expected future consumption. For example, the person with an MRTP of 12 percent would be willing to exchange 1.46 of their income in year 4 to obtain 1.00 increased consumption now. Eventually the extra consumption will lower its marginal utility and the MRTP to the market rate. In the aggregate, changes in the supply and demand for funds will alter the equilibrium interest rate as well.

MRTP in perfect market equilibrium will equal the rate at which the person will exchange available present compensation for future consumption, which is sometimes referred to as the marginal rate of substitution (MRS), and also equal to the rate at which present income can be transferred into future income, called the marginal rate of transformation (MRT). Therefore in equilibrium everyone at the margin has the same MRTP, which is equal to the return on private investment and the borrowing and lending rate (all of which are the MRT). A desirable investment is one whose rate of return exceeds this general equilibrium rate.

The previous discussion is quite logical given its assumptions, but what happens if these assumptions are relaxed? In practice it is impossible to borrow and lend at the same rate because of the risk and transaction costs borne by lenders. Uncertainty also means that the probability of bankruptcy may change as the interest rate changes (Stiglitz 1987a, 6-7). Lenders may decide to ration credit rather than raise interest rates if doing so lowers the average quality (financial soundness) of all who apply for a loan. Some people willing to borrow at current rates (which would have the effect of lowering the time preference to the market rate) cannot do so.

Further, interest rates available are a function of the amount of money a person has. Larger loans have higher interest rates and some higher yielding financial instruments require a minimum sized investment. There is also the matter of credit worthiness. A poor person or anyone subject to bankruptcy can seldom borrow enough against future income to drive MRTP to the generally available interest rate or the return on private investment. Where tax incidence is not proportional to benefits of government spending, individuals with different tax rates will have different MRTP.

For example, poor people with "a let tomorrow take care of itself" attitude may have MRTP of 20 percent, but because they cannot borrow at the private rate of 10 percent available to others their MRTP>r. Simultaneously, middle income people can have an MRTP of 8 percent, but because they cannot invest at the 10 percent available to large investors their

MRTP < r. These differences in MRTPs between individuals can persist. Government will have to choose a rate that is a compromise between the different private rates of different people.

9.2.2.   Cost of Capital Approach

Under certain circumstances, differences between individual's MRTP may not matter and decisions would be made only by references to the cost of capital. Suppose that there are two individuals with MRTPs of 6 and 15 percent, respectively, and further suppose that the cost of capital to the public agency through borrowing is 8 percent. If the agency has a project available (like project B in Table 9.1) that earns 10 percent it has the opportunity to make both of these individuals better off by building the project. The decision rule is to invest as long as returns exceed the cost of capital. Although both parties will agree that the project is desirable, they will differ as to the means of financing the project (see Sugden and Williams 1978, 47). The person with the low MRTP would prefer to be taxed for the project. The lack of other good opportunities means that person would have a higher net return with taxation than borrowing. The person with the higher MRTP would prefer borrowing.[2] Given capital rationing, individuals with different time preferences will also differ over the ranking of even externally financed projects.[3] As previously suggested, the rate they would want to use for reinvestment compounding to compare projects of different lengths would differ.

The assumptions required to use the cost of capital approach would seem to be most fully met in the case of less developed countries with external finance. But for most governments who use a mixture of borrowing and taxation, the conflicts between individuals with different MRTP remain (Feldstein 1972a).

In business, there has long been a debate over whether it mattered if corporate investment were financed from borrowing or equity stock shares. This is equivalent to the question of borrowing versus taxation in the public sector. If the source of finance matters then the attractiveness of a given private investment depends on which owner's opportunity cost is used if owners do not have the same MRTP. MRTPs will differ if risk depends on the amount borrowed and individuals face different tax rates (Atkinson and Stiglitz 1980, 150). There is a question of whose preferences would count in the private as well as in the public sector. Whether stockholder or citizen, capital market imperfections raise questions of property rights in controlling investments.

Stock ownership questions would not arise if the source of private finance did not matter. Modigliani and Miller (1958) argue that the test for investment desirability is whether the market value of a firm's shares is increased when the returns of new investment are capitalized, regardless of how the investment is actually financed and regardless of the preferences of the current owners. This *market value maximization* is not a practical guide to investment choice,[4] but it does identify the conditions under which the source of capital matters. Depending on the particular formulation, the key conditions for indifference as to source are no possibility of bankruptcy, a perfect arbitrage market, or costless functioning of financial intermediaries (Stiglitz 1974). These assumptions serve to substitute leverage (mix of equity and debt) by outsiders for any leverage practiced by the firm. The action of financial intermediaries impacts on stock values to keep cost of finance invariant of source (and more to the point here, make it possible for all stockholders to benefit from investment leading to stock price change regardless of their individual access to credit).   However real these assumptions are in private finance, they are unavailable in the public sector in which there are no stocks and no stock market. The source of capital and thus choice of whose time preference counts does matter.

9.3.   Investment Criteria

So far we have been primarily observing choice and its implied time preference, and noting the problems in public choice raised by individually different time preferences. But we have only hinted at any general rules for systematic public choice of budget size and ranking of projects.   To understand the elements of the problem, some of the commonly suggested investment criteria will be examined.

9.3.1.   Net Present Value

First, consider net present value (NPV), which is the summed discounted value of the cash flow[5] produced by the project.[6] The following formula for net present value will be familiar from the previous discussion:

$$NPV = B_o + B_1/(1+r) + B_2/(1+r)^2 + \ldots + B_n/(1+r)^n$$

or stated more generally,

$$NPV = \sum_{t=0}^{t=n} B_t/(1+r)^t$$

where B equals the net cash flow in each year and this cash flow may be zero, negative, or positive, for example, during construction there may be several years of negative flow. The $t=n$ indicates summation over the life (n) of the project and $t=0$ means that the present or initial year's negative net benefit (B_0) is not discounted (interest on borrowing is not due until the end of the year).

The criterion for choice is to invest in any project in which NPV is positive. The cost of such available projects then becomes the public budget size. The public is better off taking money from private use until the NPV of the marginal project at the opportunity cost discount rate (r) produces an NPV of zero.

An alternative method of computation is to separate the discounted negative (PVK) and positive (PVB) yearly flows, sum each separately, and then subtract one from the other to get NPV. Capital cost (K) is defined as negative net cash flow regardless of the year of occurrence. Choosing projects with positive NPV is sometimes called the *excess benefit method*, which is an apt name because it indicates whether there is any excess benefit over what would be obtained in alternate private use. All that has to be done is identify the marginal or threshold project with NPV = 0 to know if the amount of capital available is equal to that needed to finance all projects that have some positive net return (excess benefit), and all projects on the list are independent of each other (i.e., any project can be done without affecting the availability of any others--not mutually exclusive). When these conditions are not met, ranking and comparison of projects are necessary.

NPV is an absolute amount and not a rate. Therefore only projects with the same amount of capital can be compared. For example, assume projects B and B_1 in Table 9.2 are mutually exclusive. At 3 percent, B_1 has a larger NPV, 11, compared to 6 for B, but B_1 takes twice as much capital. It can be seen by comparing the benefits in year 1 that B_1 does not produce twice as much benefit as B. The NPV criterion for ranking would be erroneous if it is necessary to choose between these projects. For ranking we need some sort of rate to relate return to unit of capital (K). This could be stated as a present value ratio such as $(B - OC)/K$, which ranks project B over B_1.

The opposite but symmetrical concept to NPV is net terminal value (NTV). This utilizes compounding as already discussed.

$$NTV = \sum_{t=0}^{t=n} B_t(1+r)^t$$

The criterion for choice is to invest in any project whose NTV > 0. This is the same as saying that the terminal value of benefits (TVB), which is the sum of compounded positive B_t's, exceeds the terminal value of cost (TVK). TVK is the sum of all the compounded negative B_t's. The same point made about the need for computing a rate in the case of capital rationing applies here. (See Table 9.3 for a TV ratio.)

Some agencies that project constant annual benefits will amortize costs to obtain a constant annual cost. This ratio of annual benefits to costs is equivalent to a present value benefit-cost ratio. The amortization factor is the reciprocal of the present value of an annuity of 1 and is available in handbooks of financial tables.

9.3.2.   Internal Rate of Return

This concept directly indicates a rate. It is defined as the rate of discount that reduces the cash flow of a project to a zero net present value. More formally, the internal rate of return (IRR) is the discount rate (r) for which the sum

$$B_0 + B_1/(1+r) + B_2/(1+r)^2 + ... + B_n/(1+r)^n = 0$$

or

$$\sum_{t=0}^{t=n} B_t/(1+r)^t = 0$$

In a sense, IRR is an average rate of profit. A project that produces a given IRR is equivalent to the time flow of the given initial investment compounded forward for the given number of years at an interest rate equal to the IRR.

The method for computing IRR can be seen by taking project A in Table 9.2. The table also indicates the gross present value of the project at different discount rates (and also NPV could be calculated by subtracting capital costs). There is no formula for deriving the rate and it must be approached by trial and error either by hand computation or computer. If 3 percent had been tried it can be seen that NPV would have been 8 and not the desired zero. A larger discount rate must therefore be tried. It can be seen that at 7 percent the NPV is zero.

The criterion for choice is to invest in any project in which the IRR is greater than the opportunity cost of capital. This will identify a set of projects that maximizes the sum of net benefits.

The differences in ranking produced by different criteria[7] can be seen by reference to the list of projects in Table 9.2. In the case of no capital rationing and no mutually exclusive projects, the NPV and IRR criteria identify the same set of projects and cutoff point. For example, at 4 percent opportunity cost, projects A and B are acceptable because they have positive NPVs. Projects at the line of indifference are assumed to be rejected. The IRR criterion selects the same projects A and B because their IRR exceeds 7 percent. The optimal budget size is 200. This demonstrates that both criteria identify those projects that have some positive returns or excess benefit. But this is not good enough if capital rationing[8] or mutual exclusivity exists.

Suppose that for some reason the public authority is willing to have a budget of only 100. Or assume that project B utilizes a different technology for the same purpose and beneficiaries of project A so that building both makes no sense or is literally impossible. This is always the case when a project that is similar but at different scales is included in the list (a highly

Table 9.2 Schedule of Investment Returns at Different Interest Rates and Investment Criteria (Projects A and B are mutually exclusive)

Project	Initial Investment (K)	Net Benefits* Yr. 1	Net Benefits* Yr. 2	Internal Rate (%)	Present Value if Discounted at 2%	3%	4%	5%	7%	10%	$\frac{B - OC}{K}$ at 3%	$\frac{B}{K+OC}$ at 3%	(TVB) Terminal Value 3%	7%	10%
A	$100	0	115	7	110	108	106.3	104	100	<100	1.08	1.05	115	115	115
B	100	110	0	10	108	106	105.7	104	103	100	1.07	1.07	113	117	121
B₁	200	218	0	9	213	211	209.6	207	204	198	1.06	1.06	224	233	239
B₂	200	220	0	10	215	213	211.0	209	205	200	1.07	1.07	226	235	242
C	100	104	0	4	102	101	100.0	99	<100	<100	1.01	1.01	107	111	114
D	100	103	0	3	<100	100	<100.0	98	<100	93	1.00	1.00	106	110	113
E	100	102	0	2	100	<100	<100.0	97	<100	92	<1.00	<1.00	105	109	112

*Net benefit = gross benefit - operating costs; for example, project A has gross benefits of 168 and operating costs of 53 in year 2. Other projects have no operating costs.

desirable situation as it makes project size subject to systematic choice). A budget constraint or mutually exclusive projects make it necessary to choose between projects that are otherwise both acceptable because of positive returns. Ranking, rather than identification of the desired set of projects, is now necessary. How then do the two criteria rank the projects?

At 4 percent, the net present value of project A exceeds that of B. These projects are of the same size so we need not compute a rate, but if we did the ranking by (GPV - K)/K, the result would be the same. But if ranked by IRR, project B is superior. Most texts at this point present arguments as to why one or the other is the correct criterion with most favoring NPV (see for example Sassone and Schaffer 1978, 29). Instead, we shall explore why these and other criteria produce different rankings and then ask which set of assumptions implicit in each fits the facts and political judgments necessary to resolve conflicts among the publics.

When the two criteria produce different rankings, selection of NPV as the ranking criterion assumes a reinvestment (compounding forward) at a rate equal to that rate of discount used to compute NPV (Solomon 1956, 126). Use of IRR ranking implies reinvestment at each project's IRR. Reference to Table 9.2 illustrates the effect of different rates. Note that project B lasts only 1 year. To be comparable with the longer lived A implies that either the benefit available at the end of year 1 is consumed, which implies that it produces more utility than the returns from an alternative investment, or that it is literally transformed into a future value by another investment whose returns bring it up through year 2. As seen in earlier discussions, the question is what is this alternative investment? If the cash flow is reconstructed for project B to reflect reinvestment at the compounding rate of 4 percent, it becomes zero in year 1 and 114.4 in year 2. The terminal value is $1(1+r)$ or 110×1.04. When this reconstructed cash flow is discounted to obtain NPV, it will be smaller than that of project A, which is the ranking originally suggested by the NPV criterion at a 4 percent discount rate.

However, if the projects are made comparable by the assumption that reinvestment (or consumption) for project B is at its IRR of 10 percent, then the flow becomes zero in the first year and 1.21 in the second (i.e., its terminal value) which makes it superior in terms of net present value (100) to project A (<100), which is the rank order suggested by the IRR criterion. If the reinvestment rate equals the IRR of project B, then IRR as a ranking criterion produces the correct ranking, though this rate is not the unique rate implied by use of the criterion (Dudley 1972).

Each method is internally logically consistent, and choice depends on the opportunity cost. Table 9.2 illustrates that a reversal in ranking by NPV takes place around 5 percent. At higher rates of discount, project B is better by both NPV and IRR. The question is not which criterion is better, but rather whose opportunity cost is to count; based on the answer the method can be chosen to fit.[9] The analyst needs to be given an explicit judgment about the expected return from reinvestment (and if individuals differ in this respect, a political choice between conflicting interests is necessary).

9.3.3.   Size and Scale Comparisons

At the beginning of the chapter it was noted that projects were of different size. Ranking by the absolute size of NPV is not satisfactory in this case and some type of rate must be used. Any rate, such as IRR or one utilizing NPV, assumes the divisibility and proportionality of projects. Suppose that in Table 9.2, we had instead of project B, a project twice as large in every respect so that it looked like B_2. At a discount rate of 4 percent the GPV/K ratio (211.5/200) would be 1.057, which is inferior to A's 1.063. Use of this ratio for ranking assumes that either the larger project is perfectly divisible into two projects each costing 100, or that the smaller project can be expanded proportionately. If the larger project is divisible then we can combine project A and half of B_2 so that the summed NPV is 106.3 + 105.8 = 212.1, which is better that the entire big project B_2 at 211. Or alternatively if the smaller A can be doubled, its NPV is 2 × 106.3 = 212.6, still better than B_2. Thus, the ranking by ratios is correct when the assumptions are met. But what if A cannot be doubled and must be combined with project C (which only has an IRR of 4 percent)? Now the summed NPV is 106.3 + 100 = 206.3, which is not as good as the larger project B_2 at 211. Ranking by the ratio of the untransformed projects would be incorrect if divisibility for the necessary transformation is not possible[10] (see Mishan 1976, 194-95).

As a practical matter with hundreds of projects of widely different size it would be clumsy at best to attempt to literally combine or divide projects into some common size. Also in a large budget with many similar projects, it is reasonable to assume proportionality. Therefore, in most cases ranking by some rate of return criterion will fit the situation, but in special cases of perhaps small countries with only a few project alternatives, it may be necessary to compute returns from transformed projects reflecting actual combinatorial possibilities. It is my judgment that the determination of project scale (or optimal sets of projects) is seldom influenced by concern that the capital not used in the project in question would have to be invested at a much lower return elsewhere.

When choosing a project scale, care must be taken to avoid mistakes created by the second-best situation of capital rationing. If no capital rationing exists, the scale should be extended so that net benefit of *each* project is maximized where MC = MR. This is sanctioned by the U.S. Water Resources Council (1973).[11] But this is incorrect with capital rationing in which the scale should be extended until the ratio of MR to MC is the same as that ratio for the marginal project. In other words, if each project is pushed to MC = MR at a given discount rate (marginal B/C of unity), the marginal net returns of all projects will not be equal if there is capital rationing. Some project will be forgone that has higher marginal returns.

Table 9.3 Incorporating Reinvestment to a Terminal Value*

Project	K Cost	Benefit Year 1	Compounding Rate (%)	TV Year 2	Normalized TV Ratio TV/K'	PV of TV 10%	NPV	Normalized PV of TV/K	NIRR
A	100	0		115.0	.95	95	-5	.95	7
B	100	110	7	117.7	.97	97	-3	.97	8
B$_x$	100	110	20	133.0	1.10	110	10	1.10	15
D	100	50	10	55.0	.92	92	-8	.92	5
		53	7	56.0					
Z	100		10	121.0	Unity	100	0	Unity	10%

*All numbers have been rounded.

9.3.4. A Terminal Value Method for Systematic Choice[12]

The income generated by a project has two components--the actual flow of receipts directly from the project and the results of reinvestment of those receipts. The use of any investment criterion incorporates an assumption about reinvestment without literally displaying the resulting annual flows that make projects of unequal life comparable. It would be much more explicit if the expected project receipts and results of reinvestment were set down first, with the appropriate transformations of the initial receipts, and then a rate (ratio or IRR) derived from it, rather than trying to find a choice criterion formula that reflects the policy choices involved in a transformation, namely the rates for reinvestment (or its consumption equivalent). It is suggested that the analyst take the initial project data such as those in Table 9.2 and transform the data into a comparable set of flows (culminating in a terminal value) reflecting instructions from the political authorities as to whose opportunity cost of reinvestment (consumption) is to be utilized. This is shown in Table 9.3. For example, project A from Table 9.2 requires no transformation because it has only a terminal value and is the longest lived project. Project B lasts only 1 year and must be compounded forward to equal the length of project A. Assume that the following are consistent with policy directives. Project B produces an unmarketed consumer good in year 1, so it is assumed to be equivalent to that amount compounded forward at the politically determined rate of discount (r) of say 7 percent. This makes its year 2 or terminal value (TV) benefit equal to 117.7. For purposes of illustration, assume there is another project (B_x that is identical to B except that it is received by a different group which is poor. Policy may direct a common r for all groups or it could adopt different rates for different groups of beneficiaries. Assume that the policy is to use a rate of 20 percent for beneficiaries who are extremely poor.[13] This makes the TV of project B_x 133. This can be compared to other projects (including cash grants) only in a segmented budget for the poor group as explained in Sections 9.5 and 9.6.

The procedure can incorporate the fact that part of a project's receipts may go to different groups with different preferences and opportunities. Assume the returns of project D are partially reinvested by one group at 10 percent and partially consumed by another group at a rate equivalent to 7 percent. For example, if 50 of the 103 available in year 1 is reinvested at 10 percent it becomes 55 TV and the remaining 53 at 7 percent becomes 56 for a transformed total for project D of 111. These different rules are shown to illustrate the flexibility of the terminal value method.

9.3.5. Decision Rules

In this terminal value method the necessary transformations for projects of different maturities are made explicit by whatever rule the political authority wishes rather than being incorporated implicitly in an investment criteria such as NPV or IRR. But the criteria also do another thing implicitly that can be made explicit in the method suggested. The criteria are designed to compare the results of projects with the results that would have been obtained with alternative investments in the private sector at a single rate of discount (used to compute NPV or the cutoff IRR and thus indicate desirable projects and ranking if there is capital rationing). The terminal method is extremely flexible and a number of equivalent decision rules can be used once the cash flow is explicitly normalized to a terminal value. The terminal value of the alternative foregone private investment (or equivalent consumption) can also be explicitly listed.   The rate of compounding opportunity costs to a terminal value can be shown at whatever rate the policy makers prescribe. If it were 10 percent, this implies an alternate private project of the same size labeled Z with TV of 121 as shown in Table 9.3. This then is the opportunity cost of any $100 of capital (K) used for public investment and can be used in a TV ratio, for example, project A would be 115/121 = .95 shown in the column labeled *Normalized TV Ratio* in Table 9.3.   To summarize, the TV of K is K compounded at the time preference rate the government has chosen from among the various conflicting time preference rates of individuals (labeled K' in Table 9.3).

If it is preferred to work in terms of the more familiar NPV ratios or IRR this can also be done. The actual direct receipts are all compounded forward to the terminal year so that the transformed flow beginning in year zero is -K, 0, ..., TV. The receipts of the intervening years until the terminal year are shown as zero because they have been reinvested and transformed to the terminal year. For project B, the transformed yearly flow is now -100, 0, 117.7. The terminal value of net returns (TV in Table 9.3) can be discounted to present value and a ratio can be computed. For project B, at 10 percent the present value of the terminal value of 117.7 in year 2 is given by $1/(1 + r)^t$ = 117.7 × .826 = 97 (labeled PV of TV). Since present costs are 100 the normalized PV ratio is less than unity (.97 and labeled Normalized PV of TV/K) and the project is rejected.

If IRR is a more familiar concept, it is also possible to compute a *normalized internal rate of return* (NIRR) which is the rate of interest that reduces the transformed net cash flow to zero: -K, 0, ..., TV = 0 (Mishan 1976, 241).[14] An example of the use of the concept is project B in Table 9.3. Since a discount rate of approximately 8 percent reduces the terminal value to a PV of 100 (NPV = 0), it is the NIRR. And since the NIRR is less than the policy chosen cut-off rate (say 10 percent) for private investment, this criterion too rejects the project. If the rankings by each of these methods is compared it will be seen that each produces the same order. Once the different assumptions implicit in choice of each criterion have been superceded by transformation (i.e., the actual cash flow set down over a common period) all criteria then produce the same result. This is true regardless of what cutoff discount rate is used to calculate present value. This can be seen in Table 9.3 and more formally demonstrated by Mishan (1976, Ch. 37).

Note that the IRR calculation itself makes no assumptions about reinvestment. But choice of this as the ranking criterion is consistent with the policy objective of reflecting the opportunity cost of a group with an implied rate of reinvestment as noted in Section 9.3.2 (Dudley 1972). Given a policy judgment on reinvestment opportunities, it is time consuming to determine if choice of IRR or another criterion is consistent with that judgment. It is much more direct to use the rate given by policy to explicitly transform the cash flows, and when that is done, choice of ranking criterion makes no difference and is only a matter of what is most comfortable and familiar (subject to the qualifications of the next section). The independent analyst who cannot ask the political authority to provide the necessary compounding rates may display a sensitivity analysis at several rates. Also the results of alternative criteria can be displayed, noting the rate that would be implicit if each criteria were chosen for ranking.

The previous discussion follows the usual convention of a single rate of discount for costs and benefits. However, if it is desirable to compound project benefits forward reflecting different opportunity costs of different groups, some policy makers may wish to treat capital costs in a similar fashion. This implies a series of subbudgets, each of which has its own opportunity cost reference point, rather than one grand budget with all projects competing for a common pool of funds. This is discused further in Section 9.4.4 when the implications of the choice of discount rate are more fully explored. Suffice it to say now that the display method is flexible enough to accommodate any policy decision on time flow including different rates for forgone consumption and investment and for different groups (a separate Z project for each group) or different rates over time if time preference changes.

It should be noted that investment decisions are more complicated if the rate of annual growth in project benefits is not independent of the starting date. See Marglin (1963b) and Barzel (1968).

9.3.6.   Choice of Ratio

The point has already been made that because a project list contains projects of widely different sizes including different scales of the same general project, it is necessary to utilize some type of ratio (or transform projects to a common size if divisibility allows). But there are several kinds of ratios to choose from. Choice of the base suggests the factor which is limiting and to which returns are to be maximized. The likelihood of capital rationing means that the return to capital should be maximized. But which capital? In nations with several tiers of government each may contribute some part of the cost of a project. Many projects require complementary investments by private parties to utilize the project output properly. For example, to utilize an irrigation scheme, the farmer may have to grade fields and construct laterals. Each contributor to the total project may have to borrow the money and each may consider its own financing the most difficult to obtain. The issue can also be seen in the private sector. Do you calculate return to stockholder equity, to borrowed capital, or to both.[15] A socialist firm might turn this upside down and compute returns to human capital.

Boulding (1948, 820-21) says, "It may seem surprising that the question, 'What does the entrepreneur maximize?' (What is the measure of profitability of an enterprise?) should still be a matter of dispute, for this is perhaps the most fundamental question in all of economic theory. Nevertheless, the question is not altogether easy to answer." Indeed if the question is what should the public decision maker maximize, the answer is not a technical one but a major policy decision. And the decision reduces operationally to what is going to be put in the denominator of the ratio and what other costs are to be netted from the benefits remaining in the numerator. The issue here is one of where to include costs and not one of leaving some costs out to show a special ratio from one group's perspective.

In the project data shown so far only the net cash flows are shown. Total receipts and various outgoes were ignored. Capital (K) is defined as negative cash flow in any year. This occurs during construction when there are no receipts and perhaps later when cost of major repairs exceeds receipts for a time. It can be argued that only the years that require net borrowing or taxation are limiting. Any cost in other years can be covered by receipts in those years. The logic is similar to a grocery store with a small margin of profit on total sales. It does not maximize returns to total purchase of goods, but to its general line of credit outstanding, which is turned over many times. However, Eckstein (1961, 63-64) has argued that U.S. agencies receive a lump-sum appropriation each year to cover operating costs on existing projects and construction of new projects, and should maximize returns to this whole Federal budget. This suggests a ratio such as $B/(K + OC)$, where B is the PV of benefits, K is capital cost as defined, and OC are operating costs. The denominator includes all outgoes. The more usual NPV/K is equivalent to $(B - OC)/K$. But the mechanics of money disbursement should not be confused with the interests of the agencies' clients. These clients are not likely to regard operating costs that can be covered by receipts as they occur as limiting, and would so instruct their agent even if the agency does not automatically receive the receipts to cover operations and has to argue for them each year before Congress.

A more serious objection is raised by Kuhn (1962, 174), who notes that if OC is regarded as nonlimiting, it encourages agencies to classify given costs as OC when there is vagueness in such classification. He notes that design of projects with high OC means less net return available in future years for capital expenditure. Again, it would appear that we are faced with the need for a political judgment involving both the ability to monitor agency cost classification and a subtle trade-off between capital limits now and in the future. My own guess is that most clients would not want to regard OC as limiting (cf. Heller 1974).

If there is any OC, use of B/(K + OC) produces a lower absolute ratio than (B - OC)/K, except for negative net return projects. For example, in Table 9.2, assume project A has a gross benefit of 168 and an operating cost of 53 in year 2 (for a net benefit of 115). The present value of 168 at 3 percent is 158 and the present value of operating cost is 50. Therefore, the ratio B/(OC + K) = 158/(50 + 100) = 1.05 and project B which has no operating cost would be superior. But the ratio (B - OC)/K = 108/100 = 1.08 and project B would be inferior to A. Agencies with a high OC/K ratio do not like B/(K + OC) ratios. Such an agency does not want to be compared with other agencies in terms of NPV produced for total spending, any more than a grocery store wants to be compared in terms of total sales margin with a low volume store with high mark ups.

The IRR is similar to NPV/K in that it regards all K and only K as limiting. Recall that IRR is computed in terms of net cash flow streams and ignores how the net flow was obtained.

Although most clients agree in not wanting their agency to regard operating costs as limiting, there is no similar agreement as to whose contribution to K is to be regarded as the most limiting. A national level agency would like to have state agency K netted from receipts in the numerator as are operating costs, but the state agency may take a dim view of being regarded as freely available and taken for granted once the national money is avilable. In practice, lack of investment coordination causes some projects to fail because private capital necessary to complement the project was not forthcoming. This is related to the issue of crediting creators of indirect investment with some of the total indirect employment efforts of projects (see Chapter 6). Some factual analysis of the probable constraints in total financing may illuminate the decision on what to maximize (by putting it in the denominator), although many of the conflicts among agencies at different levels are matters of point of view and require policy judgments. It is not a technical question of which type of ratio is in the abstract, best. It depends on policy decisions, which, when made, allow the analyst to select the criteria that fits the policy objective. In the private sector, equity capital owners have been given the right to have managers make decisions in terms of maximizing return to equity capital and treat borrowed capital as a negative benefit. The question is the ownership of financial leverage.

The discussion so far may be summarized by the identification of three key variables whose characteristics are assumed to be different by various investment criteria. These variables are (1) the actual flow of cash over time, (2) the duration of this flow, and (3) the amount of capital presumed to be the limiting factor in producing the flow. Another way of expressing the first two is the question of the rate and duration of reinvestment. Once the rate is chosen, it can be incorporated into the analysis in two ways. It can be expressly used in transforming the initial nominal cash flows of projects such as in the terminal value method previously outlined or an investment criterion (algorithm) can be constructed that reflects the chosen rate(s) as applied to cost and benefits. However, in some cases it may be very difficult to construct a systematic criterion that incorporates just the combination of rates desired with the chosen limiting factor and thus explicit transformation of the cash flow in the terminal value method is the only practical method combined with the appropriate ratio using the transformed flows.

9.4.   Choice of Discount Rate

The role of the discount rate has been indicated in determining the size of the budget and choice of projects. Choice of criteria and choice of discount rate are intertwined. As shown in the previous section, to choose a certain criteria is sometimes to choose a certain group's view of the opportunity cost of reinvestment, though the choice of rate used to compute NPV or cutoff point on a list of project IRRs is a separate choice from which criteria to use. Is this vital rate a matter of data to be discovered or is it a matter of political choice to be created? The general concept of time preference was discussed earlier, but it is now necessary to consider empirical measures more closely. It is first necessary to consider forgone private investment opportunities, then to consider trade-offs between consumption and saving, and finally to inquire more deeply into possible differences between individual time preference and observed market interest rates. Some people accept the rate of interest on savings accounts, others accept the rate on government bonds, and others accept the rate on corporate stock.

9.4.1.   Investment Opportunity Costs

If a unit of resource is extracted from the private sector to build a public project, what is its opportunity cost? Rates of return on private investment should be observable and relevant. But many such rates can be observed with respect to different industries and financial instruments and these opportunities differ among individuals. Also the reported rates often have different conceptual bases. For example, Flemming et al. (1976) calculated the rate at which future earnings in the private sector are discounted in the United Kingdom capital market, namely, the ratio of real profits to market valuation of the capital stock of industry.[16] During the period 1960 to 1975, the after tax cost of capital varied between 4 and 9 percent.[17]

These figures are hard to interpret, however, because the market value is a function of expected future income and the discount rate, and there is never certainty as to whether the result is a matter of discount rate or differences in expectations. If the cost of borrowed capital (perhaps the prime rate) were to be considered there would probably be a divergence between it and the cost of capital in the market for corporate paper, bonds, and stock. Corporations are aware that at any given time there is a difference in the cost of capital between issuance of new stock and other borrowing. At times, U.S. major corporations make little use of stock to raise new capital.

For the United States, the annual rate of return in manufacturing from 1961 to 1965 was estimated to be about 15 percent (Stockfish 1969, 194; see also Krutilla and Eckstein 1958, Ch. 4; Baumol 1977; Brown and Santoni 1981). The return on private investment was about 10 percent for the period 1946-1975 (Feldstein 1977). Differences between industries are largely caused by differences in risk (Hirschleifer et al. 1960). Although there is a difference of opinion as to the riskiness of government projects (to be explored in Chapter 10), most regard these projects as relatively low risk. This would suggest that the rate of return in utilities (perhaps the bond rate on highgrade utilities) or the cost of government borrowing would be relevant.

Stockfish (1969) suggests that some of the differences between industries are the result of market disequilibrium, though he regards the difference as minor. There is disagreement among economists on this point and some believe that the barriers to entry erected by large conglomerate oligopolies make some market returns irrelevant as opportunity cost references (Solo 1982, 86). These returns are simply not available to many people.

Some analysts (e.g., McKean 1958, 74-96, 103-34) suggest that with capital rationing, the relevant opportunity cost for any public project is another public project (which does better than the market rate). Thus, the rate of discount should be the rate of return on the marginal project (MIRR).[18] This raises questions previously noted as to reinvestment assumptions. The IRR implies reinvestment at the IRR although others argue it should be at the otherwise chosen market rate used to compute NPV. Some argue that no rate will do and advocate computation of a shadow price for capital such as the B/C ratio of the marginal project (Pearce and Nash 1981, 151-53). This requires the computation of present value at some previously selected rate of discount. A present value B/C ratio is then computed. For example, if the ratio is 1.23/1.00, then 1.23 becomes the shadow price factor multiplied by the nominal capital cost of other projects and then used to recompute their NPVs used for ranking.

The guess of what will turn out to be the marginal project is subject to error. The rate of return to the marginal project is used to select among mutually exclusive projects of different size, and thus there is no certainty as to how much of the budget will be left by the time one gets down the list to the previously guessed marginal project; if the rate turns out to be wrong, the ranking is wrong. With a large number of projects there will be a wide band of projects with similar returns clustered about any possible marginal project, so that the MIRR or shadow price will not be sensitive to the exact determination of the marginal project.

9.4.2.   Rates of Return Adjusted for Taxation

Do observed rates of return on private investment indicate opportunity cost
of public investment? In Section 6.2, a question was raised as to whether the
cost of goods used and produced in a project had to be adjusted for taxation.
The same issue applies to the cost of capital. Some of the rate of return
studies use pretax earnings and others use posttax earnings.

Pearce and Nash (1981, 151) argue that pretax earnings are the measure
of net product. This implies that taxes represent a kind of tribute and
produce no utility. The language of public finance theory is highly
presumptive here and refers to tax financed consumption as a "deadweight"
or "excess burden." See, for example, Sugden and Williams (1978, 225). But
some of the corporate taxes pay for public services received and are a cost of
production like any other input (see also Section 8.10.2). Part of national
defense must be charged to business. My own preference for making
informal and directional comparison is in terms of after-tax cost of capital (or
returns). Tax on corporate profits does not necessarily reduce private
investment below the optimum. But this is in part a matter of attitude and
the question requires public choice among people with different views.

In a perfect capital market, the rate of return would be the same for both
private and public bonds and stocks of the same risk. But because of
corporation taxes, the realized private and public returns may differ (Baumol
1968).

Taxation also creates a problem in inferring individual rates of time
preference from observations of the rate at which people lend. If people are
subject to different rates of marginal taxation, then the realized rate and the
time preference differs for people in different tax brackets (Sugden and
Williams 1978, 44).

In summary, it is not so obvious which of the several observable market
rates should be used and how to interpret them. In the United States, the
fact that some drug companies realize returns of 20 percent has little
significance for the small saver who gets much less for a savings and loan
passbook account. Not only is the corporate capital market not perfect, but
the private savings market is deliberately segmented by government policy.
The government knows that if capital were completely mobile, the savings
and loan companies would have much less capital to loan for housing
mortgages. Regulation Q of the Federal Reserve made opportunity costs
unequal among individuals. The government paid 9 percent on Series EE
savings bonds available to small savers, however, it required $10,000 to buy a
higher yielding Treasury Bill in 1981. The latter might be justified in part by
differences in transactions costs, but for whatever reason, individuals have
different opportunities at the margin. This means that when some people
consume, we cannot assume they are valuing the forgone investment and
future consumption at the same rate as others. Therefore is there any
possibility that analysts can measure the time preference of these individuals

when it might be expected to be less than the yield on T-Bills and certainly less than the prime rate or corporate yields? The next section will consider this question and will discuss the possibility that some individuals collectively might reject the private returns even if they could get them.

9.4.3. Individual versus Collective Choice

It will be useful to review the factors affecting time preference and whether these might be expected to be reflected in market choice or might require collective choice. These factors include death, nearsightedness, and concern for future generations. The most obvious reason for some positive rate of time preference is that one may not be around to enjoy the future income. The probability of death can be calculated and one would then expect time preference from this source to be higher in countries with a lower life expectancy. One study derived TP rates of .4 percent for the United States and 2.15 percent for India for the median 40- to 44-year-old age group (Eckstein 1961) . The U.S. rate for the 80- to 84-year-old age group rises to 7.45 percent. Even with these data, we are left with a political choice of whether the young or the old are to count. Another study argued that U.S. investors have a time preference of 5 to 7 percent (Feldstein 1977).

People seem to discount the future because of pure nearsightedness. This is reflected in the folk saying that "a bird in the hand is worth two in the bush." Leaving out uncertainty (easier in theory than in empirical practice), some writers regard pure myopia as irrational. Pearce and Nash (1981, 154) observe that economists do not allow for irrational preferences such as those permitting indifference curves to intersect so they see no reason to allow for irrational myopia. The view taken here is that if some people are myopic and others are not, there must be a political choice to sort it out.

A third factor in time preference is expectations as to future income, both of the chooser and of future generations that the chooser cares about. The altruistic concern for future generations (Pigou 1932, 26; Dobb 1960; Sen 1961) leads us to suspect that some people will have a lower time preference than even the market return rates they can get, but it is difficult to empirically determine. It has been suggested that collective concern for future generations, when an individual knows that others are saving, also may be greater than market choice when a person is ignorant of others' choices (Marglin 1963a). Sen (1967) calls this the "isolation paradox."[19] In the case of many joint-impact goods (marginal cost = zero), individuals can provide very little for future generations acting individually. They may save more if they know others are doing likewise. This requires political choice and is not a matter for independent measurement and simple aggregation.

If the government wishes to give more weight to unborn generations, it can select lower discount rates for application to distant returns (costs) (Nash 1973). Collard (1979) has developed a more complex formulation incorporating an intergenerational discount rate emphasizing that new generations comprise different people and not merely ourselves grown older. Even a lower rate of discount for future years gives practically no value to very distant returns. One device for giving more weight to future generations is to discount only over each generation. This gives a PV for the start of each generation's cash flow to which is applied a politically chosen altruistic weight reflecting demand for intergenerational transfers. The transfer weight is effectively a price and might be expected to vary by product.

The concern for the income of future generations may be ill placed. On the basis of modern experience, we can expect them to be richer than the current choosing generation.[20]   Nevertheless, if the concern for future generations is valid it suggests a political TP less than the private rate of return, but greater than zero, if there is diminishing marginal utility for the richer generation (or even current choosers). The concept of diminishing marginal utility of consumption has two components. One is the rate of per capita consumption growth and the other is the elasticity of the utility function. Per capita growth rates offer some chance for empirical estimation but become problematic if extended very far. Further, not everyone has the same expectations of future income let alone that of future generations. So even the initially solid data of growth rates are subject to political debate between the optimists and pessimists.

The utility function component is beyond individually observable data. This has not stopped analysts from taking the U.K. data for 1957-1978 showing population growing at .39 percent and real consumption growing at 2.35 percent, asserting an elasticity of -2, and obtaining 3.8 percent as the time preference rate (Pearce and Nash 1981, 158.) The tentativeness of this offering is suggested by a comment by Dasgupta and Pearce (1972, 144) to the effect that "The question then arises as to who is to assess the most desirable elasticity." In addition, because the rate of discount affects growth, there is a fundamental conceptual problem in using the growth rate as datum to determine the discount rate (Hirschleifer (1961, 496). Perhaps this theoretical conundrum can be resolved by seeing it as an interacting process with growth rates in one period being used to form discount rates in the next.

In spite of the previous problem it seems that the long-term growth rate in real terms is a relevant input into a qualitative and directional public decision of the discount rate. For the post-World War II period, U.S. real growth was about 3.5 percent. Real interest rates were of the same general order. For example, between 1950 and 1970, a period of relatively stable prices, the real rate of interest ranged roughly between 0 and 5 percent, but some negative rates occurred in the 1970s (Wood 1981, 5). Many advocate the long-term growth rate as the cost of capital (Dobb 1969, 158-59 and 192; Arrow 1966; Gramlich 1981, 106). However, even if this is accepted, there is still the ultimate necessity for political choice between the views of individuals who expect different shares of this long-term growth rate.

Before we become too enamored of the implications of expecting the modern growth rate, the question marks on energy, natural environments, and foreign competition must be noted. Even if future generations were richer in general, they may be worse off in terms of some natural resources (MacLean 1983). Tullock (1964) and Baumol (1968) argue for a lower rate of discount for conservation projects. This is more explicitly handled by projecting rising prices of the outputs of such projects over time or by explicit intergenerational transfer weights as previously discussed. In general, it would be more explicit if all outputs were administratively priced as necessary, rather than trying to reflect future objectives in the discount rate (Fuchs and Zeckhauser 1987, 265).

Concern for the health of future generations requires additional consideration because of questions of entitlement. The present generation uses the ozone layer and groundwater for waste disposal. Shall it discount the lives of future generations, which would be saved by regulating use of these resources in the present? The question could be rephrased to whether the future generation is to be acknowledged as the owner of the resources, in which case discounting by the present user is irrelevant. If the present user does not own, there is no option to trade future benefits for present income.

Americans are concerned about their future income as a result of foreign competition (Thurow 1983). Marginal time preference can be expected to be less if future income falls. For business as usual, it is fine to insist that public projects earn today's opportunity cost of capital. But if world competition is developing major new products and you are not, the usual investment criterion will put you out of business in the future. There is no market reference for what the collective marginal rate of time preference is if lower incomes are projected without projects contributing to a nation's structural change. This requires public choice.

9.4.4. Synthetic Discount Rates: Consumption Distinguished from Investment

The opportunity cost of capital depends on where capital for projects is raised, because different people have different time preferences not made equal at the margin by similar investment opportunities. Most writers assume that taxation is at the expense of consumption and borrowing is replacing private investment. This may tend to be true but some taxation replaces investment. Investment criteria can be formulated that incorporate different assumptions as to the opportunity cost of capital and the reinvestment of benefits (both of the project and its foregone nonpublic spending). These algorithms in a sense constitute different syntheses of the investment opportunity cost and time preference concepts when a perfect capital market is not available to make them equal. In the second-best situation in which project flows cannot be borrowed against and transformed into any flow desired, there is no single rate that can represent both time preference (intertemporal aggregation) and opportunity cost.

The essence of the synthetic approach can be demonstrated by reference to the formulation by Marglin (1967, 47-71). For simplicity, the annual benefits are expressed as constant perpetuities. Assuming all costs in the present, capital (K) is divided according to whether it displaces investment (I) or consumption (C). Conventionally the foregone I is regarded as capable of earning a market related rate (p) whereas forgone C is equivalent to some publicly chosen time preference (r). Thus, capital is annualized, and forgone investment gets compounded forward at p and forgone consumption at r. Then both annuities are reduced again to PV by r. Therefore,

$$K = [(I \times p)/r] + [(C \times r)/r]$$

and since consumption carried forward by r and discounted by the same rate reduces to unity we have

$$K = [(I \times p)/r] + C$$

The same thing can be done with benefits (B), distinguishing between those benefits that are saved (b) and reinvested and those that are consumed (1 - b). The benefit side of the equation is

$$B/r [(b \times p/r) + (1 - b)]$$

This gives a shadow priced version of the usual net present value criterion to invest when PV benefits > PV costs (Pearce and Nash 1981, 161).

If the decision is made that the opportunity cost of displaced private investment is the same for all projects then it is not necessary to compute the above equations for every project. Rather it is possible to utilize a shadow price for forgone investment (K), which converts the cost to equivalent monetary units of consumption (Feldstein 1972a; Sugden and Williams 1978, 226-27).

Other authors have developed slightly different formulations incorporating different policy assumptions (Bradford 1975; Sjaastad and Wisecarver 1977). The effect on project ranking of differences in p and r depends on assumptions as to the length of time reinvestment is made, interest rate feedback, and whether society saves for the depreciation of public capital (Tresch 1981, 500-505). One of the major current problems in the United States is that benefits of some urban public works have been consumed and no money set aside for their replacement (Choate and Walter 1981). Mishan (1976, Chs. 34 and 38) notes that it all depends on what constraint (objective) is imposed on the agencies and the assumed behavior of benefit recipients and taxpayers. Thus, he shows different combinations of compounding and discounting rates for benefits and costs that can be done easily in the terminal value method of Section 9.3.4. Application of the terminal value method with two rates of reinvestment compounding can be seen in project D of Table 9.3.

In the context of developing countries, Little and Mirrlees (1974, Ch. 9) present a model that incorporates a shadow price for savings and labor. (See also Hansen 1978, Ch 6.) The model has the effect of rejecting the high time preference of poor project beneficiaries in favor of projects in which the government or private sector with a high marginal propensity to save can command the receipts for further investment. Little and Mirrlees (1974, 172) argue that much labor via transfers consumes more than its MVP and thus the economy would grow more if this consumption were taxed and shifted to investment. They do not say what happens to this labor if it is not mobile and reemployed on public projects. Death? The analyst who implements a shadow price for savings without direction by the political authorities is value presumptive. (See previous discussion of shadow pricing wages in Section 6.5.2).

The various views of the value of the alternatives forgone can be summarized. The simplest view to accommodate is when the alternative investments and consumption are valued at the same rate used to calculate PV. (Their PV ratios can be used for rankings.) This is the situation in which everyone has the same time preference and opportunity cost at the margin.[21] When there are differences among individuals and their TP and opportunity costs, various views are possible. Some may view the marginal agency project as the relevant opportunity to reinvest. This means the discount rate is the MIRR or some hybrid thereof. Others may prefer that consumption be differentiated from investment with C at r and I at p. This may be done for benefits and/or costs.[22] The split can be done once for the next year or it can continue for the chosen life span of the analysis. Some of these viewpoints can be incorporated systematically into investment criteria such as that of Marglin or more flexibly and explicitly by the transformed terminal value method described earlier.

The synthetic approach has all of the problems of opportunity cost and TP previously discussed plus the need for data on source of capital. Turvey (1971b, 13) dramatically summarizes the needed data, "So in order to ascertain the effects of a project on consumption it is necessary to know, in the first place, how much investment it displaces, what that investment would have yielded, how much of its yield would have been reinvested, and so on *ad infinitum*. In the second place, it is necessary to know how much of the output of the project will be reinvested, what this will yield, how its yield is used, and so on *ad infinitum*." He concludes that for all of its internal logic, it is impossible to apply because "the necessary knowledge is too difficult to obtain." Looking historically, it is possible in the aggregate to say what percentage of total government expenditure was paid by tax and borrowing. But what does this mean for marginal public investment? At a more basic level, it is not just a question of fact whether the marginal project came from C or I, but whose C and I.

The reader familiar with the literature in this area may wonder why no reference has been made here to social opportunity cost or social time preference. These terms are avoided because they serve as a mask for the conflicts of interest among people with different opportunities. It is appropriate for political choice, not technical discovery. The usual stance of Pareto-better BC analysis is that it is desirable to increase total wealth ignoring who receives it (and conversely who pays the cost). Any analysis that attempts to improve the measure of wealth change by making distinctions between net receipts that are consumed and invested violates the Pareto-better criterion. The advocates of the synthetic approach acknowledge that who receives the income makes a difference because they have different opportunities. But this gets glossed over in the focus on the split between C and I. Mishan (1976, 252) does in passing contemplate using a different division between C and I for different groups. It is a small step from this to the use of different rates of discount for computing the opportunity cost of capital for different groups reflecting their different rates of time preference that persist because the capital market is not and cannot be perfect. It does not make sense to make the first-best assumption of an undifferentiated pool of investment seeking the highest returns without caring where it comes from and who receives it (because distribution can be handled separately later), and then turning around and worrying about C and I splits. The reason that the value of C and I differs (and thus r and p) is that not all people have the same opportunities.

If the synthetic approach is extended to its logical conclusion to actually reflect the differences in group opportunities, it leads to the odd situation of one rate for compounding reflecting one view and another for discounting reflecting another.[23] This produces some troublesome results that are not always Pareto-better.

The implications can be illustrated by an example. Consider the projects in the transformed Table 9.3. Suppose the government decides on a single compromise rate of 10 percent as the private opportunity cost of capital (K). But suppose that group b, which is the recipient of project B, does not have the opportunity to invest at 10 percent and has a time preference of 7 percent, and is willing to be taxed for any project earning more than 7 percent. As shown in Table 9.3, short-lived project B is an unmarketable good and must be consumed (project Z at 10 percent is irrelevant); thus it is equivalent to being carried forward at 7 percent and has a TV of 117.[24] Project B_x is similar in size but the net benefits are monetized and can be reinvested in project Z at 10 percent and are received by a group with better opportunities (say 20 percent). In Table 9.3, reinvestment is carried forward at 20 percent for a TV of 133. Even at the less extreme rate of 10 percent the implications would be the same. If there is capital rationing, project B_x will be better that project B. Group b will miss the opportunity to obtain a project that does better than its otherwise poor alternatives (117/114). This is rejected because the analysis shows it as 117/121. The beneficiaries of B_x

are indifferent to a project that produces a conceptual stream of reinvestment that the government regards as wealth maximizing (reinvested at 10 percent to be 121/121), but from the recipients point of view they would have preferred to keep the original project investment for their own higher valued (20 percent) purposes and get 133/121.[25] The group that receives B_x would agree to financing the project by borrowing at any rate less than 10 percent, but not by taxation.

If the costs are borne by one group and the benefits are received by another group, the question of Pareto improvement depends on which group's discount rate is used, in other words, on whether the analysis uses the view of the taken or the taker. Again consider project B_x in Table 9.3, now, however, only group b pays the cost. If this group has a TP of 8 percent then the opportunity cost of the K = 100 is equivalent to 108 in year 1. Because the project produces 110 in year 1, the recipients can compensate group b and the result is potentially Pareto-better. But if the 110 in year 1 is discounted at the recipients' discount rate of say 20 percent, the recipients have a PV of less than 100 and cannot compensate group b which paid for the project and thus there is no Pareto improvement. As Sugden and Williams (1978, 223) conclude, "If private MTPRs differ--as they do--a social MTPR can be constructed from these private rates only in a highly arbitrary way." (MTPR is the marginal time preference rate.)

9.4.5.   Pure Time Preference and Inflation

Ideally, time preference should be separated from adjustments for inflation. If prices of benefits and costs are in real terms, then the discount rate should also be in real terms, that is, a pure time preference. Observed market rates contain an inflation premium. People would like to receive more than their pure time preference to account for inflation (but may not get it--witness periods of negative real interest rates). If an observed market rate of interest is used to discount projects, costs and benefits over time should be inflated at the expected rate of inflation (change in general price level).

The usual counsel (and the one followed by the U.S. Water Resources Council 1973) is to use current prices for both costs and benefits, unless some component of them is expected to change faster than others. Large projects constructed over a period of years seem particularly susceptible to cost overruns, which narrow realized net returns (Chitale 1981). If relative prices are expected to be unchanged, then present prices discounted by a publicly chosen pure time preference are appropriate, rather than an observed market rate containing an inflation premium (Sugden and Williams 1978, 37). The exception occurs when real relative scarcities are expected to change--for example, fossil fuels become scarce. Another exception is changes in relative demand. For example, some argue that preferences are changing and prices of wilderness experience or health products will be increasing through time.

These are not matters of inflation, but of shifts in relative prices that should be explicitly used to calculate cash flows.

9.5.   What Governments Do[26]

The practices used by goverment to aggregate benefits and costs over time have been previously noted, but can be highlighted here as follows:

1. Budget constraints are common. Budget size is not determined by determining which projects have positive rates of return above some cutoff rate.

2. Some countries use a cutoff rate to minimally qualify projects for funding. Observation of the process suggests that projects with political support seldom fail the minimal test. The agencies in these cases work hard to find enough benefits somewhere. Many countries such as the United States display some type of benefit-cost ratio. Many other countries and the World Bank are partial to calculating the internal rate of return.

3. Choice of projects is seldom a function of project ranking by any formal criterion. Ranked lists are seldom available. Selection tends to be a matter of accepting or rejecting one or a small group of projects at a time.

4. Choices in the early design stage are critical and tend to be unaltered as a result of later comparisons of rate of return. Items may be deleted or added to obtain political consensus, but not because it makes the rate of return relatively higher.

5. In the United Kingdom, the HMSO (1967) White Paper on Nationalized Industries required a rate of 10 percent with the principle being the private sector return on low risk projects. In the United States, there is no consistent discount rate used by all agencies. U.S. Office of Management and Budget (1972) Circular A-94 required 10 percent, but it was never fully implemented until President Reagan began to use 10 percent as a minimum requirement for inclusion in the Executive Budget. For so central an issue to economists, it is interesting to note the cavalier attitude of Congress giving its tacit approval to various discounting practices of its agencies rather than an explicitly legislated rate.

The one area in which the rate has been written into law is for all water resource development agencies. The principle of a floating rate equal to the average interest yield realized each year on 15-year government bonds was adopted in 1974.[27]   After many years in which the agencies without Congressional direction used the coupon rate, Congress did not want a sharp rise in rates so it mandated that the rate could not rise more than .25 percent per year. In the period of rapidly rising interest rates it never caught up to the actual bond yield and in 1981, when the prime rate reached 20 percent and U.S. government bonds reached 14 percent, the water agencies' discount rate was 7-5/8 percent. It was 8-5/8 in 1987. In addition, the agencies argued that projects originally planned under lower rates should continue to be qualified at their old rates and not reassessed.

6. U.S. regulatory agencies also use different rates. The EPA recommended a ban on some uses of asbestos and rejected the concept of discounting future lives saved (Russell 1986). The Office of Management and Budget earlier had insisted on discounting.

The reasons for these second-best behaviors are complex, but include problems of bounded rationality and preferences for distribution. In any case, some acknowledgment of the need for simplification consistent with "satisficing" behavior seems in order.

9.6.   Second-Best Segmented Budgets

Attention to different groups' opportunity costs leads to a conception of segmented, compartmentalized budgets, each with its own discount rate. If distribution could be separated from resource allocation (first-best), it would not matter who pays as the exercise is to maximize total wealth (which can then be supposedly redistributed at will). But if people face different opportunities, then the value of benefits and costs differs according to who receives and pays.[28] If this is recognized, compartmentalized budgets are necessary and the transformation display must reflect the different discount rates for both benefit and costs. Compartmentalized budgets are also consistent with consumer behavior that allocates incomes to budget categories including durables and savings and then ranks or compares only the alternatives within these categories (Earl 1983, Ch. 4). Reallocation responds only to major changes in interest rates. These simplified decision processes are consistent with bounded rationality and limited information processing capacity (Kahneman and Tversky 1979).

Once we accept that we do not have a perfect capital market and acknowledge the necessity of making sense of a second-best situation, some other questions are raised. In the usual first-best case, any divergence between r and p is a temporary disequilibrium that is interpreted as indicating there is too little total investment. Stockfish (1969, 191) (also Nichols 1970) state that even if $r<p$ it does not follow that government should use r. The problem is too little investment, and replacing high yielding private investments with lower yielding public ones does not help much. Rather the government should stimulate private investment by things such as tax policy.

But $r<p$ may have another interpretation in a second-best world. It may mean that the government does not accept the p rate, but has neither the will nor the power to put other laws into effect to alter it.[29] When a socialist government rejects the chance to get high returns in pizza parlors, it is not necessarily indicating that it wants more total investment. Rather it may want more hospitals or housing. This could be regarded as a violation of

consumer sovereignty. But consumers are sovereign only over what they have the property right to command, which is necessarily a matter of government decision. The usual welfare economics dictum is that any changes in rights must be direct redistribution. Take the case of the U.S. Federal Reserve Bank Regulation Q that once limited the yield on small savings accounts. The government was not necessarily irrational. It wanted to increase home building. A direct alternative would have been to increase taxes on those already adequately housed and to make housing grants. Instead, government effects transfers between some savers and home buyers. The justice of this is not the question here. The point is that government is as imperfect as the capital market. In principle it might get the results it wants by systematic changes in property rights such as taxing pizza parlors, controlling advertising that creates consumer demand for goods and therefore distorts demand for private and public goods, or rooting out all monopolies. Instead it sometimes crudely reduces the resources going to these private activities through general taxation and public investment at some r less than some theorist's hypothetical p. The implication is that government can persist in using its r with no implications that government is irrational if it does not lower taxes on private investment returns.

Government has the same problem of lack of system control over its own departments. The center is not able to monitor all of its agencies' estimates of project cash flows. Therefore, it may refuse to be bound by the agencies' MIRR as the rate of discount and rather impose its own in project selection and determination of budget size, or simply set budget limits on different agencies. As Little and Mirrlees (1974, 97) state, "if there was not perfect trust in the agency, then it might be desirable to make it operate within a budget ceiling." Information cost forces second-best strategies.

What then are the connections between a segmented budget and an investment criterion using a synthetic discount (compounding) rate (recall Section 9.4.4)? Choice of the segmented budget approach implies that the time preference of the program's beneficiaries are to count. That would suggest that the same rate would apply to the opportunity cost of investment and the reinvestment of any project net receipts and no synthesis would be necessary. The opportunity cost of investing any claim on the treasury is equivalent to the alternative of immediately consuming it, which is equivalent to the recipients' TP. For example, a poor group might have a TP of 20 percent and regard this as the opportunity cost of investing its share of the budget. And it would make no reinvestment of any net returns unless the yield was more than 20 percent. It would probably want to consume its share of the budget.

If the government does not want to live with the group's preferences, then perhaps it should not use a segmented budget but rather its preferred synthetic discount rate with different rates for consumption and investment components. But in an imperfect world, government may lean toward honoring the different time preferences of different program recipients, although only in part. This would mean it would need to choose two different rates for each program segment. For example, it may make a concession toward the high time preference of the poor and use 20 percent as the opportunity cost of investment (and compound value of foregone private benefits) but not fully accept the low growth rate associated with high consumption. Thus, government may use another lower rate for compounding reinvestment at the governments' investment opportunity (MIRR) assuming it has the administrative ability to actually obtain the early returns. This seems most appropriate in developing countries in which government plays a more aggressive role in influencing growth and investment.

9.7.   Summary and Conclusion

9.7.1   Implications of Differences in Marginal Rates of Time Preference

People have different marginal rates of time preferences (MRTP) because of the inherent character of financial markets (transaction and risk costs), differences in taxes, and other deliberate government policy. Property rights interacting with characteristics of goods and situations allocate different market opportunities to different people. The capital market is also structured by rights and presents people with different opportunities. It would be incredible if some perfect capital market could somehow create equal opportunities at the margin and overcome the other inequalities present in society. That is what is presumed when we suppose the young and old, rich and poor can somehow borrow and lend until their MRTPs are equal. When theory does recognize this reality it distorts the issue by focusing on the differences between consumption and investment. Inquiry into the split between C and I in the aggregate must not ignore that it is the difference between individuals that caused the opportunities for C and I to differ in the first place.

It is time for theory to evolve further to explicitly recognize individual differences. DeAlessi (1969) argues that any choice of discount rate makes an interpersonal value judgment. But once it is recognized that second-best procedures are necessary, it is not enough to ask government to select some compromise overall rate (or one for C and another for I and the percentage of cost split between them). The second-best situation makes a grand efficiency calculation nonsense. Segmented budgeting is the only sensible calculation when the trade-offs are to be explicit. The political question is who owns what part of the budget (and the opportunity to borrow). This is a matter for original jurisdiction of political choice, not something to be revealed in a market or derived from a political choice of an overall discount rate.

Vanags (1975, 142) says, "Once it is accepted that, at least in the present state of knowledge, the overall size of the public investment programme cannot be decided in a decentralized manner the discount rate serves merely to decide on the mix of projects." He refers to long- or short-lived projects. It may be that an overall budget calculation with some single compromise discount rate (or different for C and I) might fit some dominant group's time preference.[30]   But it may well suit no one.   Recall Section 9.4.4 for an example in which the compromise rate may result in project selection that suits neither the high nor low TP group. All nations' budgets are highly compartmentalized. Allocation to agencies has little to do with comparative rates of return. This is just as true for international agencies such as the World Bank that uses BCA to qualify projects, but allocates funds among countries by other criteria.

Investment ranking is more likely to affect choices of projects within an agency than allocation of budgets to agencies. If a group is going to get a certain volume of projects anyway, it does not make much sense to have project scale and time flow dictated by some national compromise discount rate. The compromise rate may be a source of inefficiency in a second-best world. If a government wants to give a certain group or region a certain volume of projects, it makes no sense to design them by some national time trade-off criteria that do not fit the recipients. This practice may account for why most of an agency's projects look the same regardless of where they are located and whom they are supposed to serve. A uniform rate may result in allocative slippage. The government tries to help a certain group by choosing its preferred rate, but inadvertently helps others as well, depending on the characteristics of available projects. Since the rate is necessarily a political choice reflecting allocative judgment, any uniform rate turns out to be an allocatively crude way to get more of the budget into the hands of the favored group.

Does practice of segmented budgets mean that no common rates should be used to compare projects among agencies? In the short run, relative rates of return have little to do with an agency's budget. In the longer run, rates of return are one of the several arguments that affect allocation of the budget. An agency with consistently lower return projects is vulnerable to attack. For this reason, a government may choose to exhibit ranking of projects using a common compromise rate of discount for all agencies for long run comparative purposes even if it does not use the same rate for selecting and designing projects within an agency or group of agencies with clients in common.

At the present time in the United States, the average or marginal rate of project return seems to have little effect on budget size. There is continual capital rationing. The relative number of unfunded projects with positive PV seems to have little to do with budget size or allocation. In the first-best case one might hope that if government sets a discount rate that implies that the budget is too small, it would either increase the budget or raise the rate. But this falls on deaf ears. Congress often wants a particular project aiding certain groups that would not meet the cutoff threshold at a higher rate. So Congress keeps the overall rate low to accommodate these wanted projects and then does not fund the total budget consistent with the low rate. But this "fictitious rate" then distorts scale and design of all projects. It might be more sensible in the second-best case to segment the budget allowing a lower rate for certain groups and a higher rate for the design of projects for others. (Of course, Congress may not want to openly defend its decision to aid a certain group and may prefer to obfuscate the issue by hiding behind a less apparently allocative choice of discount rate, and no one but economists notice the inconsistency in capital rationing anyway.)

In general, BCA or any systems analysis begins with some externally given (albeit after analytic inputs) statements of objectives. Then specific choices are calculated consistent with these objectives. A major question is how general should these objectives be stated. It was noted before that if there is only one general objective, it is going to be difficult to apply and if it is too detailed, it dictates a specific project choice and there is nothing left for analysis.

First-best theory makes budget size and its allocation a function of some rate of discount that is accepted as a generalized time preference rule externally chosen by society in the market or administratively. The generally stated rule then allows budget size to be deduced. This politically chosen rule may not make sense and it is so general that the necessary interpretation by anlaysts involves political choice among conflicting groups. As was noted, the knowledge of sources of capital (C and I splits) is impossible and choice of the combined rate is necessarily arbitrary in selecting the groupings of individuals and their opportunity cost. This suggests that the externally given property right rule for budget making should not be in terms of an abstraction such as the discount rate, but rather in terms of who owns different segments of the budget (at least which agencies have it for what purposes). This is in fact what is done. Governments as a matter of original jurisdiction allocate agency claims on the treasury just as they determine other rights issues such as abortion or pollution rights. They do not permit these claims be a derivative of some more generally stated right equivalent to the appropriate compromise rate of discount. Because it is very difficult for public representatives to fully understand the consequences of such a rights statement, they legislate budget allocations for investment by program areas and agencies (and for transfer also by program areas, agencies, and classes of individuals).

If a group is going to get a percentage of the treasury, it might as well get what fits it best. The other parties' consent can be based on a sense of fairness rather than a compromise over the discount rate, which is not instrumental in determining who gets what anyway. What a group gets is a majority decision, but the issue is the focus of that decision. Once the compromise is reached that a group gets a certain amount of spending, it seems unlikely that the rest of the nation that granted the money really cares about the time flow of the costs and benefits. Yet, under current procedures, the beneficiaries do not get their desired time preference. The point is not that the consenting majority will not extract something for its consent, but that it can be something serving its interests, rather than some meaningless compromise on the discount rate. For example, the consenting majority may insist on certain environmental constraints. The granting of rights always takes place in a broader environment of accommodation. The only issue is the "currency" of these transactions. The currency need not be a compromise of the discount rate; if it is not going to be used to set budget size and allocate projects to groups, the currency might be more useful if it were in other forms.

9.7.2.   Analyst-Politician Dialogue: System Boundaries

What sort of questions would the analyst ask of the political representatives and how would the information thus obtained be incorporated systematically (albeit a limited system)?   And what sort of aid can be given to these representatives to help guide their thinking? The first question involves what sort of budget segments are wanted. Is it to be by region, income group, agency, or program category? As was seen in Section 3.3, this naming and grouping are major political choices.

The next question involves what rate of discount to use for each segment, and whether a synthesized rate distinguishing consumption (C) and investment (I) is desired. How might the political authority consider these issues? Some overall guides include looking for differences in TP that might be expected to be related to the target group's age or income (present and future). Is there reason to think the target group has a lower TP for C than the government can achieve for it by reinvestment? (Note that we are not talking of one group's C and another's I.) Would the group appreciate more projects in which the government can keep and reinvest a major portion of returns?   A poor group would probably have TP greater than the government's reinvestment opportunity, so we are probably talking of a middle income group with moderate TP, but poor I opportunities. It does not seem realistic that the group would allow government to invest in private sector stocks and bonds to achieve the private returns available to some other groups, so the government MIRR seems relevant.   It is theoretically attractive to think of using some private rate when it exceeds MIRR as the opportunity cost for I and consider government as acting as a pooling agent for the people, something like a mutual fund overcoming transaction and information costs and obtaining the best available private rate of return (even for groups who otherwise have poor investment opportunities).   But in practice this may be hard to sell to people not used to having government play this role.

In the United States much of government investment produces consumer goods, for example, pollution control, recreation, and health care where there is no possibility of reinvestment of receipts. A criterion that favors the few market goods producing projects with returns available to the government for reinvestment would skew investment in nontraditional directions. The split of C and I seems most relevant for countries with a large publicly owned state enterprise sector producing market goods. In this case, it is possible that other things being equal, a group would prefer more state enterprise projects than projects directly producing consumption goods. The government could then reinvest the net receipts at a rate superior to what the group could get in financial markets available to it. A single discount rate for C and I would not select for this type of project.

What about the cost? When would a group want the opportunity cost of projects computed so as to distinguish between finance that came from taxes and finance that came from borrowing? Two questions are involved. The issue is not primarily one of choice among projects but a possible question of cutoff threshold and choice of means of finance. If the choice is to finance the project by borrowing or not build it at all, such as the case for many LDC projects, the discount rate for cutoff is the borrowing rate. Recall the cost of capital approach (Section 9.2.2) in which all can gain by borrowing regardless of their TP. Yet, they will differ on the preferred means of finance. If budgets are segmented and decisions are made at a more local level, there may be more homogeneity in finance method preference. Projects received by those with opportunities greater than the public cost of borrowing, and who thus prefer borrowing, can be separated from those projects whose beneficiaries have opportunities less than the public borrowing rate and prefer taxation. The later group would prefer a synthetic approach because the more tax finance is used, the more projects qualify.

In the first-best case, the system boundary is national and the opportunity cost of capital determines budget size, and if the tentative budget allocation were not used up, the tax money would be returned to individuals for private investment or equivalent consumption. This is never done in practice as there is always capital rationing. In addition, a group never has its taxes reduced by anything equivalent to the amount of projects it might refuse, so there is little incentive to refuse projects. This could be changed if the budget allocated to a group could be taken in cash grants or projects.[31] Then a project refused for not meeting a minimum cutoff return would still put money into the hands of the group. The discount rate or opportunity cost shadow price of investment then determines the project-grant mix. U.S. President Jimmy Carter's suggested reform of Federal water programs was along these lines with the states being given a budget and the power to use the budget to fund projects designed by Federal or state agencies.

9.7.3.   Physical Target Constraints

Capital markets are not only imperfect, in some cases they may be nonexistent. A poor country may not be able to borrow against a project with high yields in the future. The time flow of consumption cannot be made independent of the actual physical time flow of project output. Marglin (1967, 51) points out that if government sets a specific consumption target for a series of years (say for food) then although there may be very high yielding projects with high NPV there is no way they can be converted into the required physical flow. He says, "Nor is there any mechanism by which government can, like a private decision maker, 'borrow' consumption against the security of future benefits."

The problem is perhaps even more severe in the case of nonmarketed goods such as health. There is no way to exchange future health benefits for present ones. It is possible to describe a choice between alternative time flow projects (regulations) in terms of a time preference rate. But the rate has no implication for future choices if physical constraints are set. If government's objective is a specific consumption amount during the planning period, discounting is irrelevant. The problem becomes one only of cost minimization to achieve the fixed objective.

The comparison of alternative projects and products has already been made when constraints are imposed. The matter of constraints is difficult and economists will have to work with public representatives so boundaries for application of a given rule can be chosen intelligently. (See Henderson 1969 and Chapter 12 in this volume). As Eckstein (1961, 450) notes, "there comes a point where the assumptions are so specific that they produce 'bad' economics. Constraints can be assumed to rule out all solutions except one, which is automatically justified. On the other hand, to prohibit the use of constraints altogether is to confine economics to a very narrow--and usually utopian--range of problems."

9.7.4.   Procedural Conclusions

To facilitate systematic implementation of time-related policy objectives, the analyst can probably best serve by asking the political authority to (1) make budget allocations to regions, programs, groups, and agencies, (2) select a rate of discount for each budget segment, and (3) select the source of capital it regards as the most limiting. As most political authorities seem to prefer compartmentalized budgets with capital rationing, they might as well make the second-best of it. The discount (compounding) rates to be used can most explicitly be expressed by rules for transforming each project into a display of its cash flows over time using the provided rates to show the result of the reinvestment of intermediate returns to produce a common terminal value. For the most part, the problem raised for the use of rates for projects of different size can be ignored (see Section 9.3.3). For example, there might be a segmented budget selected from Table 9.3 of alternatives competing for a given budget aimed at group X composed of project B_x and a recomputed Z_x (consumption forgone) compounded at the group's r of 20 percent. Once the reinvestment rate has been explicitly politically chosen and terminal values computed, projects in the subbudget can be ranked by either the PV ratio or IRR, it does not matter which.

But it may matter with respect to the question of whose capital is the limiting factor to which returns are to be maximized. This is a key policy question that must be settled and the answer to the question determines what sort of rate of return concept is used. If the politicians want to make a distinction between sources of capital, IRR will not meet their objectives. Although some sets of these policy objectives fit some one of the many investment criteria formulas (algorithms) put forward in the literature, it will often be necessary to make these explicitly in the transformation display of the capital opportunity cost and the expression of it as a particular form of ratio, that is, not every component of a negative cash flow may be regarded as equally limiting and included in the ratio's denominator.

The recomputed cash flows display may not always be necessary, but in any case it may be the most explicit method, for a criterion formula can be used without being aware of its assumptions and therefore the relevant issues would never be raised with policy makers. Construction of the transformation display (terminal value method) forces the right questions to be asked in formulating the rules for reinvestment and calculation of cash flows and terminal values and for representation of the cost of forgone private consumption and investment.

Choice of a discount (compound) rate is a topic of great dispute among economists. I unequivocally side with those who regard it as a matter of public choice, not something to be discovered as prior datum.[32] A similar position is taken by Sugden and Williams (1978, 223) who say "it is not at all clear how differences in MTPR's between individuals can be reconciled." They continue by adding that "there is a strong case that the social MTPR should be a valuation postulated by decision-makers." The issue is not only one of political price versus market price but one of choice of whose market opportunities count. In some cases, the budget segmentation means the beneficiaries of a program will have more homogeneous time preferences, but differences remain to be resolved by public choice.

This is not to say that reporting of opportunities encountered by different groups is irrelevant, for it is an input into policy decision making, even if the group's aggregation is a political task. To say that economists alone do not have the answer is not to say that information is useless. An interactive, iterative process would be useful to show decision makers how the choice of discount rate and investment criteria might affect budget size and ranking (what and whose projects would be selected, but perhaps more important what projects get designed). For example, Haveman (1965, Ch. 5) applied various criteria to 147 U.S. Corps of Engineer projects. In effect, analysts can simulate the choice implications of alternative policies to see if the ranking results are sensitive. For a presentation of simulation techniques see Hufschmidt and Fiering (1966). Politicians should be reminded that the competition is not only between public and private investment, but also between public investment and public consumption. A generous public investment budget has current account public spending as its opportunity cost as well as private consumption or investment.

To summarize the departures in this chapter, it should be remembered that the emphasis has been on making the best of second-best. This means that a more modest objective of suboptimization is suggested and it will not only be more honest, but also it might lead to the design of projects better suited to the needs of the majority of project beneficiaries as to project size and time flow of benefits. The question of who owns the treasury should determine the question of project design to fit the time preference of beneficiaries.

Vanags (1975, 141) states, "The test discount rate plays virtually no part in determining the overall size of the public sector investment--it serves mainly to determine the composition of investments in different sectors once the size of the programme has been decided. This limited role seems to me to be quite proper." In practice the discount rate choice and project rank have little to do with actual choice among projects with some net return. There might be more systematic matching of projects to fit different group's time preferences if budgets were explicitly segmented, rather than the present pretense of a total systematic analysis combined with completely unsystematic political choice. Even so, the question can be asked whether even a partial system analysis is possible. There is limited demand by politicians for embarrassing explicit choice (see Chapter 11). Politicians may not want to set different time preference (discount) rates by agency or program. Although there would be more homogeneity of time preference within the groups served by an agency than between agencies, there could still be considerable conflict. Politicians may prefer to gloss over the issue and retreat to a single overall rate and claim impartiality (and then hide their inevitable partiality with ad hoc project choice).

Finally, how should the independent researcher doing an individual BCA proceed when it is not possible to question the political authority about its objectives, but the desire is still to have the study in a form usable by anyone? The results can be summarized using a range of discount (compound) rates and several investment criteria (or rather explicit reinvestment assumptions). The reader should be cautioned that comparisons with other projects must be made only on the basis of similar rates and criteria and that the optimum scale of the project depends on the discount rate. This calls attention to the fact that the usual single study is for only one selected scale, leaving returns to scale unexplored.

Notes

1. If a person consumes when there is an opportunity to invest at a given rate, the TP is at least equal to the rate of growth of that forgone opportunity. Rationality suggests that the value of present consumption is equivalent to that amount compounded at the time preference rate. TP lets us convert any flow into a comparable present or future value.

2. As noted in the previous section, a person with MRTP > MRT wants to borrow whereas the person with MRTP < MRT wants to lend.

3. The person with MRTP = 15 percent prefers project B in Table 9.1 in which the money available in years 1 and 2 can be consumed or reinvested at 15 percent. But the person with MRTP = 6 percent prefers project A as the consumption or reinvestment of B's cash flow is not as valuable. If there is capital rationing, reinvestment is possible in the marginally available public project, but its marginal IRR will not be the cost of capital.

4. Because of uncertainty, each participant in the market applies her own expectation of yield and risk premiums. A "collective" market valuation of the stock emerges that implies a rate of discount, but it is not available a priori to guide management's choice of investments.   If there were no uncertainty, the maximization of profits using a market rate of interest and the maximization of market value of shares would be identical.

5. A word of caution for those used to business accounting. No deduction from cash flows is made for depreciation or interest payments as these are already implicitly accounted for in the criteria and calculations to follow.

6. For example, for project A in Table 9.2 with a benefit of 115 in year 2 the PV is computed as follows: $1/(1 + .02)^2 = .961$. This discount factor can be found in handbooks of financial tables. Then, $.961 \times 115 = 110.52 =$ PV, and $110.52 - 100 = 10.52 =$ NPV.

7. For further background see McKean (1958, Chs. 5, 6, and 7), Henderson (1968), Turvey (1963), Jensen (1969), Lind et al. (1982), Lorie and Savage (1955), Lutz and Lutz (1951), Merrett (1965), Nash et al. (1974), Solomon (1956 and 1970), Strung (1976), and Weingartner (1963a).

8. Here single period capital rationing is assumed to demonstrate the principles. Where there is multiperiod rationing, programming techniques must be used. See (Weingartner 1963b) and (Marglin 1963b).

9. The person with a TP of 4 percent wants to use an NPV ratio at 4 percent as the ranking criteria, whereas the person with a TP of 10 percent wants to use either an NPV ratio at 10 percent or the IRR as the ranking criteria.

10. Fisher's extended yield or excess benefit method determines whether the remaining capital not used in the smaller project produces a summed excess benefit (NPV) greater than the larger project (Alchian 1955).

11. Unfortunately, the public seldom sees a display of alternative scaled projects for a particular size or purpose. Project sizing is done internally by

the agency that has a predilection for the largest possible projects. Economists have devoted most of their critical attention to the cutoff point for inefficient projects with positive net returns. Where only one project of a given kind is presented for public central budget discussion, the internal agency guidelines for scaling may be as important as the cutoff point focusing on choice among previously poorly designed projects.

12. Mishan (1981, 192) describes a "terminal value procedure," though his suggestion differs in some respects.

13. Although reinvestment opportunities are low return, some poor may have a high discount rate because they are impatient and consumption is valuable.

14. For discussion of another method for computing a modified IRR when assumption on reinvestment of intermediate cash flows is made explicit, see Marty (1970).

15. There is a great dispute over private sector accounting conventions. See Briloff (1981) and Redburn (1975).

16. Note that an investment criteria must be used to calculate rate of return. The usual practice is to relate return to equity capital, after netting out borrowed capital. See Arrow (1966), Arrow and Kurz (1970), and Mendelsohn (1981).

17. See Section 9.4.2 on how taxation effects estimates.

18. On the other hand, capital rationing may be imposed because political authorities do not trust the agency preparing the estimates, in which case they might prefer to select their own discount rate instead of the nominal MIRR.

19. See Collard's (1979, 171) comments on Sen.

20. Feldstein (1977, 117n) says that this argument is irrelevant because the investing generations could sell output to be realized after their death to future generations, but this is impossible for much of the output of public projects.

21. MRTP is the value of consumption = opportunity to invest.

22. In passing, some note of government practice is in order. The U.S. Soil Conservation Service uses a type of synthetic discount rate. Funds coming from state government taxes are discounted at a different rate from those of the federal government.

23. Or, in the terminal value procedure, one rate for compounding annual net benefits and another for net costs.

24. Note that if the project produced cash for group b and the government has another project earning 10 percent, the 10 percent becomes the relevant reinvestment opportunity. The key question is what real reinvestment opportunities are available.

25. The same problem exists if C and I are split without reference to groups of persons.

26. Sources for this summary include the author's experience in government, Birgegard (1975), Haveman (1965), Ingram (1969), and King (1967).

27. Water Resource Development Act of 1974 (P.L. 93-251, Sec. 80a).

28. This is because of differences in time preference and not differences in distribution objectives, which was the topic of Chapter 8.

29. Little and Mirrlees' (1974, Ch. 19) defense of first-best practices is based on the government's will and ability to achieve competitive behavior or earn competitive returns after taxes.

30. This question is unavoidable for high exclusion cost goods that if available for one are necessarily available to many persons.

31. The poor may prefer a cash grant to a project, but will not be willing to tax themselves or able to borrow and pay tax later. Should we use a different discount rate for a grant than for a national income oriented project when the recipients are net tax payers?

32. See, for example, Nath (1969, 175-76) who states "there is no reason why the role of national savings or the rate of discount needs to be derived from anything." They "have to be directly decided upon like any other element in a decision-making . . . social welfare function." For the opposite view see Mishan (1981, 160).

10

Uncertainty

10.1. Introduction

Public as well as private investments differ in the degree of uncertainty as to outcomes. History is replete with examples of project failures, cost overruns in the construction of public projects, and private bankruptcies (Hall 1979; Haveman 1972). Prices of both inputs and outputs may change as a result of shifts in preferences, technology, and action of competitors. In Chapter 4 the problems of predicting the production function were discussed. How then shall our measures of discounted net value over time be adjusted to reflect demand and supply uncertainty, differences among projects in the confidence of our predictions, and mean and variance trade-offs for different people.

Uncertain events have more than one possible outcome. Risky events are uncertain events of importance to the decision makers as the outcomes affect well-being. If the choices available are risky, they may be ordered according to preferences.   The ordering requires both probability of occurrences and preference information. It is not possible to state that one choice is riskier than another without specifying whose preferences count.

In the following discussion a qualitative continuum will be noted for degrees of confidence about expectations. There are situations in which it is possible to attach mathematical probabilities with some confidence to the possible outcomes, whereas in other cases confidence is low and statements of probability can only be qualitative (maybe in rank order) if made at all.

10.2. Mathematical Expectation

10.2.1. Expected Value Criterion

The analyses in previous chapters have produced information relating decisions to outcomes measured in terms of cash flows and present value. Now it is explicitly acknowledged that more than one present value outcome is possible and a subjective probability of each possible outcome can be stated. This information is summarized in the matrix shown in Table 10.1.

Table 10.1 Present Value of Net Income with Alternative Futures

| Decision | States of Nature | | EV | Variance | Standard Deviation |
	S_1 Probability .8	S_2 Probability .2			
D_1	100	-20	76	2303	48
D_2	90	30	78	575	24

The alternative decisions may involve comparing different projects or different designs and management options for the same general project. The different possible environmental conditions for the project are referred to as alternative states of nature. These might be physical conditions such as the weather or other conditions affecting the production function or social and economic conditions such as population growth or prices. Certainty has a probability of 1 and thus a probability of .1 indicates that in a large number of cases, we would expect 10 percent of the outcomes to occur as specified.

Probability is obtained from repeated observation. For example, if 50 or 100 years of rainfall records are available it is possible to specify the probability of a rainfall of a certain size during the next year. Or after repeated application of a certain drug or safety device, the probability of recovery of health or the probable accident rate may be calculated. At best, however, a statement of probability is an approximate measure. No two instances of a phenomenon are ever precisely the same. There are always judgments concerning what information is relevant. The states of nature always represent some degree of aggregation of features as does the definition of inputs and outputs as seen in Chapter 3. There is uncertainty over the probability distribution itself. For example, are 50 or 100 years of rainfall records enough? All statements of probability are fundamentally subjective. A decision must be made to proceed or wait and search for more information.

The outcome probabilities of Table 10.1 do not compel a particular decision. The highest income can come from decision 1, but if things turn out badly that decision can also result in a loss. There are other ways to describe the outcomes. The expected value (EV) or weighted average of the outcomes may be calculated by the formula $EV = \Sigma_i p_i x_i$ where x_i is the value of the ith possible outcome and p_i is the probability of its occurrence. Thus, from Table 10.1, the EV of Decision 1 is $.8 \times 100 + .2 \times (-20) = 76$ and the EV of Decision 2 is 78. On the basis of the expected value, Decision 2 appears best. When would the expected value be an acceptable criterion for decision?

The probabilities were obtained from judgments based on a series of observations. If a large number of similar projects were undertaken, the average outcome may be expected to be the same as the average of past outcomes. The expected value will become the actual or certain value. If the expected value criterion is used, the decision maker is saying that only the mean is important. The variation in outcomes does not matter as a large number of similar and independent decisions are planned. This is the principle used by insurance companies to calculate how much to collect in premiums to cover future losses and for this reason it is often referred to as *actuarial risk*. This criterion would not be used if one did not expect to be around for the long run. People may trade off increased variation in outcome to obtain a higher mean if they are able to survive during any periods of loss. This requires the ability to borrow and lend, which brings us back to the problem of the nonexistence of perfect capital markets. Transaction costs will cause the realized result to be less than the expected value.

When the number of projects is not large or there are costs of risk, the decision maker will care about the variability of outcomes as well as the expected value. Variance is equal to $\Sigma_i p_i(x_i - EV)^2$, where x_i is the value of the ith possible outcome and p_i is its probability. This is also the square of the standard deviation and the statistic is shown in Table 10.1. The decision maker may not always prefer the highest expected value if its variance is also high. It depends on the attitude toward the trade-off of expected value and variance.

10.2.2. Risk Aversion

A person who is content to act on the basis of expected value regardless of its variance is referred to as risk neutral. Such a person would be willing to play any game involving a fair gamble, such as betting on a series of coin tosses. A risk-neutral investor would pay up to the EV of a project (appropriately discounted for time preference). But it can be observed that fewer people will play such games as the possible gains and losses are raised, even though they believe they cannot on the average lose. It is possible that the utility of extra income from winning is less than the decline in utility from losing (Kahneman et al. 1982). It is reasonable to expect that there will be risk aversion even when probabilities are estimated with confidence and there are many projects. A risk-averse person will invest only if the project cost is less than the expected value, that is, the person insists on getting a positive risk premium. A risk seeker would pay more than EV if necessary.

Another condition of risk neutrality is that risks should be independent. The future states should not affect wealth regardless of the project choice. This is violated, for example, when a project's output is affected by the state of the weather, since wealth would be affected by the weather with or without the project. To summarize thus far, expected value can be used only when stakes are small and the underlying events are independent so that people are risk-neutral.   If there is evidence that people are not risk-neutral, the systematic incorporation of their preferences becomes more complex

10.2.3. Expected Utility

The previous discussion has made it clear that in some cases there is a need to determine decision makers' trade-off between expected value and its variance. This trade-off would be implicit in a utility function relating income to utility and it would incorporate any diminishing marginal utility of income as well. A utility function such as that shown in Figure 10.1 could conceivably be obtained from a type of bidding game played by decision makers.

The first step is for the analyst to arbitrarily select two levels of income, for purposes of illustration say $90 and $0 and to also arbitrarily assign two levels of utility to these incomes, say 100 units or utils for $90 and 0 utils to $0. To discover the utility of some intermediate income, for example, $30, the following question is put to the decision maker. Which would you prefer: (1) $30 with certainty or (2) a gamble in which the outcome is either $0 or $90 (corresponding to the states of nature in the matrix of Table 10.1)? The reply will depend on the probability (odds) of the two outcomes.   The interviewer varies the probability until the chooser is indifferent between the

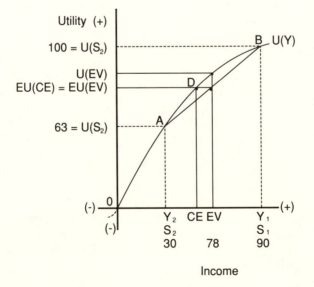

Figure 10.1 Utility Functions

two choices.[1] Suppose the probability that makes the chooser indifferent is .7 of obtaining $90 and .3 of getting nothing. Expressed as an equation this is utility of $30 = utility of probability .7 of $90 + utility of probability .3 of $0.

To transform this choice into a utility function, a key assumption must be made; namely, that utility (u) is proportional to probability (p). In the previous case this means that the utility of a .7 chance of obtaining $90 equals 70 percent of the utility of a certain $90. Or more formally, where the sum of dollars is (x) then, $Up(x) = pU(x)$. The plausibility of this assumption will be examined later.

Using the key assumption in the previous illustration, the equation can be rewritten as U($30) = (.7 × 90 utils) + (.3 × 0 utils) = 63 utils. Returning to Figure 10.1 in which we arbitrarily assigned utils to $0 and $90, it is now possible to plot the utility of $30 at 63 utils. The same type of questions can be repeated for other intervening monetary amounts until the analyst is satisfied that the relationship has been adequately described.

A better understanding of the characteristics of the utility function can be obtained by working with it. For example, take the expected value (EV) of Decision 2 from Table 10.1, which was 78, and enter it on the utility function of Figure 10.1. Further, the states of nature outcomes S_1 of $90 and S_2 of 30 can be entered. From the previous discussion we know that if the probability of each outcome were .5, the expected value would have been at the midpoint between 30 and 90. But since 90 has a higher probability, the expected value lies to the right of the midpoint. This suggests that probability is implicit in the utility function. A line (AB) drawn between the two possible outcomes, would be the locus of expected utility of the expected value, EU(EV), of the S_1 and S_2 outcomes. If outcome S_2 were certain, its utility would read from the utility function and is indicated by U (S_2) and likewise for outcome S_1 as U (S_1). But since neither of these outcomes is certain, their weighted average or expected value of 78 does not lie on the utility function, but rather on the line AB. If the expected value had a probability of one (variance of zero) its utility would lie on the utility function. As the possible outcomes become more similar, the variance is reduced and the expected utility approaches the certainty utility shown as U(EV) on Figure 10.1. As A and B become closer together, the line AB converges to a single point on the utility function. To summarize, the outcomes S_1 and S_2 have subjective probabilities that are used to calculate the expected value. The utility function incorporates the chooser's attitude toward expected value and its variance into a single unambiguous measure of expected utility that can be used to calculate rank of the projects in place of monetary units.

Once a utility function such as that shown in Figure 10.1 is obtained the utility of a given payoff can be determined. The data from the original payoff matrix shown in Table 10.1 is shown in Table 10.2 along with the utilities for these payoffs from the utility function. The expected utility is computed by multiplying the utilities by the appropriate probabilities and summing for

Table 10.2 Comparison of Expected Value and Utility

		Decision		Decision	
		D_1	D_2	D_1	D_2
Probability	State of Nature	Monetary Payoffs		Utilities	
.8	S_1	100	90	105	100[*]
.2	S_2	-20	30	-28	63
Expected value		76	78		
Expected utility				78.4	92.6

[*]Data for D_2 is shown on the utility function in Figure 10.1.

each decision. For example, for D_1, expected utility = $105 \times .8 + (-28 \times .2)$ = 78.4. The rank of expected utility indicates the choice of project D_2. In this particular case, rank by expected *utility* is the same as ranking by expected *value*.

10.2.4. Certainty Equivalents: Problems with Expected Utility Decision Rule

Some further understanding of risk relationships may be obtained from application of the concept of certainty equivalents. It was seen in Figure 10.1 that the utility of the expected value was labeled EU(EV). From the intersection of this level of utility with the utility function at point D, it can be seen that the same level of utility may be obtained from a certain income of CE or from the EV. Thus, CE is the certainty equivalent income of the expected value with its implicit variance. The concavity of the utility function in Figure 10.1 indicates the diminishing marginal utility of a risk-averse person. The greater the concavity (risk aversion), the greater the difference between CE and EV. It can be reasoned that when the possible outcomes are more similar and variance is reduced, the certainty equivalent and expected value become more similar.

The expected value minus its certainty equivalent income is the cost of risk bearing. What affects the decision maker's view of risk-bearing costs? The person who is psychologically risk-neutral still has the problem of survival during the fluctuating results of the repeated projects because of lack of perfect capital markets. These extra transaction costs are part of the cost of risk bearing. But the gambling game we asked the decision maker to play may not remind the chooser of these considerations.

The realistic evaluation of the cost of risk is a particularly troublesome aspect of the artificiality of bidding games. The chooser has not been told anything about the timing of the probable results of the repeated investments. In that case, it is impossible to plan for the needed saving and borrowing and thus impossible to know the costs of risk. In other words, the cost of uncertainty per se is unknown. This means that even if utility functions could be obtained, they would overestimate certainty equivalents for the risk-averse person. This is not to mention the key assumption that makes expected utility proportional to probability. Although this is not patently absurd, it is this author's judgment that there is no compelling reason to believe it is true for most people for most kinds of projects. See Sections 10.3.4 and 10.5. Not all 1 percent changes in the probability of death cause a 1 percent change in utility for all people.

10.2.5. Gambler's Indifference Maps

Further thought might be given to asking the political authorities to adopt a utility function. Instead of trying to construct a utility function from responses in a bidding game of chance, several examples of possible functions might be submitted to authorities for their confirmation. But since the utility function contains probability only implicitly, it would be meaningless to a political representative.

A related concept is the gambler's indifference map such as shown in Figure 10.2. This concept explicitly relates the expected value of income and its variability to utility, though it also may be difficult for a politician to choose between several of these. Individual projects (decisions) with their combinations of mean income and variation (standard deviation) are shown as dots on Figure 10.2. Any project producing a combination of mean income and variation to the left of the production possibility curve (PPC) is inferior. The mean-variance hypothesis argues that of two projects with equal expected value (such as B and C), the one with the lowest variance is preferred. If utility indifference curves (U) are politically given, the optimal project is B at the intersection of the production possibility curve and the highest possible utility curve. The concept of certainty equivalent was explained in Section 10.2.3 on the utility function. It can also be derived from the gambler's indifference map. A given project's expected value of net income and the standard deviation of its probability distribution is entered on the map, such as point B on the utility indifference curve in Figure 10.2. Then the utility indifference curve is followed until it intersects the zero variation level. The difference between the income at the point (A) that is Y_1 and the expected value of Y_2 is the certainty equivalent of the uncertain expected value and can be used to adjust project benefits.

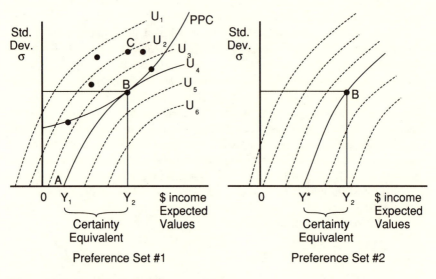

Figure 10.2 Gambler's Indifference Maps

It is conceivable that experience might confirm a number of points such as A and B in Figure 10.2. For example, there is a two-stage drawing in the Irish Sweepstakes. The winners are assigned a horse in the sweepstakes race. These horses' chances of winning have probabilities attached to them by experts and the betting of others. The payoffs to the order of finish are given. Enterprising and relatively risk-neutral bookies then offer the holders of the tickets a choice between a certain amount of money for their ticket or the uncertain chance of a higher payoff. Willingness to accept these offers could be observed. This might give a clue to analysts in deciding the shape of alternative indifference maps to be presented to decision makers for their choice. Even so, it stretches credulity to imagine politicians making meaningful choices by these maps. There is a problem in going from the magnitude of choices faced by the average person and the millions at stake in a public project. Some simple transformation is not easily justified. Still, perhaps this line of inquiry deserves more thought.

10.2.6.   Relevance of Risk in Public Decisions

Benefit-cost analysis requires data on the certainty equivalent of an uncertain project result. If people differ in their subjective probabilities, they will not agree on the appropriate certainty equivalent or risk premium. But if there were perfect and complete markets for all possible contingent claims, people could adjust their portfolios so that risk aversion for all would be equated at the margin.   Such complete and costless markets are highly unlikely

(Brainard and Dolbear 1971). This means that public choice is necessary among the conflicting views of risk assessment.

The expected value criterion may be used when risks are small and projects are not interdependent. If a large number of projects are pooled, then for the nation as a whole, the weighted average result (expected value) may be expected. The government could be regarded as a risk-neutral investor applying the expected value criterion because it can spread the risk across many people, thus making each person's risk small (Arrow and Lind 1970). But this assumes an institution for actually spreading the risk. Arrow and Lind postulate that government raises taxes in years when projects have lower than expected returns and lowers taxes for higher return periods (or accumulate and dispense surpluses). This assumes a first-best procedure whereby benefits are dispersed as national dividends in proportion to taxes (or that project benefits of whatever kind are so proportional).[2]   This is incredible. Making costs infinitely small for each person implies that people would be indifferent to infinitely small benefits as well. But this is not the case. Groups lobby for projects because of individually large possible gains. If the project they succeed in obtaining turns out badly, they have used up their political influence and may not be able to get another project. These people are not risk-neutral. In fact, they may be risk-perverse in that any benefit, even if less than cost, is advantageous since their tax share is fixed and not related to whether they obtain a project or the performance of the project. This is explored further in Section 10.8 on institutional incentives. In summary, it can not be assumed that people want government to make risky decisions as if distribution does not matter.[3]

Conceivably the financial costs of projects could be spread over all taxpayers. But some of the in-kind costs of project failures are quite limited in geographical area. The failure of a nuclear reactor for example is not necessarily small. The possibility of an airport design or siting decision having more noise (in-kind cost) than expected is not reduced by being shared by large numbers of people.

The basic proposition of Arrow and Lind (1970) is that when the number of taxpayers is large, not only are costs individually small but benefits are similarly small. But as Fisher (1973) points out, this is not necessarily the case for joint-impact goods that to some degree have marginal cost equal to zero and high exclusion costs.[4]   In that case, costs do not increase with number of users (so cost per user or taxpayer may be small), but the benefits per recipient are not reduced as the number of recipients is increased. The division of benefits among large numbers need not reduce average benefits; thus, the necessary condition for use of expected value criterion and risk neutrality may not hold. For example, the fact that many people benefit from national defense does not affect the risk of defense failure. (This is actually a poor example since the average cost of defense is not small.) A better example is any project of environmental improvement, such as air quality.

The fact that there are many breathers does not reduce the risk of an ineffectual project.

10.2.7.   Price Change and Supply Irreversibility

Demand and price change of inputs and outputs is one reason project net returns can vary. Some price changes such as those for agricultural commodities have historical cycles that are fairly well understood and that allow the attachment of mathematical probabilities. Also there are some well-understood secular trends in prices as a function of income and population. In other cases, changes in learning and discovery do not have a record of repeated observation. The changes can be large and discontinuous, leaving decision makers unwilling to state a probability distribution, whereas they might be willing to express a qualitative and directional ranking of alternatives.

In the context of uncertainty, different sorts of irreversibilities create different problems. Fixed and specialized capital has no salvage value (or much less than acquisition prices), and if output prices change from a shift in demand, the entire investment may be lost. But at least the loss is bounded. In some cases, however, the loss although not infinite, may be quite explosive. The key factor is the degree of supply response.

When supply can be expanded at some price, there is a limit on the loss that can occur if costs are incorrectly estimated. In other words, the price of an input may change as demand for it elsewhere increases. The price rise is limited if supply can increase. But if supply is fixed (any reduction in supply is irreversible), then the price change, although not infinite, could be enormous. Irreversibility creates the possibility of super errors. This can be particularly troublesome when the input in its alternative uses produces an indefinite length flow of product (i.e., it is a flow resource rather than a stock). This means that there is a long period in which learning can take place. A practical example of this problem is investment in hydroelectric projects that require a wild stream as an input. If the price of this input is based on observed prices for wilderness areas it could be quite wrong if there is a big jump in demand. If demand grows beyond the range of our experience, and supply is fixed, the cost change of this project input could be enormous.

Arrow and Fisher (1974) argue that irreversibility causes the expected value to be discounted even for a risk-neutral investor. The consumer cannot turn to a market for contingent claims when concerned that an irreversible choice may mean that a change in tastes could not be satisfied. Individual differences in option values greater or less than expected value will exist (Schmalensee 1972). This will require a public choice to resolve the differences.

Irreversibility of flow resources expands the period when learning can occur and thus exposure to changes in demand beyond our experience. This puts the situation into a realm in which we have little confidence in our subjective probabilities and further creates the possibility of super losses (greater than the size of current capital costs).

10.2.8. Components of Risk Attitudes Differ among Individuals

The criterion of expected value and the hypothesis that people act in terms of expected utility are useful because they make us question the dimensions and components of risk. The expected utility hypothesis includes specific axioms and procedures to account for subjective probability and marginal utility of money (incorporating income-variance trade-offs). As previously noted some of the axioms seem questionable and they do not incorporate the cost of uncertainty per se. Other dimensions have been identified in the literature and the search continues to determine how they might be systematically incorporated in the utility function (Robison 1982).

The first of these is the utility of risk taking itself. For some people, making risky investments is itself a thrill (or painful). The process or game itself produces utility as well as income payoffs. The usual procedure for constructing the utility function shown in Figure 10.1 takes account of marginal utility of money but not the marginal utility of the game. The concept of risk aversion or seeking must include both (Johnson 1983).

Further, it is possibile that the decision maker may have a preference for particular probabilities. Empirically we observe a "certainty effect" when outcomes with certainty are given disproportionately more weight than uncertain outcomes (Kahneman and Tversky 1979). Probabilities deserve a place in the utility function because it cannot be assumed that preference between certainty and risk is invariant when other things are equal.

Utility can be a function of a person's own wealth and relative wealth. Persons whose wealth has deteriorated relative to others may be willing to take a gamble that a stable income person would reject, even if the subjective probabilities were equal. Poor persons may reason that a small loss will not affect their life much, but the lucky realization of a large payoff could change their status. Different individuals will want their political representatives to discount different sorts of projects in different ways.

There are a number of issues related to learning. For example, some people change their risk attitudes over time. This introduces another type of uncertainty if preference maps might change.

One of the major problems in systematic representation of risk preferences is that people are unsystematic and exhibit intransitive preferences (Machina 1987). Information processing strategies are adapted to each choice. The context matters. People make decisions in a decomposed fashion using relative comparisons. Decisions are often made in isolation rather than in terms of an overall portfolio of investments. Reference points and aspiration levels (satisficing return target) are often important. Various psychological dimensions of probability judgments are observed. For example, probability assessment gets mixed up with fear or wishful thinking. Questions asking for probability in fact get answers incorporating other attitudes. Humans think in terms of representativeness, availability, and anchoring to past reference points and information (Kahneman et al. 1982). Many people are insensitive to information on prior probabilities and focus instead on the immediate and simple notion of causality.

10.3.   Risk Trade-Offs Revealed

10.3.1.   Revealed Preferences

One approach for judging the acceptability of uncertain events is to place the events in perspective by embedding the choice into normal life conditions. Perhaps it would be possible to deduce an acceptable standard of risk by observing the income-variability trade-off values actually made by people. Although some examples, such as the Irish Sweepstakes, directly relate income and its variance translating into certainty equivalents, most observations are more indirect. Variance is a proxy for the cost of risk bearing. Variable income may necessitate borrowing and lending costs that make people risk-averse (Section 10.2.4). This leads us to search for examples of trade-offs between income and costs of risk bearing.

Insurance markets produce data on willingness to pay to avoid the costs of risk bearing. The maximum premium is the difference between an individual's expected value and its certainty equivalent (Robison and Barry 1987, Ch. 7). For example, a person might compute the expected value of income with and without suffering a disability. Because the person cannot live many lives and receive the average income of all of them, the utility of a certain income could be equal to a higher, but uncertain income. On the other hand, an insurance company can spread the risk and is nearly risk neutral. The risk-averse person will trade a premium for a certain income as long as the premium is smaller than the difference between certainty equivalent and expected value. Put another way, expected value minus the premium is the certainty equivalent. If some project has an income equal to a person's lifetime income and the same variance as that income exposed to the uncertainty of disability, a measure of the willingness to pay certainty equivalent is indicated from knowledge of the expected value and the insurance premium.

There are also data on trade-offs between income and injury or death rates (Thaler and Rosen 1976; Olson 1981). Certain occupations are more hazardous than others and require higher wages to attract workers. (Though in some cases the workers are poorly paid because they have few other

Table 10.3 Occupational Risk Payoff Matrix

Occupation Decision	State of Nature	
	S_1 Life	S_2 Death
D_1 Normal	p = .99999 $9,000	p = .000001 $Zero
D_2 Steeplejack	p = .9999 $20,000	p = .0001 $Zero

opportunities for employment.) Using hypothetical data, a payoff matrix can be constructed in the usual fashion as shown in Table 10.3. In this matrix the probability (p) differs in each cell as the probability of the states of nature is a function of the decision alternatives (occupations). Casual inspection would indicate that if people were risk neutral, everyone would want to be a steeplejack where expected value income is higher. But this is unlikely as the amount is large and there is no way for the individual to play the long-run averages. The degree of risk aversion is revealed here. The certainty equivalent of $30,000 with a probability of .9999 (1 in 10,000 chance of death) is $9,000. The 9,000 may be judged as certain as the chance of death is only 1 in 1,000,000, which is the chance of death from normal exposure to disease (more on this will follow). A certainty equivalent can be inferred from the payoff matrix because it represents a choice actually made (whereas in the previous cases it displayed only potential choices).

The technique used in Chapter 5 for estimating the value of a life saved by a project uses the same kind of data but in a different way. The value of life saved of a person in the normal range of occupations is 9,000, which becomes the benefit figure that in turn might have to be adjusted if the outcome of the project is uncertain. The previous analysis of income and variance suggests one more point on the gambler's indifference map. It is not argued that this type of analysis should instruct choice, but that it can be an input into the intuitive thinking of decision makers.

An individual's probability of death from nonoccupational activities can also be observed. Starr (1969) suggests that the fatality rate from disease of one in one million people (.000001 or 10^{-6}) is the upper bound to casual acceptable risk, whereas the risk of natural disasters such as earthquakes (10^{-10}) is the lower bound below which risk is largely ignored. It can be observed that a large percentage of the population will voluntarily participate in an activity with risk equal to that of the rate of death from disease. Starr has also estimated in an approximate way the average annual benefit per person.

Such data can be used to compute certainty equivalents. The background level of average fatalities resulting from disease for the U.S. population is used as the certainty level. At this level, the benefit ranges up to $400, which is the certainty equivalent of $1,200, which is the benefit from general aviation with a risk of 1 person in 10,000 (10^{-4}) dying. Starr suggests that overall, the acceptance of risk increases with benefits in a nonlinear third power relationship.

This provides another point on the gambler's indifference map (Section 10.2.5). But many psychometric surveys deny this. Some of the rules of indifference mapping are violated with some intransitivities (crossing of indifference curves). The analyst will have to make a judgment of some likely directional representations from which the decision makers can choose.[5] Utility is multidimensional and different kinds of events with the same income and risks may be treated differently. Categorization of risky events may proceed recalling the components of risk attitudes in Section 10.2.8, several of which are singled our for further comment.

10.3.2. Voluntary and Involuntary Risk

One of the possible reasons for what some might regard as irrational behavior is that people have a different attitude toward voluntary and involuntary risk. Starr (1969) observes that people accept 1,000 times more risk when they choose the activity than when it occurs as the result of others' actions. Also see Starr and Whipple (1980).

10.3.3. Risk Control

A related factor is that of risk controllability. When people perceive that their skill may affect the risk, they accept more risk (although their perception may be wrong). This could be because of selective perception of the risk level or perhaps some extra benefit derived from the challenge of skill versus danger. This raises the question of whose perception of risk the analyst is to use (Sugden and Williams 1978, 171-74).[6] In some cases the probability is well known to experts. But there is reason to believe that many people are quite ignorant of the risks, for example, when they choose jobs, leisure time activity, or buy insurance. One area in which this is clearly demonstrated is in siting of houses in flood plains (Kates 1962). If people will not pay attention to well documented risks such as floods, what can we say in other areas? This question was briefly discussed in Section 5.3 in the context of time saving in evaluating transportation projects (does the analyst use the objective facts or what riders think?). If we use data such as Starr's, we have implicitly used an expert's knowledge of risk, as he did not ask people what their risk perception was. Whether we should is a matter of public policy. Some might instruct their government to make choices based on whatever information people have. After all, that is the basis for most consumer choice, though the government subsidizes information in some cases and producers subsidize it in most. On the other hand, it is conceivable that some people would instruct government to save them from certain of their follies. Whose preferences count is a political decision. The independent analyst will have to present the data both as perceived by experts and citizens (Fischoff et al. 1983).

10.3.4. Dramatic Risk

People have different aversions toward different sources of death even when the probability of death is the same. Dramatic deaths from radiation or chemicals create greater fear than more ordinary risks of even greater probability. People are inconsistent, however. Sometimes they ignore low-probability events such as floods even when subsidized insurance is available and at other times they focus on size of the loss even if improbable (Schoemaker 1982, 544).

To sum up available research on perception, it can be said that for any given level of benefit, greater risk is tolerated if that risk is voluntary, immediate, known precisely, controllable, and familiar (Fischoff, et al. 1978; Otway and Von Winterfeldt 1982). Risk standards (trade-offs) are likely to be compartmentalized and vary for different kinds of risk even when the numerical risk-benefit relationship is the same. Slovic (1987, 282) categorizes the factors associated with heightened risk perception and desire for environmental regulation as follows: uncontrollable, dread, global catastrophic, consequences fatal, not equitable, catastrophic, high risk to future generations, not easily reduced, risk increasing and involuntary combined with a set of factors including nonobservable, unknown to those exposed, effect delayed, new risk, and risks unknown to science.

These human behaviors are violations of the expected utility hypothesis. They make it difficult to conceive of how analysts or politicians can ask for people's risk attitudes and be confident of accurately representing the answers in a workable analytic rule. It is not clear that basic tastes and preferences really exist that are compatible with systematic representation (Hershey et al. 1982). Single parameter characterization of risk attitudes seems inappropriate. Research is proceeding on multiargument utility functions. While waiting for these issues to be resolved and in the face of complexity, it may be second-best for government to employ some of the simplifying (satisficing) heuristics and information processing rules typical of most managers and citizens rather than trying to use a sophisticated tool such as expected utility when the inputs into the calculation are of uncertain meaning. All of the previous discussion seems justified not so much to guide analysts to mathematical solutions as to provide a framework for formulating problems and guiding intuition.

10.4.   Decision Rules without Mathematical Probabilities

Experience may be insufficient for decision makers to be willing to attach numerical (cardinal) probabilities to the possible outcomes (state of nature). This is a matter of degree and judgment.   There may still be a significant amount of information available on the physical production functions that relate outcomes to combinations of decisions and states of nature.   The same payoff matrix seen in the previous discussion of risk may be available, only with the probabilities missing.   It may be judged that the likelihood of outcomes can be ranked only ordinally.   (Situations in which even the payoff matrix is missing are considered in the next section on the unknowable.) People may not be able to express their subjective judgment about likelihood in mathematical terms, but only in directional and qualitative terms.

Decision theory provides several alternative criteria for choice under uncertainty.   All imply some directional judgment on probability plus an attitude toward the trade-off between size and variance of payoff and all other relevant psychological dimensions all mixed together.   The illustrative payoff matrix to which the following criteria are applied is shown in Table 10.4.

10.4.1.   Maximax Criterion

If the decision maker is wildly optimistic, the decision with the highest payoff (maximax) might be chosen, such as D_1 in Table 10.4.   But it can be noted that this involves the chance of a negative payoff if S_2 occurs.

10.4.2.   Maximin Criterion

If the decision maker is very cautious, the decision that minimizes possible losses is in order.   It allows planning based on a level below which the outcome will not go.   The minimum payoff from each decision from Table 10.4 can then be displayed as in Table 10.5.   The project with the maximum minimum payoff (D_2) is chosen.   This maximin criterion guards against the

Table 10.4 Net Income Payoff Matrix

Decision	Present Value of Net Income for States of Nature	
	S_1	S_2
D_1	100	-20
D_2	90	30

Table 10.5 Minimum Payoff

Decision	Minimum Payoff
D_1	-20
D_2	30

Table 10.6 Regret Matrix and Maximum Regret

	States of Nature		Maximum Regret (Row Maxima of Potential Losses)
Decision	S_1	S_2	
D_1	100 - 100 = 0	30 - (- 20) = 50	50
D_2	100 - 90 = 10	30 - 30 = 0	10

worst at the cost of ignoring decisions that might do very much better with only slightly less probable outcomes. But that is the whole point if one has no confidence in estimates of the probabilities or believes they are unlikely to be improved. One might postpone decision and go to a learning mode, or, if the decision is forced, use the maximin.

10.4.3. Minimax Regret Criterion

If the decision maker wishes to be cautious but somewhat less so than in the previous criterion, the decision that minimizes the maximum regrets (losses) can be chosen. The maximum regret or loss is defined as the difference between the actual payoff and what the payoff would have been had the correct decision been made. This requires the computation of the regret matrix shown in Table 10.6. If the decision maker had known in advance that the true state of nature was going to be S_1 then D_1 is the correct choice. Thus, D_1 implies no regret. The regret is computed from the payoff matrix by subtracting each return from the highest number in its column.

For the first cell in the matrix the actual payoff is 100 if S_1 occurs and this is also the best possible result of any decision if S_1 occurs, so 100 - 100 = 0. After similar computations for other S and D combinations the maximum regret for each decision is noted (last column of Table 10.6). The best choice is seen to be D_2, which minimizes the maximum regret (10).

This criterion ignores the absolute magnitudes of the returns and focuses only on the comparative consequences of the alternative decisions. It highlights the outcomes of each decision as compared with the maximum attainable in each state of nature.

The results of application of the minimax regret criterion can be affected by the addition of alternatives.[7] This is regarded by Dorfman (1974, 365-66) and Dasgupta and Pearce (1972, 191-92) as a defect. But Mishan (1976, 349-51) argues that the availability of options should affect results. The issue is a judgment over the relevance of certain decision options.

The judgments involved in the maximin and minimax regret criteria can be compared by noting that the ultraconservative maximin may sacrifice large potential gains for a little extra security against a larger than planned for minimum result. The minimax regret criterion although less conservative involves the opposite danger, namely, that it may give up a satisfying gain in the hope of getting only slightly more.[8] An illustration of this is provided by Mishan (1976, 349). Employment of the criterion implies that the chooser is not a "satisficer."

10.4.4. Directional Risk Adjustments

Some directional adjustment must often be made for different kinds of risk. The situation lends itself to "satisficing" models in the context of bounded rationality and limited information (Simon 1978). This still leaves the question of how best to incorporate these qualitative judgments. One of the traditional devices often advocated is to add some sort of risk premium to the discount rate chosen to compute present value (hopefully added by the political authority and not the analyst). This is appealing because of computational convenience. But it has the effect of reducing the expected value at a compound rate, which implies that risk increases systematically with age of the project. This might be true in some, but surely not all cases. It also reduces the size of negative outcomes, which is nonsensical. There is also some theoretical difficulty in mixing the two concepts of time preference and probability (see Sugden and Williams 1978, 61). The other device much used in practice by private business of making a judgment on a cutoff date (pay-back period) has some of the same difficulties of assuming risk is just a function of time and makes the rather severe assumption that projects cease to have benefits (or costs) after a given date. One directional concept that does not suffer from these problems is that of the loss function (Dorfman 1974, 390-91).

Another directional device is the safety-first principle (Nelson et al. 1978). People may have in mind a minimal performance and an acceptable probability of exceeding the minimum, perhaps related to survival. The first priority of choice is to find the investment (or regulation) to achieve the minimum income (or disease rate) needed and, once that is satisfied, maximize expected net income from the remaining alternatives. The problem with these heuristics is that their axiomatic bases are not clear and it is not certain what attitudes must exist to utilize them. This is discussed further in Section 10.6.

10.5. The Unknowable

Now for the unspeakable: There are some proposed projects about which even the experts have no idea of the outcome. There can be uncertainty not only about which prelabeled state will be obtained, but also about which states are possible. There is structural as well as parameter uncertainty. Many high-technology projects are in this category, along with innovative social programs. The usual response to complete ignorance, when even the production function is unknown, is to advocate a pilot project. The project is primarily an investment in obtaining experience on which to base some future probability estimates.

This brings us back to a theme of Chapter 4, which is concerned with estimating production functions. It might be helpful if both analysts and politicians would admit to more ignorance and propose to spend some money on projects whose only purpose is to reduce this ignorance. But how much do you spend to reduce ignorance when you do not know how much ignorance can be reduced? Although there are some data on returns to a particular line of research or average returns to categories of research, it is very difficult to extend these data to predict the future returns to any marginal increment. Research is in part an act of faith. It is driven more by a lack of other alternatives than a comparison of desirable outcomes in the search for the best. Because expenditure on research is a small part of any government's budget, it is probably a good example of areas in which people are willing to make small bets for potentially large payoffs. Scholars, therefore, have a stake in a certain amount of propagation of a cultural attitude of the thrill of gambling!

10.6. Matching Risk Decision Rules to People's Judgments

All of the previous decision rules such as maximin, minimax, risk premiums, pay-back periods, and safety-first principle incorporate attitudes toward risk in a qualitative and directional manner. They mix judgments of probability, size and variance trade-offs, and contextual attitudes.

These all can be criticized in that the characteristics of a person who would prefer one of these decision rules cannot be precisely described. This inability makes it difficult to construct and test a predictive model. But this may be less important to the problem of public choice of a risk-adjusting rule which can be systematically applied. If analysts can rank the decision rules in terms ordinal, qualitative risk adjustments, it may be sufficient to establish logical connections to politically chosen decision guidelines. Cautious groups can argue for a more conservative rule than that currently used or that supported by the optimists. This is not scientifically satisfying, but in a second-best world a sense of qualitative direction may be the best that can be obtained.

10.6.1. Practical Political Participation

All of the decision criteria for uncertainty previously discussed contain two implicit judgments: (1) A directional subjective probability[9] of the possible outcomes, and (2) trade-off between income and its variability. Choice of criteria varies for each person and for each project (see Robison 1982). We expect the political authority to resolve the conflicts among people.

It seems impractical to have the politicians examining the likelihood of each project and combining this with their judgment of income and variance trade-off. These judgments could be separated. If this were done, the technical experts could provide subjective probabilities for each decision option as this is not generalizable unless, as Mishan (1976, 351) notes, people are "cautious to a fault" or "recklessly opportunistic." Then the politicians could provide the generalizable system rule of income-variability trade-off. This could take the form of the expected value criterion if they are risk-neutral or some other decision rule if they are risk-averse. It may be necessary to supplement this with some sort of thresholds (or regret function) in which projects with variability beyond a certain point are completely unacceptable.

But the division of responsibility between politician and the physical scientist is never clear and a more interactive mode of decision making may be necessary. Can we find a method that has a reasonable level of information and transaction cost? This probably means that the decision rules must be directional and qualitative. If so, can they still be systematic enough to allow checks for consistency? The answer is deferred until we examine, in Section 10.7, what governments are now actually doing.

The practicality of implementing any kind of systematic subjective probability choice depends on conceptualizing the payoff matrix. This parallels the discussion of choosing program information categories in Chapter 3. The payoff matrices previously used have been simple with only a few decision options and possible states of nature. In reality there are many, particularly when there are many inputs and outputs and possible prices and the possibility of change in any year. The cells in the matrix quickly explode to unmanageable number. Mishan (1976, Ch. 54) suggests this is why no applied project analyses make formal use of game theory. However, this problem need not be crippling for directional analysis. Much useful economic analyses such as empirical aggregate production functions utilize a high level of aggregation. The analyst is forced to combine a large number of variables into several plausible combinations to display in a payoff matrix. In other words, a 10 percent change in all prices plus a change in some underlying physical variable might be one of the hybrid states of nature examined.

The formulation of these categories provides opportunity for reasonable analysts to differ and also for biased manipulation. This brings us back to whatever protection is available in professional standards and open debate. The choice is never between the ideal and the possible, but between the possibles, and the suggestions here are hopefully better than tossing a coin (which itself involves the problem of who names the options).

10.6.2. Confidence in Size and Variation Estimates

It should be remembered that all probability statements are subjective. Given the same data, different people will attach different probabilities to outcomes depending on the confidence they have in their observations or deductions. For example, in attaching probabilities to flood heights or cancer deaths, one person may assign the same probability to the outcomes of two alternative projects even if the number of years of observation are different, while another person will attach different probabilities. This means that the plots of mean and variance in Figure 10.2 are not the same for all individuals, just as the utility function trading off mean and variance is not the same for all persons.   It is not clear how much attitude toward risk affects the assessment of probability.

It is common in government safety regulation to appoint a committee of experts and ask them for their consensus on the probabilities or most likely outcomes. The politician could specify a utility function and projects could then be chosen systematically. Although this two-step procedure is possible, both steps involve a political value choice because individuals can have different opinions in each step.

One of the purposes of systematic analysis is to facilitate citizens in determining whether public decisions are consistent with explicitly stated values and objectives. Suppose that chemical A is banned and B is not (recall Section 3.4). Is it because of differences in the probability of death from their use or differences in the value of the effects on different persons? The analyst cannot say that the ban decision was inconsistent any more than it is possible to say that the outputs of agencies X and Y are the same (in which case cost effectiveness would decide budget allocation).   Both involve political choice to settle perception conflicts. Assessment of probability is as subjective as assessment of product differences. It is not a matter of being right or wrong, but of facilitating debate over the judgments to be made.

10.7. What Governments Do

In the search for reasonable rules of choice (rather than the impossible optimal rules) it is useful to review what governments actually do to accommodate to risk and uncertainty (Hey 1981). Some rules are better than others and the consequences of using them should be noted if possible. No systematic observation of what governments do is available but some personally observed practices are suggestive.

10.7.1. Contingency Allowance

Directional risk adjustments with respect to construction costs are common in U.S. water resource development agencies. For example, the U.S. Army Corps of Engineers (1980, D16-17) adds a contingency allowance ranging from 5 to 20 percent of various components of construction cost. This reflects the engineers qualitative judgment of the likelihood of field conditions or price changes causing costs to increase.

10.7.2. Use of Expected Values

There are some areas in which many years of records are available and agencies use these records to estimate expected values. One such area is flood control projects. The historical flood frequencies are used to estimate flood damage frequencies, which can then be reduced by a reservoir, as constructed by the U.S. Army Corps of Engineers and others (see Eckstein 1965, 121; Vondruska 1969).

The expected value of flood damage reduction is used to calculate net benefits but not always to select the optimal scale of the project (storage capacity and degree of safety) (Eckstein 1965, 135-41). If maximization of net expected value of a given constrained budget were practiced, dams would be built to handle smaller floods that occur most frequently rather than infrequent very large floods, the control of which adds little to net benefits. But this would leave the population exposed to the risk of disasters. There has never been any congressional or presidential directives as to the basis for trading off maximization of expected net values and concern for variance.

10.7.3. Incentives for Construction Safety

The U.S. Army Corps of Engineers tends to build dams to control what is sometimes derisively called the "Moses Flood" (in terms of reservoir capacity) and the dams have large safety margins in terms of strength. This strategy is akin to the maximin criterion or is at least designed to minimize regret. It may be surmised that politically there is a threat to agency survival if a dam should fail. This fear seems to outweigh any political advantage of serving more clients with smaller and less costly dams. Even from a strictly life saving viewpoint, more lives might be saved by more dams rather than fewer supersafe ones. Agency rejection of this line of thought may be a recognition of the asymmetry of dramatic versus ordinary risks (similar to congressional guidelines in the emotional area of cancer versus more ordinary health risks).

Part of the drive for extra safety margins is noncalculating and is a heuristic built into the training of engineers. It is standard practice in private construction as well to compute the required strength for bridges and boilers and then add a conventional margin of safety. Still, roofs do collapse in snow storms and cables break on mountain gondolas.

There are differences in decision-making strategy between agencies. The Corps of Engineers has never had a dam failure, whereas some dams constructed by local governments and private irrigation suppliers have failed. This makes sense in terms of the risk aversion associated with the relative sizes of the gambles.

10.7.4. Population and Utilization Projections

It is common in U.S. water resource agencies to make simple projections of past trends in population and utilization in estimating future demand. For example, estimations of future flood damages may be predicted on the expectation that past population growth in the flood plain will continue. There is a bit of circularity here as past growth may have been based on ignorance of the risk of damage or on the assumption that government investment would control or compensate for the damage.

The agencies tend not to use price in their projections as much as economists would like. Thus, the rate of water use growth is projected to continue even when the cost of the contemplated project implies a higher marginal supply price. It is difficult to determine whether these practices are rules of thumb in the face of uncertainty or deliberate attempts to make the agency's projects look good.

10.7.5. Prices

All of the water resource agencies in the United States use the same prices for outputs and inputs for agricultural projects. These are provided by a coordinating body called the U.S. Water Resources Council and are termed "normalized prices." A linear trend line is fitted to the last 10 years of price data and future prices are then assumed to be the same as the most recent year of the fitted line after modification by some ad hoc judgments. The process does dampen the effect of short-term supply and demand fluctuations but has been criticized by Niehaus (1978) for not separating out the effect of government programs or being based on a plausible model of economic behavior. It is curious that these prices have attracted little attention from economists who spend far more time criticizing the discount rate. To the extent that these normalized prices are a moving average, it is conceptually similar to use of an expected value that is a probability weighted average.

Private firms may make investments when profit opportunities are indicated, only to discover later that other firms made similar investment and there is then over-supply disequilibrium (Richardson 1960). Governments sometimes act in terms of administrative prices and guarantee these prices to private producers, guarantee bank loans, or construct public projects using these administrative prices as a guide (not necessarily a prediciton). An example was U.S. investment in synthetic fuels projects after the oil crisis.

10.7.6. Sensitivity Analysis and Bracketed Estimates

Many government analyses display something called the "best estimate" bracketed by "low" and "high" estimates. This type of qualitative assessment is more common than any numerical probability statements. Because rates of return are seldom the basis for project choice, once a project qualifies as having some positive return, an agency can afford to display three levels of estimates for key variables and always choose the lowest one (if it still qualifies the project), thus exhibiting itself as very conservative.

Some analyses such as that shown in Figure 3.1 display point estimates. However the actual experimental data on pesticide impact on humans show a range of lifetime dosage levels and a range of costs for each.

Many public agencies such as the World Bank apply a sensitivity analysis to see how changes in various components such as prices and costs affect the rate of return. A switching value can be computed showing how much a variable can change before negative returns are created. The main use of sensitivity analysis is to identify critical variables so that extra managerial steps can be taken to increase their maintenance at projected levels. Sensitivity analysis by itself does nothing to implement any systematic project ranking and trade-off of outcomes and their variability.

10.7.7. Objective Probability versus Consumer Perception

It is perhaps not surprising that transportation agencies (and health agencies to the extent they use any analysis at all) tend to utilize available factual records of intermodal safety, and accident probability, rather than consumer perception of these outcomes.

It would appear that the strategies used by government agencies to accommodate to risk and uncertainty tend to be aimed at internal project design rather than anything the central budget agency could use to choose among different projects. The latter probably takes the form of disbelief in the proposals of certain agencies with overall reductions in funding rather than choice among its projects.

10.7.8. Regulation and Risk Assessment

Uncertainty prevails in health-related regulation. The U.S. Food and Drug Administration (FDA) and the Environmental Protection Agency (EPA) have the responsibility to protect citizens from disease-causing agents in their food and environment. For illustration, the discussion will be in terms of pesticides and cancer. The degree of harm is a function of the dose-response relationship multiplied by the exposure to the chemical. The exposure is a function of the dose level (residue in food) and how much people eat. A key production function is the relationship between dose (level of exposure) and response (carcinogenic effects). In the case of pesticides, the dose is expressed as milligrams of pesticide per kilogram of body weight per day. The regulatory agencies would like to know the threshold below which the material would not cause cancer in humans. This cannot be derived from experimental tests on humans and therefore the testing must be done on animals. The relationship between the dose that causes cancer in rats and the dose that would cause cancer in humans is inherently uncertain (McGarity 1979, 734).

For reasons of economy in testing, animals are fed high doses. This necessitates an estimate of effects at the lower doses that will actually occur. EPA makes a mathematical linearized extrapolation of the animal high-dose-response observations to lower doses (National Research Council 1987, 54 and 194). Wishing to be conservative and expressing risk aversion, EPA uses a 95 percent upper bound confidence limit for predicted tumor incidence. This probability refers to the variation around the observed relationship in the high-dose animal data. It is not the probability of the relationship for low doses or in humans. The product of dose-response and exposure may be wrong (at any confidence limit) if there are ingredients in the pesticide with unknown effects, the linear model is wrong, some routes of exposure are omitted, or there is synergy among compounds. The scientists assume a worst-case scenario for some variables, such as all of the food crop that can be treated will be treated. But some of the states of nature are not even specified. A judgment is made that specified worst cases will offset any unknown relevant states of nature. The peer reviewers are not asked to state their subjective probability estimates of the dose-response relationship, but only to make a conservative selection from a range of estimates. EPA then takes this selection and combines it with other considerations to place a chemical in one of five groups of relative evidence sufficiency (National Research Council 1987, 67).

Interpretations and judgments must be made all along the way that are never wholly technical issues. As van Ravenswaay (1983, 355) states:

> There are few, if any, unique numbers in regulatory decision-making. The task of weighing risks and benefits is not separate from the tasks which precede it. The weights which are assigned to

risks and benefits implicitly determine how policy is applied in the tasks of collecting data, interpreting data, and drawing inferences about the magnitude of risks and benefits. Policy weights are not simply applied to numbers, they are used to determine numbers.

The complexity here is immense because there are models behind the dose-response relationship. For example, what criteria shall be applied in determining whether the rats got cancer? The performance measure problem of Chapter 3 arises in deciding whether to count only malignant tumors or whether to also count benign tumors or just cancer cells. There are in turn models guiding interpretation of the experimental results and occasionally there is political input into choice of models (Ashford et al. 1983). This complexity makes public monitoring of risk trade-offs very difficult as scientific and policy judgments overlap.

How does the framework of regulatory decision making relate to the payoff matrices previously discussed, such as in Table 10.3? The decision alternatives are in terms of rules related to what level of a material (tolerance) is to be allowed in food or the environment. The states of nature might refer to things such as which of several models of the dose-response production function or exposure might prevail. The values in the matrix refer to cancer incidence per unit of population as predicted by the models. It is a rate of occurrence and as such is often referred to as the probability of occurrence for an individual. But the probability of the rate actually occurring is a separate matter. An individual risks being the one in a million who gets cancer as seen in Table 10.7 as well as being uncertain about whether it might really be 20 per million. Subjective probability must be attached to the different models of the production function if a formal mathematical probability decision rule is to be used. This seems impractical. Public officials are not comfortable with such explicit judgments.

In Table 10.7, the use of a qualitative decision rule such as maximin would choose decision (or dose) D_2 because it produces the best result if the worst-scenario of state of nature S_2 prevails. D_1 allows the chemical to be used at some tolerance level. The level produces a benefit (which D_2 does not) and produces no cancers if S_1 or the nonlinear dose-response model prevails, but has harmful results if S_2 prevails. In practice, EPA may or may not have a rate of disease incidence. Considering the weight of the evidence, it makes a decision to allow the chemical to be considered safe or to place it in one of several classes of human carcinogens with differing sufficiency of evidence.

The regulatory decision implicitly combines the probability of a rate of disease with a valuation of its avoidance (value of life). The 1958 Delaney Amendment to the Federal Food, Drug and Cosmetic Act provides that no food or feed additive may be approved for use by the FDA (or pesticide by EPA) that is found to induce cancer in test animals when residues

Table 10.7 Payoff Matrix for Pesticide Regulations (cancer death rate per unit of population)

Regulatory Decision	Nonlinear Model S_1	Linear Model S_2
D_1 (allow)	Zero/million	One/million
D_2 (prohibit)	Zero/million	Zero/million

concentrate in processed food. Congress did not specify dosage level, number of studies, sample size, or length of tests. But it has provided a sense of direction. The estimate of the certainty of disease involves an extrapolation from animal data to humans. The Delaney Amendment could be interpreted as saying that if the chemical causes cancer in animals, human cancer is to be considered certain. Further, whatever the rate of disease, the value of its avoidance is greater than its cost (e.g., extra costs of food production). This interpretation of the Delaney Amendment approximates the maximin rule, which errs on the side of safety. The agencies interpret congressional intent and use conservative exposure and dose-response models.

When the Delaney Amendment does not apply, the regulatory agencies have sometimes ruled that estimated upper range cancer risks not exceeding one in one million (10^{-6}) are acceptable. A National Research Council (1987) committee has suggested that a negligible risk standard be applied in all pesticide cases, rather than the Delaney zero risk standard to some cases. Late in 1988 the EPA adopted this standard. Such a policy recommendation could be interpreted as saying one death in a million has less value than the benefits of the chemical. Or it could mean that in terms of uncertainty, it is impossible to distinguish 10^{-6} from zero, that is, both are zero. The probability and value questions are difficult to distinguish.

The Federal Insecticide, Fungicide and Rodenticide Act and the Occupational Safety and Health Act seem to express a somewhat reduced expectation of performance than that suggested by the Delaney Amendment. Congress required balancing of harms and benefits. These acts clearly intend to reduce exposure to harmful materials, but not to be "cautious to a fault." The agencies involved seem not to have adopted something approaching maximin or minimize regret rules, but more research will be needed to determine what rules they do use, if indeed any systematic rule is used. In practice, delay in regulatory implementation is one way to recognize benefits.

Congress is not able to express its judgment in terms of mathematical probability and is not even likely to suggest a qualitative decision rule. The agencies do take congressional indications of the direction of intended results into account in determining their choice rules. I believe tentatively that these can be described and applied systematically in such a way as to better allow observers to determine consistency, but the process remains problematic because of its complexity.

10.8. Institutions and Incentives

The previous discussion of what public agencies do has indicated that incentives do exist to avoid physical collapse of a project that might endanger lives. But where are the incentives to achieve benefits greater than costs over time? Have you ever heard of a project designer being fired for a cost overrun or failure to reach targeted net incomes? To the contrary, there are a number of cases in which people were fired for calling attention to cost overruns. The case of Ernest Fitzgerald in the U.S. Department of Defense is a prime example (Newman 1969). Project engineers are promoted for designing projects that are funded, not those that perform close to expectation. U.S. Senator William Proxmire gave his Golden Fleece Awards for projects he considered to be a waste of taxpayers' money, but he was unique.

Why is there so little public pressure for agencies to develop strategies that better cope with uncertainty? As previously noted, Arrow and Lind argue that risk spreading means that no risk adjustment to benefits is necessary. But problems arise when risk spreading is coupled with the fact that if a group gets any benefits at all they applaud their political representatives, as their taxes are not affected by the project's net returns. This leads neither to risk neutrality nor even to thrill gambling, but to risk perversion. The opposite conclusion from Arrow and Lind can be argued, namely, that public investment as now practiced at the national level is more risky than private investment because there is no incentive to learn from past mistakes even when those mistakes are instructive.

Since this is a book about project analysis and not institutional analysis, the possible institutional changes that could alter performance can only be briefly discussed (Brandl 1988). Wherever possible it would be useful for the beneficiaries to see their present costs tied to promised benefits. Presidents Jimmy Carter and Ronald Reagan tried to move in this direction by requiring the states to pay a larger share of water project costs. Although this is still one step removed from the taxpayer, at least there is some party who has some stake in how projects actually perform. Bureaucrats checking on each other is better than no one checking at all.

10.9. Project Implementation and Management: The Case for Flexibility

Cost-benefit analysis is a tool of agency heads and central budget planners in choosing projects for funding. But the ultimate impact of public spending is not only in choosing the best projects but also in implementing and managing them. This topic is emphasized in public administration and economic development literature, but largely ignored in BCA. It could be argued that the balance between attention to project choice and implementation is misplaced in the face of uncertainty. It may be more important to make whatever projects are chosen work. The ability to adapt a project to changing conditions and to provide all of its complementary inputs when needed may be more important to economic growth than choosing the optimal project from a list whose ranking is sensitive to uncertain parameters (see Mack 1971, 221; Murelius 1981).

The ability to salvage something from the project can improve long-term performance. For example, if the prices of agricultural products change for an irrigation project, it would be useful if the layout allows other crops to be grown. Flexibility itself has a cost and judgment is still required on how much to spend. Again it is a directional matter. But, on the whole, it is this author's judgment that at the margin, long-term national income would be more enhanced by flexibility in design and continual management than by anything the central budget agency can do in any formal system for adapting project choice to risk and uncertainty. For a discussion of project monitoring, see Casley and Lury (1982) and Imboden (1978).

There is a role for some of the ingredients of BCA in sector planning, implementation, and management even if some of its more sophisticated system use is unachievable. For example, in Chapter 6, input-output analysis is used to adjust net benefits for the utilization of unemployed resources. But the same tools can be used for planning and implementation. The interindustry relationship provides a convenient check-list of needed complementary inputs necessary to the project's success, such as transportation or manpower skills. It may be a more important use of scarce analytic personnel to take steps to see that arrangements are made for the timely provision of related project inputs than to make sure the precisely optimal project and scale are chosen. The same can be said for the subsequent processing and marketing of the project stimulated outputs. The institutional arrangements necessary to ensure this complementarity is another topic (Schmid and Faas 1975). The key to success is not just to chose the right project from the available list, but to encourage the technician who designs projects to look for those projects that can utilize surplus labor if it exists.

Another example is provided by the material in Chapter 9 on discounting and investment criteria. The point was made that the investment criteria reflect a policy judgment on whose costs are most limiting. The point for planning and implementation would be to identify possible capital rationing problems found by project participants.   The timely delivery of a credit program relative to the project's suppliers and users again may be more important to success than the choice of the "right" project.   The valuation of projects over time makes us sensitive to the time flow of costs and returns. The choice of discount rate should not take all of our time away from the design of education programs that could affect the user adoption rate.   In general the point is that analysis can be used to affect the design of projects and thus the content of budget choice and the reality of projects' projected cash flows as well as the optimal choice from a given list of alternatives.

In the context of fundamental uncertainty, it may be more important to be able to learn and adapt as we go along than to choose the apparently optimal project (Korten 1980).   This also means that management and control of the environment must partially supplement even the best predictive model.

This chapter is related to the previous chapter on time trade-offs. If a system of segmented budgets is utilized, risk strategies can vary by subarea where learning can be enhanced. If the central budget agency is dominated by a concern for total budget size, it uses the discount rate and risk adjustments to control the supply of eligible projects. But with the decision of budget size previously determined, the central agency could spend more time sampling and supervising project preparation and design.

10.10. The Need for Political Choice

The trade-off between income (or other performance) and its variation is similar to the trade-off between present and future income, or any other nonmarket price in BCA. When there are second-best differences in these and other risk variables among individuals and no market allowing individuals to adjust their quantity demanded to price, there must be some political choice of whose preferences count.   Each citizen cannot independently adjust a portfolio of public projects or regulations to obtain the desired risk exposure (or to obtain the desired time preference).

Some analysts are frustrated whenever they cannot derive political oughts from observing the excreta of the economy.   But the modest economist has much to offer in using these data to help politicians decide among conflicting preferences and choose a satisficing, directional risk adjustment. As part of this modesty, it must be admitted that there are some project areas involving unique decisions to which systematic analysis cannot apply. There is nothing to be consistent with.

In conclusion, politicians can give different qualitative guidelines for different programs. It will not be possible to tie these guidelines precisely to the particular decision rule that an agency might choose to implement the guidelines. But the directional and ordinal fit can be logically argued, and it appears that challenges to consistency in these terms are the kind of thing that a court of law could adjudicate.

Notes

1. Expected utility hypothesis games are played with the experimenter giving the subject the probabilities attached to a project choice. In the real world, the subject is also choosing the probabilities that confounds interpretation.

2. This is equivalent to a perfect complete insurance market in which any risk can be spread, which is assumed by Hirschleifer (1966) who recommends the expected value criterion. See also Graham (1981).

3. There is the further problem that the distribution of project risk to individuals is itself uncertain.

4. Sometimes prejudicially called "public goods." See Schmid (1987, Ch. 5). Fisher (1973) argues that the Arrow-Lind theorem applies only to incompatible use (private) goods. But this is not true as some joint impact goods have small individual benefits.

5. This corresponds to the "editing phase" of prospect theory (Kahneman and Tversky 1979).

6. Use of objective estimates was also an issue in the valuation of time saved in section 5.3.1. Both require a policy choice.

7. This is also true of the Bayesian criterion.

8. Minimax is still conservative relative to the optimistic maximax.

9. For a review of theoretical considerations in the use of subjective probability, see Dasgupta and Pearce (1972, 179-85).

11

The Political Economy of Budgeting

11.1. Appropriations Decision Structure and Performance

It is the purpose of this chapter to analyze the effect that benefit-cost analysis can have and has had on public decision making in practice. Does the use of BCA make any difference in budget choices? In Chapter 1 it was noted that the demand for BCA is limited. The reasons for this need to be explored further.

To describe budget documentation systems it is necessary to review briefly the components of BCA. As noted in Chapter 3, the most widely used budget format contains line item costs for each project input--such as personnel, travel, or construction. The next component is evaluation, which designates some categories of input and output to be used to estimate a production function. This evaluation can be as simple as a single level of spending and related output or can be extended to relate increments of spending to increments of output. The output can be an intermediate or a final good. This first step toward a systems analysis is a giant one. Many agencies have no idea how the agency's products affect citizens as a function of incremental spending.

The next step toward systems analysis is the program budget. It utilizes the evaluation data to compare spending alternatives on the basis of some common output or measure of effect (information structure). The boundary of relevant alternatives is a matter of degree, and the alternatives may be available within an agency or across several agencies. The comparisons are made formally by cost-effectiveness analysis to determine which project can produce a given amount of a given output most cheaply.

The most complete systems analysis is benefit-cost analysis. Although one of the earlier steps is called evaluation, there is no valuation or pricing of outputs until BCA is reached. Uniform systems rules are used by all agencies, and the most ambitious approach would be to rank all alternatives.

It is possible to combine these components in various ways and apply them over various boundaries. For example, a significant reform of the budget process was made under Robert McNamara in the U.S. Department of Defense and was extended to other departments by President Lyndon Johnson in the 1960s (U.S. Congress 1967 and 1969). Some idea of the effect of systematic analysis can be obtained by comparing the performance of the budget process over time. Before 1965, the line item input budget was the rule, although some agencies used parts of BCA. For example, the water agencies were required to estimate costs and benefits, and guidelines were developed by an interagency commission and ostensibly followed by all agencies. However, the resulting project rankings were never used for budget choice within agencies, let alone across agencies. This system might be described as an input-output evaluation with more or less common valuation rules but without a program budget. Even this limited procedure was never widely used outside the water resource agencies.

McNamara had to choose among conflicting priorities arising from interservice rivalry in the Department of Defense (Sanders 1973). Program planning and budgeting (PPB), as it was then called, promised some way to compare the cost effectiveness of the alternative weapons systems championed by each of the military services. Output categories included population fatalities and industrial capacity destroyed under various strategic alternatives. Subsequent secretaries of defense used this type of analysis for other issues, such as alternative ways to move forces from one area to another. Strategic evaluations were organized by the National Security Council during President Richard Nixon's administration. The focus and management of information systems depend on the decision-making styles of top policy makers.

President Jimmy Carter had his own system called zero based budgeting (ZBB), although it was never fully implemented. In principle, ZBB reviews and justifies selected current program elements, starting near but not necessarily at zero (Sarant 1978). It requires periodic justification of some part of the current level of funding (the base) as well as increments of new programs. It asks managers at all levels to evaluate the cost effectiveness of their activities and alternatives. Sunset legislation requires the legislature periodically and explicitly to examine programs from a zero base. ZBB asks high-level policy makers to establish objectives with input from lower level managers. Each unit in the agency then puts together "decision packages" relating incremental budget size to performance. In other words, knowledge of some portion of the production function is required. Whether the function goes from zero input to maximum output is not critical. The objective can be changed periodically as the environment changes. The program categories are primarily determined by departmental organization charts, and reorganization is an integral part of budget formulation as political leadership changes.

Each level of management is asked to rank the decision package, or spending increments (and associated output), within its jurisdiction. It highlights trade-offs by showing that a higher achievement of some output in program A is at the expense of a lower output in program B for a given budget level. The bottom line for a department is a display of all the decision packages in rank order showing cumulative spending. The minimum level below which a program cannot be conducted effectively must always be ranked higher than any less costly increment for the same decision unit but not for another unit. At higher levels, packages are consolidated.

If importance weights were added to the project (decision package) ranking, prices per unit of output would be implicit when the budget level by department was chosen. This would make ZBB a full systems analysis as outlined in Section 5.8, and the public could organize its lobbying conveniently by relating these administrative prices to familiar market prices for private goods.

Budget reforms are made in the legislative as well as the executive branch. In 1974 Congress passed the Congressional Budget and Impoundment Control Act (Havemann 1978; Pfiffner 1979), which established House and Senate Budget Committees and a staff and analytic function in the Congressional Budget Office. The act required Congress to set spending targets by program areas at the beginning of each budget year. The appropriation committees were then to keep their detailed decisions within these targets. The purpose was to force Congress explicitly to consider trade-offs among programs and the resulting necessary taxes (and deficit). This procedure replaced one in which appropriations by each committee responsible for a set of agencies were made serially, with the total unknown until the last bill was passed. In practice, the spending targets seem to have been generous and to have forced few hard choices among program areas (Schick 1980, 313). In terms of budget growth and deficits, reform seems to have had little effect. Schick (1980, 573) concludes that, "at the margins, budget outcomes can be changed by the process, but dramatic shifts should not be expected." He further notes that "no system based on cooperation among peers could long survive if one side won or lost all the time" (p. 578).

Evaluating the effect of budget reforms is very difficult (Merewitz and Sosnick 1971). If measured in terms of spending trends, the result is affected more by the total environment than any procedural change. The desirability of spending decisions is in the eye of the beholder. If you like the outcome, you tend to like the process. It is difficult for participants to visualize the with and without situations. Because each participant learns from whatever is available, it is difficult to imagine what would have been done if different information were available. When participants are interviewed, they report that PPB, ZBB, and the Congressional Budget Act made little difference. After examining these surveys, Wildavsky (1969, 207-14) unequivocally concluded that the changes made no difference (see also Nelson 1987, 72-80; Rosen 1984; Wildavsky 1988).

A detailed examination of the implementation of PPB for recreation programs was made by Nienaber and Wildavsky (1973). They found no substantial use of the PPB system by agency or departmental heads and also found that the Congress was antagonistic toward the system. Although program budget formats were created and demanded considerable staff resources, there was a question as to their substantive content in practice. After several years of producing these formats, Nienaber and Wildavsky (1973, 136) observed that "elements of analysis still lacking include definition of benefits or effectiveness, quantitative goals, specification of problems, investigations of alternatives, and therefore, broad range trade-off analysis between one program and another....The program budget was supposed to contribute new analytical perspectives, and that it did not do."

It appears that in practice PPB existed mostly as a new set of forms with which to assemble the previous data into program categories. Even the categories chosen often failed to raise issues of comparison. The bottom line seems to be that it is easy to reassemble existing numbers under some new groupings, but this does not supply an information base for different political decisions. Evaluation (production function) data are scarce, and until their supply increases significantly, the character of the struggle over the treasury is not going to change. Nienaber and Wildavsky (1973) argue that if the scarce staff becomes involved in day-to-day budget battles, there may be even less evaluation.

It might be expected that the use and production of program budgets and BCA would vary by agency and department. Many executives have no interest in leadership and will decide issues only if open conflict erupts among subordinates or interest groups. Their budgets tend to develop incrementally of their own inertia. Reallocations are reactive and are made only with an eye to survival. Many observers agree that analysis was used most frequently in the Department of Defense under Robert McNamara. Some argue that this type of analysis is inherently suited to Defense Department programs, but its implementation may have resulted more from the strong will of McNamara, who instituted it, than from any intrinsic usefulness. If a policy manager wants to lead rather than react, there is no alternative to the use of some type of system analysis to provide comparisons and to serve as the basis for asking new questions and exploring alternatives. These themes are further examined in this chapter through some examples of how information is used in politics.

Weiss (1987, 42) reviewed 25 years of evaluation studies and concluded that they "seemed to have little effect on either budgetary allocations or the selection of programs for expansion or reduction." It is sobering to note that in spite of years of analysis applied to elementary and secondary education, no clear relationship exists between expenditures and student performance (Hanushek 1986). Perhaps the best evidence that past budget reform has made little difference is the 1985 passage of the Balanced Budget and Emergency Deficit Control Act (Gramm-Rudman-Hollings, PL 99-177). This act sets a schedule for arriving at a zero budget deficit in fiscal 1991 (later postponed to 1993). If the deficit is projected to exceed the limit, then automatic across-the-board spending cuts are made, with a 50/50 split between defense and nondefense programs. Congress seems to agree that budget deficits are undesirable but abrogates setting program priorities.

When budgets are being reduced, it might be expected that there would be increased demand for BCA to establish priorities.   Instead, the same percentage cuts may be applied to all programs.

Program budgeting has largely disappeared in both federal and state governments.   Earlier schemes for developing impact measures applicable across agencies have been replaced by simpler output measures for each agency (Sallack and Allen 1987).   Benefit-cost studies of individual investment projects are made in various departments and in Congress.[1]   But the attention has shifted to regulatory applications.

11.1.1.   Regulatory Application

President Carter required regulatory analysis to show the consequences of regulation and identification of least burdensome alternatives (Executive Order 21044, March 1978).   President Reagan went further and made benefit-cost analysis and a finding of net benefits requirements for new regulation (Executive Order 12291, February 17, 1981).   He hoped that requiring accounting of the costs of regulation would result in fewer regulations being promulgated (Smith 1984). The Office of Management and Budget exempted changes that relaxed regulations (Smith 1984).   The clearest effect was to create more transaction costs to delay regulatory expansion, but not for regulatory relaxation.   Regulations were in fact relaxed and fewer new ones imposed, but this might have occurred in response to presidential objectives without formal analysis.   Whether the analysis succeeded in identifying regulations with the largest net benefits that would not otherwise have been identified or in preventing regulations with less net benefit from being passed is not clear.

Some episodic evidence of the impact of regulatory analysis is provided by the decision of the National Highway Traffic Safety Administration to eliminate requirements for passive safety restraints in automobiles.   This decision was overturned and the court cited the Regulatory Impact Analysis in its argument for contradicting the administration's claim that the safety restraints were unjustified (Whittington and Grubb 1984, 66; Litan and Nordhaus 1983).

Reagan's antiregulatory thrust was blunted by the U.S. Supreme Court in *American Textile Manufacturers Institute v. Donovan* (1981).   The Court ruled that the Department of Labor did not have to meet a net benefit test in health and safety regulations (Karpf 1982).   These conflicting directives make it difficult to determine whether changes in the application of cost-benefit analysis have made a difference.

With respect to public investments, both the Johnson and Carter administrations had pushed the water resources agencies toward greater consistency and explicit valuation.   This culminated in the U.S. Water Resources Council Principles and Standards of 1973, revised in 1979 and 1980.   These guidelines were promulgated in such a way that agencies that did not follow them could be sued. The agencies were particularly concerned about the requirement that they formulate and document nonstructural and non-market-oriented water projects. Reagan abolished these detailed public water investment rules in 1982 under a general rationale of streamlining government, despite the fact that in 1981 he had ordered benefit-cost analysis to be used in all regulatory analysis.

If you want to reduce regulation, it is politically more expedient to create paper work barriers to regulatory expansion and to encourage agencies to emphasize costs rather than to explicitly lower the value of human life in systematic benefit-cost guidelines. It is also easier to exclude water projects from executive budget recommendations (which both Carter and Reagan did) than to get the agencies to follow evaluation guidelines that would theoretically reduce the number of projects with net benefits eligible for funding. The guidelines provided by the Office of Management and Budget were minimal and those developed by individual agencies gave few detailed system rules (U.S. Environmental Protection Agency 1983 and 1988). For examples of the studies produced, see U.S. Department of Transportation (1982) and U.S. Department of Labor (1981).

11.2.   Bargaining, Decision Levels, and Program Budgeting

11.2.1.   Government as a Bargaining System

The government is a hierarchical command system more in name than in reality. For example, the president is supreme over all executive agencies, yet each agency has its own constituents and basis of power (Neustadt 1960). These sources of power must be dealt with by the president in a process of bargaining, negotiation, and accommodation that in many ways is similar to market bargaining. The contents of the trades are often difficult to identify and may only constitute IOUs to be collected later.

An example will illustrate that the government is not a simple hierarchy. President Johnson let it be known that he wanted a higher discount rate used in the evaluation of Federal water resource projects. In his budget message in January 1968, he went on record as favoring the increase and stated that administrative action was underway. The interagency Water Resources Council reluctantly approved the change in November 1968. The agencies did not welcome it, and their powerful allies in Congress resisted it, so this was not a simple matter of a presidential order to subordinates. The change finally came, combined with a move to revise other evaluation practices, offsetting the decreased benefits caused by higher interest rates. The change in interest rate was not a one-way command but came about as a result of bargaining (implicit and explicit). The discount rate is an important system rule and the present procedure is a result of negotiation nominally within the executive branch but in fact with consideration of key congressional parties. Political trades are popularly spoken of in derogatory terms, yet the process of democracy follows the same give-and-take bargaining as found in the marketplace.

It is significant that such an important budget formulation system rule as the discount rate should be left to administrative determination for so many years (see Section 9.7.4). Although Congress is an ever present party to administrative determination, it has avoided making the existing system rules a matter of formal law. Congress can provide a list of projects each year for funding but rarely acts in terms of directives for benefit evaluation.

It could be said that Congress gets what it wants through informal bargaining with the executive agencies, but the matter goes much deeper. Political participants dislike overt confrontation and conflict. It is easier to get agreement on a list of projects than on more general criteria and rules. Project choice can change in response to changing interest groups without sacrifice of principle. If decisions are left to the executive agencies, the issues can be masked as technical matters rather than policy judgments. It is an advantage when defending a budget to deny that any political maneuvering was necessary and to let it appear that all issues were settled by technical expertise within the relevant agency. This strategy makes it difficult for opponents to counter with dissenting arguments, even if they can manage to produce their own experts, which is costly. Most observers seem to agree that Congress and the executive agencies are not familiar with and do not embrace a focus on general criteria and systems rules (Nienaber and Wildavsky 1973). At the state level, governors hesitate to set priorities in terms of measurable objectives (Sallack and Allen 1987, 46).

Bargaining is characteristic between and among cabinet secretaries, agencies, the president, and Congress. In addition there is often bargaining between different levels of decision within an agency, including its central and field offices. Each of these levels is a point in the information flow system, and each has slightly different constituencies and interests to resolve.

Academicians frequently assume that it is always useful to have more information, and they distribute it, when available, as widely as possible. In the language of market structure theory, access is unlimited and open. In political (and market) negotiation, information is made available as it suits the party possessing it (Bartlett 1973). The resolution of conflicts is the job of politicians (elected officials as well as bureaucrats). But conflict depends on perception, and perception is related to information. In short, expanded information systems may create conflict when none was perceived before. Most people do not like to create extra work for themselves and therefore prefer to let sleeping dogs lie. With this as background, let us further examine experience with program budget reforms.

11.2.2.   Effect of Program Budgeting on Bargaining

The effect of program budgeting systems perhaps can best be seen in the context of specific examples. Suppose a cabinet department secretary or congressman is examining the budget recommendations of an agency head; included is a request for $2 million to rehabilitate a lock and dam. When asked for justification, the agency claims that this is an emergency; there is danger the whole lock will fail with great damage to life and property. This argument arose in the Corps of Engineers appropriations hearings (U.S. Congress 1969, p. 1949). Congressman Howard Robison (R-New York) noted that the Newark Bay project, which involved the danger of ship collisions and loss of life, was at least one other emergency project. But President Nixon had cut President Johnson's recommended funding from $3 million to only $500,000 for the Newark project and Robison was not sure whether the most pressing emergency was simply a convenient argument for a project chosen on some other basis. The Corps, or any other agency, always has the best and most detailed information. It has a competitive advantage on an ad hoc basis and can make the case very well. It will not present system information that would weaken its case. There was no system rule for incorporating the emergency variable. Robison did not pursue the point and indeed could not in the context of the information available to him.

Control over information is a source of power for people at various levels of the bureaucratic structure (and their particular constituents). This power falls to them through the largely unwritten procedures by which budget information is presented, rather than by constitutional or other law. Those in possession of this power will not be indifferent to attempts to alter information flows. This is as true of agency bureaucrats as of presidential staff members, budget bureau personnel, or members of Congress.

Critics of program budgeting argue that it leads to centralization (or in market structure terminology, monopoly) by a few top decision makers (Campen 1986, 131-35). This criticism is valid in the sense that higher level decision makers, whether in Congress or the executive branch, are often lost in case-by-case details and cannot exercise judgment. The various decision makers, however, could all participate in formulation of the generally applicable rules, just as they now do on projects and specific budget line items. But politicians' power would be directly related to how well they represent and articulate group interests rather than their ability to control information. In any case, changes in access to and the form of information affect performance and the power of different groups to influence outcomes. Decentralization should not be confused with pluralism. Under present rules some local groups have great power, and more centralization might actually open access for new local groups and thus be more pluralistic (cf. Lord and Smith 1969).

Congress is concerned with its influence relative to the executive branch. Congressional committees hope to control program impacts by sampling a detailed object-classified budget (Fenno 1968, 184). The implication is that if the legislative-executive dialogue is only in terms of programs, the committees will lose control. This is not a necessary result of PPB if that program discussion were to focus on concrete objectives and the links to specific expenditures. These expenditures can then be sampled for their ability to meet the objectives. But if the specific project details are examined without concern for the overall framework, Congress is deluding itself that it has control. Although Congress may derive self-satisfaction from cutting a specific detailed budget item, the victory is empty if the main direction of the program is chosen and managed by others. Although Congress and the executive branch claim that watching budget detail is the only way to control the substantive direction of programs, many on both sides have little interest (or motivation) in controlling overall direction and are content with the rewards that come from serving very particular interests with a specific budget detail. It is clear that use of PPB affects interest groups differently, but the major difference need not change the relative power of Congress and the White House if both have an interest in overall control.

A frequent criticism of public works programs is that once they are set into motion, everyone wants a piece of the action. If there is going to be a given development appropriation, each state wants a share. Thus, more money may be spent on public works than the public really wants to spend. It is difficult to formulate a performance criterion in these terms, but it is possible to observe behavior under different structures. Just as it is not clear which project will be dropped if an "emergency" project is put into the budget, it is not clear which broad programs are traded off in Congress. The Congressional Budget Act of 1974 was designed to continually remind Congress of the necessity to make comprehensive budget trade-offs, but as noted it has been less than successful.

When an unranked list of projects is presented for approval, it is not clear which project just made the list and which just missed. Systems analysis would identify the marginal project and would identify the specific parties who barely win and barely lose as the margin is changed. Systems analysis is painful and focuses animosities.

At the individual project design level two distinctly different kinds of information systems can be presented to the public. One emphasizes explicit alternatives and trade-offs among features and their beneficiaries. The other tries to anticipate majority public reaction and assembles the features in a single recommended project design. Both involve negotiation and bargaining, but the structure and performance are quite different. As indicated earlier, the agency always has the best information relative to higher level administration, Congress, or the public. Opponents of a single recommended project plan will find it difficult to present technical documentation for another alternative to equal the agency's documentation. If the agency decides that it knows the best plan, it is not likely to aid the opponents by providing a technically sound alternative. Again, no agency will look on information system rule changes with indifference.

The public can handle only a limited number of alternatives and details. Some argue that presentation of alternative policies and performance results would confuse people and prevent any decision from being made. The public has the same problem as a cabinet secretary, president, or Congress. A person cannot make a judgment on two alternative lists of 20 projects but might be able to make a broad directional choice. Some experiments with group workshops and computer simulations suggest further possibilities for involving the public in complex decisions (Holling 1978).

One issue in this discussion is the appropriate level for political compromise. No politician appreciates an agency that gets constituents stirred up and divided over several alternative plans. The politician then must choose and in doing so will alienate some voters. The political representative probably prefers that the agency work out as many compromises as possible and accept responsibility for the compromises before the issue reaches the congressional level. This preference would probably exist even if the compromise were based on ignorance of results by some constituents. The political system has a tendency toward heat transfer and outright avoidance of responsibility where possible.

11.2.3.   Effect of Segmented Budgets

Perhaps some compromise is possible between political proclivity and the requirements of systematic analysis as usually practiced. Legislatures in fact allocate money to groups whether in the name of effective demand or redistribution. But government guidelines pretend this is only a derived decision following choice of grand objectives, when in fact projects are never funded on the basis of ranked returns. Systems analysis might be of more practical use if it served the interests of the "owners" of subbudgets. Freed of the need to control budget size, which it is not allowed to do anyway, each segment could have a different discount rate and other appropriate system rules.

For example, a legislator or executive would not have to pretend that a project was given priority because of its emergency life-saving characteristics when this was only an excuse to give effect to a group's claim on the treasury. The segmented budget approach would allow the project to be designed for the appropriate owners, for example, scaled consistent with regional time preference. If a group's budget were already established, it would not have to get its share of the treasury by getting a piece of what it might consider a low-priority project.

President Carter advocated allocating dollars to a program area (e.g., water) for each state and then letting agencies compete with projects for this subbudget. An assistant secretary of the Army advocated a regional budget approach for the Corps of Engineers (Dola 1971). The choice of subbudget categories would be critical, for example, by regional or other interest groups. The categorical level can be coterminous with the project, leaving no room for further choice, or with national income, giving unmanageable scope for choice.

Legislators seem most comfortable when giving dollar claims to certain groups. If this were done more openly, BCA might be of more use. Project rank might be the basis for project funding by politicians for the first time if system boundaries within which ranking were applied were more modest as in the case of segmented budgets. If theoreticians keep insisting on their first-best definition of national efficiency, it dooms system analysis to its present nonuse as politicians insist on their distributional prerogatives. Congress may be uncertain who gets what if they were to choose only broad rules and objectives applied to the whole budget.

Congress did experiment with one type of segmented budget when it tried general revenue sharing, giving the states money for broad program areas with specific projects chosen and implemented by the states. This scheme was dropped in 1986 because Congress apparently wanted the citizen to know who to thank for specific local projects. Segmented budgets deserve consideration, but no single change in the budget making system is a panacea.

11.3. Rewards for Display of Alternatives

Much of the previous discussion suggests important reasons agencies are not motivated to display alternatives systematically. This reluctance is particularly evident for cost-effectiveness analysis. Agencies tend to present only one funding proposal and to suggest that unless the recommendation is followed nothing should or can be done. Incremental displays of cost and output are not common. The reason is quite simple: There are no rewards for this type of presentation. In fact, there are costs. It gives opponents information they otherwise could not easily obtain. It is convenient for the budget bureau to cut agency budgets when ready-made increments are clearly visible.

In some cases, the legislature and the chief executive make very specific budget reallocations, even down to the project level. At other times the allocations are left to the agencies. Often the president's main interest is in total budget size, and the allocation is less important. The president and budget bureau find it difficult to acquire enough information to act intelligently. For example, individual ongoing projects may present unique scheduling problems understood only by the agency. The point is that the superior information position of the agency is a source of political power and the display of systematic, incremental data changes that power.

The self-evaluating agency is not likely to develop if provision of systems performance data is always used to threaten agency survival. If, however, the budget bureau were to use the systems data not merely to cut the budget wherever possible but to make reallocations within an agency's budget, there would be greater motivation to provide the data. If a lower cost alternative were selected from several increments in one area, the bureau could show that it had been done to allow the selection of a higher level of funding for another area of the agency's program. In short, systems data must be used for systems decisions and not on a piecemeal basis, or the data will not be produced. The previous discussion should not be interpreted as an argument that PPB cannot be used for interagency budget decisions; rather if it is used only to reduce an agency's budget, the system will not be provided with quality inputs.

If we look at individual motivation, many of the same factors apply. Individuals who emphasize alternatives and opportunity costs proceed at their own peril, particularly in the introduction of a new system. The manner in which the system is begun and inserted in the political process is critical for the system's survival.

An example of personal peril is the case of Ernest Fitzgerald, deputy for management systems, Office of the Assistant Secretary of the Air Force (financial management). In November 1968 he disclosed to a congressional committee that the cost of a certain C-5A airplane was going to be much higher than the official department estimate (Newman 1969). One year later, his position was abolished in an announced "economy move." Even a sympathetic senator could not save him, in spite of an unusual amount of publicity. Is the position of the systems analyst inherently tenuous even if practiced with the utmost political skill?

11.4.   Program Budgeting and Value Judgments

11.4.1.   Budgeting as Consumer Information

Critics of program budgeting point out that it does not solve problems of relative value. This is typified in the following quotation from William Gorham (1967), former assistant secretary, Department of Health, Education and Welfare:

> No amount of analysis is going to tell us whether the Nation benefits more from sending a slum child to preschool, providing medical care to an old man, or enabling a disabled housewife to resume her normal activities. The "grand decisions"--how much health, how much education, how much welfare and which groups in the population shall benefit--are questions of value judgments and politics. The analyst cannot make much contribution to their resolution.

Why does the above argument paralyze us so? If put in a slightly different form, it appears true but trite. It is the same as saying that no amount of analysis is "going to tell" the consumer whether to prefer apples or lipstick. People must make up their own minds and, after this value decision is made, tell the market what to produce. But what "tells" the consumer what to want? Values are a function of information, among other things. People have a perception of what an apple or a lipstick will do for them. They do not just have tastes, they acquire them through learning and information. Product information in the market does not short-circuit the market communication system and "tell" producers what to make, but it helps consumers decide what to demand. The same is true of government products. Systems data do not tell the agency what to produce, but they help voters (consumers) and their representatives decide what to demand.

Consumer information, whether relevant to market or government goods, is scarce in our economy,. There are some who like it that way and others who confuse the issue by making it sound as if program budgeting is a technical system that tells agencies what to produce rather than an information system that serves consumers and their representatives. Analysis does not simply assume certain values and make deductions to guide producers. It helps people decide on values in an iterative, evolutionary sense. PPB does not replace consumer judgment or political judgment about what consumers want. Rather, it highlights these judgments and makes them explicit.

In a sense, private producers are much less fearful of helping (from their view) consumers evaluate a product through advertising than public officials are of distributing product information. Both kinds of information, to date, have been all too selectively available and nonsystem-oriented. Still the amount of available information has been growing. Agencies such as the U.S. Forest Service (1980) conduct extensive program planning with substantial local public input as required by the Resources Planning Act of 1974. However, when budgets are funded in Washington, the planning information is not systematically used.

Gorham (1967) and Baram (1980) argue that the "grand decisions" of government cannot be systematized. Should these decisions be nonexplicit simply because they are grand? Nothing is so grand or ultimate that it is not related to something else, and that is what systems analysis is all about.

Wildavsky (1969) in an article entitled "Rescuing Policy Analysis from PPBS," argues that "there are other policies in which presently unquantifiable benefits, like pleasure in seeing others better off or reduction of anxiety following a visible decrease in social hostility, should be controlling." If these and other important variables are indeed uncategorizable and unquantifiable, we can never make explicit, conscious decisions. We might as well toss a coin as have a representative, president, or Congress participate in these decisions. In the context of present information systems there is too great a tendency to abdicate our freedom of choice, set up authorities, and let them tell us that a certain program is good, that is, leave it to the generals, engineers, or whoever to increase our security or provide any product. With present information systems, we must accept their assertion that we are in fact more secure as a result of following their advice, that is, until we all perish, and the results are painfully obvious and quantifiable.

All of the preceding discussion has focused on what might be termed consumer information systems. We will now consider systems for communicating the resulting consumer valuations.

11.4.2. Budgeting as Demand Communication

When consumer preferences cannot be communicated by market institutions, resulting discussions about these preferences are often confusing. If we cannot observe market prices, shall we mumble something about value judgments and leave the field to polemicists and preachers? There are serious problems in constructing institutions for demand communication for public goods (Schmid 1967). The point here is that some economists (and others) mistake the legitimacy of market prices. In a sense, some economists are akin to agency bureaucrats and hide behind technical discussions of prices (and the calculus thereof), pretending that no political choice is involved in market activity.

Prices emerging from market bargaining are no more real and legitimate than exchange ratios emerging from political bargaining (Schmid 1969a). In either case, economists can study the structure of the bargaining rules, which in both cases transform someone's consumer values into orders for goods and services. A particular exchange ratio that results from a market bargain does not validate the structure of that market system, nor does a particular exchange ratio resulting from a political bargain validate those political rules. There is no objective way of knowing the will of the public. That will is reflected only through yet another decision structure that influences which of the many conflicting publics will count.

Gorham (1967, 80-81) argues that for the large, important objectives there is a "difficulty of getting and finding a national consensus." This fact should not paralyze us. There is no consensus within the market either. All consumers do not want the same thing, but we operate within a market system in which various products are produced and trades made. The political system follows the same pattern. The common element is that there must be majority agreement over the bargaining rules. People can become familiar with thinking about and choosing alternative systems rules and performance objectives for both markets and politics, just as they are familiar with piecemeal selection of apples and lipstick, on the one hand, and candidates for the Senate, on the other.

There are two polar extremes in decision making. Analysts could ask politicians to declare a supreme good from which all investment and regulatory choices could be deduced.   This suggestion seems quite impractical and would still create a large area of choice by analysts, paralleling the problem of construct validity discussed in Chapter 4 to get from the general to the specific.   At the other extreme, each project or program could be regarded as unique, in which case there can be no systems analysis or rules that require like things to be treated (traded off) in a consistent manner.   Agreement on middle level objectives necessary to formulate budget system rules seems reachable, particularly if budget segmentation is planned.   This text has asked politicians to decide on things such as the size of transfer targeted to groups, discount rates, degree of price differentiation, range of relevant substitutes, and the job rights of existing labor.   This level of generality seems manageable.   Furthermore, in this author's judgment, political choice and bargaining at this level need not contribute to any more internecine conflict than we already have--and it just might increase public confidence in government.

An overly ambitious systems analysis presents not only unmanageable information problems but also political and social problems.   For an agency to be effective, it needs the loyalty and commitment of its employees.   A program analysis comparing the performance of one agency with another threatens people committed to the performance of a certain activity.   But is it necessary that the loyalty and commitment be to an activity rather than to a program area and the changing needs of its clientele?   It is easier to change activities of existing agencies than to destroy and create them, although neither is easy.   In any case there seems to be a strong rationale for limited systems analysis of budget segments rather than for trying to build an overreaching grand system.   Program analysis can be useful in the context of periodic examinations of directional issues.

The emerging pattern seems to be one of special studies and planning exercises of varying breadth performed by executive departments and agencies, budget bureaus, special executive interagency groups (such as the National Security Council), legislative staffs of subcommittees, and, at the general level, institutions such as the Congressional Budget Office and the General Accounting Office (Kloman 1979; Chelimsky 1987).   In the United Kingdom similar dispersed patterns have developed, including the Public Expenditures Survey Committee of the House of Commons, the Central Policy Review Staff, and the Committee of Public Accounts of the House of Commons with input from the comptroller and auditor general (Robinson 1978; Sandford 1979).   For similar experiences in France see Ducros (1976) and in Australia see Wellor and Cutt (1976).   Systems analysis is always bounded. Its boundaries can change over time and be of varying size but still be functional.   If the boundary is drawn too widely or narrowly, the system is dysfunctional or empty.

11.5.   Conclusion

Economists and policy analysts have been frustrated policy advisors. Although they are widely courted, their recommendations for sound evaluation practices have often been ignored. One of the reasons for the lack of success may be that these practices have been treated as technical questions, when in fact they frequently involve a choice among alternative political bargaining structures. If systems structure is to be reformed, it will be because some interest groups find the structure to their advantage and not because of its inherent logic from an assumed premise.

The point can be illustrated with a final specific case. Economists have long recognized that the evaluation of flood control benefits by the Corps of Engineers was in error. The Corps (and other agencies) currently counts the difference in value of the floodplain land before and after the project as a benefit. This ignores upland sites that might have developed without the project. The correct concept, which is well understood by agency economists, is the difference in rents between the protected floodplain site and the other sites that would be built on if the floodplain were not protected. The present information systems tell floodplain landowners that they can realize large financial gains if the protection project is built. No one supplies the rest of the system information and tells the upland owners that their land values may not increase as much if the project is built. The floodplain owners are an effective political force and greatly influence agency and congressional action. The upland owners are not. Only the economist speaking abstractly about efficiency is cognizant of the upland owners' position. That voice does not carry very far. The reason is that economists have assumed the upland owners should count, that is, should have a property right to be heard. The evaluation procedure used by the Corps is often criticized as leading to inefficiency, but this is presumptuous as efficiency follows from resolution of the rights conflict. Systems analysis raises issues of rights allocation about which politicians must openly decide. If the issue of analytic rules cum property right is not raised, the contest over rights is settled by default. A clear method of establishing rights to the treasury would be the explicit grants budget discussed in Section 8.9 and the segmented budget discussed in Section 9.5.

Government is unable to reform itself and become self-evaluating. It cannot alone produce the information necessary for reform. The systems now in place cannot be sustained unless help is forthcoming from the outside. Many dedicated and enlightened public servants are supplying new kinds of budget information, but the effort cannot grow unless outside political groups recognize that the information serves their advantage. Economists have focused on the supply function but ignored the demand function for information. Nongovernmental educational institutions can help. They can provide more specific information to consumers of this information than has been the case in much past research and education. But it will be necessary to get new groups to demand the present output of BCA efforts and to urge future changes in the BCA system.[2]

Policy formation is like a wide and ever-changing river. Analytic modesty is in order for those hoping to shape that river. As Weiss (1987, 44-45) states, "Decisions in organizations and in political arenas do not hinge solely on information. Too many other things matter--costs, ideology, self-interest, public reaction, the rules and standard operating procedures of the institution." Policy is seldom the result of some discrete piece of information. It evolves from long term learning. The impact of evaluations is indirect and diffuse as the information produced becomes an ingredient in shaping the broad generalizations and ideologies that give direction to policy.

Information and education will not solve all the problems of either the rich or poor. But they do seem to be necessary ingredients. Analysts can simply help provide (1) consumer information on governmental products and (2) information on the relation of political and bureaucratic structure to overall performance. After this, people must decide and interact on the basis of their total experience.

Notes

1.   One of the newest and still expanding legislative requirements for programmatic utilization of BCA came in the Resources Planning Act of 1974 directing the U.S. Forest Service (1980) to use BCA in choosing land management plans.

2.   For additional perspective on the role of analysts, politicians, and the public, see Self (1975) and Yates (1982).

12

Conclusion: Systematic Analysis in Perspective

12.1. The Role of Analysis

What is the role for benefit-cost analysis in a democratic society? BCA is a framework for systematically displaying the consequences of alternative spending and regulations in such a manner that the ranking of these alternatives is the result of applying politically chosen rules reflecting explicit performance objectives. The rules are systematically applied over some program categories, not necessarily the entire budget. The previous chapters have detailed the instrumental points at which the analyst must ask questions of the politicians and discussed how the answers can be applied to indicate a ranking of the alternatives.

It is impossible in practice for a society to separate income distribution and efficiency. It is impossible to achieve a desired distribution and then just arrange the market, government spending, and regulation to serve the consumers made sovereign by that distribution. Lump-sum redistributions are not feasible, taxes will be distorting, government will regulate resource flows such that inputs are taken and outputs provided at less than previous opportunity costs, monopoly and monopsony are present so that prices exceed opportunity cost, and the government will operate under a budget constraint. These and other conditions and practices cannot be corrected to implement some previously determined income distribution, but rather are part of the implementation of the evolving politically determined distribution. These practices are part of the arguments in a social welfare function and not exceptions to them. If government wants to change income distribution it can alter private property rights (including regulation), make income transfers, or change the rules for public investment.

BCA is not a device for telling government what it must do to avoid being labeled irrational (often stated as being "political"). It does not further market or economic values over other values. Indeed, this distinction between values is meaningless. It is not a way to prevent market (or governmental) failure. Failure is relative to someone's goals, and when goals conflict, calling something a failure is only to choose sides. BCA can illuminate the character of the conflict and make it easier for observers to tell whether, once the conflict is settled, the resolution is in fact truly implemented. Explicitness and consistency are the main values incorporated into BCA.

BCA is an efficiency analysis, whether of the independent Paretian type or the interdependent analyst-politician (decision-making) type. But in the latter approach the selection of the input-output categories to be maximized is explicitly political rather than implicit in economic theory and analytical assumption. There is no dichotomy between being efficient and being political. The issue is, rather, about what to be efficient.

BCA is a dialogue between analyst and public decision makers. It is not something the analyst does alone and presents finished to the world, summarized as a single rate of return. Such isolated, sweeping, and noninteractive analysis invites piecemeal, ad hoc decisions as politicians change the analyst's often unintended presumptuous resolution of value conflicts. Decision makers are not always ready to answer the questions put to them by analysts. In many cases their objectives have not been thought out. Analysts must do more than project analysis. They must prepare displays indicating the directional performance of the public sector if various combinations of objectives and the rules that incorporate them are to be applied. This interactive dialogue is part of the creation of objectives as well as part of their systematic application in system rules.

What, then, is the role of the analyst not employed by government (or another client who can supply the performance objectives)? The independent analyst can raise the necessary questions requiring political resolution of conflicting interests and simulate a range of likely answers. The sensitivity of the rate of return to alternate combinations of system rules can be demonstrated. This admittedly makes the presentation of results of ex-ante or ex-post project analysis more complex. It will not be sufficient to indicate the rate of return at several discount rates or to apply several investment criteria formulas. The burden of this text has been to show that there are many more policy variables. A matrix of results from applying different combinations of systems rules could quickly grow to confusing size. Another theme of this book has been the necessity of second-best analytic compromise when confronting information overload. The independent analyst will have to make a judgment to display only a few salient combinations of possible system rules. The reader of the results must be cautioned that comparisons with other projects done by other analysts can be made only for the same combination of rules reflecting possible alternative political trade-offs.

Agency planning studies displaying trade-offs are inputs into the choice of system rules by responsible officials. These then can be applied in full BCA and budget choice. In practice, the planning process and exploration of the consequences of different sets of prices for project outputs have never been tied to actual appropriations.

There is no presumption that politicians or citizens always prefer explicitness or consistency. As discussed in Chapter 11, politicians confronted with a divided public may prefer obfuscation, and the public confronted with difficult choices may prefer escapism. BCA may actually increase conflict by presenting issues that arouse those who otherwise would have remained dormant. But it is this author's judgment that BCA is part of the process of accountability and participation in democratic government. BCA's benefits can outweigh its costs, but for that to be true, the analyst must be modest and cognizant of data and decision costs. The previous discussion at various points has suggested compromises, such as deliberately compartmentalized budgets, to keep the decision process manageable and practical.

Some note of the relationship of BCA to policy analysis and other subdisciplines of economics is in order. BCA is not a separate subfield of economics but a setting in which all fields are applied, from micro to macro theory to international trade, industrial organization, regional economics, and capital theory. Is all economic analysis of public policy issues BCA? Policy and project analyses are an input into BCA, which carries these forward into a format facilitating broad comparisons and ranking of alternatives. BCA is distinguished by a bottom line rate of return and transfer ratio. It is also substantive in the sense of providing a quantitative representation of who gets what, rather than an abstract, formal theoretical analysis of why welfare is (not) lessened by alternative policies, such as tariffs, pollution standards (charges), or food stamps (cash grants).

At the present time, public decisions are highly fragmented. Budget making is not well integrated into regulatory activity, even though regulations change the flow of resources to accomplish certain performances, just as does public spending. The redistributive public spending transfers of money are not easily compared with transfers providing goods in-kind, and the transfers via tax benefits are not related to those via spending benefits. BCA is a format for comparing and relating these various activities, and it requires analytic rules to make these activities comparable and rankable in terms of benefits relative to costs or in the relative efficiency of transfer. It is not suggested that every activity of government could be listed and ranked. But it would be possible to compare a broader range of policy alternatives aimed at selected functional or population groupings by applying the procedures of this book.

Economists are divided on the proper role of systematic analysis. Some accept the values implicit in the Pareto criterion and see analysis as independent of and instructing political choice (Mishan 1976; Harberger 1971; Anderson and Settle 1977). Others have adopted what is becoming known as the decision-making approach, incorporating an interactive dialogue between analyst and politician (Sugden and Williams 1978; Peacock 1973). The difficulty of the problem is demonstrated by the fact that Mishan (1982) has tentatively championed the independent Pareto efficiency approach at the same time arguing that "prescriptive economics will have to go into cold storage" (1981, 264). Various other writers have struck a middle ground and use Pareto efficiency but add some politically chosen income distribution weights, and they particularly regard the system rule for the discount rate as a political matter (Little and Mirrlees 1974; Dasgupta et al. 1972).

The values implicit in the Pareto criterion or the liberal philosophy of freedom are too general to provide budget choice guidance even if they were widely accepted. It is the argument of this author that operational values can be obtained only from politicians supplying answers to the many specific questions leading to a choice of system rules outlined in this book. The decision-making approach is pushed into new areas formerly seen as only technical issues and thus may be termed a "political economy approach." The approach is not only interactive between analysts and politicians but also iterative in the sense that the rules are applied, budget impacts observed, and the rules re-evaluated. In summary and conclusion, the steps in BCA outlined in this chapter indicate the kinds of questions analysts must ask of public decision makers to specify the rules that incorporate judgments on distributive objectives and the resolution of conflict over what economic growth is all about.

12.2.   Program Information Structure

Distributive decisions in BCA are first made in the choice of program information structure (Chapter 3). It is not possible to analyze value questions without input and output categories whose contents can be counted. The naming and categorization of project ingredients shape the subsequent design and valuation process. BCA is an analysis of alternatives, but the first step is to conceive of the alternatives. Do different projects perhaps managed by different agencies produce essentially the same or different outputs? It is impossible to debate the issue if data are presented only in input budgets rather than in terms of outputs and performance.

In the private sector, competition is thwarted by undue product differentiation. But a policy judgment is required to decide if advertising has created differentiation that is misleading the evaluation of essential product features affecting product utility; and different consumers may not agree on the essential characteristics that determine substitutability. The courts allow private producers to claim their products are different (except for lies easily detected through testing), and consumers then individually decide whether the claimed difference justifies any price difference. In the public sector, agencies also claim their products are different. A program or performance budget is not unlike a court ruling that certain claimed differences are illegitimate; it can reveal that two or more products produced by different agencies are actually substitutes. If this is done, one of the agencies may be eliminated on the basis of higher cost per unit. The program budget enforces competition and can eliminate a producer from the running even before the ultimate question can be asked: Is this product worth its cost? The consumer-citizens and their representatives thus have a shorter list of producers (products) from which to choose.

Physical things do not come neatly categorized. Any product category is an aggregation of features with a permitted range of variation in each feature. These boundaries and levels of aggregation are matters of social choice that affect the character of political debate on budgets.

Not every input or every product feature can be noted. The requirement for environmental impact statements is one device for ensuring political input into what is to be documented. To omit an input or output is in effect to assign zero value to it. To define the range over which a feature may vary without changing the name and count of the input and output is in effect to put weights on different characteristics of a multiple characteristic good. But, at some point, lengthening the list of features to be noted becomes too costly, and information overload can produce confusion.

The program information structure is an input into the next step of explicit valuation (pricing). The analyst cannot ask the public and politicians for value judgments without a list of commodities. For example, shall analysts ask about the value of removing one part per million of chemical X or chemical Y from the environment? Or can analysts ask for the value of a unit change in risk of human death? Different interests in the public are affected by the way the question is framed. The frame shapes the character of debate and determines what projects and agencies are seen as competing alternatives and also raises or submerges questions of consistency in application of values.

Everyone in government is part of the political process, the hired analyst as well as the elected politician. The analyst as a practical matter cannot have every detail of a program information structure ratified by the legislative body. Still, awareness of the conflicts involved in choice of the input and output categories does lead to a different politician-analyst dialogue than if the issue is seen as wholly technical. The analyst can present analyses that raise questions about whether nominally different goods should be regarded as similar.

In the real world of bounded rationality and scarce analytic resources, there are few comparisons and rankings of well-documented project alternatives in terms of benefit and cost flows. Project design gets locked in early in project conception and planning stages, and formal ranking is not common. Major directional choices are not made among project alternatives in terms of rate of return, but rather in the formulative stages when the problem is defined, the general approach is chosen, and citizen demand is qualitatively (ordinally) assessed. The thinking that goes into choice of the program information structure is the most important and often the only step in analysis that makes any real difference for project choice.

12.3.   Estimating Project Effects

After the categories and units of input and output have been chosen, the next step is to establish the connection between the two. Chapter 4 introduced methods for estimating the production function so that decision makers can predict how changes in project inputs lead to changes in performance. Choice of the experimental design necessary to control for nonproject changes that might affect performance is a technical decision. But because no design can produce a certain connection between inputs and outputs, there is always an element of judgment as to when to collect more data or proceed with a budgeting or regulatory decision. There is also a judgment in choosing among project alternatives that trade-off the degree of confidence in understanding the production function and the size of the estimated net benefits. An argument is presented for a qualitative judgment based on the weight of the evidence.

Although the analyst can get some indication from politicians on tolerance for uncertainty in knowledge of the production function, the complexity of the issues leaves the analyst unescapably responsible for some judgment as a part of the political process. This raises institutional questions of how experts are selected as much as what techniques they possess. Other dimensions of uncertainty will be noted.

12.4.   Pricing Benefits and Costs

For various reasons, the outputs of public projects are not (or cannot be) priced in the market. The same may be true for some of the inputs to a project (nonbudget costs). The analyst is called on to supply the missing prices. Chapter 5 discussed various methods with which to infer willingness to pay from market-related data even if the project output itself is not sold (or the input is not purchased).

These methods are the economist's stock-in-trade and the debate over these applications is quite technical. But even here there is a role for political input when distributive issues arise. For example, in the market analogy and alternate cost methods, prices and costs of substitutes are used to indicate relative values, but this requires a judgment as to the substitutability of the project output for its marketed substitute. What one person regards as a substitute may be inadequate for another.

The intermediate good method deduces the value of a nonmarketed project output, which in turn is an input into a product that is marketed. One use of this technique is to value a project that reduces threats to life. A safety project or regulation affects lifetime income realized from human capital. This pricing method requires a judgment concerning rights and the morality of effective demand, which can make a project that saves the life of a young doctor more valuable than a project that aids retired ditch diggers. One way to avoid the need for political input at this point is to argue that prices should always reflect the existing distribution of income. The analysis then suggests investments that can best serve those consumer-citizens with effective demand. If politicians do not like the distribution of income (lifetime earning potential in this case), they can directly redistribute income independently of public projects.

But as was explored in various contexts throughout this book, politicians may not want or be able to accomplish a theoretically first-best general redistribution. Nevertheless, they may not be prepared to live with all the implications of the existing distribution as it applies to specific areas, such as life expectancy. Analysts must ask some questions here of public policy makers if they are not to presume a resolution of the conflicts that arise between general and specific distribution.

The cost savings method of estimating the value of benefits has wide application, such as to transportation projects that save a rider's time. Judgment comes in deciding whether to use the analyst's objective measure of the savings or the rider's subjective perceptions. Political input is needed on how to weight the preferences of the well-informed as compared to the impressionistic user. Do you give people what they want or what you think they would want if better informed? Sugden and Williams (1978, 179) label these "merit goods," that is, a good whose price would be different if people better understood their best interest. When information costs are high, citizens may want their representatives to act for them. Many applications to health and safety regulations involve this question. Experts may regard the value of a life saved by a project to be the same whether lost life results from cancer or auto accidents, but some people would disagree. Note that the opportunity to place different prices on different subcategories of a project output or to regard them as homogeneous was shaped in the decision on information structure.

Some public projects produce outputs (or require inputs) that have no market reference points from which willingness to pay can be inferred. In this case the analyst might utilize a survey or bidding game. When none of the methods previously discussed can be used, bidding games are the last resort before the political system must be asked to originate its own prices. However, the bidding game is itself a type of voting technique rather than a device that makes politics unnecessary in estimating willingness to pay. Much depends on survey sample, type of question asked, explicitness of trade-offs, and methods of aggregation. These cannot be solely technical choices. A key question in designing a bidding game is whether the desired value is willingness to pay or to sell. The implied starting place property right is quite different in some cases, and choice of perspective requires a political input. What the public wants is always filtered through some set of rules that influences whose preferences get counted. This is true of political referenda, bidding games, and the market.

Even the most imperialistic economist usually leaves some room for political prices.   Section 5.8 discusses a procedure for obtaining and incorporating these administrative prices into systematic choice of projects. The process emphasizes choosing prices in a manner that facilitates public participation and determining whether these prices are consistently applied.

When there is widespread support for public action, the politicians vote the money and make regulations without feeling any need for economic analysis. But when people are divided, the sheltering warmth of the analytic high priests is sought.   Politicians ask, "Can't you tell us there are some economic benefits from these non-market-related outputs to offset these economic losses that industry keeps reminding us about?" Putting an explicit political price on environmental quality and health benefits is uncomfortable. Many economists are skeptical, and others have learned a negative reaction for different reasons. In some circles, pricing is a negative word as it suggests markets and profits, which sound a bit immoral (Kelman 1981). This is an unfortunate, narrow association.   Any time a choice results in something being produced and something being forgone, a pricing decision is made. This applies to markets, government, and family decisions. To choose is to price.

A second popular confusion surrounding the idea of price is that somehow market prices are natural, whereas government choices and regulations are unnatural, at best, and immoral, at worst. This is a great delusion. Market prices, whether directly observed or inferred, are what they are because of public policy decisions. The market value of transportation, research, flood control, and irrigation benefits depends on public policies (not just tariffs, subsidies, and control programs, but cooperative, labor, monetary, and antitrust policies, to name only a few). Anyone who knows how the long-term agricultural prices used in project evaluation are put together by the U.S. Department of Agriculture economists suffers under no delusion that these prices are natural.   Still, politicians keep asking technicians to derive some formula to determine the worth of environmental or health products. They ask because of the myth that market prices are somehow natural and right. They fear that if they say that preservation of a waterfall is worth $500,000, they will be accused of arbitrariness, soft headedness, and interference with consumer sovereignty.

The market price of wheat is a function of many public policy decisions (including tax policy as well as other things affecting the distribution of income). Why, then, are we willing to give a benefit-cost ratio composed of such policy-influenced market prices so much honor and yet be so skeptical of a direct, politically determined price of a waterfall? The prices of wheat and waterfalls are not the result of some technical formula, but are based on the policy choices of legislatures, courts, the executive branch, and people who buy market products and vote for their representatives.

Therefore, there is no technical reason politicians should fear pricing any kind of public project output or input. They do not need the crutch of an economic or scientific formula derived without political input; these formulas are often a lie or a mask for the personal preferences of the economist who derived them.

A politically set price is an explicit price, whereas a politically chosen set of private market property rights and contract rules eventually produces an implicit price. Since the market price emerges out of the system and is chosen by no one person at no one point in time, it has a semblance of naturalness and spontaneity. However, if we focus on the political rules of access to government, those rules become implicit, and the political decision on prices for public projects yields explicit prices. In other words, political price becomes a composite decision of many representatives conditioned by political rules, just as a market price is a composite decision of many consumers conditioned by the publicly chosen market rules.

This is not an argument for public over private sector investment. The government can make stupid mistakes and unreasonable choices in its administrative pricing, in regulation, or in the other specifications of private property rights. The only point is that citizens live with whatever interpersonal utility comparisons government makes in all these areas. Perhaps if the government's responsibilities in choosing among these alternatives were made more explicit, at least the climate of conflict could be clarified and participation in decision making broadened.

12.4.1. BCA and Regulatory Decisions

Analysis can be applied not only to public spending but also to regulations. The methods and concepts are the same, and this text has not differentiated between these applications. A regulation directs spending without first taking public ownership of the funds via taxation. It should be emphasized that an independent, isolated BCA cannot justify a regulation any more than it can determine a ranking of investments. Both require political input establishing the right, which in turn generates the costs and benefits to be compared and the net to be maximized. A law requiring a private party to install a safety device can be justified by comparing the costs to A and the benefits to B; but the antecedent question is what rights shall be incorporated in calculating these costs and benefits. A regulation is both the means for reflecting a benefit and of determining its magnitude via decision on the use of the human capital approach, willingness to buy or sell, and the other items previously discussed.

12.5. Adjusting Opportunity Cost

Even if market-related prices are available, they may not reflect opportunity costs. Chapter 6 describes the adjustments that are often necessary because of taxation, monopoly, subsidies, foreign exchange, and labor policies. Yet, these policies are there for a reason and the reason needs to be examined before the resulting observed price is rejected and a shadow price put in its place.   This is the basis for additional analyst-politician dialogue. Opportunity cost is is chosen, not simply found. When interests conflict, the issue is *whose opportunity cost counts*. For example, taxes can distort relative values of project components.   Yet, if the tax is intended as a partial redistribution of income, it cannot be ignored by the analyst without the analyst presuming resolution of the distributive conflict. Government could alter income distribution via general redistribution, which would result in altered product prices, but it may prefer to do this via direct alteration of prices facing consumers.   The analyst can remind government of its alternatives but then must accept its judgments. Similar questions arise in the context of tariffs and foreign exchange policies.

One common adjustment reflecting opportunity costs occurs when there is unemployed labor. This is an area in which there are many technical problems and more data on labor markets are needed. But there is also need for political resolution of distributive conflicts in the context of market disequilibrium. The price of labor on public projects cannot be separated from the objectives of macro policy. If government wants to force wages down to restore full employment, then nominal wages should be used on public projects so that government does not add to demand for labor. But if the rights of those already employed to maintain wages are recognized, government, by shadow pricing labor, may have more high return projects and increase labor demand. If it nevertheless actually pays going wages, the unemployed receive a transfer above their opportunity cost. The text outlines various situations in which the opportunity cost is subject to interpretation and in which the acceptance or modification of nominal wages and other prices requires a policy judgment. The same issues would apply to public programs to create private sector jobs, such as subsidized credit, tax breaks, and free public services.

The management of regional economic growth is another matter. A key element in opportunity cost specification is how to handle immobile assets. For example, the shadow pricing of labor in effect determines whether public investment will bring capital to resources that do not want to move or whether the owners of the resources must suffer if they will not move.

Politicians dearly love any public project that provides the home folks with tangible proof of their representative's ability to help them. Politicians have asked analysts to incorporate local employment benefits into their analysis. But economists have pointed out that, under full employment, public investment or aid to private firms just moves resources around and adds nothing to the direct benefits to project output users already estimated. Although there are more jobs in one region and rents earned by local merchants and landowners are increased, if the money had been spent elsewhere, the same thing would have happened, only elsewhere. It is not enough, however, to point out that these benefits cancel out. They are part of the distributive processes of government, and they need to be incorporated and compared with the effects of other transfer policies. The only issues are whether it will be explicit and consistently applied, and whether public jobs and public aid to private jobs will be systematically evaluated in terms of relative efficiency.

12.6.   Nonmarginal Projects

Some projects (and regulations) are large enough to affect output or input prices as discussed in Chapter 7. For example, a public irrigation scheme may increase output sufficiently to lower farm product prices. There may be no change in farmer net income to indicate any benefits, but consumers may benefit from lower prices. This can be measured by the saving in production costs for the old level of output, indicating benefits with no conflicts, unless the saved resources are immobile.

The nonmarginal increase in output reveals the downward sloping demand curve not evident to the marginal competitive firm. This curve suggests that a perfectly discriminating seller could extract more revenues from buyers than a seller charging the same price to all buyers. Should this apparent added willingness to pay (consumer surplus) be counted as an extra benefit? At this point conflict arises. In the private sector of the U.S. economy, price differentiation is prohibited if it is used to gain an advantage over a competitor. In all other cases, consumers have to accept it if sellers are able to segment their markets. In any case, it usually makes people angry when they are charged a price that is different from what other people pay. Where the government does not sell at all, the consumer surplus is never put to actual test, but taxes are collected in its name.

The total willingness of consumers to pay is often substantially larger than the value indicated by a single price to all buyers, so it can affect project ranking. In some cases it may be the difference between negative and positive net returns. In the face of seeing their favorite project receive a low priority, some buyers may be willing to pay more than their neighbors. There are no economic data that the technician can observe to determine this willingness to be exposed to price differentiation. The results of a bidding game would be worthless if the respondent were told that the price or tax to be paid would be different from that paid by others, depending on the bid made. The politician is also in a dilemma when public products are not sold. Citizens supporting the project claim they would not mind paying higher taxes than others, but in reality they know they cannot be required to do so (except as special assessments are possible).

Even if we could satisfy ourselves with a consumer surplus measure, there is the distributive question of loss of producer surplus in substitute products whose demand is affected by the differential pricing of the project's output. This raises a problem of interpersonal welfare comparisons.

Consumer surplus is one of the most complex areas of BCA and one that divides economists. It involves both empirical difficulties and unresolved theoretical problems. In the face of this, this applied economist leaves the extra net "benefits" implied by the possibility of price differentiation for public choice.

12.7.   Distributional Comparisons

Several dimensions of project design and finance alter the distribution of income. Chapter 8 showed how BCA can compare the efficiency with which projects and other transfer instruments deliver income to target groups. If politicians choose the size of the transfer they want to make to particular groups, a grants performance budget can then compare the effectiveness of alternative means (grants efficiency). This would be a large departure from present government practice, which seldom compares direct cash grants with other projects or financing alternatives. Since projects can affect distribution in ways that never show as treasury costs, a systematic procedure is needed to incorporate all distributive dimensions. If this is not done, the government may take credit for helping a group with one hand and reduce the group's income with the other hand.

Just because a target group is given a grant, does not mean that they can spend it any way they want. It is still subject to the rules of anlaysis which give content to the interests of others via the effect on costs and benefits or act as direct constraints.

12.8.   Valuation over Time

It is the rate of discount (or of compounding) that makes projects with different benefit and cost flows over time comparable as discussed in Chapter 9. A public project is desirable only if it produces a return equal to its opportunity cost. If there could be perfect capital markets, everyone would have the same time preference at the margin. In practice, everyone does not have the same investment opportunities and return at the margin, and thus there are differences in preferred investments among groups. This capital market disequilibrium creates conflict that requires a political choice. The issue is parallel to that created by disequilibrium in labor markets, discussed in Section 12.5.

Different investment criteria, such as net present value or internal rate of return, imply a different choice of what (whose) investment opportunities are to count. The criteria also imply whose capital is most limiting. All of economics is about maximization, but the input to which returns are to be maximized requires a public choice. The related issue of whose complementary capital investments are to be credited for using formerly unemployed resources was discussed in Section 6.5.7.

Some of the public may not regard anyone's market-related rate of return as relevant to choice of budget size. If returns are higher in the private sector, should public investments be reduced? Or do higher private returns tell us that expenditures for advertising are much higher for private than publicly produced goods? Or do they tell us that antitrust policies have failed? One corrective is to regulate advertising and invoke rigorous antitrust proceedings. But such sweeping reforms are difficult, and to restrict change to them is often to argue for the status quo. A lower discount rate and larger government budget take some funds away from the private sector without a frontal attack on the sources of the higher returns there. Just as interest rates are a policy choice by central banks resolving various conflicts between consumption, growth, and inflation, the size of the public sector is ultimately a political choice.

Although this text presents the case for systems analysis, we must be mindful of decision costs. A deliberately segmented budget with politically chosen allocation to program areas is suggested as a manageable compromise. The analysis would rank projects only within subbudgets. This would allow projects to be selected with net benefit time flows more appropriate to the actual opportunities of program recipients. The bottom line political decision for all to see is who owns how much of the public treasury. This is ultimately a matter of original jurisdiction and cannot be derived from market observations.

It is not responsible to ask the political authority to confirm its devotion to maximization of national income as a whole and leave the details to analysts. If the politicians are to lift their sights above the project level at all, it will be to some intermediate system boundary (budget segmentation). If we are to have any systems analysis, the boundary of the system must be realistic.

12.9.   Uncertainty

All the estimates produced in BCA are predicted values and thus are uncertain. Uncertainty is present in the first steps, in estimating the physical production function relating inputs to outputs, and all along the way, in predicting future demand and prices. This means there is a trade-off in project choice between the size of the net benefit and its variation. Individuals can be expected to differ in their attitudes toward risk aversion, and this requires a political resolution.

It is not easy to design manageable questions for politicians so that risk judgments can be systematically incorporated into project choice. Some specific techniques are discussed in Chapter 10 as well as some less systematic directional and qualitative devices. More theoretical and applied research is needed in this area before ad hoc choice by both analysts and politicians can be reduced.

12.10. Public Choice Affects Relational Values

Some of the previous discussions can be integrated and further summarized by noting that value is relational and not independent of its measurement framework.[1] Because there are many possible relationships and frameworks, they are subject to public choice. This proposition can be illustrated by recalling several previous topics.

One method reviewed in Chapter 5 for estimating the value of nonmarketed goods was a bidding game. People are asked to express their bid for a hypothetical product. This bid, however, is not prior, independent data. It is influenced by the manner and sequence of questions that are inescapably intertwined with the learning and evolution of a respondent's preferences. The choice of bidding game format is as much a policy decision as is the implementation of the results. Just as there are publicly chosen market rules shaping the struggle for placement of products on the supermarket shelf, there are rules for the sequences and placement of nonmarket bids that affect the learning about substitutes and complements.

Chapter 7 contains a discussion of the value of projects that add enough to supply to lower prices. The new resulting price is the value of the marginal unit and not necessarily the intramarginal units. What would a consumer pay for the latter? The answer, again, depends on the context. Market rules determine consumer exposure to differential prices for public (or private) good B. Because there is no way for the consumer to pay consumer surplus for all products, the order in which the maximum willingness to pay is extracted affects the maximum willingness to pay for any given product. Many bankrupt private firms would have survived if they had been able to use differential pricing, which would have affected the market price of other privately produced products and the inferred demand for products publicly produced. A product has no value independent of the choice of rules for pricing its complements and substitutes. The degree of exposure to differential prices (taxes) is part of one's wealth (opportunity set) and affects returns to alternative investments.

Indirect employment effects are another area in which value is relational. Chapter 6 discussed how a public investment can create new demands for inputs and further processing of outputs, which create new employment. How much of the net value added by the linked inputs and outputs should be added to a project's direct benefits? The answer depends on how much credit is given to the entrepreneurial energy represented by these complementary investments. For example, a public transportation project can be associated with new private investments in factories and even other public investments in education and health care for the employees. The factory or school employment can be seen as determined by the transport project or vice versa. But it is not possible for the public transportation agency to claim all linked employment benefits when the public education agency asserts that the causality runs the other way, that is, once people are properly trained, the road and industrial projects are feasible. The return to project A is relational to the employment effects claimed by interdependent project B. Funding decisions must take cognizance of the value interdependence, or high priority may be given to project A and no funding to project B, which provides the projected employment that is part of A's projected high returns.

A similar problem arises in the choice of investment criteria (Chapter 9). There are many varieties of costs, and they are paid by different people. Each set of decision makers may try to maximize returns to its own budget by putting its costs into the denominator of the benefit-cost ratio and regarding other costs as negative benefits in the numerator. Efficiency is of essence a relational concept. Public choice is required to determine the ratio's base. The ranking of projects (relative returns) is not independent of the form of the ratio.

A final example is provided by the problem of joint cost allocation, which determines which beneficiaries pay for facilities that produce more than one product simultaneously. Users of product A can be assumed to pay as much as the product would cost if produced in a single purpose project alternative, and then users of product B can be asked to pay only marginal costs or vice versa. Public choice of an allocational base is required. A product's cost is not wholly an isolated, independent fact, but a relational matter influenced by the stance taken for its measurement.

Economic analysis focuses on marginal relationships, but these margins are frequently matters to be defined by public choice and not just simply givens and prior data. The observer is part of the system being measured and thus must receive some policy guidance as to how the measurement context is to be constructed.

12.11. Role of Property Rights in Exchange and Grants: Externalities

Boulding (1973, 63) has observed that "bad definitions and the failure of perceptual discrimination is perhaps the most important single source of bad politics." This is nowhere clearer than in the field of public investments. Some benefit-cost analyses masquerade as scientific, value-free tests of change in national income that would arise if market exchange worked (Hanke and Walker 1974). The government becomes both parties in a transaction--the buyer acting as agent for beneficiaries and the seller producing the project and making payment to designated input suppliers.

Some of these inputs are referred to as externalities, and those who lose are to be compensated. First-best analysis takes a global view and distinguishes sharply between exchange and grants results. Of course, the grants elements have always had to bear a heavy burden of legitimacy, whereas those who get their income by exchange simulations are largely unquestioned. But the current rules of benefit-cost analysis derived from first-best economic theory are the most implicit grants mechanism of all. These rules could be matters of explicit political choice, but now are out of sight, hidden in dusty manuals, and are seldom debated by politicians.

Let us review what has already been said in this context by reference to an example. When a transportation project is built that destroys the environment, does the government's action in building the project represent an implicit grant from environmentalists to project beneficiaries? Or is it just a case of a rightful property owner finally exercising previous rights after a period of forbearance? Consider the following analogy. There is an empty lot in back of my house on which my children play. One day the owner will build on it, and my environment will deteriorate. Is this an externality to be compensated? Is this action a negative grant or theft? I was using his lot by his forbearance. He had actually been giving me a grant all along, and if he decides to take it back, I have no legal claim. If I want to continue my use of his lot, I must make an offer of exchange. If I cannot make a sufficient bid, his action is a cost to me as a result of his ownership. A private ownership right is the opportunity to inflict a variety of negative grants (externalities) by withholding that which others want but do not own.

If the government builds a dam for irrigation, is it acting as agent for irrigators who own the stream and who have formerly forgone any use of the stream and made temporary grants to canoeists? If that is the case, the only criticism that might be made is that the government failed to organize a bid from canoeists in an effort to persuade the irrigators to sell their right. When a grant stops, exchange can continue the old use. Alternatively, we might regard the canoeists as the owner. If government builds the dam anyway, without their consent, this is a negative implicit grant. If condemnation is not allowed, then government acting as agents for the irrigators will have to increase project costs by the amount of the bid to the canoeists in exchange for their rights.

Labeling an effect an "externality" is either presumptuous of ownership or provides no help (see Section 2.4). The pure competition market model is silent on which party owns things as long as there is no monopoly. If there were an explicit legislative act to designate a wild river or regulate irrigation, it would immediately be seen as an implicit grant question. The same is true for a court case in which canoeists sue, claiming theft of their water. Yet, some technical assumption of ownership can be made in the benefit-cost rules, and no one notices, but these BCA rules are just as distributive as any court contest over ownership.

The same analysis can be applied to the issue of national and regional benefits. If a group does not own the right to sell a certain amount of good, then when a project increases supply and losses occur, they have no claim. All they can do is ask for an explicit grant of charity. But if they do own the right, then the treasury cost of building a new transportation or irrigation project goes up. This is of interest to environmentalists who do not want development. People's interests are protected in strange and complex ways-- patterns of interacting rights. If we were debating a prohibition of all dams on canoe streams, everyone would see it as an implicit grant (actually, relatively explicit, although not so much so as charity). But environmentalists may not realize they could also achieve fewer dams by implementing a benefit-cost rule that made the reduced prices and loss of asset values suffered by nonirrigated farmers a new irrigation project cost. That is the power of implicit grants: They are difficult to see and affect groups indirectly.

12.12. Systems Analysis and Public Choice

The political application of BCA involves two questions: (1) What is the boundary of the systems analysis? (2) Who provides the system rules? At present in the United States, the World Bank, and many other governmental agencies around the world, the boundary of the system is narrow. Analysis is allowed to define only a threshold of eligible projects and is not used to determine budget size or choice among the eligible projects.

The official systems rules are largely those suggested by first-best welfare economics theory. Some exceptions in the United States are a congressionally mandated discount rate, minimum price for a water recreation day, and the use of average rather than marginal costs in determining the value of a navigation project that would replace rail service. In practice, Congress utilizes budget constraints and does not use project rank to select projects. This suggests the hypothesis that Congress will not accept the BCA rankings if it has not participated in the making of the system rules or when its mandated rules have been branded as irrational.

What are possible reasons for politicians to substitute choice at the project level for choice of system rules and implementation over all agencies? First, when politicians have been asked about objectives, they have been given only limited alternatives by those economists who simply ask if government wants to maximize national income. This can be answered only affirmatively. The only relief offered is that the politicians could have a distributive objective to be implemented by applying weights to benefits received by different groups.

Sugden and Williams (1978, 186) go a bit further and suggest that politicians can postulate administrative prices. What possible reasons are there for politicians not to seize this invitation? Is it because they find it difficult to categorize and price complex outputs with multiple attributes? It is difficult to list all the attributes that are preferred and the rates of substitution among them and it is costly to specify preferences in such a way that the technician could deliver precisely what was wanted. It saves time to choose among projects rather than to price attributes, but the design technicians are left to make less visible trade-offs among the attributes. This was the issue in Chapter 3.

When analytic rules are applied they aggregate to produce an overall level of welfare for various groups. In principle, politicians and analysts could iterate between choice of a matrix of rules and the overall result politicians desire. But there is always uncertainty and they may wish to avoid the iteration and try to choose the end result more directly in the form of projects. Decision makers have the same problem when legislating regulations and private property rights. These rights as between individuals or groups often overlap and the real end value of an opportunity depends on the actual and somewhat unpredictable use of opportunities by others.

System rules and system boundaries are sometimes complements and sometimes substitutes for each other over certain ranges. Presently choice is at the project level and the rules of analysis produce a dichotomy between eligible and ineligible projects leaving choice among the eligible projects unsystematic. Perhaps there is a middle ground between a project and total system boundaries. Money is sometimes appropriated to budget segments defined in various ways such as by program, commodity, income group, or region. This provides a degree of performance predictability while leaving the details of which projects to fund to be guided by general rules.

From the perspective of first-best prior, legitimate property rights, segmented budgets appear to be irrational. If income distribution were settled and a project built when its beneficiaries were not willing to pay enough to make it equal to the rate of return from another segment, then the budget of the first segment was too large and national income suffers. But if the desired income distribution cannot be achieved by costless transfers, the system rules act as property rights to achieve the desired income distribution.

Suppose that the rule is to utilize the human capital approach to valuing life in choosing health projects. Congress has two choices if it finds the results unacceptable. It can change the rule and set an administrative price on human life that does not distinguish between people of different ages or income. Or it can allocate a certain amount of money to life-saving projects for the poor so that regardless of willingness to pay, a certain amount will be spent for this purpose. A variation of this is to target a grant to the poor and let projects compete for delivery of benefits valued by the recipient or by the giver. Either way, government is altering the distribution of income and this could alter willingness to pay such that the project would be economic. But it is a constrained redistribution. Governments often do not give the poor money and ask what they would like most. The way they spend the money is tied to whether the redistribution is acceptable. Ownership is validated in the context of end results.

When legislators are debating between giving money to farmers for flood control and giving money to labor for retraining, they may not want the decision to depend on the beneficiaries respective willingness to pay any more than they wanted the decision in the case of the poor to depend on the poor's willingness to pay for their lives. Government may want to give labor benefits as a matter of original wealth ownership in the same way it gives property rights in the electromagnetic spectrum to TV stations, in off-shore oil, or in use of the atmosphere for coal burning and acid rain. But even so, ruling coalitions may not be willing to transfer income if the recipients spend it for just anything. So recipients can have the money only for retraining. The scope of the budget segments is part of the political decision that builds consent for any action.

Whether Congress sees this as a charitable transfer instructed by those with present income, or as a resolution of an ownership conflict over the social dividend is a matter of perception. This is not something to be deduced from data on the world of commodities, but rather chosen from the world of social relationships.

A segmented budget is not irrational. It is a grant of ownership in the national dividend that is validated in part by restricting what it is used for. It is also instructed by a sense that there would be willingness to pay if these groups had more money. It is not a reduction in national income, but a part of the definition of the prices and quantities that make up national income.

The analytic rules for BCA are themselves matters of ownership definition. Congress could choose some combination of rules and explicit grants that would achieve the same results as any segmented budget. But the linkage would be difficult to predict and the results uncertain. So Congress quite rationally wants some level of segmentation to better predict the performance results. The degree and kind of segmentation and system rules together determine ownership.

Part of the validation (coalition building) of this ownership depends on the manipulation of symbols, including trying to make it appear that the rules that favor one group over another are technical matters. Politicians from ignorance or design may not want to decide system rules. Each analyst will have to make his or her own choice. Just because politicians do not want to do their job, economists do not have to do it for them. This is not a simple decision. What is technical and what is a matter of ownership requiring political input is a question over which reasonable people may differ. This is nowhere clearer than in the continuing arguments over consumer surplus. This book is an argument for asking more questions of politicians, but just where the line gets drawn is a matter of prevailing practice in the community of economists. Economists are part of the policy process and although they may not get answers to all of their questions, what they choose to ask is part of the evolution of the game.

The quality of political agreement on budget segments and rules varies in terms of the degree to which it is informed or consensual. This is no less true for economists. When Harberger (1971) asked the economics profession to agree on three rules of welfare analysis, his first-best proposal for equal weight to gainers and losers prevails in government manuals, but its relevance in a second-best world is still debatable. Politicians have some chance of being held directly accountable for their decisions, whereas academic debate evolves according to its own rules. At the same time, political choice of any kind has as one of its ingredients symbolic manipulation including hiding value conflicts behind various smokescreens (including, but not limited to some kinds of economics) that happen to serve particular interests.

12.13. Conclusion

You cannot make a grant unless you have a right. Do not take the ability to grant for granted. The same is true for exchange. You cannot trade something or give it away if you do not own it. Samuels (1975, 342) puts it well: "The grants economy helps to produce the power structure within which exchange takes place, including income and wealth distributions; and exchange produces the power structure within which grants take place, including income and wealth distributions."

The same points apply to government investment and regulation. Sometimes they act to facilitate exchange, sometimes they bring about voluntary grants, and sometimes they engender nonvoluntary grants. Which is which depends on what one considers to be the legitimate norm of rights ownership. These rights are implemented by the rules of benefit-cost analysis. Research could focus on how private rights and rights equivalencies in the procedures of public investment analysis are substitutes and complements for accomplishing the same real income distribution. If we want to aid a certain group, what mix of new private property rights and public investment rules will do the job? This is a question of positive science, and applying the labels grant and exchange is largely a matter of where one focuses in the social dynamic. Again, as Samuels (1975, 342) puts it, "grants determine the *status quo* (or starting) point from which exchange proceeds and, in turn, from which the next set of grants are made, and so on."

The question of labels becomes important in political debate. An exchange facilitated by government group action has an aura of legitimacy. If you can get your source of income labeled as an exchange, you are ahead of the person who gets a grant. Grant flows are not protected by the courts and can be cut off at any time, as can the beneficiaries of police power regulations. But a property right to exchange is protected and requires compensation if changed. Of course, the best property right to have is one hidden in the procedures of an agency doing benefit-cost analysis. It is protected by a hidden assumption that economists can be relied on to distinguish a grant from an exchange and so instruct government. In fact, only public choice can do that, although positive economics may be able to show the substantive consequences of alternative public choices in terms of income to different parties, rather than make some presumptive claim of detached and independent total welfare maximization, as does normative economics.

This book should not be interpreted as a defense or critique of present benefit-cost practices. The point is that these are the source of some people's income as surely as an explicit transfer payment or private property right. To call these rules either exchange facilitating or grant making is to presume an answer to the question of whose efficiency is being sought. If people understood how these rules affect income flows, some might cease their support and others might commence supporting these rules. Boulding's (1973, 10) law of political irony is indeed relevant here: "Political conflict rests to a very large extent on a universal ignorance of consequences, as the people who are benefited by any particular policy are rarely those who have struggled for it, and the people who are injured are rarely those who opposed it." Some would have us believe that cost-benefit analysis is value free and that government must justify its departures from efficiency. But it must be realized that the BCA rules are themselves property rights instituting value judgments, which in turn determine what is efficient.

Efficiency cannot be a guide to justifying the selection of a particular set of BCA rules, as those rules define efficiency. This does not mean that economists cannot distinguish between efficiency and redistribution. It does mean that any discussion of efficiency presumes a set of property rights. Economists can tell government how output can be increased given a set of rights. But it cannot label a political decision to build an "inefficient" project as stupid without making an explicit value judgment that the existing rights that define the inefficiency are valid. Congress may choose to institute rights via project selection and the rules of cost-benefit analysis, through taxes, or regulations, or by declaring new private property rights in resources. We need more information on how different varieties of these institutions affect who gets what rather than further refinement of benefit-cost techniques and presumptive pseudoscientific criticism of political choices.

A major theme of this book has been that analysts must be more interactive with politicians and other clientele if analysis is to play its role in demonstrating the systematic effects of implementing more generally stated objectives. The analyst need not be apologetic for asking questions rather than supplying independently determinative project values and rankings. The philosophic position is one of pragmatic means-ends interaction. The decision rules, such as time preference, consumer surplus, and indirect effects, are not assumed to be fixed prior to analysis of effects. Systems analysis requires only that the rules and trade-offs and the boundaries within which they are applied be constant over some set of choices for some period.

If BCA follows political objectives, project ranking can be expected to change with changes in occupants of the seats of power. If people want stable ranking, then they will reelect existing politicians. BCA can be part of the process of public accountability. Demonstration of the effect of applying a given set of analytic rules is an input into political choice of those rules and resolution of the conflict of interests that they represent. The analyst helps formulate rules and applies them as well. An interactive iterative systems analysis can be incorporated into public choice. To conclude, there is no way politicians can regard BCA as independent information to be weighed, somehow, along with other inputs to make a decision. BCA is either the politician's decision, or it is nothing at all.

Notes

1.   This perspective has some parallels to quantum physics. As Capra (1975, 867) says, "In atomic physics the observed phenomena can be understood only as correlations between processes of observation and measurement, and the end of this chain of process lies always in the consciousness of the human observer. . . . In atomic physics the sharp Cartesian distinction between mind and matter, between the observer and the observed, can no longer be maintained."

References and Bibliography

Aaron, Henry, and Martin McGuire. 1970. Public Goods and Income Distribution. *Econometrics* 38:907-20.

Aboucher, Alan. 1985. *Project Decision Making in the Public Sector*. Lexington, Mass.: Heath.

Achen, Christopher H. 1987. *The Statistical Analysis of Quasi-Experiments*. Berkeley: University of California Press.

ACIR. 1988. *Significant Features of Fiscal Federalism*, Vol. II. Washington: Advisory Commission of Intergovernmental Affairs.

Ackerman, Bruce A. 1971. Regulating Slum Housing Markets on Behalf of the Poor. *Yale Law Journal* 80:1093-1197.

Acton, Jan. 1973. *Evaluating Public Programs to Save Lives: The Case of Heart Attacks*. Santa Monica: Rand Corporation.

Adler, Hans A. 1971. *Economic Appraisal of Transport Projects: A Manual with Case Studies*. Bloomington: Indiana University Press.

Akehurst, R. L., and A. J. Culyer. 1974. On the Economic Surplus and the Value of Life. *Bulletin of Economic Research* 26:63-78.

Alchian, A. A. 1955. The Rate of Interest, Fisher's Rate of Return over Costs and Keynes Internal Rate of Return. *American Economic Review* 45:938-42.

American Association of State Highway Officials. 1960. *Road User Benefit Analysis for Highway Improvements*. Washington.

Anas, Alex. 1984. Land Market Theory and Methodology in Wildland Management. In *Valuation of Wildland Benefits*, ed. George L. Peterson and Alan Randall, 89-114. Boulder: Westview.

Anderson, J. R., J. L. Dillon, and J. B. Hardaker. 1977. *Agricultural Decision Analysis*. Ames: Iowa State University Press.

Anderson, L. G., and R. F. Settle. 1977. *Benefit-Cost Analysis: A Practical Guide*. Lexington, Mass.: Lexington Books.

Anderson, R. J., and T. D. Crocker. 1971. Air Pollution and Residential Property Values. *Urban Studies* 8:171-80.

Arrow, K. J. 1966. Discounting and Public Investment Criteria. In *Water Research*, ed. A. V. Kneese and S. C. Smith, 13-32. Baltimore: Johns Hopkins University Press.

_____. 1976. The Rate of Discount for Long Term Public Investment. In *Energy and the Environment: A Risk-Benefit Approach*, ed. Holt Ashley, Richard L. Rudman, and Christopher Whipple, 113-40. New York: Pergamon.

Arrow, K. J., and A. C. Fisher. 1974. Environmental Preservation, Uncertainty and Irreversibility. *Quarterly Journal of Economics* 88:312-19.

Arrow, K. J., and Mordecai Kurz. 1970. *Public Investment, the Rate of Return and Optimal Fiscal Policy.* Baltimore: Johns Hopkins University Press.

Arrow, K. J., and R. C. Lind. 1970. Uncertainty and the Evaluation of Public Investment Decisions. *American Economic Review* 60:364-78.

Arthur, W. B. 1981. The Economics of Risks to Life. *American Economic Review* 71:54-64.

Ashford, N. A., C. W. Ryan, and C. C. Caldart. 1983. Law and Science Policy in Federal Regulation of Formaldehyde. *Science* 222:894-900.

Atkinson, A. B., and J. E. Stiglitz. 1980. *Lectures on Public Economics.* New York: McGraw-Hill.

Austin, James E. 1981. *Agroindustrial Project Analysis.* Baltimore: Johns Hopkins University Press.

Azzi, Corry F., and James C. Cox. 1973. Equity and Efficiency in Evaluation of Public Programs. *Quarterly Journal of Economics* 87:495-502.

Babunakis, Michael. 1982. *Budget Reform for Government: A Comprehensive Allocation and Management System.* Westport, Conn.: Quorum Books.

Bacha, Edmar, and Lance Taylor. 1971. Foreign Exchange Shadow Price: A Critical Review of Current Theories. *Quarterly Journal of Economics* 85:197-224.

Bain, J. S., et al. 1966. *Northern California's Water Industry.* Baltimore: Johns Hopkins University Press.

Baram, Michael S. 1980. Cost-Benefit Analysis: An Inadequate Basis for Health, Safety, and Environmental Regulatory Decisionmaking. *Ecology Law Quarterly* 8:473-529.

Bartlett, Randall. 1973. *Economic Foundations of Political Power.* New York: Free Press.

Barzel, Yoram. 1968. Optimal Timing of Innovations. *Review of Economics and Statistics* 50:348-55.

Bates, Robert H. 1983. Government and Agricultural Markets in Africa. In *The Role of Markets in the World Food Economy,* ed. D. Gale Johnson and G. Edward Schuh, 153-83. Boulder: Westview.

Baumol, William J. 1968. On the Social Rate of Discount. *American Economic Review* 58:788-802.

_____ 1977. On the Discount Rate for Public Projects. In *Public Expenditure Analysis,* ed. R. H. Haveman and Julius Margolis, 161-179. Chicago: Rand-McNally.

Beardsley, P. L., D. M. Kovenock, and W. C. Reynolds. 1974. *Measuring Public Opinion on National Priorities: A Report on a Pilot Study.* Beverly Hills: Sage.

Beardsley, Wendell. 1971. Bias and Noncompatibility in Recreation Evaluation Models. *Land Economics* 47:175-80.

Beesley, M. E. 1965. The Value of Time Spent Traveling: Some New Evidence. *Economics* (May):32.

Bell, C. L. G., and P. B. R. Hazell. 1980. Measuring the Indirect Effects of an Agricultural Investment Project. *American Journal of Agricultural Economics* 62:75-86.

Bergmann, H., and J. M. Boussard. 1976. *Guide de l'Evaluation des Projets d'Irrigation*. Paris: Organization for Economic Cooperation and Development.

Birch, Alfred L., and A. Allan Schmid. 1980. Public Opinion Surveys as Guides to Public Policy and Spending. *Social Indicators Research* 7:299-311.

Bird, Richard M., and Lue H. DeWulf. 1973. *Taxation and Income Distribution in Latin America: A Critical Review of Empirical Studies*. International Monetary Fund Staff Papers 20:639-82.

Birgegard, Lars-Erik. 1975. *The Project Selection Process in Developing Countries*. Stockholm: Economic Research Institute, Stockholm School of Economics.

Bish, Robert. 1969. Public Housing: The Magnitude and Distribution of Direct Benefits and Effects on Housing Consumption. *Journal of Regional Science* 9:425-38.

Bishop, Richard C., and Thomas A. Heberlein. 1979. Measuring Values of Extramarket Goods: Are Indirect Measures Biased? *American Journal of Agricultural Economics* 61:926-30.

Blomquist, Glenn C. 1979. The Value of Life Saving: Implications of Consumption Activity. *Journal of Political Economy* 87:540-58.

Blomquist, Glenn C., and Lawrence Worley. 1979. Hedonic Prices, Demands for Housing Amenities, and Benefit Estimates. Paper read at the annual meeting of the American Real Estate and Urban Economics Association, 28-30 December.

Boadway, Robin W. 1974. The Welfare Foundation of Cost-Benefit Analysis. *Economics Journal* 84:926-39.

_____. 1976. Integrating Equity and Efficiency in Applied Welfare Economics. *Quarterly Journal of Economics* 90:541-56.

Boadway, Robin W., and Neil Bruce. 1984. *Welfare Economics*. Oxford: Basil Blackwell.

Bockstael, Nancy E., and Ivar E. Strand. 1985. Distribution Issues and Nonmarket Benefit Measurement. *Western Journal of Agricultural Economics* 10:162-69.

Bockstael, Nancy E., Ivar E. Strand, and Michael Hanemann. 1987. Time and the Recreation Demand Model. *American Journal of Agricultural Economics* 69:293-302.

Bohm, Peter. 1972. Estimating Demand for Public Goods: An Experiment. *European Economic Review* 3:111-30.

Bonnen, James T. 1975. Improving Information on Agriculture and Rural Life. *American Journal of Agricultural Economics* 57:753-63.

Booth, James H. 1975. *Michigan Operation Hitchhike: A Cooperative Effort in Rural Manpower Programming Between Michigan State University and the Michigan Employment Security Commission, Final Report*. East Lansing: Center for Rural Manpower and Public Affairs, Michigan State University.

Boring, E. G. 1954. The Nature and the History of Experimental Control. *American Journal of Psychology* 67:573-89.

Boskin, Michael J. 1978. Taxation, Saving and the Rate of Interest. *Journal of Political Economy* 86:523-27.

Boulding, Kenneth E. 1948. *Economic Analysis.* New York: Harper & Row.

_____. 1973. *The Economy of Love and Fear.* Belmont, Cal.: Wadsworth.

Bouma, F. 1976. Some Models for Determining the Value of Recreation Areas. In *Environmental Economics*, Vol. 2, Methods, ed. Peter Nijkamp. Leiden: Martinus Nijhoff.

Boyle, Kevin J., and Richard C. Bishop. 1988. Welfare Measurements Using Contingent Valuation: A Comparison of Techniques. *American Journal of Agricultural Economics* 70:20-28.

Bradford, David F. 1975. Constraints on Government Investment Opportunities and the Choice of the Discount Rate. *American Economic Review* 65:887-99.

Brainard, William, and F. T. Dolbear. 1971. Social Risk and Financial Markets. *American Economic Review* 61:360-70.

Brandl, John. 1988. On Politics and Policy Analysis as the Design and Assessment of Institutions. *Journal of Policy Analysis and Management* 7:419-24.

Break, George F. 1974. *The Incidences and Economic Effects of Taxation.* Washington: Brookings.

_____. 1980. *Financing Government in a Federal System.* Washington: Brookings.

Bridier, Manuel. 1980. *Guide pratique d'analyse de projets: analyse economique et financiere de projet dans les pays en voie de developpement.* Paris: Economica.

Briloff, Abraham J. 1981. *The Truth about Corporate Accounting.* New York: Harper & Row.

Bromley, Daniel, A. Allan Schmid, and William Lord. 1971. *Public Water Resource Project Planning and Evaluation: Impacts, Incidence and Institutions.* Madison: Center for Resource Policy Studies and Programs, University of Wisconsin.

Brookshire, David S., and Don L. Coursey. 1987. Measuring the Value of a Public Good: An Empirical Comparison of Elicitation Procedures. *American Economic Review* 77:554-66.

Brookshire, David S., Berry C. Ives, and William D. Schulze. 1976. The Valuation of Aesthetic Preferences. *Journal of Environmental Economics and Management* 3:325-46.

Brookshire, David S., Alan Randall, and J. R. Stoll. 1980. Valuing Increments and Decrements in Natural Resource Service Flow. *American Journal of Agricultural Economics* 62:478-88.

Brookshire, David S., et al. 1982. Valuing Public Goods: A Comparison of Survey and Hedonic Approaches. *American Economic Review* 72:165-76.

Brown, C. V., and P. M. Jackson. 1978. *Public Sector Economics.* Oxford: Martin Robertson.

Brown, William G., and Farid Nawas. 1973. Impact of Aggregation on the Estimation of Outdoor Recreation Demand Function. *American Journal of Agricultural Economics* 55:246-49.

Brown, William G., Ajmer Singh, and Emery N. Castle. 1964. *An Economic Evaluation of the Oregon Salmon and Steelhead Sport Fishery.* Agricultural Experiment Station, Technical Bulletin No. 78. Corvallis: Oregon State University.

Brown, W. W., and G. J. Santoni. 1981. Unreal Estimates of the Real Rate of Interest. *Review, Federal Reserve Bank of St. Louis* 63:18-26.

Brownrigg, Mark. 1974. *A Study of Economic Impact, The University of Stirling.* New York: Wiley.

Bruce, Colin. 1976. *Social Cost-Benefit Analysis: A Guide for Country and Project Economists to the Derivation and Application of Economic and Social Accounting Prices.* World Bank Working Paper No. 239. Washington: International Bank for Reconstruction and Development.

Bryden, John M. 1973. *Tourism and Development, A Case Study of the Commonwealth Caribbean.* London: Cambridge University Press.

Bullock, J. Bruce, and Clement E. Ward. 1981. *Economic Impacts of Regulations on Mechanically Deboned Red Meats.* Report P-815. Stillwater: Oklahoma State University, Agricultural Experiment Station.

Burke, A. W. 1977. *Change, Cause, Reason: An Inquiry into the Nature of Scientific Evidence.* Chicago: University of Chicago Press.

Burns, Michael E. 1973. A Note on the Concept and Measurement of Consumer Surplus. *American Economic Review* 63:335-44.

Campbell, Donald T. 1969. Reform as Experiments. *American Psychologist* 24:409-29.

Campbell, Donald T., and Julian C. Stanley. 1963. *Experimental and Quasi-Experimental Designs for Research.* Chicago: Rand-McNally.

Campen, James T. 1986. *Benefit, Cost, and Beyond.* Cambridge: Ballinger.

Caporaso, James A., and Leslie L. Roos, Jr. 1973. *Quasi-Experimental Approaches.* Evanston: Northwestern University Press.

Capra, Fritjof. 1975. *The Tao of Physics.* New York: Bantam Books.

Carlson, J. E. 1976. *Public Preferences Towards Natural Resources Use in Idaho.* Agricultural Experiment Station, Research Bulletin No. 94. Moscow: University of Idaho.

Carpenter, Edwin H., and Larry G. Blackwood. 1977. *The Effect of Question Position on Responses to Attitudinal Questions: A Look at Four Different Scaling Metrics.* Experiment Station Journal Paper No. 2800. Tucson: Department of Agricultural Economics, University of Arizona.

Carr-Hill, Roy A. 1984. The Political Choice of Social Indicators and Radicalising Survey Methodology. *Quality and Quantity* 18:173-91.

Carver, Ronald P. 1978. The Case Against Statistical Significance Testing. *Harvard Educational Review* 48:378-99.

Casley, D. J., and D. A. Lury. 1982. *Monitoring and Evaluation of Agriculture and Rural Development Projects.* Baltimore: Johns Hopkins University Press.

Cesario, Frank J. 1976. Value of Time in Recreation Benefit Studies. *Land Economics* 55:32-41.

_____. 1980. Congestion and the Valuation of Recreation Benefits. *Land Economics* 56:329-38.

Cesario, Frank J., and Jack L. Knetsch. 1970. Time Bias in Recreation Benefit Estimates. *Water Resources Research* 6:700-704.

_____. 1976. A Recreation Site Demand and Benefit Estimation Model. *Regional Studies* 10:97-104.

Chapin, F. S. 1955. *Experimental Designs in Sociological Research*. New York: Harper.

Chelimsky, Eleanor. 1987. The Politics of Program Evaluation. *Society* (November/December):24-32.

Chenery, H. P., and Larry E. Westphal. 1969. Economies of Scale and Investment over Time. In *Public Economics*, ed. Julius Margolis and Henri Guitton. New York: St. Martin.

Chervel, Marc. 1977. The Rationale of the Effects Method: A Reply to Bela Balassa. *Oxford Bulletin of Economics and Statistics* 39:333-44.

Chipman, J. S., and J. C. Moore. 1980. Compensating Variation, Consumer's Surplus, and Welfare. *American Economic Review* 70:933-49.

Chitale, V. P. 1981. *Project Viability in Inflationary Conditions--A Study of Capital Cost and Project Viability*. New Delhi: Vikas Publishing House.

Choate, Pat, and Susan Walter. 1981. *Amercia in Ruins*. Washington: Council of State Planning Agencies.

Christiansen, Vidar, and Eliv S. Jansen. 1978. Implicit Social Preferences in the Norwegian System of Indirect Taxation. *Journal of Public Economics* 10:217-45.

Cicchetti, C. J. 1973. *Forecasting Recreation in the United States*. Lexington, Mass.: Lexington Books.

Cicchetti, C. J., A. C. Fisher, and V. K. Smith. 1976. An Econometric Evaluation of a Generalized Consumer Surplus Measure: The Mineral King Controversy. *Econometrica* 44:1259-75.

Cicchetti, C. J., and V. K. Smith. 1976. *The Costs of Congestion*. Cambridge, Mass.: Ballinger.

CIDA. 1980a. *Methodology Guide for Project Teams Responsible for Managing Evaluations*. Ottawa: Canadian International Development Agency.

_____. 1980b. *Guide for the Use of the Logical Framework Approach in the Management and Evaluation of CIDA's International Development Projects*. Ottawa: Canadian International Development Agency.

Clark, Terry N. 1974. Can You Cut a Budget Pie? *Policy and Politics* 3:3-31.

_____. 1976. *Citizen Preferences and Urban Public Policy*. Beverly Hills: Sage.

Clawson, Marion, and Jack L. Knetsch. 1966. *Economics of Outdoor Recreation*. Baltimore: Johns Hopkins University Press.

Coburn, T. M., M. E. Beesley, and D. J. Reynolds. 1960. *The London-Birmingham Motorway: Traffic and Economics*. Road Research Technical Paper No. 46. London: HMSO.

Cocheba, Donald J., and William A. Langford. 1978. Wildlife Valuation: The Collective Good Aspect of Hunting. *Land Economics* 54:490-504.

Cohn, Elchanan. 1972. *Public Expenditure Analysis*. Lexington, Mass.: Heath.

Coleman, James. 1966. *Equality of Educational Opportunity*. Washington: U.S.GPO.

Collard, David. 1979. *Faustian Projects and the Social Rate of Discount. Papers in Political Economy*, Working Paper No. 1179. Bath, U.K.: University of Bath.

Conley, Bryan C. 1976. The Value of Human Life in the Demand for Safety. *American Economic Review* 66:45-55.

Cook, Thomas D., and Donald T. Campbell. 1979. *Quasi-Experimentation*. Boston: Houghton-Mifflin.

Cooke, Stephen. 1985. *A Theory of Consumer Surplus and Economic Rent and an Application for Measuring the Benefits from the Mechanical Cucumber Harvestor*. Ph.D. dissertation, Michigan State University.

Cooper, B. S., and D. P. Rice. 1976. The Economic Cost of Illness Revisited. *Social Security Bulletin* 39:21-36.

Cornbach, Lee. 1982. *Designing Evaluations of Educational and Social Programs*. San Francisco: Jossey-Bass.

Crouch, E. A., and Richard Wilson. 1982. *Risk/Benefit Analysis*. Cambridge: Ballinger.

Crowther vs. *Seaborg*, 312 F. Supp. 1205 (D. Colo. 1970).

Cummings, Ronald G., David S. Brookshire, and William D. Schulze, eds. 1986. *Valuing Environmental Goods*. Totowa, N.J.: Rowman & Allanheld.

Currie, J. M., J. A. Murphy, and Andrew Schmitz. 1971. The Concept of Economic Surplus and Its Use in Economic Analysis. *Economic Journal* 81:741-99.

Dardis, Rachel. 1980. The Value of Life: New Evidence from the Marketplace. *American Economic Review* 70:1077-82.

Dasgupta, A. K., and D. W. Pearce. 1972. *Cost Benefit Analysis: Theory and Practice*. London: Macmillan.

Dasgupta, Partha, A. K. Sen, and Stephen Marglin. 1972. *Guidelines for Project Evaluation*. New York: United Nations.

David, Elizabeth L. 1968. Lakeshore Property Values: A Guide to Public Investment in Recreation. *Water Resources* 4:697-707.

Dawson, R. F. F. 1971. *Current Costs of Road Accidents in Great Britain*. London: U.K. Department of Environment, Road Research Laboratory.

DeAlessi, Louis. 1969. Some Implications of Property Rights Structures for Investment Choices within Government. *American Economic Review* 59:13-24.

DeGarmo, E. Paul. 1967. *Engineering Economy*. New York: Macmillan.

DeGrasse, Robert W., Jr. 1983. *Military Expansion, Economic Decline: The Impact of Military Spending on U.S. Economic Performance*. Armonk, N.Y.: M.E. Sharpe.

Deutscher, Irwin. 1973. *What We Say, What We Do*. Glenview, Ill.: Scott, Foresman.

Diamond, P. A. 1975. A Many Person Ramsey Tax Rule. *Journal of Public Economics* 4:335-42.

Diamond, P. A., and J. A. Mirrlees. 1971. Optimal Taxation and Public Production, Part I: Production Efficiency and Part II: Tax Rules. *American Economic Review* 61:8-27 and 261-78.

Diewert, Walter E. 1983. Cost-Benefit Analysis and Project Evaluation: A Comparison of Alternative Approaches. *Journal of Public Economics* 22:265-302.

_____. 1986. *The Measurement of the Economic Benefits of Infrastructure Services*. Berlin: Springer-Verlag.

Dobb, Maurice. 1960. *An Essay on Economic Growth and Planning*. New York: Monthly Review.

_____. 1969. *Welfare Economic and Economics of Socialism*. London: Cambridge University Press.

Dola, Steven. 1971. The Evolution of a Funding Policy. *Water Spectrum (Army Corps of Engineers)* Fall:1-6.

Dorfman, Robert, ed. 1965. *Measuring the Benefits of Government Expenditures*. Washington: Brookings.

_____. 1974. Decision Rules under Uncertainty. In *Cost-Benefit Analysis*, ed. Richard Layard. Harmondsworth, England: Penguin.

Dreze, Jacques. 1962. L'Utilite Social d'une Vie Humaine. *Review Francaise de Recherche Operationelle* 6:93-118.

Ducros, Jean-Claude. 1976. The Influence of RCB on Parliament's Role in Budgetary Affairs (France). In *The Power of the Purse*, ed. David L. Coombes, et al. London: Allen & Unwin.

Dudley, Carlton L., Jr. 1972. A Note on Reinvestment Assumptions in Choosing Between Net Present Value and Internal Rate of Return. *Journal of Finance* 27:907-15.

Dwyer, J. F., J. R. Kelly, and M. D. Bowes. 1977. *Improved Procedures for Valuation of the Contribution of Recreation to National Economic Development*. W.R.C. Research Report. Urbana: University of Illinois, Water Resources Center.

Earl, Peter E. 1983. *The Economic Imagination: Towards a Behavioral Analysis of Choice*. New York: M. E. Sharpe.

Eckhouse, Richard S. 1973. Estimation of Returns to Education with Hourly Standardized Incomes. *Quarterly Journal of Economics* 87:121-31.

Eckstein, Otto. 1961. A Survey of the Theory of Public Expenditure Criteria. In *Public Finances: Needs, Sources, and Utilization*. Princeton, N.J.: National Bureau of Economic Research, Princeton University Press.

_____. 1965. *Water Resource Development*. Cambridge: Harvard University Press.

Epp, D. J. 1977. *Identification and Specification of Inputs for Benefit-Cost Modeling of Pesticide Use*. Socioeconomic Environmental Studies Series EPA-600/5-77-012. Washington: U.S. Environmental Protection Agency.

_____. 1979. Unemployment and Benefit-Cost Analysis: A Case Study Test of a Haveman-Krutilla Hypothesis. *Land Economics* 55:397-404.

Feenberg, Daniel, and Edwin S. Mills. 1980. *Measuring the Benefits of Water Pollution Abatement*. New York: Academic Press.

Feldstein, Martin. 1972a. The Inadequacy of Weighted Discount Rates. In *Cost-Benefit Analysis*, ed. Richard Layard, 245-69. Harmondsworth, England: Penguin.

_____. 1972b. Distributional Equity and the Optimal Structure of Public Prices. *American Economic Review* 62:32-36.

_____. 1977. Does the United States Save Too Little? *American Economic Review* 67:116-21.

Fenno, Richard F. 1968. The Impact of PPBS on the Congressional Appropriation Process. In *Information Support, Program Budgeting, and the Congress*, ed. Robert Chartrand, Kenneth Janda, and Michael Hugo, 175-87. New York: Spartan Books.

Fischoff, Baruch, et al. 1978. How Safe Is Safe Enough? A Psychometric Study of Attitudes Towards Technological Risks and Benefits. *Policy Science* 8:127-52.

Fischoff, Baruch, Paul Slovic, and Sarah Lichtenstein. 1983. The Public vs.'The Experts': Perceived vs. Actual Disagreements about Risks of Nuclear Power. In *The Analysis of Actual Versus Perceived Risks*, ed. Vincent T. Covello, et al. New York: Plenum Press.

Fisher, A. C. 1973. Environmental Externalities and the Arrow-Lind Theorem. *American Economic Review* 63:722-25.

_____. 1976. Econometric Evaluation of a Generalized Consumer Surplus Measure: The Mineral King Controversy. *Econometrica* 44:1259-76.

Fisher, A. C., and J. V. Krutilla. 1972. Determination of Optimal Capacity of Resource-Based Recreation Facilities. In *Natural Environments: Studies in Theoretical and Applied Analysis*, ed. J. V. Krutilla. Baltimore: Johns Hopkins University Press.

FitzGerald, E. V. K. 1977. The Public Investment Criterion and the Role of the State. *Journal of Development Studies* 13:365-72.

Fleischer, G. A. 1962. *The Economic Utilization of Commercial Vehicle Time Saved as the Result of Highway Improvements*. Stanford: Stanford University.

Flemming, J. S., et al. 1976. The Cost of Capital, Finance and Investment. *Bank of England Bulletin* 16(2).

Foster, C. D. 1966. Social Welfare Functions in Cost-Benefit Analysis. In *Operational Research and the Social Sciences*, ed. J. R. Lawrence. London: Tavistock.

_____. 1973. A Note on the Treatment of Taxation in Cost Benefit Analysis. In *Cost-Benefit and Cost Effectiveness*, ed. J. N. Wolfe, 63-74. London: Allen & Unwin.

Freeman, A. Myrick, III. 1972. Distribution of Environmental Quality. In *Environmental Quality Analysis*, ed. Allen V. Kneese and Blair T. Bower. Baltimore: Johns Hopkins University Press.

_____. 1974. On Estimating Air Pollution Control Benefits from Land Value Studies. *Journal of Environmental Economics and Management* 1:74-83.

_____. 1975. Spatial Equilibrium, the Theory of Rents, and the Measurement of Benefits from Public Programs: A Comment. *Quarterly Journal of Economics* 89:470-73.

_____. 1977. Project Design and Evaluation with Multiple Objectives. In *Public Expenditures and Policy Analysis*, 2d ed., ed. Robert H. Haveman and Julius Margolis, Ch. 10. Chicago: Markham.

_____. 1979. *The Benefits of Environmental Improvement*. Baltimore: Johns Hopkins University Press.

_____. 1982. *Air and Water Pollution Control: A Benefit-Cost Assessment*. New York: John Wiley.

Freeman, A. Myrick, III, and Robert H. Haveman. 1977. Congestion Quality Deterioration, and Heterogeneous Tastes. *Journal of Public Economics* 8:225-32.

Friedman, Lee S. 1984. *Microeconomic Policy Analysis*. New York: McGraw-Hill.

Fuchs, Victor R., and Richard Zeckhauser. 1987. Valuing Health--A "Priceless" Commodity. *American Economic Review* 77(2): 263-68.

Galtung, Johan. 1967. *Theory and Methods of Social Research*. New York: Columbia University Press.

Garn, Harvey A., et al. 1976. *Models for Indicator Development: A Framework for Policy Analysis*. Washington: Urban Institute.

Gillespie, W. Irwin. 1976. On the Redistribution of Income in Canada. *Canadian Tax Journal* 24:417-50.

Gittinger, J. P. 1982. *Economic Analysis of Agricultural Projects*. Baltimore: Johns Hopkins University Press.

Gittinger, J. P., et al. 1982. *Current Use of Project Analysis Tools in the World Bank and the Inter-American Development Bank*. Economic Development Institute Training Materials, Course Note Series No. 86. Washington: International Bank for Reconstruction and Development.

Goodman, Robert. 1982. *The Last Entrepreneurs: America's Regional Wars for Jobs and Dollars*. Boston: South End Press.

Goodwin, P. B. 1976. Human Effort and the Value of Time. *Journal of Transport Economics and Policy* 10:3-15.

Gordon, Irene M., and J. L. Knetsch. 1979. Consumer's Surplus Measures and the Evaluation of Resources. *Land Economics* 55:1-10.

Gorham, William. 1967. In U.S. Congress, Joint Economic Committee. *Hearings on The Planning-Programming-Budgeting System: Progress and Potentials*. 90th Congress, 1st session.

Graham, D. A. 1981. Cost-Benefit Analysis under Uncertainty. *American Economic Review* 71:715-25.

Graham, J. D. and J. W. Vaupel. 1981. The Value of a Life: What Difference Does It Make? In *Risk/Benefit Analysis in Water Resources Planning and Management*, ed. Yacov Y. Haimes. New York: Plenum Press.

Graham-Tomasi, Theodore, and Robert J. Myers. 1986. *On Uncertainty and the Measurement of Welfare Change*. Department of Agricultural Economics Staff Paper No. 86-94. East Lansing: Michigan State University.

Gramlich, Edward M. 1981. *Benefit-Cost Analysis of Government Programs*. Englewood Ciffs, N.J.: Prentice-Hall.

_____. 1985. Reforming U.S. Federal Fiscal Arrangements. In *American Domestic Priorities*, ed. John M. Quigley and Daniel L. Rubinfeld. Berkeley: University of California Press.

Gramlich, Edward M., and Michael J. Wolkoff. 1979. A Procedure for Evaluating Income Distribution Policies. *Journal of Human Resources* 14:319-50.

Green, H. A. John. 1975. Two Models of Optimal Pricing and Taxation. *Oxford Economic Papers* 27:352-82.

Green, P. E., and Yorum Wind. 1973. *Multiattribute Decisions in Marketing: A Measurement Approach*. Hinsdale, Ill.: Dryden.

Griliches, Zvi. 1958. Research Costs and Social Returns: Hybrid Corn and Related Innovations. *Journal of Political Economy* 66:419-31.

Gum, Russel L., and William E. Martin. 1975. Problem and Solution in Estimating the Demand for and Value of Rural Outdoor Recreation. *American Journal of Agricultural Economics* 57:558-66.

Guttentag, Marcia, and Kurt Snapper. 1974. Plans, Evaluations, and Decisions. *Evaluation* 2(1):58-64 and 73-74.

Haimes, Yacov Y., ed. 1981. *Risk/Benefit Analysis in Water Resources Planning and Management*. New York: Plenum.

Hall, Peter, 1979. *Great Planning Disasters*. Harmondsworth, England: Penguin.

Halvorsen, Robert, and Michael Ruby. 1981. *Benefit-Cost Analysis of Air Pollution Control*. Lexington, Mass.: Heath.

Hammack, Judd, and Gardner M. Brown. 1974. *Waterfowl and Wetlands: Toward Bioeconomic Analysis*. Baltimore: Johns Hopkins University Press.

Hanemann, W. Michael. 1984. Welfare Evaluations in Contingent Valuation Experiments with Discrete Responses. *American Journal of Agricultural Economics* 66:332-41.

Hanke, Steven H., and R. A. Walker. 1974. Benefit-Cost Analysis Reconsidered: An Evaluation of the Mid-State Project. *Water Resources Research* 10:898-908.

Hansen, J. R. 1978. *A Guide to Practical Project Appraisal*. New York: United Nations.

Hansen, W. Lee, and Burton Weisbrod. 1969. The Distribution of Costs and Direct Benefits of Public Higher Education. *Journal of Human Resources* 4:176-91.

Hanushek, Eric A. 1986. The Economics of Schooling. *Journal of Economic Literature* 24:1141-77.

Hapgood, Fred. 1979. Risk-Benefit Analysis: Putting a Price on Life. *The Atlantic Monthly* 243(1):33-38.

Harberger, Arnold C. 1971. Three Basic Postulates for Applied Welfare Economics. *Journal of Economic Literature* 9:785-97.

_____. 1978. On the Use of Distributional Weights in Social Cost-Benefit Analysis. *Journal of Political Economy* 86(2, Pt.2):S87-S120.

Hardin, Einar, and Michael E. Borus. 1971. *The Economic Benefits and Costs of Retraining*. Lexington, Mass.: Heath Lexington.

Hargrove, Erwin C. 1980. The Bureaucratic Politics of Evaluation: A Case Study of the Department of Labor. *Public Administration Review* 40:150-59.

Harris, John R., and Michael P. Todaro. 1970. Migration, Unemployment and Development: A Two-Sector Analysis. *American Economic Review* 60:126-42.

Harris, Louis. 1977. Would Cut U.S. Spending. *The State Journal*. Lansing, Michigan, September 19.

Harrison, A. J. 1974. *The Economics of Transport Appraisal*. New York: Wiley.

Harrison, A. J., and D. A. Quarmby. 1974. The Value of Time. In *Cost-Benefit Analysis*, ed. Richard Layard. Baltimore: Penguin.

Harrison, David, Jr., and D. L. Rubinfeld. 1978a. The Air Pollution and Property Value Debate: Some Empirical Evidence. *Review of Economics and Statistics* 60:635-38.

_____. 1978b. Hedonic Housing Prices and the Demand for Clean Air. *Journal of Environmental Economics and Management* 5:81-102.

Hartunian, Nelson, et al. 1981. *The Evidence and Economic Costs of Major Health Impairments*. Lexington, Mass.: Heath.

Hartwick, John M. 1978. Optimal Price Discrimination. *Journal of Public Economics* 9:83-89.

Hausman, J. A. 1981. Exact Consumer Surplus and Deadweight Loss. *American Economic Review* 71:662-76.

Haveman, Robert H. 1965. *Water Resource Investment and the Public Interest*. Nashville: Vanderbilt University Press.

_____. 1968. Comments: Income Redistribution Effects and Benefit-Cost Analysis. In *Problems in Public Expenditure Analysis*, ed. Samuel B. Chase, Jr. 209-13. Washington: Brookings.

_____. 1972. *The Economic Performance of Public Investments: An Ex-Post Evaluation of Water Resource Investments*. Baltimore: Johns Hopkins University Press.

_____. 1977. Evaluating Public Expenditures under Conditions of Unemployment. In *Public Expenditure and Policy Analysis*, 2d edition, ed. Robert Haveman and Julius Margolis, Ch. 9. Chicago: Rand-McNally.

Haveman, Robert H., and J. V. Krutilla. 1968. *Unemployment, Idle Capacity and the Evaluation of Public Expenditures*. Baltimore: Johns Hopkins University Press.

Havemann, Joel. 1978. *Congress and the Budget*. Bloomington: Indiana University Press.

Havens, Harry S. 1983. Looking Back at PPBS, Image vs. Substance. In *Public Budgeting and Finance, Behavioral, Theoretical and Technical Perspective*, ed. Robert T. Golembieski and Jack Rabin. New York: Dekker.

Heller, Peter S. 1974. Public Investment in LDC's with Recurrent Cost Constraint: The Kenyan Case. *Quarterly Journal of Economics* 88:251-77.

Helmers, F. L. C. H. 1979. *Project Planning and Income Distribution*. Boston: Martinus Nijhoff.

Henderson, P. D. 1968. Investment Criteria for Public Enterprise. In *Public Enterprise*, ed. Ralph Turvey. Harmondsworth, England: Penguin.

_____. 1969. Political and Budgetary Constraints: Some Characteristics and Implications. In *Public Economics*, ed. Julius Margolis and Henri Guitton. London: Macmillan.

Hershey, John C., Howard C. Kunreuther, and Paul J. H. Schoemaker. 1982. Sources of Bias in Assessment Procedures for Utility Functions. *Management Science* 28:936-54.

Hey, J. D. 1981. Are Optimal Search Rules Reasonable? And Vice Versa? (and Does It Matter Anyway?). *Journal of Economic Behavior and Organization* 2:47-70.

Hight, Joseph E., and Richard Pollock. 1973. Income Distribution Effects of Higher Education Expenditures in California, Florida and Hawaii. *Journal of Human Resources* 8:318-30.

Hirschleifer, Jack. 1961. Comment to Otto Eckstein. In *Public Finances, Sources and Utilization*, ed. Otto Eckstein. Princeton: National Bureau of Economic Research and Princeton University Press.

———. 1966. Investment Decision under Uncertainty: Applications of the State-Preference Approach. *Quarterly Journal of Economics* 80:252-77.

Hirschleifer, Jack, James de Haven, and Jerome W. Milliman. 1960. *Water Supply*. Chicago: University of Chicago Press.

HMSO. 1967. *Nationalized Industries: A Review of Economic and Financial Objectives*. Cmnd. 3437. London: HMSO.

Hochstim, Joseph R. 1967. A Critical Comparison of Three Strategies of Collecting Data from Households. *Journal of the American Statistical Association* 62:976-89.

Hoehn, John P., Mark C. Berger, and Glenn C. Blomquist. 1987. A Hedonic Model of Interregional Wages, Rents, and Amenity Values. *Journal of Regional Science* 27:605-20.

Hoehn, John P., and Alan Randall. 1987. A Satisfactory Benefit Cost Indicator from Contingent Valuation. *Journal of Environmental Economics and Management* 14:226-47.

Holling, C. S., ed. 1978. *Adaptive Environmental Assessment and Modeling*. Chichester, England: John Wiley.

House, E. R. 1980. *Evaluating with Validity*. Beverly Hills: Sage.

———, ed. 1983. *Philosophy of Evaluation*. San Francisco: Jossey-Bass.

Howe, C. W. 1971. *Benefit-Cost Analysis for Water System Planning*. Washington: American Geophysical Union.

Howe, J. D. 1976. Valuing Time Savings in Developing Countries. *Journal of Transport Economics and Policy* 10:113-25.

Hufschmidt, Maynard M., and Myron B. Fiering. 1966. *Simulation Techniques for Design of Water-Resource Systems*. Cambridge: Harvard University Press.

Hufschmidt, Maynard M., et al. 1983. *Environment, Natural Systems, and Development: An Economic Valuation Guide*. Baltimore: John Hopkins University Press.

Hutchison, T. W. 1964. *Positive Economics and Policy Objectives*. Cambridge: Harvard University Press.

Hylland, Aanund, and Richard Zeckhauser. 1979. Distributional Objectives Should Affect Taxes But Not Program Choice or Design. *The Scandinavian Journal of Economics* 81:264-84.

Imboden, N. 1978. *A Management Approach to Project Appraisal and Evaluation*. Paris: Organization for Economic Cooperation and Development.

Ingram, Helen M. 1969. *Patterns of Politics in Water Resources Development*. Albuquerque: University of New Mexico, Division of Government Research.

Irvin, George. 1978. *Modern Cost-Benefit Methods*. New York: Barnes & Noble.

Isard, Walter. 1960. *Methods of Regional Analysis*. New York: Wiley and M.I.T. Press.

Izac, A-M. N. 1981. *Economic Theory and Measurement of Unpriced Natural Resources*. Ph.D. dissertation, University of Western Australia, Nedlands.

Jacobs, James J., and George L. Casler. 1979. Internalizing Externalities of Phosphorus Discharges from Crop Production to Surface Water: Effluent Taxes versus Uniform Reductions. *American Journal of Agricultural Economics* 61:309-12.

Jensen, R. C. 1969. Some Characteristics of Investment Criteria. *Journal of Agricultural Economics* 51:251-68.

Johnson, G. L. 1983. Risk Aversion vs. Aversion for Losses and Risk Preferences vs. Preference for Gain. *Annuals of Agricultural Sciences*, Series G. Warsaw: Polish Academy of Science.

Johnson, G. L., and Leroy Quance, eds. 1972. *The Overproduction Trap in U.S. Agriculture*. Baltimore: Johns Hopkins University Press.

Johnson, P. O., and R. W. B. Jackson. 1959. *Modern Statistical Method: Descriptive and Inductive*. Chicago: Rand-McNally.

Jones-Lee, M. W. 1976. *The Value of Life: An Economic Analysis*. Chicago: University of Chicago Press.

_____, ed. 1982. *The Value of Life and Safety*. New York: North Holland.

Just, R. E., and D. L. Hueth. 1979. Multimarket Welfare Measurement. *American Economic Review* 69:947-54.

Just, R. E., D. L. Hueth, and Andrew Schmitz. 1982. *Applied Welfare Economics and Public Policy*. Englewood Cliffs, N.J.: Prentice-Hall.

Kahneman, Daniel, Paul Slovic, and Amos Tversky. 1982. *Judgment under Uncertainty: Heuristics and Biases*. New York: Cambridge University Press.

Kahneman, Daniel, and Amos Tversky. 1979. Prospect Theory: An Analysis of Decisions under Risk. *Econometrica* 47:263-91.

Kalter, Robert J., and Thomas H. Stevens. 1971. Resource Investments, Impact Distribution, and Evaluation Concepts. *American Journal of Agricultural Economics* 53:206-15.

Karpf, Beth. 1982. American Textile Manufacturers Institute v. Donovan. *Ecology Law Quarterly* 10:87-96.

Kasl, Stanislav. 1972. The Optimal Measures of the Impact of Manpower Programs on Health. In *Evaluating the Impact of Manpower Programs*, ed. Michael Borus. Lexington, Mass.: Heath.

Kates, Robert W. 1962. *Hazard and Choice Perception in Flood Plain Management*. Department of Geography Research Paper No. 78. Chicago: University of Chicago.

Kearsley, Greg. 1982. *Costs, Benefits, and Productivity in Training Systems*. Reading, Mass.: Addison-Wesley.

Kelman, Mark. 1987. *A Guide to Critical Legal Studies*. Cambridge: Harvard University Press.

Kelman, Steven. 1981. Cost-Benefit Analysis, An Ethical Critique. *Regulation* 5(January/February):33-40.

Kendall, M. G., ed. 1971. *Cost-Benefit Analysis*. New York: American Elsevier.

_____.1971. The Estimation of Benefits from Recreation Sites and the Provision of a New Recreational Facility. *Regional Studies* 5:55-69.

Marglin, Stephen. 1963a. The Social Rate of Discount and the Optimal Rate of Investment. *Quarterly Journal of Economics* 77:95-111.

_____. 1963b. *Approaches to Dynamic Investment Planning*. Amsterdam: North Holland.

_____. 1967. *Public Investment Criteria*. Cambridge: M.I.T. Press.

Marty, Robert. 1970. The Composite Internal Rate of Return. *Forest Science* 16:276-79.

Mathur, Om Prakash. 1985. *Project Analysis for Local Development*. Boulder: Westview.

McCloskey, Donald N. 1985. *The Rhetoric of Economics*. Madison: University of Wisconsin Press.

McConnell, Kenneth. 1975. Some Problems in Estimating the Demand for Outdoor Recreation. *American Journal of Agricultural Economics* 57:330-39.

_____. 1976. Some Problems in Estimating the Demand for Outdoor Recreation: Reply. *American Journal of Agricultural Economics* 58:598-99.

McGarity, T. O. 1979. Substantive and Procedural Discretion in Administrative Resolution of Science Policy Questions: Regulating Carcinogens in EPA and OSHA. *Georgetown Law Review* 67:729-811.

McGuire, Joseph W. 1978. The Distribution of Subsidy to Students in California Public Higher Education. *Journal of Human Resources* 11:343-53.

McIver, J. P., and Elinor Ostrom. 1976. Using Budget Pies to Reveal Preferences: Validation of a Survey Instrument. *Policy and Politics* 4:87.

McKean, R. N. 1958. *Efficiency in Government Through Systems Analysis*. New York: Wiley.

McKenzie, George W. 1983. *Measuring Economic Welfare: New Methods*. New York: Cambridge University Press.

McKillop, William. 1974. *Economic Impacts of an Intensified Timber Management Program*. Division of Forest Economics and Marketing Research, Research Paper No. WO-23. Washington: U.S. Department of Agriculture, Forest Service.

Meade, J. E.. 1972. Review of Cost-Benefit Analysis by E. J. Mishan. *Economic Journal* 82:244-46.

Meerman, Jacob. 1979. *Public Expenditures in Malaysia: Who Benefits and Why*. New York: Oxford University Press.

Mendelsohn, Robert. 1981. The Choice of Discount Rates for Public Investment. *American Economic Review* 71:239-41.

_____. 1983. An Application of the Hedonic Travel Cost Framework for Recreation Modeling to the Valuation of Deer. In *Advances in Applied Microeconomics*, Vol. 3, ed. V. K. Smith. Greenwich, Conn.: JAI Press.

Merewitz, Leonard, and Stephen H. Sosnick. 1971. *The Budget's New Clothes*. Chicago: Markham.

Merrett, A. J. 1965. Net Present Value vs. the Internal Rate of Return, Yet Again. *Scottish Journal of Political Economy* 12:116-18.

Merrett, A. J., and Allen Sykes. 1963. *The Finance and Analysis of Capital Projects*. New York: Wiley.

Meyer, J. R., and M. R. Straszheim. 1971. *Techniques of Transport Planning*, Vol. 1. Washington: Brookings.

Meyer, Philip A. 1979. Publicly Vested Values for Fish and Wildlife: Criteria for Economic Welfare and Interface with the Law. *Land Economics* 55: 223-35.

Michigan. 1973. *A Guide to Michigan's Program Budget Evaluation System*. Lansing: Bureau of Programs and Budget.

_____. 1974. *Executive Budget, Fiscal Year Ending, June*. Lansing: Executive Office.

_____. House Fiscal Agency. 1975. *Program Budget Review, 1970-71 to 1974-5*. Lansing: House of Representatives, Committee on Appropriations.

Miller, Delbert C. 1977. *Handbook of Research Design and Social Measurement*. New York: McKay.

Miller, James. C., III, and Bruce Yandle. 1979. *Benefit-Cost Analyses of Social Regulation--Case Studies from the Council on Wage and Price Stability*. Washington: American Enterprise.

Milliman, Jerome W. 1969. Beneficiary Charges and Efficient Public Expenditure Decisions. *The Analysis and Evaluation of Public Expenditure: The PPB System*, Vol. 1, 291-318. U.S. Congress, Joint Economic Committee, Subcommittee on Economy in Government. 91st Congress, 1st session.

Mills, Edwin S. 1972. Markets and Efficient Resource Allocation in Urban Areas. *Swedish Journal of Economics* 74:100-13.

Minsky, Hyman P. 1978. *The Financial Instability Hypothesis: A Restatement*. Thames Papers in Political Economy. London: Thames Polytechnic.

Mirrlees, J. A. 1975. Optimal Commodity Taxation in a Two-Class Economy. *Journal of Public Economics* 4:27-33.

Mishan, E. J. 1968. What Is Producer Surplus? *American Economic Review* 58:1269-82.

_____. 1976. *Cost-Benefit Analysis*, 2d ed. New York: Praeger.

_____. 1981. *Economic Efficiency and Social Welfare*. London: Allen & Unwin.

_____. 1982. The New Controversy about the Rationale of Economic Evaluation. *Journal of Economic Issues* 16:29-47.

Modigliani, Franco, and M. H. Miller. 1958. The Cost of Capital, Corporation Finance and the Theory of Investment. *American Economic Review* 48:261-97.

Mohring, Herbert. 1965. Urban Highway Investments. In *Measuring the Benefits of Government Investments*, ed. Robert Dorfman. Washington: Brookings.

Morey, Edward R. 1984. Confuser Surplus. *American Economic Review* 74:163-73.

Morrison, Denton E. and R. E. Henkel, eds. 1970. *The Significance Test Controversy-- A Reader*. Chicago: Aldine.

Morse G. M., and L. J. Hushak. 1979. *Income and Fiscal Impacts of Manufacturing Plants in Southeast Ohio*. Research Bulletin No. 1108. Wooster: Ohio Agricultural Research and Development Center.

Moser, C. A., and G. Kalton. 1972. *Survey Methods in Social Investigation*. New York: Basic Books.

Moses, Leon, and Harold F. Williamson, Jr. 1963. Value of Time, Choice of Mode, and the Subsidy Issue in Urban Transportation. *Journal of Political Economy* 71:247-64.

Mowitz, Robert. 1980. *The Design of Public Decision Systems*. Baltimore: University Park Press.

Munley, Vincent, and V. Kerry Smith. 1976. Learning by Doing and Experience: The Case of Whitewater Recreation. *Land Economics* 52:545-53.

Murelius, Olaf. 1981. *An Institutional Approach to Project Analysis in Developing Countries*. Paris: Organization for Economic Cooperation and Development.

Musgrave, Richard A. 1969. Cost-Benefit Analysis and the Theory of Public Finance. *Journal of Economic Literature* 7:797-806.

Musgrave, Richard A., et al. 1974. The Distribution of Fiscal Burdens and Benefits. *Public Finance Quarterly* 2:259-311.

Nachmias, David. 1979. *Public Policy Evaluation*. New York: St. Martin.

Nash, C. A. 1973. Future Generations and the Social Rate of Discount. *Environment and Planning* 5:611-17.

Nash, C. A., D. W. Pearce, and John Stanley. 1974. An Evaluation of Cost-Benefit Analysis Criteria. *Scottish Journal of Political Economy* 22:121-34.

Nath, S. K. 1969. *A Reappraisal of Welfare Economics*. London: Routledge and Kegan Paul.

National Research Council. 1975. *Decision Making for Regulating Chemicals in the Environment*. Washington: National Academy of Science.

_____. 1977. *Consideration of Health Benefit-Cost Analysis for Activities Involving Ionizing Radiation Exposure and Alternatives*. Committee on the Biological Effects of Ionizing Radiation. EPA Report No. 520/4-77-003. Washington: Environmental Protection Agency.

_____. 1980. *Regulating Pesticides*. Washington: National Academy Press.

_____. 1987. *Regulating Pesticides in Food*. Washington: National Academy Press.

Nelson, A. G., G. L. Caler, and O. L. Walker. 1978. *Making Farm Decisions in a Risky World: A Guidebook*. Corvallis: Oregon State University Extension Service.

Nelson, Jon P. 1980. Airports and Property Values: A Survey of Recent Evidence. *Journal of Transport Economics and Policy* 14:37-52.

Nelson, Robert. 1987. The Economics Profession and the Making of Public Policy. *Journal of Economic Literature* 25:49-91.

Neustadt, Richard E. 1960. *Presidential Power*. New York: John Wiley.

Newman, Barbara. 1969. The Cost of Courage: The Loneliest Man in the Pentagon. *The Washington Monthly* 1(July):30-33.

Nichols, Alan. 1970. The Optimal Rate of Investment in a Firm: Comment. *Journal of Finance* 25:682-84.

Niehaus, Robert D. 1978. *Normalized Prices for Resources Planning: A Comparison of Alternatives*. ESCS-39. Washington: U.S. Department of Agriculture.

Nienaber, Jeanne, and Aaron Wildavsky. 1973. *The Budgeting and Evaluation of Federal Recreation Programs or Money Doesn't Grow on Trees*. New York: Basic Books.

Niskanen, W. A., and Steven H. Hanke. 1977. Land Prices Substantially Underestimate the Value of Environmental Quality. *Review of Economics and Statistics* 59:375-77.

Nunnally, Jum C. 1978. *Psychometric Theory*. New York: McGraw-Hill.

O'Higgins, Michael. 1980. The Distributive Effects of Public Expenditure and Taxation: An Agnostic View of the CSO Analysis. In *Taxation and Social Policy*, ed. Cedric Sandford, et al., 28-46. London: Heinemann.

O'Higgins, Michael, and Patricia Ruggles. 1981. The Distribution of Public Expenditures and Taxes among Households in the United Kingdom. *Review of Income and Wealth* 27:298-326.

Okun, Arthur M. 1975. *Equality and Efficiency: The Big Trade-Off*. Washington: Brookings.

Olson, Craig A. 1981. An Analysis of Wage Differentials Received by Workers on Dangerous Jobs. *Journal of Human Resources* 16:167-85.

Oppenheim, Abraham N. 1966. *Questionnaire Design and Attitude Measurement*. New York: Basic Books.

Otway, Harry J., and Detlof Von Winterfeldt. 1982. Beyond Acceptable Risk: On the Social Acceptability of Technologies. *Policy Science* 14:247-56.

Patinkin, Don. 1963. Demand Curves and Consumer Surplus. In *Measurement in Economics*, ed. Carl F. Christ, et al. Stanford: Stanford University Press.

Pattison, John C. 1973. Some Aspects of Price Discrimination in the Airline Industry. *Journal of Economic Issues* 7:136-47.

Patton, Michael Quinn. 1980. *Qualitative Evaluation Methods*. Beverly Hills: Sage.

Payne, Stanley L. 1951. *The Art of Asking Questions*. Princeton, N.J.: Princeton University Press.

Peacock, Alan. 1973. Cost-Benefit Analysis and the Political Control of Public Investment. In *Cost-Benefit and Effectiveness--Studies and Analysis*, ed. J. N. Wolfe, 17-29. London: Allen & Unwin.

_____. 1974. The Treatment of Government Expenditures in Studies of Income Redistribution. In *Public Finance and Stablization Policy*, ed. W. L. Smith and J. M. Culbertson, 151-67. Amsterdam: North Holland.

Pearce, D. W. 1984. *Cost-Benefit Analysis*, 2d ed. New York: St. Martin.

Pearce, D. W., and C. A. Nash. 1973. The Evaluation of Urban Motorway Schemes: A Case Study-Southampton. *Urban Studies* 10:129-43.

_____. 1981. *Social Appraisal of Projects: A Text in Cost-Benefit Analysis*. London: Macmillan.

Pechman, J. A., and B. A. Okner. 1974. *Who Bears the Tax Burden?* Washington: Brookings.

Pfiffner, James. 1979. *The President, the Budget, and Congress: Impoundment and the 1974 Budget Act*. Boulder: Westview.

Pigou, A. C. 1932. *The Economics of Welfare*, 4th ed. London: Macmillan.

Piore, Michael J. 1979. Qualitative Research Techniques in Economics. *Administrative Science Quarterly* 24:560-69.

Polinsky, A. M., and Steven Shavell. 1975. The Air Pollution and Property Value Debate. *Review of Economics and Statistics* 57:100-04.

Powers, Terry A., ed. 1981. *Estimating Accounting Prices for Project Appraisal*. Washington: Inter-American Development Bank.

Prescott, James R. 1974. *Economic Aspects of Public Housing*. Beverly Hills: Sage.

Prest, A. R. 1968. The Budget and Interpersonal Distribution. *Public Finance* 27:80-98.

Prest, A. R., and Ralph Turvey. 1965. Cost-Benefit Analysis: A Survey. *Economic Journal* 75:683-735.

Prou, Charles, and Marc Chervel. 1970. *Etablissement des Programmes en Economie Sous-Developpe*, Vol. 3, *l'etude des grappes de projets*. Paris: Dunod.

Provus, Malcolm. 1971. *Discrepency Evaluation: For Educational Program Improvement and Assessment*. Berkeley: McCutchan.

Randall, Alan. 1981. *Resource Economics*. Columbus: Grid Publishing.

Randall, Alan, John P. Hoehn, and George S. Tolley. 1981. Structure of Contingent Markets, Some Results of a Recent Experiment. Paper read at annual meeting of American Economic Association, Washington.

Randall, Alan, Berry Ives, and Clyde Eastman. 1974. *Benefits of Abating Aesthetic Environmental Damage from the Four Corners Power Plant, Fruitland, New Mexico*. Agricultural Experiment Station Bulletin No. 618. Las Cruces: New Mexico State University.

Raphaelson, Arnold H. 1983. The Davis-Bacon Act. In *What Role for Government*, ed. R. J. Zeckhauser and Derek Leebart. Durham: Duke University Press.

Raucher, Robert. L. 1986. The Benefits and Costs of Policies Related to Groundwater Contamination. *Land Economics* 62:33-45.

Rausser, Gordon. 1982. Political Economic Markets: PERTS and PESTS in Food and Agriculture. *American Journal of Agricultural Economics* 64:821-33.

Ray, Anandarup. 1984. *Cost-Benefit Analysis: Issues and Methodologies*. Baltimore: Johns Hopkins University Press.

Redburn, Thomas. 1975. Accountants: Those Wonderful People Who Gave You Maurice Stans. *The Washington Monthly* 6(February):4-16.

Reid, T. R. 1980. *Congressional Odyssey: The Saga of a Senate Bill*. San Francisco: W. H. Freeman.

Richardson, G. B. 1960. *Information and Investment*. Oxford: Oxford University Press.

Richardson, Harry W. 1972. *Input-Output and Regional Economics*. London: Weidenfeld and Nicolson.

Richter, Donald K. 1977. Games Pythagoreans Play. *Public Finance Quarterly* 5:495-515.

Robinson, A. 1978. *Parliament and Public Spending*. London: Heinemann.

Robison, L. J. 1982. An Appraisal of Expected Utility Hypothesis Tests Constructed from Responses to Hypothetical Questions and Experimental Choices. *American Journal of Agricultural Economics* 64:367-75.

Robison, L. J., and Peter Barry. 1987. *The Competitive Firms's Response to Risk*. New York: Macmillan.

Roemer, Michael, and J. J. Stern. 1975. *The Appraisal of Development Projects--A Practical Guide to Project Analysis with Case Studies and Solutions*. New York: Praeger.

Rose, Roger N. 1980. Supply Shifts and Research Benefits: Comment. *American Journal of Agricultural Economics* 62:834-37.

Rosen, Sherwin. 1974. Hedonic Prices and Implicit Markets: Product Differentiation in Pure Competition, *Journal of Political Economy* 82:34-55.

Rosen, Stephen. 1984. Systems Analysis and the Quest for Rational Defense. *Public Interest* 76:3-17.

Rossi, P. H., and Sonia R. Wright. 1977. Evaluation Research: An Assessment of Theory, Practices and Politics. *Evaluation Quarterly* 1:5-52.

Rothenberg, Jerome. 1961. *The Measurement of Social Welfare*. Englewood Cliffs, N.J.: Prentice-Hall.

_____. 1975. Cost-Benefit Analyis: A Methodological Exposition. In *Handbook of Evaluation Research*, Vol. 2, ed. Marcia Guttentag and E. L. Stuening. Beverly Hills: Sage.

Rowe, R. D., et al. 1980. An Experiment on the Economic Value of Visibility. *Journal of Environmental Economics and Management* 7:1-19.

Ruggles, Nancy. 1949. Recent Developments in the Theory of Marginal Cost Pricing. *The Review of Economic Studies* 17:107-26.

Ruggles, Patricia, and Michael O'Higgins. 1981. The Distribution of Public Expenditure among Households in the United States. *Review of Income and Wealth* 27:137-64.

Rundquist, Barry S. 1980. *Political Benefits: Empirical Studies of American Public Programs*. Lexington, Mass.: Lexington Books.

Russell, Clifford S. 1986. Discounting Human Life. *Resources* Winter, No. 82:8-10.

Sagan, L. A. 1972. Human Costs of Nuclear Power. *Science* 177:487-93.

Sallack, David, and David N. Allen. 1987. From Impact to Output: Pennsylvania's Planning-Programming Budgeting System in Transition. *Public Budgeting and Finance* 7:38-50.

Samples, Karl C. 1985. A Note on the Existence of Starting Point Bias in Interactive Bidding Games. *Western Journal of Agricultural Economics* 10:32-40.

Samuels, Warren J. 1975. Grants and Theory of Power. *Public Finance Quarterly* 3:320-45.

Samuelson, P. A. [1947] 1963. *Foundations of Economic Analysis*. Cambridge: Harvard University Press.

Sanders, Ralph. 1973. *The Politics of Defense Analysis*. New York: Dunellen.

Sandford, Cedric, ed. 1979. *Control of Public Expenditure*. Centre for Fiscal Studies Occasional Paper No. 14. Bath: University of Bath.

Sarant, Peter C. 1978. *Zero-Base Budgeting in the Public Sector--A Pragmatic Approach*. Reading, Mass.: Addison-Wesley.

Sasaki, Komei, and Hiroo Shibata. 1984. Nonsurvey Methods for Projecting the Input-Output System at a Small-Region Level: Two Alternative Approaches. *Journal of Regional Science* 24:35-50.

Sassone, Peter, and William Schaffer. 1978. *Cost Benefit Analysis*. New York: Academic Press.

Schick, Allen. 1966. The Road to PBB: The Stages of Budget Reforms. *Public Administration Review* 26:243-58.

_____. 1971. *Budget Innovation in the States*. Washington: Brookings.

_____. 1980. *Congress and Money*. Washington: Urban Institute.

Schick, Allen, et al. 1980. *Zero-Base Budgeting in Practice: State and Local Government Experiments in New Budgeting System*. Washington: Urban Institute.

Schmalensee, Richard. 1972. Option Demand and Consumer Surplus: Valuing Price Changes under Uncertainty. *American Economic Review* 62:813-24.

Schmid, A. Allan. 1967. Nonmarket Values in Efficiency of Public Investments in Water Resources. *American Economic Review* 57:158-68.

_____. 1969a. Natural Resources and Growth: Towards a Non-Marginal Political Economics. *American Journal of Agricultural Economics* 51:1304-13.

_____. 1969b. Effective Public Policy and the Government Budget: A Uniform Treatment of Public Expenditures and Public Rules. *The Analysis and Evaluation of Public Expenditures: The PPB System*, Vol. 1, 579-91. U.S. Congress, Joint Economic Committee, Subcommittee on Economy in Government. 91st Congress, 1st session.

_____. 1972. Changed Distribution of Income vs. Redistribution in Public Project Evaluation: Comment. *American Journal of Agricultural Economics* 54:135-36.

_____. 1975. Systematic Choice among Multiple Outputs of Public Projects without Prices. *Social Indicators Research* 2:275-86.

_____. 1982. Symbolic Barriers to Full Employment: The Role of Public Debt. *Journal of Economic Issues* 16:281-94.

_____. 1987. *Property, Power and Public Choice*, 2d ed. New York: Praeger.

Schmid, A. Allan, and Ronald C. Fass. 1975. A Research Approach to Institutional Alternatives in the Administration of Agrarian Development Programs. *Agricultural Administration* 2:285-305.

Schmid, A. Allan, Werner Kiene, and Gail Updegraff. 1973. *A Comprehensive Rural Health Clinic: Case Study of Public Program Evaluation Methodology*. Department of Agricultural Economics Report No. 260. East Lansing: Michigan State University.

Schmid, A. Allan, and William A. Ward. 1970. *A Test of Federal Water Project Evaluation Procedures with Emphasis on Regional Income and Environmental Quality: Detroit River, Trenton Navigation Channel*. Department of Agricultural Economics Report No. 158. East Lansing: Michigan State University.

Schmitz, Andrew, and David Seckler. 1970. Mechanized Agriculture and Social Welfare: The Case of the Tomato Harvester. *American Journal of Agricultural Economics* 52:569-77.

Schoemaker, P. J. H. 1982. The Expected Utility Model: Its Varients, Purposes, Evidence and Limitations. *Journal of Economic Literature* 20:529-63.

Schon, David A. 1974. Planning and Managing Change. *The Bureaucrat* 3:153-61.

Schulze, William D., Ralph d'Arge, and David S. Brookshire. 1981. Valuing Environmental Commodities: Some Recent Experiments. *Land Economics* 57(2):151-72.

Scitovsky, Tibor. 1941. A Note on Welfare Propositions in Economics. *Review of Economic Studies* 9:77-88.

Seers, Dudley. 1976. The Political Economy of National Accounting. In *Employment, Income Distribution and Development Stategy: Problems of the Developing Countries*, ed. Alec Cairncross and Mohinder Puri, 193-209. New York: Holmes & Meier.

Self, Peter. 1975. *Econocrats and the Policy Process: The Politics and Philosophy of Cost Benefit Analysis*. London: Macmillan.

Sellin, Thorstein, and Marvin E. Wolfgang. 1964. *The Measurement of Delinquency*. New York: Wiley.

Selowsky, Marcelo. 1979. *Who Benefits from Government Expenditure? A Case Study of Columbia*. New York: Oxford University Press.

Sen, A. K. 1961. On Optimizing the Rate of Saving. *Economic Journal* 71:479-96.

_____. 1967. Isolation, Assurance and the Social Rate of Discount. *Quarterly Journal of Economics* 81:112-24.

Shabman, Leonard, and Robert J. Kalter. 1969. *The Effects of New York State Administered Outdoor Recreation Expenditures on the Distribution of Personal Income*. Department of Agricultural Economics Research Paper No. 298. Ithaca: Cornell University.

Silberberg, Eugene. 1972. Duality and the Many Consumer Surpluses. *American Economic Review* 62:942-52.

Simon Herbert A. 1978. Rationality as a Process and as a Product of Thought. *American Economic Review* 68:1-15.

Simon, Julian. 1970. Family Planning Prospects in Less-Developed Countries and a Cost-Benefit Analysis of Various Alternatives. *Economic Journal* 80:58-71.

Sinden, John A. 1974. A Utility Approach to the Valuation of Recreational and Aesthetic Experience. *American Journal of Agricultural Economics* 56:61-72.

Sinden, John A., and Albert C. Worrell. 1979. *Unpriced Values: Decisions without Market Prices*. New York: Wiley.

Sjaastad, Larry, and Daniel Wisecarver. 1977. The Social Cost of Public Finance. *Journal of Political Economy* 85:513-47.

Slovic, Paul. 1987. Perception of Risk. *Science* 236:280-285.

Small, K. A. 1975. Air Pollution and Property Values: Further Comment. *Review of Economics and Statistics* 47:105-07.

Smith, R. S. 1976. *The Occupational Safety and Health Act: Its Goals and Its Achievements*. Washington: American Enterprise.

Smith, V. Kerry, ed. 1984. *Environmental Policy under Reagan's Executive Policy*. Chapel Hill: University of North Carolina Press.

Smith, V. Kerry. 1986. A Conceptual Overview of the Foundation of Benefit-Cost Analysis. In *Benefits Assessment, the State of the Art*, ed. Judith D. Bentkover, Vincent Covello, and Jerry Mumpower. Dordrecht, Holland: D. Reidal Publishing.

Smith, V. Kerry, and William H. Desvousges. 1986. *Measuring Water Quality Benefits*. Boston: Kluwer-Nijhoff.

Solo, Robert A. 1982. *The Positive State*. Cincinnati: Southwestern Publishing.

Solomon, Ezra. 1956. The Arithmetic of Capital-Budgeting Decisions. *Journal of Business* 29:124-29.

_____.1970. Rate of Return Concepts and Their Implications for Utility Regulation. *Bell Journal of Economics and Management Science* 1:65-81.

Squire, Lyn, and Herman G. van der Tak. 1975. *Economic Analysis of Projects*. Baltimore: Johns Hopkins University Press.

Stanford Research Institute. 1966. *Route Selection and Feasibility Analysis of the Tanzam Highway*. Final Report, Contract No. AID/afr-364, September.

Starr, Chauncey. 1969. Social Benefit versus Technological Risk. *Science* 165:1232-38.

Starr, Chauncey, and Chris Whipple. 1980. Risks of Risk Decisions. *Science* 208:1114-19.

Steiner, Peter O. 1966. The Role of Alternative Cost in Project Design and Selection, In Water Research, ed. A. V. Kneese and Stephen C. Smith. Baltimore: Johns Hopkins University Press.

Stiglitz, J. E. 1974. On the Irrelevance of Corporate Financial Policy. *American Economic Review* 64:851-66.

_____. 1987a. The Causes and Consequences of the Dependence of Quality on Price. *Journal of Economic Literature* 25:1-48.

_____.1987b. The Wage-Productivity Hypothesis: Its Economic and Policy Implications. In *Modern Developments in Public Finance,* ed. Michael Boskin. Oxford: Basil Blackwell.

Stockfish, Jacob A. 1969. The Interest Rate Applicable to Government Investment Projects. In *Program Budgeting and Benefit-Cost Analysis*, ed. Harley Hinrichs and Graeme Taylor. Pacific Palisades, Cal.: Goodyear.

Stoevener, Herbert H., et al. 1972. *Multi-Disciplinary Study of Water Quality Relationships: A Case Study of Yaquina Bay, Oregon*. Agricultural Experiment Station Special Report No. 348. Corvallis: Oregon State University.

Strung, Joseph. 1976. The Internal Rate of Return and the Reinvestment Presumptions. *Appraisal Journal* 44:23-33.

Stuart-Alexander, D. E., and R. K. Mark. 1977. Disasters as a Necessary Part of Benefit-Cost Analysis. *Science* 197:1160-62.

Sudman, Seymour. 1976. *Applied Sampling*. New York: Academic Press.

Sugden, Robert, and Alan Williams. 1978. *The Principles of Practical Cost-Benefit Analysis*. Oxford: Oxford University Press.

Swatzman, Daniel, et al. 1982. *Cost Benefit Analysis and Environmental Regulations*. Washington: Conservation Foundation.

Szakolczai, Gy. 1980. Limits to Redistribution: The Hungarian Experience. In *Income Distribution: The Limits to Redistribution*, ed. David Collard, et al. Bristol: Scientechnia (John Wright).

Thaler, Richard, and Sherwin Rosen. 1976. The Value of Saving a Life: Evidence from the Labor Market. In *Household Production and Consumption*, ed. N. E. Terleckyj. New York: Columbia University Press.

Thaler, Richard, and H. M. Shefrin. 1981. An Economic Theory of Self-Control. *Journal of Political Economy* 89:392-406.

Thomas, Harold A. 1963. The Animal Farm: A Mathematical Model for the Discussion of Social Standards for Control of the Environment. *Quarterly Journal of Economics* 77:143-48.

Thomas, T. C. 1968. *The Value of Time for Passenger Cars: An Experimental Study of Commuters Values.* Highway Research Record, No. 245. Washington: Highway Research Board.

Thompson, Mark. 1980. *Benefit-Cost Analysis for Program Evaluation.* Beverly Hills: Sage.

Thurow, L. C. 1983. *Dangerous Currents, the State of Economics.* New York: Random House.

Tiebout, Charles. 1962. *The Community Economic Base Study.* Supplementary Paper No. 16. New York: Committee for Economic Development.

Tobin, James. 1975 Keynesian Models of Recession and Depression. *American Economic Review* 65(2):195-202.

Tolley, George S. 1959. Reclamation's Influence on the Rest of Agriculture. *Land Economics* 35:176-80.

Torrance, George W. 1986. Measurement of Health State Utilities for Economic Appraisal. *Journal of Health Economics* 5:1-30.

Tresch, Richard W. 1981. *Public Finance: A Normative Theory.* Plano, Texas: Business Publications.

Tucker, J. Dean, and Stanley R. Thompson. 1979. *Economic Effect of Rural Road Development on Grain Assembly Costs: The Case of Lenawee County, Michigan.* Department of Agricultural Economics Report No. 367. East Lansing: Michigan State University.

Tullock, Gordon. 1964. The Social Rate of Discount and Optimal Rate of Investment: Comment. *Quarterly Journal of Economics* 78:33-36.

Turvey, Ralph. 1963. Present Value versus Internal Rate of Return--An Essay in the Theory of Third Best. *Economic Journal* 73:93-98.

_____. 1971a. *Economic Analysis and Public Enterprises.* London: Allen & Unwin.

_____. 1971b. On the Development of Cost-Benefit Analysis. In *Cost-Benefit Analysis,* ed. M. G. Kendall. New York: American Elsevier.

U.S. Army Corps of Engineers. 1980. *Little Colorado River at Holbrok Arizona, Review Report for Flood Control.* Washington: Army Corps of Engineers.

U.S. Congress. 1967. Joint Economic Committee. *The Planning Programming-Budgeting System: Progress and Potentials, Hearings.* 90th Congress, 1st session.

_____. 1969. Joint Economic Committee. *The Analysis and Evaluation of Public Expenditures: The PPB System.* Vols. 1, 2, and 3. 91st Congress, 1st session.

_____. 1977. Joint Economic Committee. SubCommittee on Economic Growth and Stabilization. *Assessment of Public Opinion and Public Expectations Concerning the Government and the Economy, Hearings.* 95th Congress, 1st session.

U.S. Congress. House. 1969. Committee on Appropriations. *Public Works Appropriations for 1970 for Water and Power Resources Development, Hearings.* 91st Congress, 1st session, Part 2.

U.S. Congress. Office of Technology Assessment. 1970. *Environmental Contamination in Food*. Washington: U.S.GPO.

U.S. Congress. Senate. 1962. *Policies, Standards and Procedures in the Formulation, Evaluation, and Review of Plans for Use and Development of Water and Related Land Resources*. S. Doc. 97. 87th Congress, 2d session.

U.S. Department of Agriculture. 1987. *Estimating Prices for Access to Opportunities for Hunting, Fishing, and Viewing Wildlife on Public and Private Lands*. Washington: Natural Resources and Environment Steering Committee on Wildlife and Fish Access Prices, Final Report, May 15.

U.S. Department of Health, Education and Welfare. 1966a. *Disease Control Programs: Motor Vechicle Injury Prevention Program*. Washington, August.

———. 1966b. *Selected Disease Control Programs*. Program Analysis Series 1966-5. Washington: Office of Assistant Secretary for Programming Coordination, September.

U.S. Department of Interior. 1986. Natural Resource Damage Assessments. *Federal Register* 51(148):27674-753.

U.S. Department of Labor. 1981. *Final Regulatory Analysis of the Hearing Conservation Amendment*. Washington: Occupational Safety and Health Administration, January.

U.S. Department of Transportation. 1976a. *Social and Economic Impact of Highways*. Federal Highway Administration. Washington: U.S.GPO.

———. 1976b. *Societal Costs of Motor Vehicle Accidents*. Washington: National Highway Traffic Safety Administration, December.

———. 1982. *Final Regulatory Impact Analysis, Part 581 Bumper Standard*. Washington: National Highway Traffic Safety Administration, Office of Program and Rulemaking Analysis, May.

U.S. Environmental Protection Agency. 1983. *Guidelines for Performing Regulatory Impact Analysis*. EPA-230-01-84-003. Washington: Office of Policy Analysis.

———. 1985. *Costs and Benefits of Reducing Lead in Gasoline, Final Regulatory Impact Analysis*. EPA-230-05-85-006. Washington: Office of Policy Analysis.

———. 1988. *Guidelines for Preparing Regulatory Impact Analysis*, Appendix A, Analysis of Benefits. Washington: Office of Policy Analysis.

U.S. Forest Service. 1980. *A Recommended Renewable Resources Program*. Washington: U.S.GPO.

———. 1987. *Resource Pricing and Valuation Guidelines for the 1990 RPA Program*. Report of the Chief's Technical Coordinating Committee on Resource Values for the 1990 RPA. Washington, March 17.

U.S. Inter-Agency Committee on Water Resources. 1958. *Proposed Practices for Economic Analysis of River Basin Projects*. Washington, May.

U.S. National Bureau of Standards. 1977. *Preliminary Report on Evaluating Alternatives for Reducing Upholstered Furniture Fire Losses*, NBSIR-77-1381. Washington, November.

U.S. Office of Management and Budget. 1972. *Discount Rates to be Used in Evaluating Time-Distributed Benefits and Costs*. Circular A-94. Washington, March.

U.S. Water Resources Council. 1973. Water and Related Land Resources, Establishment of Principles and Standards. *Federal Register* 38(174), 10 September, 24778.

_____. 1975. *Recommendations of the Water Resources Council to the President: Planning and Costs Sharing Policy*. Washington, November.

_____. 1979a. Procedures for Evaluation of National Economic Development (NED) Benefits and Costs in Water Resources Planning (Level C) and Proposed Revisions to the Standards for Planning Water and Related Land Resources. *Federal Register* 44(102), 24 May, 30194-258.

_____. 1979b. Procedures for Evaluation of National Economic Development (NED) Benefits and Costs in Water Resources Planning: Final Rule. *Federal Register* 44(242) 14 December, 72892-976.

_____. 1980a. Proposed Rules; Principles, Standards and Procedures for Planning Water and Related Land. *Federal Register* 45(73), 14 April, 25302-48.

_____. 1980b. Procedures for Evaluation of National Economic Development Benefits and Costs: Final Rule. *Federal Register* 45(190), 29 September, 64448-66.

_____. 1982. Economic and Environmental Principles and Guidelines for Water and Related Land Resources Implementation Studies. *Federal Register* 47(55), 22 March, 12296-307.

Vanags, A. H. 1975. A Reappraisal of Public Investment Rules. In *Current Economic Problems*, ed. Michael Parkin and A. R. Nobay, 119-48. New York: Cambridge University Press.

van der Tak, Herman G., and Jan de Weille. 1969. *Reappraisal of a Road Project in Iran*. World Bank Staff Occasional Paper No. 7. Washington: International Bank for Reconstruction and Development.

van Ravenswaay, E. O. 1983. The Science Policy Interface in Regulatory Decision-Making. In *PCB's Human and Environmental Hazards*, ed. F. N. D'Itri and M. A. Kamrin, 353-65. Woburn, Mass.: Butterworth.

Vartia, Y. O. 1983. Efficient Methods of Measuring Welfare Change and Compensated Income in Terms of Ordinary Demand Functions. *Econometrica* 51:79-98.

Vickerman, Roger. 1972. The Demand for Non-Work Travel. *Journal of Transport Economics and Policy* 6:176-210.

Viner, Jacob. 1932. Cost Curves and Supply Curves. *Zeitschrift fur Nationalokonomie* 3:23-46.

Vondruska, John. 1969. *Estimating Small Watershed Project Benefits: A Computer Systemization of SCS Procedures*. Department of Agricultural Economics Report No. 120. East Lansing: Michigan State University.

Wabe, J. S. 1971. A Study of House Prices as a Means of Establishing the Value of Time, the Rates of Time Preference and the Valuation of Some Aspects of Environment in the London Metropolitan Region. *Applied Economics* 3:247-55.

Walsh, Richard G. 1985. *Recreation Economic Decisions*. Fort Collins, Colo.: privately published.

Walsh, Richard G., et al. 1978. *Option Values, Presevation Values and Recreational Benefits of Improved Water Quality: A Case Study of South Platte River Basin, Colorado.* EPA-600/5-78-001. Research Triangle, N.C.: U.S. Environmental Protection Agency.

Ward, William A. 1976. *Adjusting for Over-Valued Local Currency: Shadow Exchange Rates and Conversion Factors.* Economic Development Institute Course Notes No. 28. Washington: International Bank for Reconstruction and Development.

Watson, P. L. 1974. *The Value of Time: Behavioral Models of Mode Choice.* Lexington, Mass.: Lexington Books.

Watson, W. D., and J. A. Jaksch. 1982. Air Pollution, Household Soiling and Consumer Welfare Losses. *Journal of Environmental Economics and Management* 9:248-62.

Webb, E. J., et al. 1966. *Unobtrusive Measures: Nonreactive Research in the Social Sciences.* Chicago: Rand-McNally.

Weckstein, R. S. 1972. Shadow Prices and Project Evaluation in Less Developed Countries. *Economic Development and Cultural Change* 20:474-94.

Weingartner, H. M. 1963a. The Excess Present Value Index--A Theoretical Basis and Critique. *Journal of Accounting Research* 1:213-24.

_____. 1963b. *Mathematical Programming and the Analysis of Capital Budgeting Problems.* Englewood Cliffs, N.J.: Prentice-Hall.

Weisbrod, Burton A. 1968. Income Redistribution Effects and Benefit-Cost Analysis. In *Problems in Public Expenditures Analysis,* ed. Samuel B. Chase, Jr. Washington: Brookings.

Weiss, Carol H. 1987. Evaluating Social Programs: What Have We Learned? *Society* (November/December):40-45.

Wellor, Patrick, and James Cutt. 1976. *Treasury Control in Australia, A Study in Bureaucratic Politics.* Sydney: Ian Novak.

Westley, Glenn. 1981. *Guidelines for the Appraisal of Farm Development Projects.* Papers on Project Analysis No. 13. Washington: Inter-American Development Bank.

Wetzstein, Michael E., and John G. McNeely. 1980. Specification Errors and Inference in Recreation Demand Models. *American Journal of Agricultural Economics* 62:798-800.

Whittington, Dale, and W. Norton Grubb. 1984. Economic Analysis In Regulatory Decisions: The Implications of Executive Order 12291. *Science, Technology and Human Values* 9:63-71.

Whittington, Dale, and Duncan MacRae, Jr. 1986. The Issue of Standing in Cost-Benefit Analysis. *Journal of Policy Analysis and Management* 5:665-82.

Wildavsky, Aaron. 1969. Rescuing Policy Analysis from PPBS. *Public Administration Review* 29:198-220.

_____. 1974. *The Politics of the Budgetary Process.* Boston: Little.

_____. 1988. *The New Politics of the Budgetary Process.* Glenview, Il.: Scott, Foresman.

Willig, Robert D. 1976. Consumer's Surplus without Apology. *American Economic Review* 66:589-97.

Wolfe, J. N., ed. 1973. *Cost Benefit and Cost Effectiveness*. London: Allen & Unwin.

Wood, John H. 1981. Interest Rates and Inflation. *Economic Perspectives* 5(3):3-12.

Yates, Douglas. 1982. *The Search for Democracy and Efficiency in American Government*. Cambridge: Harvard University Press.

Young, Robert A., and S. Lee Gray. 1985. Input-Output Models, Economic Surplus, and the Evaluation of State or Regional Water Plans. *Water Resources Research* 21:1819-23.

Zaidan, G. C. 1971. *The Costs and Benefits of Family Planning Programs*. Baltimore: Johns Hopkins University Press.

Author Index

Aaron, Henry, 184, 190
Aboucher, Alan, 7
Achen, Christopher H., 52
ACIR, 162
Ackerman, Bruce A., 169
Acton, Jan, 88, 103
Adler, Hans A., 67, 68, 73
Akehurst, R. L., 64
Alchian, A. A., 231
Allen, David N., 271, 273
American Association of State Highway
    Officials, 73
Anas, Alex, 81, 103
Anderson, J.R., 307
Anderson, L. G., 71, 287
Anderson, R. J., 83, 103
Arrow, K. J., 17, 214, 232, 243, 244, 262
Arthur, W. B., 64
Ashford, N. A., 260
Atkinson, A. B., 197
Austin, James E., 7
Azzi, Corry F., 188

Babunakis, Michael, 30
Bacha, Edmar, 115
Bain, J. S., 154, 159
Baram, Michael S., 102, 279
Barry, Peter, 246
Bartlett, Randall, 273
Barzel, Yoram, 207
Bates, Robert H., 110
Baumol, William J., 211, 212, 215
Beardsley, P. L., 74, 93
Beardsley, Wendell, 308
Beesley, M. E., 69
Bell, C. L. G., 129

Berger, Mark C., 319
Bergmann, H., 309
Birch, Alfred L., 103
Bird, Richard M., 180
Birgegard, Lars-Erik, 133, 233
Bish, Robert, 171
Bishop, Richard C., 91, 92
Blackwood, Larry G., 89
Blomquist, Glenn C., 61, 83
Boadway, Robin W., 11, 146, 186
Bockstael, Nancy E., 77, 145
Bohm, Peter, 88
Bonnen, James T., 44
Booth, James H., 45
Boring, E. G., 49
Borus, Michael E., 45, 62
Boskin, Michael J., 310
Boulding, Kenneth E., 208, 299, 305
Bouma, F., 78
Boussard, J. M., 309
Bowes, M. D., 314
Boyle, Kevin J., 92
Bradford, David F., 216
Brainard, William, 243
Brandl, John, 262
Break, George F., 162, 167
Bridier, Manuel, 310
Briloff, Abraham J., 232
Bromley, Daniel, 81
Brookshire, David S., 81, 92
Brown, C. V., 107
Brown, Gardner M., 91
Brown, R. E., 321
Brown, William G., 74, 75, 78
Brown, W. W., 211
Brownrigg, Mark, 132

Bruce, Colin, 120, 135
Bruce, Neil, 11, 146
Bryden, John M., 132
Bullock, J. Bruce, 152
Burke, A. W., 311
Burns, Michael E., 142

Caldart, C. C., 308
Caler, G. L., 325
Campbell, Donald T., 27, 48, 52, 55, 57
Campen, James T., 274
Caporaso, James A., 52
Capra, Fritjof, 306
Carlson, J. E., 90
Carpenter, Edwin H., 89
Carr-Hill, Roy A., 21
Carver, Ronald P., 54
Casler, George L., 65
Casley, D. J., 263
Castle, Emery N., 311
Cesario, Frank J., 68, 72, 74, 76, 77, 78
Chapin, F. S., 50
Chelimsky, Eleanor, 281
Chenery, H. P., 120
Chervel, Marc, 118, 121
Chipman, J. S., 141
Chitale, V. P., 219
Choate, Pat, 216
Christiansen, Vidar, 171
Cicchetti, C. J., 75, 77, 78
CIDA, 22
Clark, Terry N., 90, 93
Clawson, Marion, 74
Coburn, T. M., 106
Cocheba, Donald J., 91
Cohn, Elchanan, 7
Coleman, James, 43
Collard, David, 213, 232
Conley, B. C., 102
Cook, Thomas D., 27, 52
Cooke, Stephen, 141, 148
Cooper, B. S., 64
Cornbach, Lee, 47, 88
Coursey, Don L., 92
Cox, James C., 188

Crocker, T. D., 83, 103
Crouch, E. A., 39
Culyer, A. J., 64
Cummings, Ronald G., 91
Currie, J. M., 146
Cutt, James, 281

d'Arge, Ralph, 329
Dardis, Rachel, 61
Dasgupta, A. K., 214, 252, 265
Dasgupta, Partha, 104, 105, 112, 114, 171,
    288
David, Elizabeth L., 83
Davis, Robert K., 91
Dawson, R. F. F., 63
de Haven, James, 319
de Weille, Jan, 67
DeAlessi, Louis, 223
DeGarmo, E. Paul, 7
DeGrasse, Robert W., Jr., 117
Desvousges, William H., 7
Deutscher, Irwin, 313
DeWulf, Lue H., 180
Diamond, P. A., 186
Diewert, Walter E., 142
Dillon, J.L., 307
Dobb, Maurice, 213, 214
Dola, Steven, 276
Dolbear, F. T., 243
Dorfman, Robert, 7, 252
Dreze, Jacques, 64
Ducros, Jean-Claude, 281
Dudley, Carlton L., Jr., 202, 207
Dwyer, J. F., 94

Earl, Peter E., 221
Eastman, Clyde, 327
Eckhouse, Richard S., 56
Eckstein, Otto, 162, 166, 171, 208, 211,
    213, 228, 256
Epp, D. J., 43, 135

Faas, Ronald C., 263
Feenberg, Daniel, 67

Feldstein, Martin, 186, 197, 211, 213, 216, 232
Fenno, Richard F., 275
Fiering, Myron B., 230
Fischoff, Baruch, 249
Fisher, A. C., 78, 243, 244, 265
FitzGerald, E. V. K., 110
Fleischer, G. A., 67
Flemming, J. S., 210
Foster, C. D., 109, 189
Freeman, A. Myrick, III, 61, 65, 67, 76, 78, 81, 82, 83, 103, 185
Friedman, Lee S., 169
Fuchs, Victor R., 215

Galtung, Johan, 54
Garn, Harvey A., 37
Gillespie, W. Irwin, 180, 183
Gittinger, J. P., 115, 133
Goodman, Robert, 132
Goodwin, P. B., 71
Gordon, Irene M., 91
Gorham, William, 278, 279, 280
Graham, D. A., 265
Graham, J. D., 42, 102
Graham-Tomasi, Theodore, 145
Gramlich, Edward M., 116, 145, 162, 168, 170, 178, 190, 214
Gray, S. Lee, 120
Green, H. A. John, 186
Green, P. E., 82
Griliches, Zvi, 146, 147, 155
Grubb, W. Norton, 271
Gum, Russel L., 75
Guttentag, Marcia, 103

Haimes, Yacov Y., 39
Hall, Peter, 235
Halvorsen, Robert, 67
Hammack, Judd, 91
Hanemann, W. Michael, 77, 92
Hanke, Steven H., 79, 299
Hansen, J. R., 217
Hansen, W. J., 321
Hansen, W. Lee, 183

Hanushek, Eric A., 43, 270
Hapgood, Fred, 102
Harberger, Arnold C., 144, 155, 184, 185, 186, 287, 304
Hardaker, J.B., 307
Hardin, Einar, 45, 62
Hargrove, Erwin C., 45
Harris, John R., 120, 121
Harris, Louis, 90
Harrison, A. J., 67, 68, 71, 72, 73
Harrison, David, Jr., 82, 83, 103
Hartunian, Nelson, 102
Hartwick, John M., 186
Hausman, J. A., 142
Haveman, Robert H., 78, 120, 128, 129, 171, 177, 229, 233, 235
Havemann, Joel, 269
Havens, Harry S., 30
Hazell, P. B. R., 129
Heberlein, Thomas A., 91
Heller, Peter S., 208
Helmers, F. L. C. H., 171
Henderson, P. D., 228, 231
Henkel, R. E., 54
Hershey, John C., 249
Hey, J. D., 256
Hight, Joseph E., 183
Hirschleifer, Jack, 211, 214, 265
HMSO, 220
Hochstim, Joseph R., 88
Hoehn, John P., 82, 91
Holling, C. S., 276
House, E. R., 88
Howe, C. W., 7
Howe, J. D., 71
Hueth, D. L., 149
Hufschmidt, Maynard M., 7, 230
Hushak, L. J., 132
Hutchison, T. W., 2
Hylland, Aanund, 190

Imboden, N., 263
Ingram, Helen M., 233
Irvin, George, 113
Isard, Walter, 124, 135

Ives, Berry, 310
Izac, A-M. N., 104

Jackson, P. M., 107
Jackson, R. W. B., 52
Jacobs, James J., 65
Jaksch, J. A., 67
Jansen, Eliv S., 171
Jarrett, F. G., 155
Jensen, R. C., 231
Johnson, G. L., 155, 245
Johnson, P. O., 52
Johnson, Ronald W., 45
Jones-Lee, M. W., 64, 102
Just, R. E., 142, 149, 152

Kahneman, Daniel, 221, 237, 245, 246, 265
Kalter, Robert J., 177, 189
Kalton, G., 89
Karpf, Beth, 64, 271
Kasl, Stanislav, 30
Kates, Robert W., 248
Kearsley, Greg, 320
Kelly, J. R., 314
Kelman, Mark, 64, 91, 92
Kelman, Steven, 292
Kendall, M. G., 7
Kennedy, Duncan, 2
Kiene, Werner, 30
King, J. A., 233
Kloman, E. J., 281
Knetsch, J. L., 74, 77, 78, 91
Kokoski, Mary F., 142
Korten, D. C., 264
Kovenock, D. M., 308
Krutilla, J. V., 78, 128, 211
Kuhn, T. E., 73, 208
Kunreuther, Howard C., 65
Kurz, Mordecai, 232

Lal, Deepak, 7
Landefeld, J. S., 103
Langford, William A., 91
Lansing, John B., 88
Lave, L. B., 67

Leamer, Edward, 53
Lee, Robert D., Jr., 45
Lewis, Arthur, 120
Lichtenstein, Sarah, 315
Lind, R. C., 17, 80, 81, 103, 231, 243, 262
Linder, R. K., 155
Litan, Robert F., 271
Little, I. M. D., 107, 110, 118, 134, 144,
    145, 154, 160, 217, 222, 233, 288
Lord, William, 274
Lorie, James H., 231
Loughlin, James C., 161
Lury, D. A., 263
Lutz, F. A., 231
Lutz, Vera, 231

Machina, Mark J., 245
Mack, Ruth, 263
MacLean, Douglas, 215
MacRae, Duncan, Jr., 11, 44
Maital, Schlomo, 190
Maler, Karl-Goran, 67, 85, 103
Mansfield, N. W., 72, 78, 167
Marglin, Stephen, 170, 172, 189, 207, 213,
    216, 228, 231
Mark, R.K., 331
Martin, William E.,75
Marty, Robert, 232
Mathur, Om Prakash, 7
McCloskey, Donald N., 53, 57
McConnell, Kenneth, 76, 77
McGarity, T. O., 259
McGuire, Joseph W., 183
McGuire, Martin C., 184, 190
McIver, J. P., 93
McKean, R. N., 167, 211, 231
McKenzie, George W., 7
McKillop, William, 132
McNeely, John G., 103
Meade, J. E., 91
Meerman, Jacob, 180, 181, 182, 183, 184,
    185
Mendelsohn, Robert, 82, 232
Merewitz, Leonard, 269
Merrett, A. J., 231

Meyer, J. R., 73
Meyer, Philip A., 91
Michigan, 35, 45
Miller, Delbert C., 57
Miller, James. C., III, 190
Miller, M. H., 197
Milliman, Jerome W., 161
Mills, Edwin S., 67, 81
Minsky, Hyman P., 116
Mirrlees, J. A., 107, 110, 118, 134, 186, 217,
    222, 233, 288
Mishan, E. J., 72, 91, 148, 188, 203, 206,
    216, 218, 232, 233, 252, 254, 287
Modigliani, Franco, 197
Mohring, Herbert., 71
Moore, J. C., 141
Morey, Edward R., 142
Morgan, James N., 88
Morrison, Denton E., 54
Morse, G. M., 132
Moser, C. A., 89
Moses, Leon, 68
Mowitz, Robert, 22
Munley, Vincent, 78
Murelius, Olaf, 263
Murphy, J. A., 313
Musgrave, Richard A., 2, 177, 180
Myers, Robert J., 145

Nachmias, David, 26, 43, 103
Nash, C. A., 10, 107, 117, 171, 211, 212,
    213, 214, 216, 231
Nath, S. K., 233
National Research Council, 39, 41, 45, 57,
    259, 261
Nawas, Farid, 74
Nelson, A. G., 252
Nelson, Jon P., 83, 103
Nelson, Robert, 269
Neustadt, Richard E., 272
Newman, Barbara, 262, 278
Nichols, Alan, 221
Niehaus, Robert D., 257
Nienaber, Jeanne, 45, 269, 270, 273
Niskanen, W. A., 79

Nordhaus, William D., 271
Nunnally, Jum C., 42

O'Higgins, Michael, 180, 181, 182, 183, 189
Okner, B. A., 181
Okun, Arthur M., 178
Olson, Craig A., 61, 246
Oppenheim, Abraham N., 88, 103
Ostrom, Elinor, 93
Otway, Harry J., 249

Patinkin, Don, 140, 155
Pattison, John C., 326
Patton, Michael Quinn, 28
Payne, Stanley L., 89
Peacock, Alan, 177, 182, 287
Pearce, D. W., 7, 10, 107, 117, 171, 211,
    212, 213, 214, 216, 252, 265
Pechman, J. A., 181
Pfiffner, James, 269
Pigou, A. C., 213
Piore, Michael J., 45
Polinsky, A. M., 103
Pollock, Richard, 183
Powers, Terry A., 113, 120, 134
Prescott, James R., 169
Prest, A. R., 181
Prou, Charles, 121
Provus, Malcolm, 57

Quance, C. Leroy, 155
Quarmby, D. A., 68, 71, 72, 73

Randall, Alan, 84, 90, 91, 93
Raphaelson, Arnold H., 117
Raucher, Robert. L., 67
Rausser, Gordon, 187
Ray, Anandarup, 135
Redburn, Thomas, 232
Reid, T. R., 327
Reynolds, D. J., 312
Reynolds, W. C., 308
Rice, D. P., 64
Richardson, G. B., 258
Richardson, Harry W., 327

Richter, Donald K., 142, 154
Robinson, A., 281
Robison, L. J., 245, 246, 254
Roemer, Michael, 7
Roos, Leslie L., Jr., 52
Rose, Roger N., 155
Rosen, Sherwin, 61, 82, 246
Rosen, Stephen, 269
Rossi, P. H., 55
Rothenberg, Jerome, 328
Rowe, R. D., 89
Rubinfeld, D. L., 82, 83, 103
Ruby, Michael, 67
Ruggles, Nancy, 160
Ruggles, Patricia, 180, 182, 183, 189
Rundquist, Barry S., 328
Russell, Clifford S., 221
Ryan, C. W., 308

Sagan, L. A., 64
Sallack, David, 271, 273
Samples, Karl C., 92
Samuels, Warren J., 304
Samuelson, P. A., 144
Sanders, Ralph, 268
Sandford, Cedric, 281
Santoni, G. J., 211
Sarant, Peter C., 268
Sasaki, Komei, 135
Sassone, Peter, 202
Savage, Leonard, J., 231
Schaffer, William, 202
Schick, Allen, 30, 31, 269
Schmalensee, Richard, 244
Schmid, A. Allan, 20, 30, 66, 95, 103, 104,
       118, 158, 167, 168, 170, 175, 263, 265,
       280
Schmitz, Andrew, 148
Schoemaker, P. J. H., 249
Schon, David A., 36
Schulze, William D., 88
Scitovsky, Tibor, 189
Seckler, David, 148
Seers, Dudley, 44
Self, Peter, 283

Sellin, Thorstein, 45
Selowsky, Marcelo, 180, 182, 184
Sen, A. K., 213
Seskin, E. P., 67, 103
Settle, R. F., 71, 287
Shabman, Leonard, 177
Shavell, Steven, 103
Shefrin, H. M., 331
Shibata, Hiroo, 135
Silberberg, Eugene, 141, 142
Simon, Herbert A., 252
Simon, Julian, 102
Sinden, John A., 7, 90, 91
Singh, Ajmer, 311
Sjaastad, Larry, 216
Slovic, Paul, 65, 249
Small, K. A., 103
Smith, R. S., 61
Smith, Stephen, 274
Smith, V. Kerry, 7, 78, 142, 271
Snapper, Kurt, 103
Solo, Robert A., 211
Solomon, Ezra, 202, 231
Sosnick, Stephen H., 269
Squire, Lyn, 7, 135
Stanford Research Institute, 103
Stanley, John, 325
Stanley, Julian C., 48
Starr, Chauncey, 247, 248
Steiner, Peter O., 84
Stern, J. J., 7
Stevens, Thomas H., 189
Stiglitz, J. E., 14, 115, 120, 121, 196, 197,
       198
Stockfish, Jacob A., 211, 221
Stoevener, Herbert H., 74, 78
Stoll, J. R., 310
Strand, Ivar E., 77, 145
Straszheim, M. R., 73
Strung, Joseph, 231
Stuart-Alexander, D.E., 331
Sudman, Seymour, 88
Sugden, Robert, 20, 99, 103, 104, 155, 171,
       186, 197, 212, 216, 219, 229, 248, 252,
       287, 291, 301

Swatzman, Daniel, 331
Sykes, Allen, 324
Szakolczai, Gy, 158, 184

Taylor, Lance, 115
Thaler, Richard, 61, 246
Thomas, Harold A., 104
Thomas, T. C., 71, 73
Thompson, Mark, 7
Thompson, Stanley R., 67
Thurow, L. C., 115, 215
Tiebout, Charles, 135
Tobin, James, 332
Todaro, Michael P., 120, 121
Tolley, George S., 167
Torrance, George W., 30
Tresch, Richard W., 2, 19, 141, 142, 143, 145, 154, 155, 186, 216
Tucker, J. Dean, 67
Tullock, Gordon, 215
Turvey, Ralph, 7, 217, 231
Tversky, Amos, 221, 245, 265

U.S. Army Corps of Engineers, 66, 187, 256
U.S. Congress, 40, 103, 267, 274
U.S. Department of Agriculture, 153
U.S. Department of Health, Education and Welfare, 30, 63, 67
U.S. Department of Interior, 153
U.S. Department of Labor, 272
U.S. Department of Transportation, 63, 272
U.S. Environmental Protection Agency, 102, 153, 272
U.S. Forest Service, 152, 279, 283
U.S. Interagency Committee on Water Resources, 164
U.S. National Bureau of Standards, 333
U.S. Office of Management and Budget, 220
U.S. Water Resources Council, 78, 106, 111, 133, 152, 161, 185, 203, 219
Updegraff, Gail, 329

Vanags, A. H., 224, 230
van der Tak, Herman G., 7, 67, 135
van Ravenswaay, E. O., 259
Vartia, Y. O., 154
Vaupel, J.W., 42, 102
Vickerman, Roger, 71
Viner, Jacob, 148
Von Winterfeldt, Detlof, 249
Vondruska, John, 79, 256

Wabe, J. S., 83
Walker, O. L., 325
Walker, R. A., 299
Walsh, Richard G., 7, 90
Walter, Susan, 216
Ward, Clement E., 152
Ward, William A., 66, 113
Watson, P. L., 68
Watson, W. D., 67
Webb, E. J., 55
Weckstein, R. S., 107
Weingartner, H. M., 231
Weisbrod, Burton A., 171, 183
Weiss, Carol H., 270, 283
Wellor, Patrick, 281
Westley, Glenn, 135
Westphal, Larry E., 120
Wetzstein, Michael E., 103
Whipple, Chris, 248
Whittington, Dale, 11, 271
Wildavsky, Aaron, 45, 172, 269, 270, 273, 279
Williams, Alan, 20, 99, 103, 104, 155, 171, 186, 197, 212, 216, 219, 229, 248, 252, 287, 291, 301
Williamson, Harold F., Jr., 68
Willig, Robert D., 141, 142
Wilson, Richard, 39
Wind, Yorum, 82
Wisecarver, Daniel, 216
Wolfe, J. N., 7
Wolfgang, Marvin E., 45
Wolkoff, Michael J., 190
Wood, John H., 214
Worley, Lawrence, 83

Worrell, Albert C., 7
Wright, Sonia R., 55
Wyzga, R. E., 67

Yandle, Bruce, 190

Yates, Douglas, 283
Young, Robert A., 120

Zaidan, G. C., 102
Zeckhauser, Richard, 190, 215

Subject Index

Access cost-quantity method, 73-79

Accountability, 23, 62, 287, 304, 306

Accounting price ratio. See Shadow price

Adverse selection, 14

Aggregate demand, 116, 117, 123, 131, 133, 170. See also Monetary policy

Agricultural projects, 26, 39, 54, 62, 89, 110, 120-21, 133, 137, 146, 150, 159, 167, 176, 184, 185, 207, 257, 263

Air quality projects, 63, 67, 79, 82, 91, 168, 243

Alienation, 17

Allocation branch, 1, 10, 59, 167, 221, 300, 304. See also Distribution branch under Income distribution; Efficiency

Alternate cost method, 67, 84-86, 110, 290

Alternatives,
    display of, 277-78, 288
    selection of. See Ranking of projects

Altruism, 183, 186, 213, 214

American Textile Manufacturers case, 64-65, 271

Amortization, 199

Analyst (technical), role of, 1, 44, 57, 59, 73, 95, 105, 121, 134, 166, 171, 172, 181, 182, 184, 188, 202, 205, 226-27, 229, 252, 254, 255, 277, 280-81, 283, 285-89, 294, 303-06. See also Political foundations of benefit cost analysis

Antitrust, 3, 292, 297. See also Monopoly

Attitudinal surveys, 89-90

Balance of trade. See Trade deficit

Beesley method, 69-71

Behavioral economics, 92, 113, 179, 246, 248. See also Cognition

Benefit-cost ratio, choice of, 207-10, 299

Benefit measurement. See Access cost-quantity method; Beesley method; Contingent valuation method; Cost saving method; Hedonic pricing; Intermediate good method; Market analogy method; Rent method

Bidding games (contingent valuation method), 81, 91-94, 100, 102, 140, 238, 241, 291, 295, 298,

Birth control projects, 102n

Border prices. See Price

Borrowing rate of interest, 195, 227. See also Capital, cost of

Bounded rationality, 221, 252, 276, 286, 289,

Budget pie, 93

Budgetary process, 227, 228-30, 262, 267, 275, 303

Budgets, 21, 25, 93,
    constrained, 3, 14, 19, 77, 89, 118, 173, 179, 197, 199, 200, 202, 203, 207, 211, 220, 224, 227, 285, 301
    grants, 172, 173, 177, 178, 179, 187-88, 282, 296
    program, 19, 22-25, 30-38,
    segmented, 19, 205, 221-23, 264, 276-77, 281, 282, 297, 302, 303
    size, 19, 93, 99, 100, 171, 198, 200, 210, 220, 222, 224, 227, 264, 268, 276, 297
    unbalanced (deficits), 177, 270
    zero-based, 31

Capital
  cost (K), 199, 210
  cost of, approach, 197-98, 229
  market, 17, 195, 197, 210, 212, 215, 221,
    223, 237, 240, 296
  rationing. See Budgets, constrained;
    Shadow price, of capital
Carter, Jimmy, 30, 227, 262, 268, 272, 276
Cash flow, 191-95, 198, 202,
Cash transfers. See Transfer payments
Causal validity, threats to, 5, 34, 47-48
C.C.F. See Consumption conversion
    factor
Central bank policy. See Monetary policy
Certainty equivalent income, 240-41, 248
C.I.F. See Cost, Insurance and Freight
Civil rights projects, 21, 35-39
Clawson method. See Access cost-
    quantity method
Cognition, 74, 75, 76, 88, 90, 94. See also
    Bounded rationality, Learning,
    Satisficing, Subjective vs. objective
    measures
Combinations of projects, 203
Compensated demand curve. See
    Demand curve
Compensating variation (CV), 91, 139-40,
    142, 145
Compensation principle. See Pareto
    improvement
Competitive economy, 11, 16, 62, 80, 85,
    143, 147, 158, 160, 167, 300. See also
    Monopoly
Complementarity, 61, 79, 93, 141, 144, 298
Complementary investments, 130, 132,
    209, 263, 298
Compounding, 195, 199, 200, 202
Congestion, 78, 120
Conjoint analysis, 82
Consistency in valuation, 18, 40, 95, 133,
    171, 254, 255, 265, 271, 281, 286, 287,
    289. See also Systems analysis
Conspicuous consumption, 76
Constraints, 168, 172, 187, 296
  physical target, 228,

  See also Budgets, constrained
Construct validity, 26-27, 30, 34-36, 44, 53,
    88, 90, 275, 281
Consumer sovereignty, 2, 9-10, 222, 285,
    292
Consumer surplus (CS), 13-14, 78, 83,
    103n, 110, 134n, 137, 160, 175, 184,
    185-86, 295-96, 298, 303
Consumption conversion factor (CCF),
    115, 134n, 135n
Consumption (C) vs. investment (I). See
    Source of finance
Content validity, 28, 30
Contingency allowance, 256
Contingent claims market, 244
Contingent valuation method. See
    Bidding games
Corps of Engineers, 66, 78, 130, 161, 177,
    187, 229, 256, 257, 274, 276, 282,
Cost
  average, 66, 111
  of capital approach, 197-98
  category, 24, 43-44, 54
  fixed, 110, 163, 175
  joint cost allocation, 162-67, 175, 183-
    84, 299
  marginal, 13, 62, 76, 106, 110, 141, 150,
    158, 159, 160, 162, 301
  operating, 129, 163, 208-09,
  opportunity, 5, 62, 65, 66, 105, 111, 114,
    115-16, 119, 128, 133-34, 155, 170,
    175, 176, 202, 210-11, 293-95
  of risk bearing, 240
  saving, 146-50, 173
  sharing, 90, 132, 161-62, 175, 262
Cost-effectiveness analysis, 18-19, 24, 35,
    40, 61, 84, 228, 267, 268, 277
Cost, Insurance and Freight (C.I.F.), 110,
    113
  defined, 135n
Costsaving method, 66-73, 85, 106, 111,
    147, 291
Credit, 114, 118, 127, 131, 177, 264, 294
  rationing, 14, 196

Crime prevention projects, 24, 28, 29-30, 32

Davis-Bacon Act, 117
Deadweight loss, 143, 152, 178, 185, 186-87, 212
Decision costs. See Transaction costs
Decision maker (political authority), 1, 9, 44, 60, 100, 171, 173, 191, 208, 229, 237, 238, 245, 286
  incentives, 262, 277-78, 279-80
Decision making approach, 20n, 286, 287
Decreasing cost industry. See Scale economies
Defense, 25, 90, 117, 180, 183, 212, 243, 268, 270
Delaney amendment, 45n 261
Demand curve, 40, 66, 74-79, 84-85, 91, 101, 145, 154, 162, 185
  all or nothing, 139-40
  compensated, 140, 143, 154
  elasticity, 61, 107, 141, 143, 146, 151, 153, 184, 186
  Marshallian, 140
  shift, 130, 178, 186, 219, 244
  uncertainty, 77
Depreciation, 155, 216, 231
Devaluation, 112-14. See also Exchange Rates
Direct effects, 59, 130, 135n, 157
Discounting, 192-93. See also Present value
Discount rate, 65, 192, 200, 206, 210-20, 223, 227, 229, 230, 272, 296, 301
  risk premium on, 252
  social, 213-15, 218
  synthetic, 215-19, 222, 226
Disease control. See Health
Disequilibrium, 14, 77, 111, 115, 120-21, 134, 170, 196-97, 211, 212, 215, 219, 221, 223, 242, 258, 294, 296
Displacement effect, 132, 167
Distributional weights. See Income distribution

Distribution branch. See Income distribution
Double counting, 130-31, 294
Dual economy, 129
Duality theory, 141

Economic base multiplier, 123-24, 127
Economic growth, 111, 115, 118, 129-30, 214, 217, 223, 263, 288, 294
Economies of scale. See Scale economies
Economist, role of. See Analyst
Education projects, 15, 22-23, 43, 51, 56, 62, 90, 96, 109, 130, 132, 137, 161, 162, 183, 184, 264, 270, 278, 282, 298
Efficiency, 11, 17, 134, 186, 223, 282, 305. See also Allocation branch; Relational value
Electricity, 85, 90, 106, 163, 244
Employment. See Unemployment
Energy projects, 258
Enterprise budgets, 62, 132
Entitlements, 161, 172
Environment, 78, 83, 85, 168, 185, 219, 243, 244, 249, 300. See also Pollution control
Environmental impact statements, 43, 185, 289
Environmental Protection Agency, 40, 153, 221, 259, 260
Equivalent variation (EV), 91
Evaluation, 47, 270
Excess benefit method, 199
Excess burden. See Deadweight loss
Exchange rates, 111-15
Exclusion costs, 12, 88, 154, 183, 243
Expectation, mathematical. See Probability, mathematical
Expected utility, 238-41, 245, 249
Expected value criterion, 235-37, 240, 245, 252, 254, 256, 258
Experimental design, 48-54, 87-89, 97, 133, 259, 290
Explicitness, 87, 89, 99, 281, 286, 287
Exports. See Exchange rates

Externalities, 5, 15-16, 44, 107, 119, 145, 167, 168-69, 176, 182, 183, 188, 299-301

External validity, 54-55, 62-63, 78, 88

Factor (input) prices, 107-09, 121, 152, 167, 244

Fairness, 88, 90, 154, 160, 225

Finance. See Source of finance

Financial analysis, 9, 11

Financial leverage, 209

First-best economy, 3, 13, 16, 106, 142, 159, 179, 218, 221, 224, 225, 227, 243, 277, 291, 300, 301, 302, 304. See also Second-best theory

Fiscal policy, 118, 131, 133, 294. See also Budgets, unbalanced

Fixed factor, 63, 150

Flexibility, 263-64

Flood control projects, 11, 63, 66-67, 79, 130, 161, 163, 165, 187, 249, 255, 256, 257, 282

F.O.B., defined, 135n

Food policy, 112, 121, 228

Food safety, 40, 259

Forced rider problem. See Unwilling riders

Foreign competition, 117, 215

Foreign exchange. See Exchange rates

Forest Service, 152, 279

Framing, 89, 92, 289

Free riders, 11, 168. See also Exclusion costs

Frictions, 129. See also Immobile assets

Gambler's indifference map, 241-42, 247

Game theory, 88, 254

Grades and standards, 26-27

Grant efficiency ratio, 166, 173, 177, 178, 179, 187, 188, 296

Grants, 67, 169, 170, 172, 177, 185, 299-301, 302, 304. See also Transfer payments

Grants account, 172-77, 188

Grants budget. See under Budgets

Gravity models, 71, 74

Gross national product, 143. See also National income

Growth. See Economic growth

Health, 28, 32, 63-64, 67, 90, 95-96, 130, 184, 219, 227, 228, 236, 257, 258, 271, 292, 298, 302

Hedonic pricing, 82-84

History of benefit cost analysis, 4, 30, 268

Household production function, 76

Housing, 27, 60, 80, 169, 171, 187, 222

Human capital, 63-64, 101, 167, 208, 290, 293, 302

Ideal economy. See First-best economy

Immobile assets, 68, 80, 82, 84, 120, 129-30, 131, 134, 145, 146-50, 151, 153, 160, 167, 217, 244, 294

Impact indicator, 22-25, 34, 55, 271

Implementation, 263-64

Import substitution, 61, 85

Imports, shadow prices of. See Exchange rates

Income distribution, 9-10, 16-17, 27, 32, 64, 77, 81, 84, 91, 107, 112, 115, 117, 131, 134, 142, 144-45, 146, 148, 154, 285, 291, 294, 296, 302, 304

distribution branch, 1, 186, 304

distributive weights, 170-72, 188, 214, 215, 288, 301

goals, 134, 170, 177, 188. See also Objectives

macro studies, 179-81, 184, 188

redistribution vs. change in income distribution, 158

See also Transfer payments

Income elasticity of demand. See Demand curve, elasticity

Income transfers. See Grants account; Income distribution; Transfer payments

India, 213

Indirect effects, 59, 105, 121-23, 127, 131-32, 167, 185, 298 rounds of, 124, 126, 128, 129-30, 132, 133

Individual vs. collective choice, 11, 16-17, 213-15

Induced effects, 127, 129, 131

Inflation, 11, 111, 117, 124, 219-20

Information cost, 14, 65, 73, 94, 120, 162, 208, 222, 226, 252, 273, 277, 283, 291

In-kind transfers. See under Transfer payments

Input-output analysis, 124-31, 134n, 263

Input vs. output budgets, 22-25, 33, 38

Insurance, 237, 246, 249, 265

Interdependent projects.   See Mutually exclusive projects

Interest rate. See Discount rate

Intergovernmental grants, 161, 173, 175, 180

Intermediate good method, 62-66, 79, 101

Internal rate of return. See under Investment criteria

Internal validity, 47-48, 87-88, 90

International trade, 110. See also Exchange rates; Prices, border

Interpersonal utility comparison, 84, 101, 160, 184, 186, 223, 293, 295

Inter-regional interdependence, 80, 124, 132

Inter-sectoral interdependence, 121-23, 127, 135n, 154, 263, 298

Investment
    complementarity, 120, 127-30
    coordination, 120
    See also Source of finance

Investment criteria, 198-210, 229, 263-64, 286, 296, 299
    excess benefit-cost ratio, 199
    internal rate of return (IRR), 200-03, 209, 211, 296
    net present value, 64, 79, 198-99
    normalized internal rate of return (NIRR), 206
    normalized terminal value ratio, 206
    pay-back period, 252

synthetic, 215-19. See also under Discount rate
    See also Terminal value

Isolation paradox. See Individual vs. collective choice

Job training, 62, 117, 161, 303

Johnson, Lyndon, 30, 267, 271, 272, 274

Joint cost. See under Cost

Joint-impact goods, 12-13, 88, 162, 213, 243, 265

Kaldor-Hicks test. See Pareto improvement

Keynesian multiplier, 123

Labor, 176, 263, 294, 303
    intensive projects, 133
    shadow price for. See Shadow price
    supply theory, 68, 77, 109
    unions, 9, 116, 117, 120
    See also Unemployment: Job training

Land value, 63, 79-82, 282

Laspeyres price index, 140-41

Learning, 48, 78, 92-94, 244, 245, 264, 279, 298

Legal liability, 15, 60, 102n, 160, 168, 225, 293, 300. See also Externalities

Less developed countries (LDC), 102n, 110, 111-15, 120-21, 129, 133, 159, 197, 217, 227, 228. See also World Bank

Life, value of, 19, 42, 61, 63-64, 88, 101, 247, 256, 261, 290, 302

Linear programming, 65, 120

Localization coefficient, 128

Lump sum transfers. See under Tax

Marginal cost equal zero. See Joint-impact goods

Marginal use change, response to price, 66. See also Price, change in

Marginal utility of income, 68, 184, 186, 214, 238, 245

Market analogy method, 60-61, 65, 85, 290

Market price, 59-60, 280
Maximax criterion, 250
Maximin criterion, 250-51, 256, 260, 261
Merit goods, 73, 291
Migration, 80, 82, 120-21, 131
Minimax criterion, 251-52, 261
Mobility. See Immobile assets; Open-city
     assumption;
Monetary policy, 17, 112, 114, 117, 170
Monopoly, 3, 16, 109, 110, 159, 211, 222,
     285. See also Antitrust
Multipliers, 126-27, 128, 129, 130, 132, 133.
     See also Keynesian multiplier; Type I
     and II multiplier
Mutually exclusive projects, 199, 202
Myopia, 213

National income, 67, 81, 127, 130-31, 134,
     147, 151, 153, 166, 167, 172, 175, 263,
     297, 299, 301
  accounting, 44n, 84, 131, 167, 173, 187,
     190
Navigation projects. See under
     Transportation projects
Net benefits (income), 62, 79, 137
Net locational advantage, 81, 131, 155.
     See also Resources saved
Net present value. See under Investment
     criteria
Nominal scale, 25-26
Nonmarginal projects. See Consumer
     surplus
Nonmarket values, 59, 95-101, 173, 176,
     184-85, 264, 272, 290
Normalization procedure. See Terminal
     value method
Numeraire, 105-06, 113, 133, 141. See also
     Accounting price ratio under Shadow
     price

Objectives, 1, 3, 9, 17, 25-28, 33, 44, 95,
     105, 110, 115, 117, 158, 161, 166, 167,
     171, 179, 225, 255, 273, 280, 301
Occupational Safety and Health Act, 261
Open-city assumption, 80-83

Operating cost. See under Cost
Opportunity cost. See under Cost
Optimal output (scale). See Size of
     project
Option demand, 244
Output index, 26-27, 29, 40, 96, 99, 289
Output categories, 21, 25-30, 34, 35, 90, 94,
     95-96, 238, 268, 286, 288

(p) Private rate of return, 216, 217, 221
Paasche price index, 140-41
Paretian approach, 11, 286, 287
Pareto improvement, 2, 10, 12, 13, 17, 145,
     146, 186, 188, 218, 219
Park projects, 74-79, 93, 169, 175
Path dependence, 141
Pay-off matrix, 261
Peak load, 120, 160
Pecuniary effect, 81, 131, 145, 149, 157,
     167, 176, 178, 185
Perception. See Cognition
Perfect knowledge, 65. See also
     Information cost
Perfect mobility. See Open-city
     assumption; Immobile assets
Pesticide regulation, 19, 39-42, 258-62
Planning, 113, 263, 264, 281, 286, 289. See
     also Investment coordination
Police. See Crime prevention projects
Policy validity, 89
Political economy approach, 11, 288
Political foundations of benefit-cost
     analysis, 1, 44, 64, 87, 109, 254, 282,
     301-06. See also Public choice;
     Analyst, role of
Pollution control, 15, 65, 227. See also Air
     quality projects
Population estimation, 85, 236, 257
Population planning. See Birth control
Postal service, 158
Predictive validity, 28
Preferences, 3, 10, 17, 75, 86, 89, 94, 142,
     185, 222, 280. See also Revealed
     preferences

Present value, 192-93, 252. See also
    Investment criteria
Price
    acquisition, 244. See also Immobile
        assets
    administrative, 28, 40, 78, 84, 95-101,
        114, 168, 176, 215, 258, 269, 280, 292,
        301
    border, 85, 106, 110, 115
    change in, 14, 109, 139-41, 153, 176,
        178. See also Consumer surplus
    control, 111, 170, 184, 190
    differentiation, 13, 143, 144, 145, 150,
        153, 159, 175, 186, 295, 298
    discrimination, 14,
    as measure of marginal cost and
        valuation, 110, 301
    projections, 257-58
    shadow. See Shadow price
    uncertainty, 244, 257-58
    See also Subsidies
Pricing rule, 110, 111, 154, 159, 184
Probability, 88
    mathematical, 57, 235-46, 260
    ordinal, 244, 248, 250
    subjective, 57, 235, 242, 245, 254, 255
Producer's surplus. See Rent
Production function, 5, 22, 47, 55, 62, 109,
    120, 236, 253, 254, 259, 267, 290, 297
Profit, 125, 137, 145, 149, 151, 153, 162,
    181, 200, 210, 258
Program budgeting, 30-39, 61, 267, 270,
    272-77, 278-82, 288
Program information structure, 4, 21-45,
    94, 226, 254, 260, 270, 280, 288-89.
    See also Output categories; Impact
    indicator
Property rights (ownership), 2, 9, 15, 44,
    60, 64, 91, 101, 107, 117, 143, 148,
    157-60, 166-70, 172, 173, 178, 179,
    181, 182, 184, 186, 197, 222, 223, 225,
    282, 285, 290, 291, 293, 299-306
Property value. See Land value
Public (political) choice, 11, 17-18, 40, 43,
    57, 64, 73, 84, 87, 89, 91, 94-95, 95-
    101, 107, 109, 114, 118, 119, 121, 130,
    134, 154, 163, 169, 170, 175, 179, 181,
    184, 186, 189, 195, 203, 212-15, 223,
    229, 243, 244, 255, 264-65, 281, 296,
    298-306
Public enterprise rationales, 11-18, 110,
    120, 285
Public good. See Joint-impact good
Public opinion, 86, 89-90, 94, 153
Public participation, 3, 21, 25, 292
Public transport. See Transportation
    projects

(r) Public time preference rate, 216, 217,
    221
Ranking of projects, 18-19, 88, 99, 166,
    179, 198, 199, 200, 202, 203, 206, 207,
    216, 220, 224, 230, 239, 258, 268, 275,
    285, 287, 289, 299, 301
Rate of return, 196, 212-13, 287
Rationing. See Budgets, constrained;
    under Credit
Reagan, Ronald, 220, 262, 271, 272
Recreation, 60, 74, 78, 91, 167, 227. See
    also Park projects
Redistribution. See Income distribution
Regional development, 5, 80, 119-21, 123-
    24, 301. See also Inter-regional
    interdependence
Regulation, 3, 19, 39-42, 61, 63, 66, 82, 100,
    121, 152, 169, 170, 221, 249, 252, 255,
    259, 264, 271-72, 287, 290, 291, 293,
    302, 305
Regulation Q, 212, 222
Reinvestment, 194-95, 197, 202, 205, 218,
    222
Relational value, 298-99, 306n
Rent, 72, 79-82, 131, 144-45, 149, 150, 151,
    167, 185, 282, 294, 295
Rent method, 79-82
Resources saved, 146-50. See also Net
    locational advantage; Cost, saving
Revealed preferences, 61, 68, 171, 246-47
Risk,
    actuarial, 237

assessment, 88, 259-62

attitudes, 245-46, 249, 253-54

aversion, 61, 65, 237-38, 240, 254, 259, 297

control, 248-49

decision rules, 250-53

dramatic, 249, 257

neutral, 237, 243

perversion, 243, 262

premium, 252

spreading, 262. See also Insurance

trade-offs, 61, 246-48

voluntary, 247, 248

Risk-benefit analysis, 39-42, 100, 255

Rules for systematic analysis, 10, 17-19, 40, 100, 228, 249, 254, 261, 267, 272-73, 274, 276, 280-82, 285, 286, 300, 301-04

Safety first principle, 252

Salvage value, 244 See also Immobile assets

Sampling, 54, 87, 88, 94, 261, 264, 274, 291

Satisficing, 245, 249, 252, 264

Saving, 111, 118, 193, 241

Scale economies, 24, 110, 120, 129, 132, 135n, 159-60, 175, 184, 200, 203

Scale of project. See Size of project

Scales, 25, 42-43, 89-90

Scope of benefit-cost analysis. See System boundaries

Second-best theory, 3, 4, 11, 16, 19, 77, 110, 111, 118, 120, 186, 203, 215, 221, 223-25, 228, 230, 249, 254, 258, 264, 286, 304

Sensitivity analysis, 207, 258, 286

Shadow price, 105, 294

accounting price ratio, 113-14, 128

of capital, 129, 211, 216

of foreign currency, 111-15,

of imports. See Exchange rates

of labor, 107-09, 113, 115-33, 217, 294

and monopoly, 109

and price controls, 111

and price support, 109

and tariffs, 106-09

and taxation, 106-09, 212-13

Size of project, 230, 256, 263

Smith auction process, 92

Social discount rate. See under Discount rate

Social indicators, 49. See also Impact indicator

Socialist firm, 158, 208, 221

Social trap, 117

Social welfare function, 11, 186, 233, 285

Source of finance (capital)

borrowing or taxation, 197-98, 227

consumption or investment, 215-19, 223, 225, 226-27, 229

Specification of models, 53

State owned enterprise, 110. See also Socialist firm

Strategic behavior, 88

Subjective vs. objective measures, 64, 65, 73, 97, 101-02, 248, 258, 291. See also Cognition

Subsidies, 107, 109-12, 120, 130, 131-32, 158, 166, 170, 184, 248, 249, 293

Substitutes, 27, 60-61, 66, 71, 75, 81, 85, 93, 110, 141, 144-45, 152, 160, 167, 181, 288, 290, 295, 298

Sunk cost. See Cost, fixed

Supply change, nonmarginal, 61, 80, 83-84, 109. See also Consumer surplus

Supply irreversability, 151, 244-45

Switching value, 258

System boundaries, 18, 226, 227, 277, 297. See also Budgets, segmented

System rules. See Rules for systematic analysis

Systems analysis, 3, 4, 18, 40, 42, 89, 95, 117, 119, 205, 225, 230, 263, 267, 269, 270, 275, 276, 281, 297, 301-04

interactive, iterative, 134, 188, 229, 254, 264, 279, 286-88, 302, 306

Tariffs, 107, 112, 113, 294

Tastes, changes in, 244. See also Demand curve shift; Learning; Uncertainty

Tax, 79, 90, 115, 128, 131-32, 140, 143, 146,
    152, 157, 161, 168, 176, 227, 269, 294,
    305
    allocation, 109, 180
    cut, 117, 131, 133, 170
    expenditures, 132, 190
    incidence, 110, 154, 160, 161, 171, 196
    and income distribution, 107
    lump-sum, 2, 9, 13, 106, 107, 121, 146,
    159, 176, 185, 186, 188, 285
    subsidy, 132
    See also under Shadow pricing;
    Transfer payments
Terminal value, 199, 202
Terminal value method, 205-06, 209, 216,
    217, 229
Time, value of, 66, 77, 265
Time horizon. See Reinvestment
Time preference (TP), 118, 188, 191-98,
    212, 213, 219-20, 223-26, 264, 276
    differences among individuals, 195-97,
    206, 217
    social. See Discount rate, social
Tourism, 132. See also Recreation
Traded goods (international), 113, 115
Trade deficit, 112-13
Transaction costs, 9, 15, 119, 168, 185, 212,
    226, 237, 240, 271
Transfer payments, 67, 91, 118, 154, 158,
    173, 181, 182, 217
    between generations, 182, 195, 213
    cash transfers, 170, 171, 173, 175, 178,
    179, 205, 227
    cost of, 185-87, 198
    in cash vs. in kind, 16, 169-70, 187
    in-kind, 162, 287
    lump-sum. See under Tax
    tax, 166, 168, 175, 177-78
    See also Income distribution
Transportation projects, 66, 67-73, 79, 128,
    133, 159, 160, 161, 258, 263, 291, 298,
    300
    navigation, 66, 81, 110, 111, 121, 165
Travel cost method. See Access cost-
    quantity method

Travel time, 66, 67-73, 74
Type I multiplier, 127, 129
Type II multiplier, 127, 128, 129, 131

Uncertainty, 14, 38, 109, 113, 115, 129, 132,
    145, 195, 235-65, 290, 297-98. See
    also Risk; Expected utility; Expected
    value; Variance of outcome
Unemployment, 14, 109, 115, 128-29, 130,
    133, 170, 185, 294
    cyclic, 116-19, 159
    structural, 119-21
    See also Shadow price, of labor
United States, 84, 110, 111, 112, 120, 132,
    159, 161, 167, 168, 180, 211, 212, 220,
    224, 227, 257, 301
United Kingdom, 63, 106, 161, 180, 210,
    214, 220, 281
Unwilling riders, 12, 154
User charges (fees), 157, 159, 160, 161,
    172, 175, 177, 184
U.S. Food and Drug Administration, 259,
Utility function, 238, 241, 245, 255

Valuation. See Benefit measurement
Value judgments, 12, 16, 28, 44, 63, 91, 95-
    96, 144, 151, 153, 154, 160, 186-87,
    278-82, 289, 305
Variance of outcome, 72, 237, 238, 250,
    256, 297
Voting, 86-89, 93, 94-95

Wages. See Shadow price, of labor
Water supply projects, 62, 84, 128, 132,
    150, 154, 162, 177, 272
Weighting. See Income distribution
Welfare economics, 2, 9-11, 13, 91, 110,
    143, 145, 148, 154, 212, 287, 304. See
    also Pareto improvement
Welfare programs, 181-82. See also
    Income distribution
Willingness to pay (WTP), 40, 59-60, 64,
    66, 79-80, 84, 88, 90, 91-94, 112, 139,
    143, 146, 290, 302

vs. willingness to sell, 60, 88, 91-92,
    102, 107, 119, 142, 169, 291
World Bank, 4, 115, 133, 187, 220, 224,
    258, 301

Zero-based budgeting, 30, 268